An Introduction to Spanish Literature

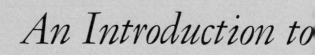

An Introduction to

by GEORGE TYLER NORTHUP

Third Edition Revised by

NICHOLSON B. ADAMS

Spanish Literature

THE UNIVERSITY OF CHICAGO PRESS

Chicago and London

ISBN: 0-226-59442-4 (clothbound); 0-226-59443-2 (paperbound)

THE UNIVERSITY OF CHICAGO PRESS, CHICAGO 60637
The University of Chicago Press, Ltd., London

Preface

This book is an attempt to clarify Spanish literature, to present a picture of it as a whole, stressing the evolution and development of its great genres, and, when possible, grouping authors in their respective schools. An effort has been made, too, to relate Spanish literature to the geographic, ethnic, social, and historical facts which have determined it. It is not my aim to present a mass of detailed information respecting each writer studied. In order that the trees may not obscure the forest, I have omitted courageously. Many secondary writers of considerable importance have been passed over. Neither has it been possible to mention all the works of all the authors included. My constant purpose has been to give the general reader and the university student an account of Spanish literature which may serve to give him his bearings on first acquaintance with the subject. Spanish-American writers are mentioned only when by residence in Spain they have identified themselves with Spanish literature, or when their influence has been too great to neglect. More intensive study will necessitate the use of the many histories of Spanish literature of more extensive scope. The Bibliography, too, is selective. It seemed needless to duplicate and extend such lists as those given by Fitzmaurice-Kelly, Hurtado and Palencia, Cejador y Frauca, and others. I merely indicate the best editions of important works, sometimes adding the most accessible edition and the most indispensable studies on each subject and author.

Preface.

I desire to express my thanks to Mr. R. H. Keniston, who, having had in mind a similar book, and finding that his plans did not permit early collaboration with me, most generously withdrew in my favor. It is to be hoped that he will later write his own history of Spanish literature. I also thank Mr. Thomas Walsh and Mrs. W. S. Hendrix for permitting me to use certain of their translations of Spanish lyrics, and Mr. E. P. Dargan for his kindness in reading portions of my manuscript, and Mr. Gordon J. Laing, general editor of the University of Chicago Press, for his never failing helpfulness. In revising this work, I owe much to my various reviewers and to the following friends in particular: S. G. Morley, F. C. Tarr, A. R. Nykl, and Carlos Castillo.

G. T. NORTHUP

UNIVERSITY OF CHICAGO

Professor Northup's *Introduction to Spanish Literature* has been deservedly popular for more than a generation. During the years since its first publication and the somewhat later revision, Hispanic scholarship has added to our knowledge, and Spanish literature has been enriched by the works of younger creative artists. This revision endeavors to take both facts into account. The book is otherwise in all essentials the same as planned and composed by Professor Northup.

For the revision I have been offered numerous suggestions by scholarly colleagues and friends in various parts of this country and abroad. I have heeded their words and—without incriminating them in the final results—I give them my sincere thanks. The reader will observe that the corrections which have been made, within the space available, practically all refer to matters of detail. The bibliographies have been completely revised and many more recent titles have been added. In the text, attention has been paid to new discoveries, such as that of the delightful and important *kharjas*.

I wish to thank Professor Northup for his scholarly, kind, and co-operative participation throughout the course of this revision. In a very few cases in which I ventured to differ in point of view from my esteemed senior friend, I have so indicated.

The last chapter, which seeks to bring this account of

Preface to
Third Edition

Spanish literature up to date, is entirely my own, and I am solely responsible for the imperfections to which any treatment of contemporary literature is notoriously liable. No blame attaches to those who read and criticized it. I can only hope that it adds to the utility of the volume as a whole.

NICHOLSON B. ADAMS

UNIVERSITY OF NORTH CAROLINA

Contents

The Characteristics of Spanish Literature as Determined by Geography, History, and Race

The peninsular state—*Españolismo*—Spain a diversified country—A glance at the provinces—Regionalism—A glance at the history of Spain—Spanish literary characteristics as determined by history—Racial elements—Havelock Ellis' theory—Stoicism—Dignity—Laziness—Individualism—Democracy—Humor—Summary.

Just as the traveler in Spain notes that country's striking individuality, so the reader of Spanish literature is constantly impressed by the fact that it differs from any other literature known to him. Let us try to account for some of its peculiar traits.

GEOGRAPHY

The peninsular state.—The fact that Spain is a peninsula, at one extreme of Europe, bounded by two seas, and separated from its nearest neighbor by the lofty Pyrenees, is of primary importance. Ángel Ganivet, in his *Idearium español*, has pointed out that the island state, safeguarded from invasion and free to expend its energies abroad, is, in the long run, most likely to succeed in colonization and imperialistic enterprise (England, Japan). On the contrary, the continental state is always apprehensive of invasion. The defensive is its proper rôle. If it essays imperialism, it may for a time succeed; but disaster eventually overtakes it (France, Germany). Since the

Battle of Hastings, British soldiers have fought their foreign foes abroad; French and German soldiers usually fight near their own frontiers. There is, continues Ganivet, a third type, the peninsular state, represented by Spain, more secure than the continental and less so than the island state. Spanish soil has frequently been invaded by the enemy and defended by Spaniards with characteristic obstinacy. At other times Spain has felt as secure as the island state to undertake foreign adventure—a departure from her proper rôle. At moments of her history Spain has been almost a hermit nation—at other times an active participant in world-politics, making her influence felt in the remote corners of the globe. Though Ganivet's theory needs qualification, it seems sound in the main.

Españolismo.—Spain's remote situation has made her literature less subject than others to influence from abroad. In ancient times the Iberic peninsula never developed a culture comparable to those of Greece and Italy, because of remoteness from oriental influences. Under Rome, Spain's culture was purely Roman; in modern times she has been far from European centers of thought. To be sure, her literature has been influenced by those of Italy, France, England, etc.; but such influences were thoroughly absorbed. They coincided usually with those political events which brought Spain into contact with other nations. The Renaissance exerted a less vital influence upon Spain than upon France, Germany, and England. France, geographically most capable of exerting influence, was viewed with that prejudice which one so easily entertains toward a next-door neighbor. The Pyrenees tended to become a wall of China. This remote-

ness has created in Spaniards a characteristic which they
term *españolismo*, by which they mean a complacent self-
satisfaction with everything Spanish, accompanied with a
disdain for everything foreign. The "peninsularity" of
the Spanish exceeds the insularity of the British. During
the period of Spain's greatness, *españolismo* was an almost
universal trait among Spaniards. It has many manifestations in literature. With the decadence many intellectuals
began to combat it. The Generation of 1898 proceeded
to assail it vigorously. "Europeanization" and "deafri-
canization" were words ever on the lips of Joaquín Costa.
Today the Spaniards are the most self-critical of peoples,
so much so as to justify Bartrina's epigram: "If you hear
a man talk, you can easily tell where he saw the light of
day: If he praises England to you, he must be English;
if he talks ill of Prussia, he is a Frenchman; if he speaks
ill of Spain, he is a Spaniard." Yet *españolismo* is still a
force to be reckoned with among the inert masses and a
few reactionary men of education. For generations it
occasioned an intellectual aloofness which deprived Spanish literature of many fecundizing ideas. However, a self-
sufficient literature, while it loses in cosmopolitan spirit,
gains individuality.

Spain a diversified country.—While France is a low-
lying country, formed by nature to be unified and homo-
geneous, Spain is crisscrossed by barriers which tend to
form several states rather than one. The important rivers
are the Ebro, flowing east into the Mediterranean; the
Miño, the Duero, and the Tagus, flowing west; and the
Guadiana and the Guadalquivir, flowing southwest into
the Atlantic. Far more formidable are the mountain
ranges. In the northwest the Cantabrian Sierra separates

a narrow, well-watered seaboard from the almost rainless steppes of the interior; the Guadarramas roughly divide Old and New Castile; the Sierra Morena separates Andalusia from Northern Spain; and in the southeast the Sierra Nevada shuts out the seaboard. These natural barriers rendered intercommunication far more difficult in the past than it is in the present; but even today the railways follow circuitous routes and painfully mount difficult grades. Temperature varies from the subtropic to extreme cold. Certain regions are luxuriant, others arid wastes. Though Spain achieved a nominal political unity in 1469, the country is still a federation of *reinos* rather than a single realm. The old designation, *Las Españas*, is still descriptive.

A glance at the provinces.—Modern Spain is divided into fifty provinces. It is still convenient to disregard these and consider the old, historic provinces or kingdoms. In the extreme northwest is Galicia, wooded, well-watered, mountainous, picturesque. The dialect is akin to both Spanish and Portuguese. The race is an amalgam of elements chiefly Celtic and Germanic. The peasantry is backward and stupid, unless it be that their superior imaginativeness merely makes them seem so to the natives of other provinces. The Gallego is the hewer of wood and the carrier of water for all Spain. He is a universal butt of ridicule; but his hardy virtues are famous. He reaps the harvests of Central Spain. Galician labor excavated the Panama Canal after negro and Italian labor had failed. Galicia was an early home of Spanish lyric song. Its folklore is interesting. It is the province which fairies most frequent; and in recent times the plaintive verse of Rosalía de Castro shows that the Celtic imagination is still at work. Chief cities—La Coruña, Ponte-vedra, Santiago de Compostela.

Eastward on the Bay of Biscay lies the "never-con-quered" province of Asturias. Here at the time of the Arabic invasion the irreconcilables made their stand, and from this point extended their conquests. Every inhabit-ant boasted of "clean blood" and considered himself a noble. Asturias is the cradle of the modern Spanish nation. It is one of Spain's most picturesque and charm-ing regions. Chief city—Oviedo.

Next to the east is the Montaña district. Its coastal inhabitants are simple fishermen; its hill-dwellers, primi-tive farmers. The chief city, Santander, is a delightful watering-place as well as a commercial emporium.

Then come the Basque provinces. The Basques are, supposedly, the primitive Iberians. The race straddles the Pyrenees. Some are therefore Spanish, others French. Their language is unrelated to any of the Indo-European group, and may be the oldest tongue now spoken in Europe. The Basques are thrifty, hard working, progressive. Their material condition is better than that of most Spaniards. They have always manifested a spirit of revolt when cher-ished privileges are attacked. As a people they seldom produce a genius. Ignatius Loyola is the greatest Basque who has figured in history. The region is a center of min-ing, and the capital, Bilbao, is a modern, industrial city.

Navarra, next to the east, was an ancient kingdom which also straddled the Pyrenees. The smaller, northern portion has gone to France. There are many Basques in this province, and the other inhabitants resemble the Aragonese in character. Navarra is a sterile region. Pamplona is the principal city.

6

Aragon lies east of Navarra and south of the Pyrenees. Its landscape resembles that of New Mexico. It is
sterile except for its remarkably fertile river basins. The
Aragonese are in some respects the noblest Spanish breed.
When a Spaniard says, "You are very Aragonese," he
means, "You are very pig-headed." Stubbornness is the
dominant Aragonese trait; but the Aragonese know how
to apply their obstinacy to a righteous purpose. Though
stubborn defense of the soil is a common Spanish characteristic, the Aragonese are supreme in this. The siege of
Saragossa is the classic example; but their noblest struggle
has been in behalf of liberty. Their various social classes
have shown a solidarity, a spirit of compromise, an ability
to sink individual ends in furtherance of a common cause,
all of which are quite un-Spanish. During the Middle
Ages they were leaders in constitutional progress. Before
the time of Magna Charta they had already won valuable
privileges. Their two great charters of liberty, the General Privilege, 1283, and the Privilege of Union, 1287,
are outstanding documents in the history of European
jurisprudence. Significant of the Aragonese attitude
toward royalty is the oath of allegiance to the king sworn
by the representatives of the four estates: "We who are as
good as you swear to you who are no better than we, to
accept you as our king and sovereign lord, provided you
observe all our liberties and laws; but if not, not." This
formula is a good sample of Aragonese style; for the Aragonese are the Spartans of Spain, in laconicism as well as
in simplicity and endurance. The writers of this province
are tersely vigorous (Gracián, Costa), lacking the ver-
bosity characteristic of Spaniards in general.

In the extreme northeast lies the province of Catalonia, fertile and favored with an ideal climate. Its capital, Barcelona, is a great, modern, industrial city—but the most beautiful of industrial cities. The Catalans are a nervous, energetic race, discontented, radical, seditious. There is cause for their dissatisfaction. They feel that their province should possess the leadership, that they are the producers of wealth and the race best fitted to make Spain a modern nation. Castile, owing to central position, tradition, and linguistic reasons, still possesses the hegemony, hence the separatism of Catalonia. The Catalan tongue is allied to the Provençal, and the Catalans possess a literature of their own.

Following down the Mediterranean shore, one enters the other two Levantine provinces, Valencia and Murcia The natives speak their own dialects. They tend to republicanism and socialism. As one travels south, the Arabic strain is more observable. Valencia, an earthly paradise, is center of a rich, well-irrigated, agricultural region.

In Central Spain there lie from west to east the three semidesert provinces of León, and Old and New Castile. These are high plateaus, intersected by mountain ranges, extremely cold in winter, sun parched in summer. The arid soil yields its scanty crop grudgingly. The region is almost entirely deforested. Erosion has carved the hills into curious forms. Except for a brief season, green is absent from the landscape. A tawny plain in the foreground, blue hills in the background. Over all a cloudless, indigo sky. Critics like to see the austere grandeur of the Castilian plains reflected in the characteristic works of Castilian genius. The Central Spaniard is the typical Spaniard, courteous, chivalric, quixotic. We shall have him chiefly in mind when we generalize concerning Spanish character. Chief cities of León—Zamora, Salamanca; of Old Castile—Burgos, Valladolid, Segovia, Ávila; of New Castile—Madrid, Toledo.

South of León lies Extremadura. Though less barren than the three last considered, the characteristics of the province and its inhabitants are similar. León and the Castiles bred heroes in the epic days of the Reconquest; Extremadura provided them for the conquest of America. Chief cities—Badajoz, Cáceres, Mérida.

Andalusia is the southern region of Spain. Here the climate is kindly, though often very hot in summer, and the soil fertile. This is the Spain of fruit and flowers, the guitar and the castanet. Northern Spaniards are graver, more stoical; Andalusians are gayer, more epicurean. They know the art of living; their tastes are simple; they incline to laziness. They are adaptable and subtle, and, like the French *méridional*, prone to exaggeration. The provinces which compose Andalusia are Almería, Granada, Malaga, Jaén, Cordova, Seville, Cadiz, and Huelva.

Regionalism.—Thus Spain is not merely shut off from Europe, but is divided into compartments as well. Regionalism, entailing separatistic movements, has always been a force to reckon with in Spanish politics. But that is not all. Within the provinces there are many sub-dialects. Each town has its peculiar physiognomy. From valley to valley the peasant costumes change; even the designs of the water-jugs vary. *Españolismo*, regionalism, particularism, individualism—these tendencies are all very Spanish. In literature the *patria chica* has often loomed larger in a writer's imagination than the *patria grande*. The very configuration of the land renders it difficult for a Spanish writer to envisage his country as a whole.

A GLANCE AT THE HISTORY OF SPAIN

Spain's peculiarly adventurous history has in large measure determined the characteristics of her literature. Let us consider how.

The fusion of races.—Like most European races, the Spaniards are of a very composite stock. The primitive Iberians mingled with the North African Berbers. Then came a Celtic invasion about the sixth century B.C., and a fusion of races, producing the Celto-Iberian stock. The Celtic strain was most pronounced in Galicia and Portugal, the Iberic in the east; in the center the fusion was most complete. Many centuries before the coming of the Celts, Phoenicians, Greeks, and lastly Carthaginians had established trading-posts along the coasts. Ambitious schemes of conquest on the part of Carthage were finally defeated by the Romans with the ending of the Second Punic War, 206 B.C. In the four previous centuries Carthage had been the dominating power in the peninsula.

The Romans proceeded to subdue and colonize Spain systematically. According to Strabo, this would have been difficult but for the excessive pride and individualism of the Iberians. Petty jealousies prevented concerted action; yet the Iberians were formidable for their guerrilla tactics, that form of warfare in which Spaniards have always excelled. The principal seats of Roman power were the eastern capital, Tarragona, the western, Mérida, and garrison towns like Saragossa, León, Toledo, Cordova, and Itálica, near Seville. These were connected by roads, and adorned with aqueducts, theaters, temples, baths, and other enduring monuments. *Obra de Romanos* is a proverbial expression to denote any huge undertaking. Roman law and administration introduced a degree of civilization hitherto unknown in Hispania. Culture followed. The schools of the south produced some of the greatest writers of the Silver Age of Latin literature: Lucan, Seneca, Martial, Quintilian, and later Prudentius. Many of the Peninsular writers in Latin already display a tendency toward that euphuism so characteristic of the Spanish literature of later periods. Spanish literature, too, has maintained the gravity of its Roman origin far more than is the case with the French and Italian literatures. The greatest gift of Rome to Spain was her language, which soon became all but general. The Celts readily adopted the new tongue. Only the Basques, in their mountain fastnesses, have clung to their primitive speech.

The Germanic invasions.—The Roman period lasted until 409 A.D., when three tribes, the Suevi, the Alani, and the Vandals, swept Spain with fire and sword. The Suevi settled in Galicia, the Alani in what is now Portugal, and the Vandals in Andalusia. The Visigoths followed hard after in 414. They came in greater numbers and organized their victory. They had long been in touch with Latin culture and were both civilized and Christian. This was not so much a conquest as a social revolution welcomed by all the oppressed. The Goths maintained the old Roman organization, adding new blood and vigor. They were comparatively few in number, but powerful enough to set up a new line of kings, found a new aristocracy, and assume most of the posts of leadership. They added few words to the language, rapidly losing their own tongue and identifying their interests with those of Spain. The influence of Germanic law and custom is very noticeable in Spanish medieval literature.

The Moslem invasion, under Tarik, begins in 711. Apparently the Moors were introduced as auxiliaries by the sons of Witiza, who had been denied the throne by Rodrigo and his followers; but the Moors, seeing how easily the country could be captured, proceeded to take possession. In a few years they had organized their conquest of the whole peninsula, except the mountainous region of the northwest, which was not only difficult to subdue, but did not seem worth the effort. It must not be thought that many Spaniards fled to the north. The irreconcilables were few. Most reconciled themselves to their lot and lived among the invaders, who treated them with toleration and interfered only slightly with their religious observances. The bigotry which subsequently became so marked on both sides was of a much later date.

Arabic civilization.—The century-long Reconquest started almost immediately with the skirmish of Covadonga, a victory of sentimental importance won by Pelayo in 718. Soon the little kingdom of Asturias was formed, and before the end of the century Oviedo had been made the capital. Meanwhile the Moors had organized their power with Cordova as capital. The caliphate of Cordova lasted from 758 to 1031. Those were the palmy days of the Moors in Spain. Cordova became the second center of culture in all Europe. Only Byzantium stood higher. The Arabs had come into contact with Greek civilization. Their architecture was Byzantine in its origins. They possessed many Greek writings unknown to Western Europeans until they were translated out of Arabic translations into Latin. The Moors of Spain were famous mathematicians. The clumsy Roman system of notation was replaced by the more convenient

Arabic system which we use. (The Roman had no symbol for zero.) Moorish engineers made Southern Spain a garden, by means of extensive systems of irrigation. Their doctors were the best in Europe. Progress was made in many arts and handicrafts. The Mosque of Cordova and the Alhambra still stand as evidence of their architectural triumphs. Compared with the invading race, the Christian Spaniards were at the outset barbarians. They advanced by imitating their conquerors' methods. The Moslem invasion came in several waves, and later arrivals were less civilized and more fanatic. The invaders enriched the language and the life of Spain in many ways, but direct literary influence was slight.

The Reconquest.—The early stages of the Reconquest were characterized by desultory border warfare. Several little Christian kingdoms had formed in the north which waged war with each other as freely as against the infidel. Nothing like a formal campaign occurred until the French monks of Cluny organized a European crusade against the Moors. With foreign aid Alfonso VI captured Toledo in 1085, a victory which effectually loosened the Moorish hold upon the north. Rodrigo Díaz (the Cid), Alfonso's great vassal, captured Valencia in 1094, though after his death the Christians were forced to relinquish it in 1102. Another European crusade resulted in the notable victory of Las Navas de Tolosa, 1212, under Alfonso VII. Cordova and Seville fell to Fernando III in 1236 and 1248, respectively. Meanwhile, the Aragonese under Jaime el Batallador had been pushing their conquests down the east coast. Valencia was definitively taken in 1238, and the final conquest of Murcia, which fell to Castile in 1266, left only the kingdom of Granada in Moorish hands. These victories would have been impossible if the Moors had been able to maintain the strongly centralized government of the caliphate of Cordova; but Moorish Spain had split early into mutually warring kingdoms, just as had been the case with Christian Spain. Obviously, the final victory would fall to that side which should first achieve national unity. Gradually, Castile and Aragon emerged as the two most important kingdoms, drawing into their orbits the lesser, adjacent states. When Fernando of Aragon married Isabel of Castile in 1469, Christian unity was achieved. Granada fell in 1492.

A fantastic picture.—To understand the significance of this long-drawn-out struggle, let us take a hint from Washington Irving and draw a fanciful picture, projecting the history of Spain upon that of England. The Normans gained England in 1066, but left the Scotch virtually independent in their highland fastnesses. Let us suppose, then, that the Scotch, as far behind the Normans in civilization as the Asturians were inferior to the Moors, were able to organize an effective resistance. They win minor border forays. The Normans do not consider the waste lands of the north worth a strong defense. The Scotch grow in power and capture York (Toledo) in 1460. They win London (corresponding to Cordova) in 1591. Brighton, Southampton, and the southern littoral fall in 1603. The Normans are now hemmed in in the kingdom of Canterbury (Granada), where they maintain themselves until 1847. Imagine all this, and then try to conceive the effect upon English literature if England had suffered a civil war lasting nearly eight centuries.

Later events.—It would seem that with the fall of

Granada Spain had at last earned the right to a peaceful, normal development—the more so as Fernando and Isabel had, like Louis XI of France, succeeded in curbing the power of the great nobles, establishing law and order, and were active in fomenting trade, industry, culture, and the arts. But this very date, 1492, marks a new departure, the discovery, conquest, and colonization of America. New avenues were opened for Spain's adventurous spirit. In 1516 Charles V came to the throne. Three years later he was elected German emperor, which caused Spain to play a leading rôle in European politics. With the outbreak of the Reformation in Germany, Spain became the champion of Catholicism against heresy throughout the world. This burden was too great for the country's population and finances, and Spanish power, even at this period of her greatness, was more apparent than real. Charles's policies were continued by his son, Philip II. Spain's decline may be said to date from the defeat of the "Invincible Armada" in this reign. Few statesmen in Europe then understood the true sources of wealth, but the economic administration of Spain during this period is the classic example in the world's history of inept financiering. Decadence set in rapidly under Philip III and Philip IV, whose reigns, nevertheless, represent the greatest period of Spanish literature. Throughout all these reigns the Inquisition had hampered freedom of thought. Under the French Bourbons of the eighteenth century Spain was a prostrate nation. In the nineteenth century come the Napoleonic invasion, the struggle for a constitution, involving the second French invasion of 1823, numerous civil wars, revolutions, a change of dynasty, and a short-lived republic. Since the restoration of the

Bourbon dynasty in 1874, Spain has been torn by two disasters: the war with the United States in 1898 and the Civil War of 1936–39. She fortunately remained neutral during World Wars I and II.

The dictatorships under the last king of Spain, Alfonso XIII, proved unsuccessful, and Alfonso fled the country in 1931. An idealistically minded but politically inept Second Republic came to grief in 1936. In that year Francisco Franco and fellow generals, fundamentally representing the forces of conservatism, rebelled against their government. The Civil War was one of the most sanguinary in history, costing about a million lives.

Franco assumed dictatorial powers as chief of state. The Church and the army regained their lost powers. In 1953 a new Concordat was signed with the Holy See, and an agreement was signed with the United States for the establishment of naval and air bases and for economic aid. Inflation nevertheless increases. As of now, Franco remains as dictator. Spain's problems are still unsolved, and it would be hazardous to predict the future.

Spanish literary characteristics determined by history.— Spain's troubled, adventurous history is reflected in her literature. The crusading spirit appears everywhere, just as the spirit of exploration is prominent in Portuguese literature. We should expect a nation devoted to heroic achievement to produce a great epic and ballad literature. Such has been the case. We should expect ideas of chivalry and military honor to prevail, as they do. Bourgeois ideals appear as rarely as one would expect in a country almost lacking in a middle class. So we find a tendency toward extravagance, less under the control of common sense than is the case with most literatures. We shall have occasion to note several purely aristocratic movements; but, in the main, Spanish literature is democratic. Centuries of fighting an alien race and creed had made all Spaniards of *sangre limpia* brothers. Distinctions of rank mattered less there than elsewhere. In the early days there was little intellectual cleavage between noble and commoner. The classes thought alike on most subjects. Therefore Spain produced the most democratic literature of all nations, but a democratic literature constantly tinged with aristocratic traits; for all the "clean-blooded" considered themselves noble. A nation which fought so many centuries for its religion prized it more highly than did other countries. Spanish literature is strongly Roman Catholic. It is supreme in the domain of mysticism and devotion. On the other hand, excess of devotion brought about bigotry, and the repressive influence of the Inquisition made Spanish literature weak in philosophy, criticism, and works of daring speculation.

THE RACE

Racial elements.—We have seen that the principal racial stocks whose fusion has produced the modern Spanish people are the Iberian or African Berber, the Phoenician-Carthaginian, Jewish, Grecian, Celtic, Roman, Germanic, and Arabic. Spaniards have more oriental blood than any other Western European race. These stocks united in varying proportions in the different localities, still further intensifying that tendency to regionalism favored by geography. The following generalizations apply most accurately to Central and Southern Spaniards.

Havelock Ellis' theory.—Havelock Ellis, in *The Soul of*

Spain, states that every race, in its development, passes out of savagery into barbarism, thence into civilization; yet every nation, whatever its present status, shows an especial aptitude for one of these three stages. The Gauls, even when barbarians, showed, he writes, a marked capacity for civilization. Conversely, the Spaniards, while undoubtedly possessed of a high civilization, show greater talent for barbarism. This is an overstatement, but it can scarcely be questioned that Spaniards possess less talent for capitalistic civilization than for a more primitive social structure. Faith suits them better than science. Their victories spring from an ardent crusading spirit, not from scientific, military organization. Ellis points out that many of the Spanish traits, stoicism, dignity, laziness, individualism, are also savage or barbaric peculiarities.

Stoicism.—In ancient times stoicism was the prevalent Spanish philosophy. Seneca was a Spaniard, and Seneca's bloody death Ellis considers typically Spanish. Certain it is that Spaniards are less moved at the sight of squalor, suffering, blood, and death than are other civilized nations. Are they therefore cruel, as commonly charged? The Inquisition is often cited as a manifestation of cruelty, but Spaniards reply that the total who lost their lives in Spain as a result of religious persecution did not exceed 23,000. This is a record which France, Germany, and England may well envy. Now that an American historian, Lea, has told the truth concerning the Inquisition, Spain should no longer be the victim of a century-old "black legend." There is little to choose between the various nations and creeds in the matter of cruelties perpetrated in the name of religion. The bull-fight, however, continues to keep alive the national reputation for cruelty. Intellectuals are unanimous in condemning it, but it continues to delight the populace. Without attempting to justify a wholly obnoxious institution, it is only fair to state that the spectators of a bull-fight do not go there to revel in the sight of blood, but it is true that the incidental horrors are viewed with indifference. The typical Spaniard is not so much cruel as stoically indifferent. He lacks imaginativeness, an ability to put himself in the place of the sufferer. He is no more innately cruel than our own ancestors whose sports were many of them brutal; but in this respect the Spaniard has lagged behind civilization. Kindness to animals has never been effectively preached to him. This is the more remarkable in that one finds everywhere in Spain so many evidences of genuine kindliness. Out of his stoicism grows the Spaniard's talent for realism. Though deficient in imagination, he has a gift for observation. His indifference to the repulsive crops out in some of the paintings of Ribera and Velázquez, the writings of Quevedo, and the picaresque novel. But, as a rule, his native kindliness and humor assert themselves. Realism is the typical form of Spanish art, but it is a realism almost always tempered by cheerfulness. It is seldom pessimistic and cynical, like so much of the realism of France and Russia. The race is still too simple and sound to have acquired a philosophy of despair.

Dignity.—Dignity is a quality closely related to stoicism. More than any other European, the Spaniard's bearing suggests that of the ancient Roman. He has a high sense of personal worth and honor. This quality is shared by all classes, even the peasant and the beggar. Spaniards are easily offended, and at times their susceptibility renders them ridiculous; but if they demand courtesy for themselves, they are no less ready to extend it to others. They are perhaps the politest people in existence. The literature of such a race is of necessity dignified, full of gracious formulas of courtesy. Hence the tendency toward ceremoniousness, magniloquence, and grandiloquence. Though dignified, they are never distant and frigid like Anglo-Saxons. Their clubs are less exclusive. Servants join naturally in conversation with their masters and their masters' guests. Snobbishness is virtually unknown to this democratic race. There exists among all classes an atmosphere of genuine kindliness in striking contrast to the tendency toward thoughtless cruelty noted above.

Laziness.—The traditional laziness of the Spaniard does not hold for the energetic Basques and Catalans, and is less applicable to the dwellers on the high, cool, central plateaus than to the Andalusians and inhabitants of the warmer regions. Even these latter display astounding outbursts of energy. There is no more active being than an energetic Spaniard (Lope de Vega, Velázquez, Menéndez Pidal, Sorolla). Havelock Ellis makes comparison with the North American Indian with whom "the love of idleness is the background for the manifestation of violent energy." This so-called laziness has a philosophic basis. The Spaniard "prefers to limit his wants rather than to work hard merely for the sake of creating artificial ones." This Mediterranean simplicity which we praise in the ancient Greeks is commonly condemned in the modern Spaniards—their attitude is so at variance with the viewpoint of a material age. But to quote Ellis again:

The Spaniard is constitutionally incapable of accepting the delusion that the best things in the world may be bought by money, or that a man's wealth consists in the abundance of his possessions. That is why in a passing phase of civilization, the Spaniard seems to belong to the past; and that is why, to some observers, he seems to belong also to the future.

The philosophical aspects of Spanish laziness are well treated by Mesonero Romanos, in the sketch, *Tengo lo que me basta.* The more reprehensible side, procrastination, is satirized by Larra in *Vuelva usted mañana.* In general, the Spaniard shows readiness to undertake vast enterprises, but lack of patience for sustained and detailed labor in completing the task begun. The effect of this in literature is a strong tendency toward improvisation and careless, rapid writing. There is charm in the unpremeditated lay, but all too often in Spanish literature a mediocre production might have been turned into a masterpiece with a little added care. Lope de Vega might have become a Shakespeare if he had avoided improvisation. There is often a lack of precision and clarity caused by indifference to niceties of grammar and style.

Individualism.—One of the Spaniard's salient characteristics is an intense individualism often accompanied with a spirit of insubordination. Ganivet distinguishes between *un pueblo guerrero* and *un pueblo militar.* The former class, to which Spain belongs, struggles against organization; the latter relies upon it. Thus Spaniards have always been guerrilla fighters, brave, defending their natal soil with tenacity, but relying upon individual effort. History has preserved to us many details of the gallant defense of Numantia, but most significantly neglects to tell who was in command there. The Cid was an insubordinate *guerrillero*. He fought kings for his private interest. Cortés and Pizarro were leaders of the same stamp. Gonzalo de Córdoba, Ganivet thinks, was rightly termed the "Great Captain," because he was a captain rather than a general. Napoleon's best troops were beaten by guerrilla tactics, not in pitched battles. There is the same individualism in the administration of law and justice. Until recently each district had its own privileges (*fueros*) and laws to which it jealously clung. One of the worst features of Spanish politics is the inability of the nation or even a single party to unite in a common cause. In literature, individualism is no less evident. Each writer tends to be a law unto himself. Literary schools are less clearly defined than elsewhere. Spanish authors, as a rule, rebel against critical precepts, and criticism has, perhaps, played a less important rôle in Spanish literature than in any other. This tendency makes for variety and color, but often leads to chaos.

Democracy.—We have seen how the course of Spanish history produced social democracy even under the most undemocratic forms of government. Spanish literature is the most democratic of all literatures. Royal and noble patronage was rarer by far than in Italy and France, and this weakness of aristocratic influence is another reason for the ineffectiveness of criticism in Spain. To be sure, there have been a few powerful patrons of literature, Alfonso el Sabio, John II, Isabel the Catholic, Cardinal Ximenes, and the less intelligent Philip IV. These and others instituted aristocratic movements. But, in the main, literature has been left to the people. The great genres of Spanish literature are the democratic genres: the epic, the ballad, the drama, the novel, and the literature of mystic devotion. One might also mention the proverb, for Spain is richer in proverbs than any other nation. The large number of them to be found in nearly all Spanish writings shows what close contact prevails between author and people. Spanish literature is weakest in criticism, history, and philosophy. Spain has produced much fine lyric poetry, and has continued to do so right up to the present moment.

Humor.—Humor is an almost universal characteristic of the Spanish race. Few of their authors are without it. That the illiterate peasant possesses this quality is shown by his numerous funny proverbs and his clever application of them. In quality Spanish humor is closely akin to that of England and the United States. Cynical wit, like that of Quevedo, is rare.

Character of the present-day Spaniard.—Many observers, Spanish as well as foreign, feel that the national character has undergone important changes. Past enterprise is contrasted with present apathy. But Spanish degeneracy is more relative than real. Spain is now more powerful, and conditions of life are better than in the days of her greatness. This fact is obscured when one notes that so many nations have since surpassed her that she now marches well toward the rear in the procession of civilization. Spain is not degenerate in a physiological or moral sense. Nevertheless, the present weakness, contrasted with past greatness, has caused racial discouragement. Ganivet diagnoses the national disease as *abulia*—a weakening of the will. The individual afflicted with this symptom, in his physical life does nothing, in his mental life heeds nothing. He develops a fixed idea and then gives way to some violent outburst. So, too, thinks Ganivet, the nation. Hence the present insistence upon *la voluntad* as the remedy needed. Azorín and his school never tire of preaching the doctrine. Most characters in recent Spanish fiction show will, often unaccompanied with scruple, in a way suggestive of Nietzscheian influence. Now that the disease is diagnosed, there is hope that the remedy will be applied. There are many encouraging signs: improved economic conditions, reforms in education, and magnificent achievements in art, music, and literature. Ganivet concludes his *Idearium español* hopefully. Each nation, he holds, has created some fictional type symbolizing its spirit. Greece created Odysseus, athletic and intellectually supple; Germany, Faust, scholarly and metaphysical; England, Robinson Crusoe, plucky, audacious, surmounting seeming impossibilities, typical of the Anglo-Saxon's adventurous but eminently practical spirit. But, he argues, Don Quijote, brave, courteous, impractical, but ever true to his ideals, is the noblest type of them all. There is no despairing of a nation which has created such a national figure.

Summary.—But Sancho Panza is as truly Spanish as Don Quijote. Just as master and man symbolize the clashing claims of the ideal and the real, so they may be made to typify the two opposed poles of Spanish literature, the idealistic and the realistic. Only Cervantes and a few others have had the genius to represent both of these tendencies. Romanticism constantly alternates with realism. Only a few writers, like Luis de León, successfully embodied the classic spirit. Spanish literature is democratic, individualistic, and for the most part undisciplined. Improvisation is too frequent. But it is elegant,

courtly, and chivalric; it abounds in humor and picturesqueness; it is human; it is racy of the soil; it is the most
colorful of literatures.

BIBLIOGRAPHY

ELLIS, HAVELOCK. *The Soul of Spain.* New ed. Boston, 1937.
ARJONA, DORIS KING. "*La voluntad* and *abulia* in Contemporary
Spanish Ideology," *Revue hispanique,* LXXIV, 593–667.
GANIVET, ÁNGEL. *Idearium español.* Madrid, 1897.
COSTA, J. *Ideario.* Madrid, n.d.
ALTAMIRA, R. *Historia de España.* . . . 4 vols. Barcelona, 1900–1911.
———. *A History of Spain.* New York, 1949. The most useful one-
vol. history of Spain.
MENÉNDEZ PIDAL, R. *The Spaniards in Their History,* trans.
WALTER STARKIE. London, 1950.
———. *Historia de España.* First vol., Madrid, 1935. A monu-
mental history in course of publication.
Diccionario de historia de España. 2 vols. Madrid, 1952. Nearly
3,000 pages of useful information.
CASTRO, A. *La realidad histórica de España.* Mexico, 1957. (Pub.
in English as *The Structure of Spanish History.* Princeton,
1954.) Stimulating meditations.
MADARIAGA, S. DE. *Spain.* New ed. New York, 1958. History
and interpretation.
LIVERMORE, H. *A History of Spain.* London, 1958.
PEERS, E. A., *et al. Spain: A Companion to Spanish Studies.* 5th
ed. London, 1956.
MALLO, J. *España: Síntesis de su civilización.* Useful class text.
Illustrated.
ADAMS, N. B. *The Heritage of Spain.* Rev. ed. New York, 1959.
Brief introduction to Spanish culture. Illustrated.
ECHEVERRÍA, L. M. *España: El país y los habitantes.* Mexico,
1949. Excellent treatment of geography, physical features,
demography, etc. Illustrated.
LEA, H. C. *A History of the Inquisition of Spain.* 4 vols. New
York and London, 1906–7.
HEMINGWAY, ERNEST. *Death in the Afternoon.* New York, 1932.
A discussion of bull-fighting by the celebrated American
aficionado.

CHAPTER II

The Epic

Birth of the Spanish language—The epic genre—Theories of epic origins—The Romantic theory—The *cantilena* theory—The theory of Germanic origin—The saga or prose-tradition theory—The saints' lives–monastery theory—The Moorish-Andalusian theory for Spain—Riquer's summary conclusions—How lost epics are restored—The epic heroes—The legend of Don Rodrigo—Bernardo del Carpio—Fernán González—Los infantes de Salas—*El cantar de Zamora*—*El cantar de Mio Cid*—*Rodrigo* and *La crónica rimada*—*Roncesvalles*.

Birth of the Spanish language.—Latin became the official language of Spain in 206 B.C. The speech of the masses was the *sermo vulgaris*, or spoken Latin, which differed significantly in vocabulary and simplicity of forms from the polished, artificial medium employed by the best Roman writers, which had become considerably Hellenized in the schools. By the time of the Moslem conquest, 711 A.D., Spanish Latin differed considerably from the variety spoken in Gaul and elsewhere. Just when Spanish came to be felt as a separate language, it is impossible to say. Most writing was done in classic Latin, or at least in a Latin which strove to conform to the standard rules of grammar; but, from the tenth century on, vernacular speech becomes more and more evident in legal documents. We are equally in the dark about when the first works of imaginative literature were written in Spanish. The earliest preserved epic monuments date from about the middle of the twelfth century,

but such a work as the *Cantar de Mio Cid* (about 1140?)
implies an antecedent epic development. It seems likely
that many Spanish epics must have been written in the
eleventh century, perhaps earlier. A folkloristic literature, for the most part oral rather than written, must
have begun even earlier.

The epic genre.—It used to be firmly believed that
epic manifestations preceded lyric in the various literatures. As far as Spain is concerned, the first surviving
literary babblings are the charming little *kharjas* written
in Hebrew or Arabic characters but in Mozarabic Spanish. They date from the eleventh century, but were not
studied until the 1940's. It is perfectly conceivable that
lyric and epic verse existed simultaneously at all periods.
The *kharjas* will be mentioned later in this book.

The word "epic" is likely to suggest to most people
Homer's *Odyssey* and *Iliad*, perhaps Hindu and Persian
epics, Virgil's *Aeneid*, Ariosto's *Orlando Furioso*, Camoens' *Lusiads*, Ercilla's *Araucana*, or Milton's *Paradise
Lost*. This is not the sort of epic with which we are now
concerned, because the poems mentioned are quite
sophisticated, and all presuppose a long period of development of the form. We are considering a more primitive sort of medieval epic, as it came into being in France
and Spain, at a date which no one can possibly pinpoint
with complete accuracy. Certainly epic songs must have
existed in France and Spain before early examples which
happened to survive, such as the *Chanson de Roland* and
the *Cantar de Mio Cid*.

Theories of epic origins.—Thousands of pages have
flowed from the pens of scholars with regard to the medieval epic. Earlier theories have been excellently summarized in such works as U. T. Holmes, Jr., *A History of*

Old French Literature; Ramón Menéndez Pidal, *L'Épopée castillane* and other works; and the more recent Martín de Riquer, *Los cantares de gesta franceses.* Theories referring to France may have parallel applicability to Spain. To those books the eager student is cordially urged to turn.

The Romantic theory.—In the early nineteenth century, certain French and German Romantics, perhaps best represented by Jacob Grimm, held the semimystic notion that all primitive epic songs sprang simply and collectively from a group, perhaps from some singing chorus of spontaneous enthusiasts. Stressing the anonymity of early poems, Grimm went so far as to say that it would have been absurd for one person to try to create an epic, because it was the people as a whole who composed it. It can be readily admitted that epic compositions did indeed represent the spirit of a whole group or tribe or people, but we may feel sure that some conscious author originally composed them. As time went on, they were no doubt modified, added to, changed, or re-worked. Such a process surely went on in Spain, with regard to both longer heroic poems and shorter ballads.

The "cantilena" theory.—Gaston Paris held that epics were formed by putting together *cantilenae,* short epico-lyric songs composed just after stirring events. The theory is no longer held as a full explanation of the rise of the epic.

The theory of Germanic origin.—In the eighties of the past century, the Italian scholar Pio Rajna, agreed with by many others, asserted that the origin of the French epic was Germanic. He stressed the fact that the Germanic epic is very old, perhaps as early as the fifth century A.D., and pointed out similarities with the epic as it later developed in France. The great dean of Spanish scholars, Ramón Menéndez Pidal, fundamentally agrees, with regard to Spain. He has maintained that the Gothic tribes, after establishing themselves in Spain, lost their language but not their love of epic song, and that the Spanish epic began as early as the tenth century. Later surviving Spanish examples unquestionably show many references to Germanic names, law, and customs. The Visigoths were dominant in Spain for about three centuries, and their spirit was not quenched by the victorious Moors from North Africa.

The saga or prose-tradition theory.—Some scholars maintained that the medieval epic was really based, not on poems arising from striking events, but on prose or oral traditions, versified as early as the ninth or tenth centuries. This theory would amount mainly to replacing Gaston Paris' *cantilenae* with prose narrations.

The saints' lives–monastery theory.—Some held early in the nineteenth century that the epic really arose under the influence of the numerous lives of saints; but it remained for Joseph Bédier, of the Collège de France, to elaborate the theory profusely and skilfully from 1904 onward. He persuasively suggested that medieval monasteries unconsciously became a sort of advertising fraternity, inspiring minstrel-bards to poetize the deeds of heroes whose relics were held within their walls, mighty men of yore who fought with the sword for the Cross. Popularity might thus be gained for monasteries, especially along the routes trod by devout pilgrims, or at least requiring only a short detour. Pious listeners (and so few could read!) might like to think of revered heroes like Charlemagne or Fernán González or the Cid (the last two only in Spain) as possessed of religious convictions as sturdy as their doughty right arms. The Spanish of it is *"A Dios rogando, y con el mazo dando."* The cynical modern who chances to read a medieval epic is likely to conclude that, if the poem under his eye is meant for propaganda somehow in favor of some religious establishment or other, the author involved showed no great skill as an advertiser. Bédier further maintained that the medieval epic was of semilearned provenience, and relatively late in date, not before the year 1000. His theory was attacked by Ferdinand Lot and others and is now by no means accepted *in toto*. One must not forget that the epics served as excellent propaganda for heroic military enterprise of all sorts.

The Moorish-Andalusian theory for Spain.—Passing mention may be made of the contention of the enthusiastic Spanish Arabist Julián Ribera, who endeavored to prove the existence of an epic produced by Mozarabic Christians in occupied southern Spain, in contact with the far more sophisticated Arabic civilization there. Ribera's efforts remained quite unsupported by other scholars as far as the epic is concerned. This is by no means to deny the general impact of Arabic culture, but the earliest surviving records are in connection with the lyric, and, as we shall see, the contact of the two civilizations was most fruitful in that regard.

Riquer's summary conclusions.—In the middle of the present century, Professor Martín de Riquer of Barcelona viewed the whole matter with a different focus, in considering the French epics and their relationship with Spain. He does not endeavor to refute or sustain the rival theories of epic origins which raged for more than a century in limited academic circles—theories which, by the way, are not all mutually exclusive. He insists that the fundamental element in the origin of the epic poem is the creative impulse of the composer: *"El cantar de gesta nace el día que un poeta se decide a escribir sobre una leyenda."* He has at his disposal many sources: actual history, its transformation into legend; saints' lives; older short poems such as the *cantilenae;* oral tradition; and his own artistic imagination. He applies them all to his chosen hero.

The earliest French epics are in lines with assonance, but with a regular number of syllables per line. The early surviving Spanish epics—the *Cid*, the *Crónica rimada*, and the *Roncesvalles*—are more primitive and show a chaotic irregularity in length of line.

How lost epics are restored.—The only examples of the popular Spanish epic which have come down to us are the three named above; but the content of many lost ones is known. The compilers of the *Primera crónica general,* 1270, and later chroniclers accepted the *cantares de gesta* as bona fide historical sources. They therefore incorporated a number of these into their text, turning them into prose. The full account of the Cid follows a version close to the MS preserved to us, and other passages devoted to other national heroes are just as evidently based upon poetic narratives. This we know from the large number of assonances preserved in the prose. Whole lines of the original verse are sometimes incorporated without change, as Menéndez Pidal shows in his *Leyenda de los Infantes de Lara.* The ballads, too, often the débris of lost epics, preserve much epic material. Thus, we are familiar with the content of many lost poems, even though their original form be lost. The "prosifications" in the early chronicles permit us to reconstruct epics of the best period; the late chronicles, particularly the so-called *Crónica de 1344,* incorporated *cantares* of the period of degeneracy.

The epic heroes.—The principal epic heroes around whom cycles developed were as follows: (1) Roderick the Goth; (2) Bernardo del Carpio; (3) El Conde Fernán González; (4) the latter's successors, Garci Fernández, Sancho García, El Infante Don García, and the sons of Don Sancho el Mayor; (5) Los Infantes de Salas; (6) El Cid, Rodrigo Díaz. There is also evidence that *cantares* existed to celebrate the deeds of the Gothic king, Wamba, the Cid's companion, Álvar Fáñez, Pedro Ansures, founder of Valladolid, and many another. It is important for the student of Spanish literature to familiarize himself with the epic legends in which these worthies figure, because they appear and reappear throughout a large part of Spanish literature. Their stories, first told in the popular epic, were taken up by the chronicles and works on genealogy, then formed the theme of popular ballads, next received the attention of cultured poets and dramatists of the sixteenth and seventeenth centuries, and lastly afforded a mine of material for the Romantic poets, novelists, and dramatists of the nineteenth century.

The legend of Don Rodrigo.—Historically, Rodrigo was a usurper who won the throne away from Achila, the rightful heir. The latter's faction was probably responsible for calling the Moors into Spain; but legend had made Rodrigo the scapegoat for the disaster. There existed in Toledo an abode of magic called the "House of Hercules," a sort of Bluebeard's chamber. The kings of Spain were forbidden entrance, and each in turn put a padlock on the door until the total number was twenty-four. Rodrigo forced an entrance. He found within a chest, containing a canvas on which were painted figures of Moslems, and an inscription stating that the beholder would see his kingdom conquered by men such as these. But Rodrigo, one of the first pacifists on record, foolishly collected as many weapons as he could and had them reforged into agricultural implements. Later, he seduced La Cava, daughter of Count Julian, then governor of the Spanish stronghold of Ceuta. La Cava wrote to her father demanding vengeance. Julian organized a Moorish force and invaded Spain. Christians and Moors met in a pitched battle, in which, after a gallant resistance, the former were vanquished. This legend, like all the rest, has many variants, and Rodrigo's fate is variously described: he died fighting gallantly; he was drowned in a river; he was devoured by wild beasts; but the most popular account was that he made his way to Viseo, Portugal, where he confessed his sins to a hermit, who prescribed a penance proportionate to the sin. Rodrigo was told to enter a tomb filled with serpents. This he did, accepting the one hope of salvation for his soul. In English literature the legend of Rodrigo has been treated by Sir Walter Scott, Southey, and Washington Irving.

Bernardo del Carpio.—Bernardo is the sole epic hero of Spain who cannot be identified with a historic personage. Epic heroes are not manufactured out of whole cloth, and perhaps some day the historic prototype will be found; but one must seek it in France rather than in Spain. The name is French. There existed two distinct *cantares* on Bernardo, the one presenting a French point of view, the other a Spanish adaptation, written from a patriotic, nationalistic viewpoint. We can reconstruct the content of each with a fair degree of accuracy. Of the two twelfth-century chroniclers, Lucas de Tuy and Rodrigo de Toledo, Lucas follows the French account, Rodrigo the Spanish version. The compilers of the

Crónica general, too, were familiar with both *cantares,* and made vain attempts to reconcile discrepancies. In the French version, Bernardo is son of Doña Tiber, Charlemagne's sister, who meets Bernardo's father, El Conde Saldaña, while on a pilgrimage to Santiago de Compostela. Bernardo, on reaching maturity, visits the French court where his kinship is denied, but he forces acknowledgment by duels and feats of arms. In the Spanish version, he is Leonese and his mother is Ximena, sister of Alfonso el Casto. Alfonso, offended at the relations existing between Ximena and the Conde Saldaña, places the mother in a convent, the father in a dungeon. Their offspring, Bernardo, is cared for at court, ignorant of his parentage. On reaching maturity, he accidentally learns his parentage and his father's fate. He asks the king for Saldaña's release, but is put off with excuses. After the battle of Roncesvalles, where he figures prominently in the French defeat and saves the king's life, both Alfonso el Casto, and his successor, Alfonso III, continue to refuse the one favor he begs. Bernardo retires to his castle and becomes a typical robber baron. The king, terrorized by his rebellious vassal, at last promises to free Saldaña. The son arrives at the appointed place. A mounted knight, clad in armor and gaily plumed, is led toward him. Bernardo dismounts and clasps his father's hand only to find it cold in death. Many people know Felicia Hemans' spirited ballad on this dramatic episode. Bernardo stands for the national cause, imperiled by the poltroonery of a weak king, also for a democratic spirit of revolt.

Fernán González.—Fernán González, who died in 970, was the leader who erected Old Castile into a separate county, making it independent of León. The story goes

that King Sancho el Gordo coveted a horse and a hawk
owned by Fernán. Sancho agreed to purchase for a stipu-
lated sum which was to be doubled each day that payment
was deferred. Sancho, ignorant of the workings of geo-
metrical progression, allowed the debt to run until not all
the wealth of Spain sufficed to satisfy it. He compounded
by granting the independence of Castile, whose first count
Fernán became. Castile became a kingdom in 1035.
The old *cantar* also related the founding of the monastery
of San Pedro de Arlanza, Fernán's exploits against the
Moors, his saucy defiance of the Leonese kings, and two
escapes from prison in which he was aided by his faithful
wife, Sancha. The *cantar* which served as basis for the
"prosification" in the *Crónica de 1344* is lost, but we possess a long work called *El poema de Fernán González,*"
written just previous to 1236, and which may now be consulted in Mr. Marden's critical edition. Though based
on the old, lost epic, its tone and form are learned and
clerical. It lacks the spirited turns characteristic of the
popular epic. Its form is the "fourfold way" (*cuaderna
vía*, four-line monorhymed stanzas of fourteen-syllable
Alexandrines). Though it tells the story with tolerable
completeness, we would gladly trade the whole of this
uninspired work for a fragment of the original.

Los infantes de Salas.—The legend of the seven noble-
born sons of Salas, or Lara (the substitution of the latter
name occurred in later variants), is one of the most
famous of Spanish tales. It is the story of a medieval feud.
Nobody knows what historic deed of vengeance inspired
the epic. We only know that the names of the leading
characters occur in tenth-century legal documents and
that they lived in the localities mentioned. Like all

legends, this had many variants and underwent various stages of development. The following is the story in its developed, rather than in its primitive, form. The opening scene is Burgos, where Doña Lambra is being married to Ruy Velázquez. Her nephews, the seven sons of Gonzalo Gustios, lord of Salas, are present to participate in the wedding sports. The boys, particularly the youngest, Gonzalo González, surpass all the rest at the games and incur the anger of Álvar Sánchez, Doña Lambra's cousin, whom the young Gonzalo kills in a personal encounter. The bride grieves for her slain kinsman and considers herself personally dishonored; but a peace is patched up for the moment. Sometime later one of Doña Lambra's servants insults Gonzalo by striking him with a cucumber filled with blood. Gonzalo kills him, in spite of the fact that the servant had claimed sanctuary by placing himself beneath his mistress' mantle, according to an old Germanic custom. The breach is now irrevocable, and Doña Lambra induces her husband to act in behalf of her honor. Ruy Velázquez' first step is to send the father, Gonzalo Gustios, on an embassy to Almanzor, Moorish general of Cordova. The letter Gonzalo carries urges Almanzor to decapitate the bearer and then proceed northward with his army; but Almanzor merely holds Gonzalo prisoner. Velázquez, meanwhile, had led the *infantes* southward on a campaign and arranged with the advancing Moors to lead his nephews into an ambush. The boys are accompanied by an aged mentor (*ayo*), Nuño Salido, the finest character in the epic. This Spanish Nestor scents treason and urges his charges to escape the snare. They are too rashly brave to accept good advice, and Nuño is too loyal to desert them. All perform prodigies of valor as the battle joins, but fall fighting. The heads of Nuño and the seven boys are sent to Almanzor as trophies. The most stirring portion of the legend is where Almanzor calls upon the father to identify the heads. Gonzalo pronounces over them touching eulogies which collectively summarize the qualities expected to characterize the perfect knight: loyalty, justice, truth, valor, fidelity, generosity, a fondness for good company. While a captive, Gonzalo had had another son, Mudarra, by a noble Moorish lady named Zeula. In course of time Gonzalo is released and returns to his northern home, after first leaving with Mudarra half of a broken ring, himself retaining the other portion. Mudarra does not learn his parentage until attaining manhood. He then turns Christian and determines to avenge his half-brothers. He visits his aged father; the two parts of the ring join; he is acknowledged as a son. He encounters Ruy Velázquez and slays him in single combat. Doña Lambra is burned at the stake.

This grim legend is a faithful reflex of the rudeness of Castilian society during the Middle Ages. Menéndez Pidal, in his *Leyenda de los infantes de Lara*, has reconstructed the content of three old *cantares* written on the theme. As later editions of the *Crónica general* utilized reworkings of the original *cantar*, a study of the evolution of this legend shows how epic poetry developed from the comparatively simple to the ornate and romantic as it passed from the period of its prime to an epoch of degeneracy. Few legends have been utilized more in Spanish literature. As late as the nineteenth century, it gave the Duque de Rivas the subject of his Romantic epic, *El moro expósito*.

"*El cantar de Zamora.*"—The epic thus designated must have been by far the most artistic narrative poem of the Spanish Middle Ages, one of the most imposing works of genius which Spain ever produced, worthy to rank among the best heroic poems of the world literature. The loss of this *cantar* is a calamity, but the *Primera crónica general* has preserved its plot intact. What we lack is the *juglar's* energetic phraseology. It was superior to the often prosy *Cantar de Mio Cid*. It was a Spanish *Iliad*, treating artistically the facts of history. Some historians of literature classify it in the Cid cycle, for the Cid figures as a personage, though in a subordinate capacity. Some have thought that this epic is the missing introduction of the *Cantar de Mio Cid;* but the best authorities consider it wholly distinct. Puyol y Alonso has sought to reconstruct it with the title, *Cantar de gesta de Don Sancho II de Castilla*. The ballads on this subject were incorporated in the *Romancero del Cid*. Probably the Cid did not figure in the original redaction, but was dragged into later rehandlings of the theme when he had become a favorite with minstrels and populace. The true heroes are Diego Ordóñez, on the side of Castile, and Arias Gonzalo and his sons on that of León. The theme is the dissension between the children of Fernando I and the tragic consequences which ensued, all centering around the siege of Zamora.

Content.—Fernando I, having by war, marriage, and diplomacy effected a union of the little kingdoms of Northwestern Spain, on his deathbed partitioned his domains among his children in 1065. Sancho received Castile; Alfonso, León; García, Galicia and Northern Portugal. His daughters protested at being disinherited, and, as an afterthought, Urraca was awarded the city of Zamora, and Elvira, Toro. (Menéndez Pidal thinks that this episode, rather than beginning the *Cantar de Zamora*, closed a *Cantar del rey Don Fernando*, preserved in prose in the *Crónica de 1344*.) Sancho II soon began an attack upon his brothers and sisters to reunite the divided kingdom. First, pretending to go on a pilgrimage to Santiago, he led an army through León and defeated his brother García, who languished over twenty years in prison and died asking to be buried in his chains. Sancho next turned upon Alfonso, who was driven out of his kingdom and forced to take refuge with the Moors of Toledo. (As a matter of historic fact, León was conquered before Galicia.) Elvira surrendered Toro with slight resistance. Sancho then laid siege to Zamora with all his forces. The Cid was sent as an ambassador to Urraca demanding the surrender of the city. After holding counsel with Arias Gonzalo and her nobles, who swore unfailing loyalty, Urraca replied with a haughty refusal. Arias is a Nestor-like character, brave, prudent, loyal. Sancho made slight progress against the strong fortifications of Zamora, which even today are as lofty, if not as formidable, as in the Middle Ages. The siege continued for seven years; the inhabitants were reduced to extremes.

At this point Bellido Dolfos, one of the Zamoran nobles, offered in council to take personal measures to end the siege. To this mysterious offer Urraca replied equivocally. Bellido sallied forth through a postern and reached Sancho's camp. Feigning to be a deserter, he placed his hands in those of the king and swore fealty. A voice from the battlements warned that treason was afoot: "*¡Rey don Sancho, rey don Sancho, no digas que no* *te aviso!*" etc. (These spirited lines from a later ballad may well have been taken from the original.) But Sancho, unheeding, withdrew in private with Bellido, who stabbed him in the back with fatal result and fled. Bellido was received into the city through the same postern by which he had quitted it. The Cid pursued the traitor, but was unable to overtake him, because of being at the moment unprovided with spurs. Bellido was placed in irons, pending the outcome of the trial by combat which was sure to ensue, but nothing is told of his subsequent fate.

Then Diego Ordóñez appeared below the walls and issued his famous *reto*, or defiance. This was a solemn accusation of treason, proclaimed in accordance with Gothic law against the inhabitants of Zamora collectively. He cursed "those of high and low degree, the living and the dead, those born and those still unborn, the waters they shall drink, the clothes they shall wear, and even the stones of the wall." Such an accusation of treason, accompanied by a curse, was not to be lightly regarded in the Middle Ages. The challenger was forced to meet five champions successively in the lists. He must slay each of these, ejecting the corpse of his foe from the inclosure without himself leaving it, unless led forth by the judges. Between combats he might change horse, armor, and weapons, and taste three slices of bread dipped in wine.

Arias Gonzalo and his sons accepted in behalf of Zamora; but Urraca refused her aged *ayo* permission to risk his life. The responsibility, therefore, rested with the sons. The first son, Pedro Arias, was slain. The second, Diego Arias, met no better fate. The third son, Rodrigo Arias, was also slain, but in his last struggle wounded the

challenger's horse so that it became unmanageable and
bore its rider forth from the inclosure. What were the
judges to decide? Diego Ordóñez had killed his man,
whose corpse was lying within the inclosure; but the victor had violated the strict rule which forbade passing the
bounds. They declared a draw. Zamora was neither
proved guilty of treason nor formally acquitted of the
charge. The divine judgment was inconclusive.

Alfonso VI, who lived to become one of Spain's
greatest monarchs, was now heir to the dominions so
tragically reunited; but as he had been primarily identified with the interests of León, the Cid and other Castilian
nobles found the oath of allegiance to Sancho's foe a bitter
pill to swallow. It is a matter of historic record that the
Cid and eleven other nobles, as a condition to their allegiance, forced Alfonso to swear on the gospels that he had
not been an accomplice in his brother's murder. This
ceremony took place in the little church of Santa Gadea,
Burgos, still standing. Alfonso changed color three times
as the Cid thrice forced him to swear the oath, and on the
conclusion of the ceremony refused to allow the Cid to
kiss his hand. With this dramatic episode the *Cantar de
Zamora* ended.

Its literary value.—The old generalization that the
popular epic of Spain is an exclusively Castilian manifestation needs revision. We have seen that some believe
in the existence of an Andalusian epic. The newly discovered *Roncesvalles* fragment shows that the form was
cultivated in Navarra; and it would be surprising if there
were no Leonese epic, when Leonese and Castilians were
similar in culture. It is true that most of the *cantares de
gesta* known display a narrowly Castilian point of view

and intense prejudice toward the Leonese. The chief exception to this is the *Cantar de Zamora*, whose unknown author rose above partisan strife and became broadly national. Alfonso, and more especially, Urraca were suspected by Castilians of being guilty of Sancho's death, as is shown not only by the oath of Santa Gadea but by the Latin epitaph on Sancho's tomb at Oña, where it is formally stated that he was murdered by his sister.[1] Our anonymous author shows none of this prejudice. His is a spirit of fair play. Over against Diego Ordóñez are balanced Arias Gonzalo and his sons. Both sides are equally brave, equally loyal. It is an epic with many heroes. No one of them was singled out for exclusive admiration The author avoided offense to the Castilians convinced that King Sancho had met with foul play, though evidence seems to show that in reality he fell in a fair fight. On the other hand, he avoided offending the Leonese by refusing to declare their faction guilty. The poem seems to reflect the policy of conciliation instituted by Alfonso on coming to the throne. The poet clearly saw the folly of partitioning into little kingdoms territory hardly won from the Moors, when national unity was demanded to oppose an enemy at the doors. It is with a sense of foreboding that one reads the provisions of Fernando's will. The division of a family brings as a logical consequence internecine strife between the provinces. The larger theme, then, is

[1] "Sanctus forma Paris et ferox Hector in armis
    clauditur hac tumba, jam factus pulvis et umbra.
    Femina, mente dura, soror, hunc vita expoliavit
    jure quidem dempto, flevit fratre perempto.

"Rex iste occisus est proditore consilio sororis suae Urracae apud Numantiam civitatem per manum Belliti Adelfis magni traditoris. In Era MCX Nonis Octobris [=Oct. 7, 1072] rapuit me curis et horis."

the division and reintegration of Christian Spain. The siege of Zamora serves to give the poem unity. All is realism, all is logic, all is nice balance in this work. The facts of history are closely followed with only that amount of imagination necessary to distinguish an epic from versified history. The interest never flags. There are no prosy passages, as in most medieval poetry. If the bald prose of the *Crónica general* justifies such statements as these, one may fairly conclude that the *Cantar de Zamora* in its most perfect form must have been the noblest work of literature which twelfth-century Spain produced.

"*El Cantar de Mío Cid.*"—This is the sole considerable survival of a once widely cultivated genre. It has been preserved in a single MS which has undergone so many vicissitudes that only by a miracle has it failed to perish like so many others. It was first published by Sánchez in 1779. Menéndez Pidal in his monumental three-volume edition has given us both diplomatic and critical texts, grammar, glossary and an all but definitive study of every question which concerns this important work. That scholar finds that the date of composition was close to 1140, the period when epic poetry in Spain reached its height of development. He bases this conclusion on internal and linguistic evidence. By a study of geographical allusions, it becomes evident that the anonymous poet was a Castilian most familiar with a restricted region around Medina Celi. Whether or not he was connected with the monastery of San Pedro de Cardeña, which the Cid endowed, is uncertain. The portion preserved numbers 3,735 lines. The part lost at the beginning probably amounted to some 50 lines.

Content.—The poem is split into three divisions, after

each of which the minstrel paused for rest, reward, and his
vaso de buen vino. These divisions Menéndez entitles: (1) *el
cantar del destierro;* (2) *el cantar de las bodas;* (3) *el cantar
de Corpes.* The poem opens dramatically with the return
of Rodrigo Díaz to Burgos, where he finds every door
closed against him.

> He turned and looked upon them, and he wept very sore
> As he saw the yawning gateway and the hasps wrenched off the
> door,
> And the pegs whereon no mantle nor coat of vair there hung.
> My Lord the Cid sighed deeply, such grief was in his heart,
> And he spake well and wisely: "Oh Thou, in Heaven that art
> Our Father and our Master, now I give thanks to Thee.
> Of their wickedness my foemen have done this thing to me."
>
> —Rose and Bacon

A nine-year-old girl informs him that a letter has arrived
from King Alfonso forbidding the citizens to harbor him
or give him food. Alfonso had accused his vassal of with-
holding tribute money. The barbaric custom of killing
the bearer of evil tidings was still in vogue, and the
citizens had feared to intrust the message to a male. Sor-
rowfully the Cid left the city and camped that night on
the banks of the Arlanzón. Within a few days he must
leave Castile, an exile. His trusty henchman, Martín
Antolínez, financed the departure by raising a loan from
the Jews, Raquel and Vidas, offering as security a coffer
filled with sand, which they supposed contained the Cid's
treasure. With pockets lined, the little band of sixty
lancers went to San Pedro de Cardeña, where the Cid
intrusted his wife and daughters, Elvira and Sol, to the
keeping of the abbot of that monastery. The parting
from his family was like that of "the fingernail from the

flesh." News of the Cid's banishment had spread, and
adventurers began to flock to his standard. Now began
his adventures as a soldier of fortune, and, while there is
much monotony in this portion of the work, there are
several spirited battle-pictures like the following:

> Before their breasts the war-shields there have they buckled
>   strong,
> The lances with the pennons they laid them low along,
> And they have bowed their faces over the saddlebow,
> And thereaway to strike them with brave hearts did they go.
> He who in happy hour was born with a great voice did call:
> "For the love of the Creator, smite them, my gallants all.
> I am Roy Diaz of Bivar, the Cid, the Campeador."
> At the rank where was Per Vermudoz the mighty strokes they
>   bore.
> They are three hundred lances that each a pennon bear.
> At one blow every man of them his Moor has slaughtered there,
> And when they wheeled to charge anew as many more were slain.
> You might see great clumps of lances lowered and raised again,
> And many a shield of leather pierced and shattered by the stroke,
> And many a coat of mail run through, its meshes all to-broke,
> And many a white pennon come forth all red with blood,
> And running without master full many a charger good.
> Cried the Moors "Mahound!" The Christians shouted on Saint
>   James of Grace.
> On the field Moors thirteen hundred were slain in little space.
>
> —Rose and Bacon

Throughout the poem the Cid figures as a loyal vassal
ever seeking a reconciliation with his lord, in spite of bad
treatment. After each victory he sends rich booty to
Alfonso, and the gifts increase in value with the donor's
growing prosperity. The second division of the poem first
describes the conquest of Valencia, called even today
"Valencia del Cid." After this triumph he sent Álbar

Fáñez with a present of one-hundred horses to request Alfonso to permit Ximena and the daughters to join him in Valencia. Alfonso accepted the present and granted the request. The Cid had now become virtually an independent monarch, and sound statesmanship demanded a reconciliation. Soon a conference (*las vistas*), between king and vassal was held. The Cid completely regained his sovereign's good graces. Alfonso demanded that the Cid marry his daughters to the Infantes de Carrión. This match displeased the Cid, but he loyally carried out Alfonso's wishes. The *cantar de las bodas* ends with a description of the wedding festivities.

The Cid bestowed wealth upon his sons-in-law, and, what he prized more, his swords, Colada and Tizón. But the *infantes* proved themselves cowards in battle, and when a captive lion escaped in the Cid's palace, they became such objects of ridicule that they resolved to withdraw with their wives to their estates. The Cid dismissed them with kindliness and presents, but they were resolved to be avenged for the indignities they had suffered in Valencia. On reaching the oak grove of Corpes, they stripped their wives, bound them to trees, flogged them and rode away. The ladies were rescued by their cousin, Félez Muñoz, and restored to their father. The Cid then demanded of the king that the *infantes* be punished and amends made to his daughters and himself. Alfonso summoned a *cortes* to be held at Toledo, and both parties were ordered to appear before it. When the session opened, the Cid first demanded the return of his two swords, which the Infantes de Carrión readily consented to; they had feared a more serious request. Not satisfied with this, the Cid asked for the return of his wealth. The *infantes* complied with this demand, too, but reluctantly, under compulsion. For a third time the Cid arose and demanded that his sons-in-law be tried by judicial combat. This request, too, Alfonso granted. The Cid, who had up to this point kept his beard bound up to keep enemies from pulling it, now unbound it. All were amazed at the majesty of his presence. Emissaries from the princes of Navarra and Aragon now arrived, demanding the hands of Doña Elvira and Doña Sol, who had become automatically divorced when abandoned by their husbands. Later the duel was held between the Infantes de Carrión and the Cid's champions. The latter triumph; the divine decision proves the sons-in-law traitors and the Cid a man of honor. So the poem ends with the hero's complete vindication.

Criticism.—*El cantar de Mio Cid* was written just forty years after the hero's death, more nearly contemporaneous with the events narrated than is the case with any of the world's great epics now preserved. The natural trend of epic development is from the historic and true to the romantic and marvelous. Therefore we should expect *The Cid* to be the most realistic of epics. Such is the fact. Of all epics it shows us most exactly what heroic poetry was like in its origins. Not that it is mere rhymed history. Though many of the *juglar's* auditors had doubtless seen and conversed with the Cid, a mythical tradition concerning him had already sprung up. He was no longer the freebooting adventurer of history who occasionally fought on the Moslem side against Christians, but had become the champion of the cross against the crescent, the symbol of all Christian Spain—a symbol, also, of the democratic spirit of the nation, a vassal who had become greater than his king. Certain incidents, like those of the first marriages of the Cid's daughters and the Robledo de Corpes episode, appear fictitious. Yet the historicity of the Infantes de Carrión has been established, and we may be dealing with an instance of "epic transference." That is to say, an adventure which befell another family may have been ascribed to the Cid and his daughters. Other departures from truth may be shown, but, in the main, recent research has revealed a closer adherence to fact than had formerly been supposed. The poet interpreted history imaginatively, but his imagination was restrained. Magic does not appear; Christian miracle is introduced very sparingly. We lack completely that exaggeration so common in the French epic, where, as in the *Chanson de Roland*, whole armies fall in a faint. The Cid's personal exploits are no greater than those recorded of many knights. A dignity wholly Spanish pervades the whole work. The tone is as austerely grave as the landscape of Old Castile. The business of life is fighting. There is no element of romantic love; but to make up for it there are several pleasing pictures of conjugal love. No other epic hero is such a perfect *paterfamilias* as the Cid. The poet is interested neither in his hero's youth nor in his death. The Cid is presented in his prime, engaged in his greatest achievements. The story is arranged climactically. We meet him in adversity and part from him when he has conquered Valencia, become reconciled with his king, and won complete vindication. The scene at the Cortes de Toledo is artistically the best. The poem is a "slice of life." The laws and customs, habits of thought, mode of life of the Castilians, are portrayed with the most minute exacti-

tude. It presents a stirring picture of a rude and primitive race on the road to greatness.

Its metrical form.—That rudeness of the race is well
illustrated by the crudity of the metrical form of this
poem. Romance poetry is almost universally based upon
the principle of syllable counting. A fairly high percent-
age of lines in *The Cid* scan as Alexandrines, that is to say
they have fourteen syllables with a fixed caesura in the
middle. A lesser number are in ballad meter (*verso de
romance*), sixteen syllables with a caesura in the middle.
The stress in each half-line would fall always on the sixth
or seventh syllable, respectively in the two measures
named. But the greater number of lines are utterly irregular, some very long, others short. Some scholars
think that such irregularities cannot have stood in the
original, but are due to scribal errors. Restori has held
that the Alexandrine was the original meter, while Cornu
has sought to show that the metrical basis was ballad meter. Milá, however, advanced the theory of irregular versification which Menéndez Pidal and his school espouse.
Menéndez finds like irregularity in the *Rodrigo* and in
that portion of the *Cantar de los infantes de Lara* which
he was able to reconstruct from the *Crónica general;* and
likewise in *La crónica rimada* and the *Roncesvalles.*
Though there are still many skeptics, the theory of *versificación irregular* appears to be winning ground. With the
Arabic invasion the old Roman seats of culture were
destroyed. A new culture had to be developed slowly in
the highlands of the North. What wonder if the first
poetic attempts were halting!

The course of epic development and degeneracy.—Rude
though it be in some respects, *El cantar de Mio Cid* shows

a relative talent which implies a considerable antecedent epic development. Whether or not Menéndez is right in placing the beginning of the Spanish epic in the tenth century, there can be no doubt that many such works were written in the eleventh. The twelfth century is the period of epic flowering. The works then written showed realism, close adherence to historic fact, lack of the love element and the marvelous. The thirteenth and fourteenth centuries were a time of epic degeneration. The fictional element increases, imagination runs riot, love and the marvelous are prominent, and many of the heroes are of foreign importation. These epics, too, may frequently be reconstructed, for late editions of the *General Chronicle*, particularly the so-called *Chronicle of 1344*, drew from them instead of from the older, better *cantares.* The degenerate epic frequently dealt with the youthful exploits (*mocedades*) of a popular hero, or his last days (*vejeces*). This course of development and degeneration closely parallels what happened to the French *épopée*—a fact to be borne in mind in considering the matter of Franco-Hispanic epic relations.

The "Rodrigo."—The name *Rodrigo*, or sometimes *Las mocedades del Cid*, is given to a cantar which may be reconstructed from a "prosification" in the *Crónica de 1344*. This deals with the Cid's *primera hazaña*, the killing in a duel of Ximena's father who had insulted the Cid's own aged father. Ximena then demanded of the king the Cid's hand in marriage by way of compensation. The marriage follows. The Cid also makes a foray into France, aiding Fernando I in his aspirations to become Roman emperor. Here, too, occurs for the first time the story of the Cid's encounter with a leper whom he takes to his table and his bed, after which deeds of charity the stranger reveals himself as St. Lazarus. There are other episodes equally unhistoric and fictitious. The contrast between the romantic tone of the *Rodrigo* and the grave realism of *El cantar de Mio Cid* is complete. The author of the Rodrigo deserves to be remembered as the first writer who introduces the conflict between love and honor which rages in Ximena's heart; but the love affair is handled awkwardly, and it remained for Guillén de Castro and Corneille to develop this highly poetic situation.

"*La crónica rimada.*"—From the *Rodrigo* derived *La crónica rimada del Cid*, a crude, fragmentary poem of 1,132 lines, apparently written in *versificación irregular*, and which Menéndez Pidal dates from the beginning of the fifteenth century. This work marks a further stage in the process of degeneracy. It is less true to history than its source. The most striking departure is that the Cid has ceased to be a loyal vassal, but has become a saucy chieftain of popular revolt, indicative of the growth of democracy. From the *Rhymed Chronicle of the Cid*, its sources and related versions derive most of the old ballads in the *Romancero del Cid*.

"*Roncesvalles.*"—A most happy find disclosed in the archives of Pamplona four parchment pages containing 100 lines of verse and which on examination proved to be a fragment of a Spanish version of the *Chanson de Roland*. It is not a translation of the greatest of French epics, but a re-writing, indicating a Spanish point of view. Menéndez Pidal announced this discovery to the world of scholars in 1917. The manuscript appears to date from about 1310. The poem itself seems to have been written about the middle of the twelfth century. Menéndez estimates that the whole work was 4,000 lines in extent. As one of the oldest monuments of Spanish literature, the fragment is of interest both philologically and from a literary point of view. It appears to offer another specimen of *versificación irregular*, and preserves the episode where Charlemagne, after the battle, returns to mourn over the bodies of his deceased chieftains. Reinaldos is one of these, and his death at Roncesvalles is a distinctly Spanish, not a French, tradition. There is also evidence that the author was acquainted with the *Maynete* epic, which, by the way, was transcribed in prose in both the *Crónica general* and *La gran conquista de Ultramar*. No "prosification" of the *Roncesvalles* exists. There was no supposition that such an epic had been written in Spain. How many more like it must have passed into oblivion, and how rich must have been the development of the popular epic in Spain during the Middle Ages! How the epic died out in the fifteenth century and was replaced by popular ballads is a story to be told in a later chapter.

BIBLIOGRAPHY

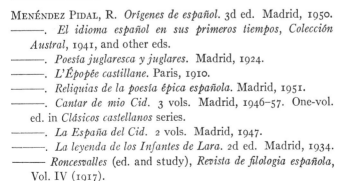

Menéndez Pidal, R. *Orígenes de español*. 3d ed. Madrid, 1950.
———. *El idioma español en sus primeros tiempos*, Colección Austral, 1941, and other eds.
———. *Poesía juglaresca y juglares*. Madrid, 1924.
———. *L'Épopée castillane*. Paris, 1910.
———. *Reliquias de la poesía épica española*. Madrid, 1951.
———. *Cantar de mio Cid*. 3 vols. Madrid, 1946–57. One-vol. ed. in *Clásicos castellanos* series.
———. *La España del Cid*. 2 vols. Madrid, 1947.
———. *La leyenda de los Infantes de Lara*. 2d ed. Madrid, 1934.
——— *Roncesvalles* (ed. and study), *Revista de filología española*, Vol. IV (1917).

MENÉNDEZ PIDAL, R. *Rodrigo el último godo.* 3 vols. Madrid, 1925-27.

————. La Chanson de Roland y el *neotradicionalismo: Orígenes de la épica románica.* Madrid, 1959.

ENTWISTLE, WM. J. *The Spanish Language.* New York, 1929.

LAPESA, R. *Historia de la lengua española.* 2d ed. Madrid and Buenos Aires, 1950.

SPAULDING, R. K. *How Spanish Grew.* 2d printing. Berkeley and Los Angeles, 1948.

HOLMES, U. T. *History of Old French Literature.* New York, 1948. Chap. vii gives an excellent summary of theories on the epic held by Jacob Grimm, Gaston Paris, Pio Rajna, Joseph Bédier, Robert Fawtier, and others.

RIQUER, MARTÍN DE. *Los cantares de gesta franceses: Sus problemas, su relación con España.* Madrid, 1952.

————. *Les Chansons de geste françaises.* 2e éd., entièrement refondue. Paris, 1957.

RIBERA, J. *Discurso en la Academia de la Historia.* Madrid, 1915.

MENÉNDEZ Y PELAYO, M. "Tratado de los romances viejos," *Antología de poetas líricos castellanos.* 10 vols. Santander, 1944-45. Contains account of epic heroes and legends.

KRAPPE, A. H. "La Légende de la maison fermée de Tolède," *Bulletin hispanique,* XXVI, 305-11.

Poema de Fernán González, ed. C. C. MARDEN. Baltimore, 1904.

PUYOL Y ALONSO, J. "Cantar de gesta de Don Sancho II de Castilla," *Archivo de investigaciones históricas,* I (1911).

DOZY, R. P. A. *Recherches sur l'histoire politique et littéraire de l'Espagne pendant le moyen âge.* 2 vols. Leyden, 1882.

"Crónica rimada del Cid," ed. B. BOURLAND, *Revue hispanique,* XXIV, 310-57.

The Poem of the Cid, trans. L. B. SIMPSON. Berkeley and Los Angeles, 1957. Prose translation.

The Lay of the Cid, trans. R. S. ROSE and LEONARD BACON. Berkeley, 1919. Verse translation.

MILLARES, CARLO A. *Literatura española hasta fines del siglo XV.* Mexico, 1950.

AMADOR DE LOS RÍOS, J. *Historia crítica de la literatura española.* 7 vols. Madrid, 1861-65. Middle Ages only.

CHAPTER III

The Beginnings of
the Drama and Early
Poetic Monuments

The liturgical drama—the three dramatic cycles—Later development—*Auto de los tres reyes magos*—*Mester de juglaría* and *mester de clerecía*—*Disputa del alma y el cuerpo*—*Razón de amor con los denuestos del agua y el vino*—*Elena y María*—*La vida de Madona Santa María Egipciaqua*—Gonzalo de Berceo—*Libro de Alexandre*—Rabbi Sem Tob—*Libro de Apolonio*—*Poema de Yuçuf*—*Poema de Alfonso Onceno*—*Danza de la muerte*.

The liturgical drama.—The origin of the drama in Spain was similar to that in other European countries. It sprang from the church liturgy. The lyric poetry of the Hebrews was parallelistic. Each thought was repeated in varied language. Such poetry, which formed the basis of the church's liturgy, was well adapted to the antiphonic, choral chant and contained within it the germ of the drama. The records of the monastery of St. Gall, Switzerland, credit the monk Tutilo with taking the next step—actual acting introduced into the service on special occasions. Tutilo in the early tenth century invented the *tropus*, a dialogue introduced into the *introitus*, or first part of the mass. This was in connection with the Easter service, and consists of an interview between the angel guarding the tomb and three priests who came to seek the body. Tutilo's dialogue was in Latin, a mosaic of scriptural passages with nothing original added.

The three dramatic cycles.—The European drama origi‹ nated, then, in connection with the Easter service. Tutilo's invention was immediately passed on to other monasteries and churches, and soon was elaborated. Mary Magdalene announced the resurrection to Peter and Paul. There were special ceremonies for Palm Sunday. The night before Easter the harrowing of hell was enacted. A procession of monks passed through the church. They paused before a door representing the gate to hell. A priest, acting the part of Christ, held speech with a deacon, the devil, who stood on the other side. After three demands the procession passed through, and later returned bearing in triumph a number of saved souls. The walk to Emmaus and Christ's rising from the tomb were also acted. Thus there was gradually formed a whole cycle of Easter plays. The Christmas cycle is nearly as old, for Tutilo also wrote a Christmas *tropus*. There was a crib behind the altar; priests played the rôles of shepherds, herald-angels, midwives, etc. The Annunciation and the Massacre of the Innocents were performed, though it is supposed that the latter event was represented symbolically. The most important of the three great cycles was the Epiphany cycle. Three priests, representing the three magi, came from different parts of the church, met under a star, exchanged greetings, and then followed the star as it slid along a rope until they were guided to the manger. Then came the adoration scene.

Later development.—The period of the liturgical drama is roughly from 900 to 1200 A.D. During these centuries there was constant development. Latin hexameters, especially from Vergil, were introduced into the text. Free composition in Latin followed. In the twelfth cen-

tury the vernacular languages were substituted for Latin
a change which greatly increased public interest. More
ambitious effects were attempted. Laymen joined with
priests as actors, and finally displaced them. New subjects were essayed. The stories of Lazarus, of the wise
and foolish virgins, of the prophet Daniel, and of many a
popular saint were cast in dramatic form. The comic element grew in importance, devils contributing most of the
humor. Finally, these representations grew unseemly
and were banished from sacred edifices. Plays were then
acted in the market-place. In France they were elaborate-
ly staged by semireligious guilds. Out of the liturgical
drama developed in the thirteenth and fourteenth centuries the great miracle and mystery plays. In the later
period of elaboration, Herod became an important figure.
He was half-man, half-devil, a ranting part whose tradition was still familiar to Elizabethans when Shakespeare
coined the phrase, "to out-Herod Herod." His astrologers,
who spoke a comic gibberish, were also popular with the
masses. The foiling of Herod by the magi appealed greatly to the risibilities. The simple dignity of the early Epiphany plays had degenerated into farce.

"*El auto de los reyes magos.*"—Spain, too, had her liturgical drama, but the genre is now represented by a single short fragment called *El auto de los reyes magos*. It was
written toward the middle of the twelfth century, within
a few years of *El cantar de Mio Cid*. It is not only the
second oldest literary monument of Spain, but is also the
second oldest example of a liturgical drama in any vernacular language. The French *Jeu d'Adam*, written earlier in
the same century, alone outdates it. In the eleventh
century there was an influx of French clergy into Spain,

and it is thought that they did much to spread dramas of the sort then being acted in the religious establishments of Northern Europe. Our play is unlike any other known Epiphany play in several particulars, but bears closest resemblance to a Latin liturgical work on the same theme written in Orleans. Each of the magi enters separately, expressing astonishment at sight of the new star in the east. Their paths converge; they exchange greetings. One bears gold, symbolic of kingly dignity; another frank-incense, symbolic of the divine nature; another myrrh, symbolic of the human nature. The magi are skeptical and seek to test the Christ-child, seeing which of these presents he will prefer. The scene changes to Herod's palace, where the magi inform that ruler that the Christ is born. They depart. The fragment breaks off during a consultation between Herod and his astrologers. Beyond a doubt, the piece ended with the adoration scene, the escape of the wise men, and the rage of Herod. The comic element is slight, but may have been more pronounced in the missing portion. The *auto* belongs to the second, or fuller, period of Epiphany play development. Unique features of this version are the separate entrances of the magi and their dismissal before, rather than after, Herod's consultation with his astrologers. The single manuscript which perpetuated the *auto* was written in the thirteenth century. It shows a variety of verse forms, lines of six, eight, and twelve syllables predominating. Rhyme, not assonance, is used. The tone is dignified, in spite of a certain naïveté.

A dramatic gap.—The *Auto de los reyes magos* is the chance survival from among many similar works which must have existed. In the *Siete partidas* of Alfonso X, a codification of the laws compiled around 1255, the clergy are forbidden to participate in *juegos de escarnios* (a form of mummery which gave rise to scandal), but encouraged to act plays representing the Nativity, Crucifixion, and Resurrection. Such chance allusions show that the drama continued to be cultivated in Spain, though it can scarcely have equaled that of France in quality or extent. We shall not again have occasion to deal with the drama until the period of the late fifteenth century is reached. The intervening three-hundred years are a blank, so far as dramatic literature is concerned.

"Mester de juglaría" and "mester de clerecía."—Poetic production of the Middle Ages falls into two main categories: that of the minstrel-poets (*juglares*), termed *mester* ("manner," "mode") *de juglaría*, narrative and lyric, and that of the clergy, *mester de clerecía*, devotional, edifying, didactic. The clerical writings were largely a literature of translation. The age showed little originality. Plagiarism was a merit, not a crime. Latin or French originals may be indicated or posited for most of the works of this school. The early literary monuments of any literature acquire a factitious importance unjustified by intrinsic merit—for they alone exist to portray their age, and permit us to glimpse the first halting attempts at literary expression.

"Disputa del alma y el cuerpo."—This work was written at the monastery of Oña early in the thirteenth century, and derives from a Latin original through the French. The "debate" was a stock device in French and Provençal poetry, and the dispute between soul and body became a common motive in European literature. The poem is a fragment of thirty-seven lines. The soul rebukes the body

for its sins, but the modern reader is unable to judge the case, because the manuscript breaks off before the body has had a chance to reply. The same theme is treated in *Revelación de un ermitaño* (1420), and there also exists another variant as late as the sixteenth century.

"*Razón de amor con los denuestos del agua y el vino.*"— This is an awkward joining of two distinct works. The first, *La razón de amor*, is a dialogue between two lovers. It is interesting as a very early lyric poem in Castilian. The second, a debate between water and wine, was a stock medieval theme. Water enumerates the sins for which wine is responsible, while wine points out how he suffers from dilution. Wine's final argument is that in the communion service he represents Christ's blood. Water's rejoinder is that without his services there can be no baptism. The debate ends with honors easy. There are 264 short lines of unequal length, rhymed in couplets.

"*Elena y María.*"—This work, too, shows metric irregularities indicative of popular origin. It consists of 402 lines of unequal length rhyming as couplets. Assonance often replaces rhyme. The dialect is Leonese. Two ladies discuss the respective merits of their lovers, an abbot and a knight. The *disputa* waxes warm, and the strongly satirical tone is popular and realistic, not courtly. This was another favorite subject for the medieval *débat*. Antecedent Latin and French poems exist on the same theme. The Spanish poem varies sufficiently to suggest intermediary lost versions. *Elena y María* is a specimen of the popularized *mester de clerecía*.

"*La vida de Madona Santa María Egipciaqua.*"—This narrative poem of 1,451 lines deals with the life and miracles of the most sinful of saints, St. Mary of Egypt, whose adventures were relished by those with a taste for pious scandal. It may be dated early in the thirteenth century, and seems related to *La vie de Sainte Marie l'Égyptienne*, attributed to Robert Grosseteste, bishop of Lincoln. Its immediate source appears to have been Provençal. Menéndez Pidal considers it another example of ametric versification.

"*Libro dels tres reis d'Orient.*"—This is a poetic account of the adoration of the magi and the flight into Egypt, told in 250 irregular verses. Like the foregoing, it dates from the thirteenth century and shows French influence.

Gonzalo de Berceo.—The oldest Spanish poet whose name has been preserved is Gonzalo de Berceo. We know that his birthplace was the town whence he derived his appellation, a hamlet in the diocese of Calahorra. He was born toward the close of the twelfth century and flourished in the first half of the thirteenth, living to an advanced age. He was made deacon in 1220 and priest in 1236. He was attached as a lay brother to the Benedictine monastery of San Millán de la Cogolla.

Cuaderna vía.—Berceo was the principal exponent of a new poetic meter which continued in vogue for over two centuries, variously called *cuaderna vía* ("fourfold way"), *mester de clerecía*, and *nueva maestría*. This consisted of four-verse, monorhymed stanzas of disagreeable monotony. Each line was divided into hemistichs, separated by a strongly marked caesura, with the final stress of each half-line invariably falling on the sixth syllable. Poets of this school boasted that they counted syllables, a statement that confirms many scholars in the belief that practitioners of the rival *mester de juglaría* did not do so.

Scholars are still uncertain whether Berceo did without syneresis and synalepha or admitted them to a slight degree. This problem has never been properly approached, for the meter occurs in Provençal poetry as early as 1100, and the Spanish poets who used it were imitating a foreign measure. It is therefore important to know the rules governing the system they copied. Berceo, then, did not invent the *cuaderna vía;* he may not have been the first Spanish poet to use it; but he did most to give it currency.

Berceo's works.—Berceo calls himself *juglar* and *trobador.* He sang or read his works like the ordinary minstrel; but he terms his productions *dictados* and *tractados* rather than *cantares.* Like the lay singer, he is not above asking for "a glass of good wine," but once at least he remembered his sacred calling and demanded a reward of paternosters. He chose Romance (Spanish) as his vehicle of expression, pleading an insufficiency of Latin; but his chief reason was the desire to reach a wide audience of simple folk:

> Quiero fer la pasion de sennor Sant Laurent
> en romaz que la pueda saber toda la gent.

Like the *juglares,* too, Berceo divides his long narratives into convenient cantos (*libriellos*), after each of which there was a pause for rest and refreshment. He was very prolific, and most of his output, thirteen thousand lines, has survived. All his writings are religious. There are three saints' lives, *Vida de Santo Domingo de Silos, Vida de San Millán de la Cogolla, Vida de Santa Oria;* three poems dedicated to the Virgin, *Loores de Nuestra Señora, Miraglos de Nuestra Señora* (his most important work), *Duelo de la Virgen el día de la pasión de su Hijo;* and three other

religious works, *El martirio de San Lorenzo, El sacrificio
de la misa,* and *Los signos que aparecerán ante del Juicio.*
There are also three short hymns. None of these works is
wholly original. Latin sources are known for some; for
the rest they are posited.

Berceo's place in literature.—Berceo is a literary primitive, a Fra Angelico of early Castilian poetry, a naïve,
pious soul who wrote for others of his kind. He is full of
unconscious humor. The descriptions of miracles wrought
by his favorite saints now cause sophisticated readers to
smile while paying tribute to his sincerity. Here and
there in the midst of dreary stretches one encounters an
unexpected bit of genuine poetry. He occasionally ex-
hibits a fine feeling for nature. But his merit is slight. He
interests the philologer primarily, the student of literature only moderately. The English reader may gain an
idea of his style from the translations made by Ticknor
in his *History of Spanish Literature* and Longfellow's
The Praise of Spring. Minor works illustrating the school
of Berceo in its decadence are the anonymous *Vida de San
Ildefonso* and the recently discovered *Libro de miseria de
homne.* The latter is a fourteenth-century work based
upon Innocent III's gloomy *De contemptu mundi.*

"Libro de Alexandre."—This romance, dealing with
the career of Alexander the Great, consists of over ten
thousand lines of verse in *cuaderna vía.* It has been preserved in two manuscripts, differing to such an extent
that Morel-Fatio despaired of the possibility of combining
them into a single critical text. The Madrid manuscript
states that the work was written by Johan Lorenço
Segura de Astorga, *bon clerigo y ondrado;* but *escreuio*
clearly signified "copied," not "composed." The Paris

MS credits Berceo with the authorship; yet subject, matter, and style differ so from those of the priest of San Millán that the attribution is discredited. The anonymous author was a priest possessed of a far wider literary culture than Berceo's.

Sources.—French narrative poetry of the Middle Ages treated one or the other of the following subjects: (1) the adventures of Charlemagne and his peers; (2) those of Arthur and the knights of the round table; (3) those of the heroes of classic antiquity. The three great French *matières* are known, respectively, as the "Carolingian Cycle," the "Arthurian Cycle," and the "Cycle of Antiquity." Numerous sources for the *Libro de Alexandre* have been discovered. It is a combination of two famous French romances of the last of the cycles named, the *Alexandreis* of Gautier de Chatillon and the *Roman d'Alexandre*, written jointly by Lambert le Tort and Alexandre de Bernai. A long, episodical passage describing the siege of Troy derives from a source used by Guido delle Colonne in his *Historia trojana*. Other less important sources have been indicated.

Content.—Alexander, as conceived by the poets of the Middle Ages, was not merely the conqueror of the oriental world, but a pattern of knightly virtue. By the recital of his deeds one might impart *bonas gestas*, and teach how to be *largo*, "generous." For Alexander was considered to be the model of liberality par excellence. As the itinerant poets of the time admired liberality for interested motives, Alexander became almost a patron saint of the guild. But he was conceived as possessing all the other virtues of a thirteenth-century knight. He was first in war, as learned as his famous master, Aristotle, an insatiable seeker after the remote. He penetrates India in quest of glory, fame, and knowledge. To explore the wonders of the deep he descends in a diving-bell. He has encounters with Amazons and the more formidable sirens who seek to allure his soldiers in the enchanted gardens of the Far East.

Criticism.—Much that is good in the *Libro de Alexandre* occurs in its sources; but the author added many original details. He had a powerful gift for description. His pictures of Alexander's tent and chariot are noteworthy. The work betrays a growing interest in the remote, an awakening occasioned by the crusades. It reveals occidental Europe amazed at contact with the superior wealth and culture of the East. And the East is painted in glowing colors. Everything there partakes of the marvelous and the fantastic. The olden days were better too. Greater heroes were produced; life was ampler, happier. Those who poetized Alexander felt humble in the presence of antiquity. Romanticism offered an escape from the mediocrity of medieval life. The *Libro de Alexandre* remains Spain's best romance of the Middle Ages. It is readable today.

"Libro de Apolonio."—The exact chronology of this twelfth-century romance in *cuaderna vía* remains in doubt. It may possibly be earlier than Berceo's writings, in which case it would be the oldest example of this meter preserved. It is a nearly complete work of 2,624 verses, and, like most other poems of the time, belongs to the literature of translation, deriving from some lost Latin or French source, which in turn went back to a Greek original. The *Libro de Apolonio* is a Milesian tale, the term by which late Greek fiction is usually designated.

The Milesian tale is a form of the romance of adventure. It reflects the hazards which accompanied intercourse between the principal centers of Magna Graecia, such cities as Tyre, Antioch, Syracuse, etc. It deals with pirates, shipwrecks, strange separations, and reunitings of lovers and kinsmen. In English literature the genre is represented by Shakespeare's *Comedy of Errors* and *Pericles, Prince of Tyre*, which latter work retells the old Apollonius story. In the Spanish version, Apolonio buries at sea his young wife, Luciana, who has just given birth to a daughter, Tarsiana. Luciana's casket floats ashore, she falls into friendly hands, is revived from her swoon, and becomes a priestess of Diana, in whose temple she serves many years. Tarsiana, on reaching maturity, is stolen by pirates, who sell her as a slave. She is a gypsy-like character, skilled in song and dance, and is thought by some to be a prototype of such later characters as Cervantes' Preciosa and Hugo's Esmeralda. After adventures which imperil her virtue, she emerges triumphant, finds a suitable husband, and Apolonio, Luciana, and the young couple are at last reunited. The charm of this work lies entirely in its romantic plot. The Spanish singer tells his tale with little art, hampered by his monotonous form. The *Libro de Apolonio* may easily be read in Mr. Marden's admirable edition.

"*Poema de Yuçuf*"(*José*).—This crude poem of 312 coplas of *cuaderna vía* relates the familiar story of Joseph down to the time of his final triumph over his brethren. A few stanzas have been lost at the end. The poet did not base his work upon the Bible, rather upon the Koran and rabbinical traditions. The two manuscripts preserving the work are *textos aljamiados,* that is to say, Arabic characters were employed to transcribe the Spanish. The dialect is strongly Aragonese.

"*Poema de Alfonso Onceno.*"—Fitzmaurice-Kelly describes this fourteenth-century work as the swan song of the *mester de juglaría*. It deals with the conquests over the Moors by Alfonso XI, consists of 2,456 quatrains of eight-syllable verse in which the first line rhymes with the third, the second with the fourth. Many lines are irregular, and in these Menéndez Pidal sees support for the theory of *versificación irregular*. Cornu, on the other hand, sees in the many traces of Galician evidence that this was the original dialect, and tries to show that metrical difficulties disappear when the lines are retranslated into Galician. However that may be, the poem shows that lyric poetry was beginning to exercise a regularizing influence upon the epic. The *Poema de Alfonso Onceno* is a connecting link between the *cantares de gesta* and the later ballad.

The Rabbi Sem Tob, the first Jew whose name appears in the list of Spanish poets, flourished in the middle of the fourteenth century. His *Proverbios morales, o Consejos y documentos* was dedicated to Peter the Cruel, a monarch who favored Hebrews. The *Proverbios* contains 686 quatrains of seven-syllable verse with crossed rhymes. The maxims are taken from the Bible, the Talmud, and various writers, mostly Jewish. A few examples will give an idea of Sem Tob's manner. The first illustrates his fondness for paradox—no peace without war, no ease without previous toil:

> La pas non se alcança
> sygno con guerrear,
> nin se gana folgança
> sy non con bien lasrar.

In the practical guidance of life he urges *mesura*, moderation and the middle course:

> Por la grande escasesa
> tener lo han en poco,
> por la mucha franquesa
> juzgarlo han por loco.

Niggardliness and prodigality are equally to be avoided. But where an essential principle of morality is involved there must be no compromise. Better truth to one's disadvantage than deceit with profit:

> Desir sienpre verdad,
> maguer dapno tenga,
> y nunca falsedad,
> aunque pro dello venga.

The Rabbi Sem Tob is the principal representative of gnomic literature in Spain during the Middle Ages. He is witty, pithy, ever sagacious, and at times reaches heights of lofty morality.

"*Danza de la muerte.*"—The "Dance of Death" was a favorite theme for writers and painters everywhere in Europe during the Middle Ages. Spain possesses the finest extant literary specimen of the genre in the *Danza de la muerte*, written in the early fifteenth century. All told there are thirty-three victims, clergy alternating with laity. Thus the emperor is balanced against the pope, the king against the cardinal, and so on down to the lowest social orders. There is much grim humor and biting satire. The dignitaries of the church fare no better than the laymen. The author pays his respects to every social category and indicates the sins of each calling The merchant, the lawyer, the doctor, the usurer, the loose-living monk, the sacristan, Jew, and Moor, types so

severely treated in the later farces and the picaresque
novel, are here flayed without mercy. The whole is written in twelve-syllable octaves and cast in dramatic form.
Each victim whines out an octave of protest to Death,
who replies with another of severe reprimand. The *Danza
de la muerte* is an impressive sample of satirical literature
in the Spanish Middle Ages.

BIBLIOGRAPHY

CREIZENACH, W. *Geschichte des neueren Dramas.* 2d ed.; 4 vols.
Halle, 1911–23. Best general history of the European drama,
extending through the Renaissance.

YOUNG, KARL. *The Drama of the Medieval Church.* New York,
1933.

SCHACK, A. F. VON. *Geschichte der dramatischen Literatur und
Kunst in Spanien.* 2d ed.; 3 vols. Frankfurt a.M., 1854.
Spanish trans. E. DE MIER. 5 vols. Madrid, 1885–87. The
standard history, though obsolete in part.

"Auto de los reyes magos," ed. R. MENÉNDEZ PIDAL, *Revista de
Archivos*, IV, 453–62. See also J. D. M. FORD's *Old Spanish
Readings.* Boston, 1906.

STURDEVANT, W. *The Misterio de los Reyes Magos: Its Position in
the Development of the Mediaeval Legend of the Three Kings.*
Baltimore, 1927.

CRAWFORD, J. P. W. *Spanish Drama before Lope de Vega.* Philadelphia, 1922.

JANER, F. "Poetas anteriores al siglo XV," *Biblioteca de autores
españoles*,[1] Vol. LVII. Contains most of the works mentioned
in this chapter.

"Disputa del alma y el cuerpo," ed. R. MENÉNDEZ PIDAL, *Revista
de archivos*, IV, 449–53.

"Razón de amor con los denuestos del agua y el vino," ed. R.
MENÉNDEZ PIDAL, *Revue hispanique*, XIII, 602–18.

"Elena y María, o disputa del clérigo y del caballero," ed. R.
MENÉNDEZ PIDAL, *Revista de filología española*, I, 3–47.

[1] Henceforth this collection will be indicated by the initials *BAE.*

BERCEO, G. DE. *La vida de Santo Domingo de Silos*, ed. J. D. FITZ-GERALD. Paris, 1904.

―――. *El sacrificio de la misa*, ed. A. G. SOLALINDE. Madrid, 1913.

―――. *Milagros de Nuestra Señora*, ed. A. G. SOLALINDE. Madrid, 1922.

―――. *Cuatro poemas de Berceo*, ed. C. C. MARDEN. Madrid, 1928.

―――. *Veintitrés milagros*, ed. C. C. MARDEN. Madrid, 1929.

FITZ-GERALD, J. D. *Versification of the Cuaderna Vía.* New York, 1905.

El Libro de Alexandre, ed. R. S. WILLIS. Princeton and Paris, 1934.

Libro de Apolonio, ed. C. C. MARDEN. 2 vols. Baltimore, Princeton, and Paris, 1917–22.

Poema de Yuçuf, ed P. MORF. Leipzig, 1883; ed. MENÉNDEZ PIDAL, *Revista de archivos*, Vol. VII.

STEIN, L. *Untersuchungen über die Proverbios morales von Santob de Carrión.* Berlin, 1900.

MENÉNDEZ Y PELAYO, M. *Antología de poetas líricos*, Vols. I–III. New ed.; 10 vols. Santander, 1944–45.

Danza de la muerte, ed. R. FOULCHÉ-DELBOSC. Barcelona, 1907.

WHYTE, F. *The Dance of Death in Spain and Catalonia.* Baltimore, 1931.

KURZ, L. P. *The Dance of Death and the Macabre Spirit in European Literature.* New York, 1934.

Poema de Alfonso Onceno, ed. YO TEN CATE. Madrid, 1956.

CHAPTER IV

Early Prose Works—
Didactic Literature,
History, and the Novel

Didacticism—Alfonso el Sabio—*Las siete partidas*—Scientific works—*Los cronicones*—*La crónica general*—*Grande e general estoria* —Other historians of the Middle Ages—The oriental apologue— *Calila e Dimna*—*Libro de los engannos*—*Barlaam and Josaphat*— Other oriental collections—The Christian exemplum—Juan Manuel—El Arcipreste de Talavera—Romances of chivalry—The romance of chivalry in France—Spanish translations of French romances—*El Caballero Çifar*—The medieval *Amadís*.

DIDACTICISM

Clerical literature was as didactic in prose as in verse. It not only sought the reader's moral improvement, but, as priests were almost the sole repositories of learning, provided much secular information as well. The didactic movement came to a head during the reign of Alfonso el Sabio, whose dates are 1220?–84, resulting in a veritable medieval Renaissance. Alfonso did for Spain, on a grander scale, what Alfred and Charlemagne had earlier done for their countries.

Alfonso el Sabio.—The reign of this monarch (1252–84), so rich for literature and learning, was politically unsuccessful. Alfonso was unable fully to consolidate the victories of his father, Fernando III, the conqueror of Cordova and Seville. Elected Holy Roman emperor, he was deprived of the possession of that office by papal intrigue. But the worst calamity of the reign was the death of his eldest son, leaving infant heirs, whose legitimate claims Alfonso's second son, later Sancho IV, el Bravo, disputed. Alfonso first weakly acknowledged Sancho as his successor, but when foreign powers began to intervene in favor of the dispossessed *infantes*, his policy wavered. The result was a disastrous civil war in which father and son were arrayed as enemies. Sancho's strength was the greater, and Alfonso died stripped of most of his power, partially justifying Mariana's epigram which states that Alfonso lost his kingdom while gazing at the stars. (*Dumque cœlum considerat observatque astra, terram amisit.*) This famous saying started a legend of political incompetence which does Alfonso injustice. He was brave and energetic in battle, but confronted with impossible situations. Another legend is still more damaging to his memory. He is represented as having said: "If God had consulted me before the creation, he would have made a different world." It was this silly anecdote which caused Emerson to view Alfonso as a monster of self-conceit:

> And, for I'm styled Alphonse the Wise,
> Ye shall not fail for sound advice.
> Before ye want a drop of rain,
> Hear the sentiment of Spain.
>
> —EMERSON, *Alphonso of Castile*

Legends do not spring up around nonentities. They prove that the man had strongly impressed himself upon his age and nation; but they create misconceptions which must be brushed away. Alfonso's ruling passion was not overweening conceit, but the true scholar's humble love of learning.

Alfonso as an organizer of culture.—It was as a patron of the arts and learning that Alfonso found his truest pleasure. Nothing comparable to the extent of his official encouragement of genius had been known in Europe since Alexander the Great had endowed Aristotle's researches. Early in the twelfth century Raymond, archbishop of Toledo, had started to translate works out of the Arabic on an extensive scale. This work Alfonso continued. The court became the rendezvous of scholars, writers, troubadours, musicians, painters, sculptors, and architects. Every monastery library of the kingdom was ransacked for its treasures. Hosts of scribes were in attendance to copy works both old and new. Alfonso founded what was for the times a vast publishing-house. The magnificent illuminations of an extant manuscript of his *Cantigas* picture *el rey sabio* presiding over this cultured court Small wonder if the rougher elements found a more congenial refuge in the camp of Sancho el Bravo. It is thought that Alfonso wrote little himself; even his share in the *Cantigas*, which seems to be his most personal work, has been questioned. But his was the directing genius. He selected the workmen, assigned them tasks, and financed them. We know that he followed the working out of his plans with eager interest, and made editorial corrections. He possessed a spirit of wide tolerance. Most of the learning of the age was locked up in Greek, Latin, Hebrew, and Arabic texts. Alfonso's contemporaries had no direct contact with Greek literature and had to be content with such Greek lore as the Arabs had preserved. No religious scruples prevented Alfonso from calling

learned Jews and Moors to his court. These he set to
work, side by side with Christian monks, translating,
popularizing, compiling from diverse sources into encyclopedic works. The significance of the medieval Renaissance is that a considerable portion of ancient and oriental learning was brought within the ken of many unversed
in Latin. The circle of readers and thinkers was extended.
And from Spain this knowledge passed to the rest of
Europe. Brunetto Latini, Dante's teacher, was the bearer
of some of this lore from Spain to Italy. Alfonso el
Sabio, therefore, did much to pave the way for the true
Renaissance of the fifteenth century. "Oh Spain," wrote
one of his collaborators, "if thou dost take the gifts which
the wisdom of the king gives thee, thou wilt shine re-
splendent, likewise thou wilt grow in fame and beauty."

"Las siete partidas."—On conquering Cordova and
Seville, Fernando III, Alfonso's father, desiring to bring his
new subjects under Castilian law, promulgated a legal code
called the *Fuero juzgo*. This, the oldest Spanish lawbook,
is a digest of Roman law with certain Gothic modifica-
tions. Its chief interest is philological and legal. One of
Alfonso's earliest projects was to continue his father's
work by completely codifying the law of all the Castilian
dominions, establishing one set of ordinances for all
his subjects. This he attempted in *Las siete partidas*,
begun in 1256 and completed some seven or nine years
later. The work derives its name from the seven parts
into which it falls. Each division is indicated by one of
the seven letters of the name Alfonso. *Las siete partidas*
has literary qualities, though it is most interesting from
the viewpoint of culture history. It is more than a codification of laws; it sets forth the primitive constitution of

thirteenth-century Spain. The duties and privileges of
the king, how he should be educated, how he should act
in given circumstances, the rights and obligations of the
great nobles, jurists, clergy, burgesses, and slaves—all
these things are distinctly demarcated. The laws themselves interest for their curious provisions, so illustrative
of medieval ideas. In short, a complete picture of society
is offered. We see in operation the lumbering machinery
of Alfonso's government, how artisan and peasant lived
and suffered, and the part which woman played.

Scientific works.—Alfonso, like his age, does not
distinguish between science and pseudo-science. His
earliest work, the *Lapidario*, describes precious stones,
and catalogues the mysterious curative and magical
qualities each was supposed to possess. His mathematical
inclinations are evidenced by two works on the astrolabe
and *El libro de la esfera*. The science of his predilection
was astronomy, not wholly free from astrology, and one of
his chief productions was *Libros del saber de astronomía*.
This is a revision of the work of the Greek astronomer,
Ptolemy. Another astronomical work was the *Libro de
las tablas alphonsíes*. A Columbus visiting this learned
court would have had no need to argue that the world is
round. Alfonso even caused to be translated the Koran,
Talmud, and other religious writings of the Arabs and
Jews—so insatiably curious was his mind, and free from
prejudice.

HISTORY

"Los cronicones."—From the fifth century on, it was
the practice of most religious establishments to write
Latin chronicles of important happenings. Often these
were the briefest of annals, listing under each year battles,

famines, and the deaths of important personages. **When**
an ambitious writer attempted more than a brief skeleton
of history, he rarely succeeded in adding the slightest
touch of human interest. Several Castilian chronicles of
the same sort have been preserved. These crude works are
called derogatively *cronicones*. It was not until the early
thirteenth century that two prelates, writing in Latin,
produced histories of real merit. Lucas de Tuy (d. 1249),
bishop of Tuy, in his *Chronicon mundi* traces the history
of Spain from its legendary origins to the conquest of
Cordova by Fernando III, 1236. Rodrigo Jiménez de
Rada (1170–1247), who, as archbishop of Toledo, is
usually designated Rodrigo de Toledo, wrote a *Historia
gothica*, or, as it is sometimes known, *De rebus Hispaniæ*.
This covers the same ground down to the victory of Las
Navas de Tolosa, 1212. The example of these two men
inspired Alfonso to compile in the vernacular a far more
ambitious chronicle.

"*La crónica general.*"—-This was by far the most important work of history anywhere undertaken during the
Middle Ages. No other nation can boast a similar work
comparable either as to magnitude or merit. Stylistically,
it is important as an official attempt to fix the Castilian
tongue, and to matters of style the royal editor devoted
much personal attention. As with all such works of the
period, the critical spirit is lacking. The compilers accepted with naïve faith myth and fable. They failed to
distinguish between poetic fancy and sober fact. They
drew from Vergil as freely as from Suetonius, and, while
conscientiously seeking the best authorities, their gulli-
bility inclined them to favor the picturesque. Consequently, no book is more interesting to the lover of ro-

mance. Its interest never flags. Let him open it at random and the reader is sure to be rewarded. For sheer pageantry the *Crónica general* is rivaled only by the much later chronicles of Froissart.

Contents.—The story begins with the deluge, the wanderings of Japheth, the fabled adventures of Hercules in Spain, the rule of Greeks and Carthaginians. Next comes the story of the founding of Rome, and Vergil is drawn upon for an extensive *historia de Dido.* There follow the Punic wars, the deeds of Pompey and Caesar, and accounts of the more illustrious emperors down to the fall of Rome. Here the compilers are following Latin historians. Plainly, Spaniards felt a solidarity with Rome. No history of Spain would be complete without sketching in the Roman background. But they felt no less solidarity with the Goths. The wanderings of the Gothic tribe with their descent upon Spain are related at length. The reigns of the Gothic kings are treated in detail. Of these Wamba was the favorite, as Rodrigo was the most hated. After relating the loss of Spain to the Moors, the first volume ends with two noble outbursts of eloquence, not original but taken from Lucas of Tuy. First is the *Loor de España.* We are told of Spain's lofty mountains and mighty rivers, its favored climate, its fertile soil, its mineral wealth, the bravery, intelligence, and loyalty of its sons. And then the fervent outcry: *"¡Ay España! non ha lengua que pueda contar tu bien!"* Next comes the *Duelo de España,* the expression of a nation's anguish under the great calamity. Thus the first volume ends with a note of tragic despair. The second volume begins with Pelayo's victory at Covadonga. The Reconquest starts. The reigns of the kings of the little Christian

kingdoms are narrated, but the information to be gleaned
from the Moorish historians was not neglected. Several
important Arabic sources, now lost, were utilized. This
was Spain's heroic period, and one by one come the prose
versions of the old *cantares*. These "prosifications" are
the most interesting portion of the work. Nothing analogous is found in any other European chronicles. Spaniards of the time looked upon their epics as faithful
purveyors of fact. The narrative is continued through
the reign of Fernando III, el Santo. If the first division of
Alfonso's history ends with despair, the whole work concludes with a note of optimism. With Cordova and Seville
in Christian hands, the struggle with the Moors was almost over.

Later editions.—The work just described is called *La
primera crónica general* to distinguish it from later versions. Menéndez Pidal has published (Madrid, 1906), a
critical edition of this which closely approximates the
original. He finds that the first part was begun in 1270,
and the second half, obviously later as to language, was
begun in 1289 under Sancho IV. There exist many
manuscripts, each differing from the others in important
respects. Few scribes were content merely to copy; most
were revisers, adding, omitting, changing. Thus if we ex-
amine the *Segunda crónica general*, more commonly called
La crónica de 1344, we find that the epic "prosifications"
are based, not on the splendid *cantares* of the twelfth century, but on the degenerate redactions of these which prevailed in the fourteenth century. It is regrettable that this
manuscript, so important for the study of the Spanish
epic and balladry, has not found an editor. It is preserved
in the Biblioteca Real. From another lost redaction

sprang the *Tercera crónica general,* which was printed by
Florián Ocampo in 1541, a later edition appearing in
1602. The Ocampo edition, careless and inadequate as it
is, is important, first because until 1906 it was the sole
printed edition of Alfonso's chronicle as a whole, and
second because it was the source book from which dramatists, erudite balladists, and other writers drew.

"*General estoria.*"—Vast as was the *Crónica,* Alfonso
conceived a work much more extensive in scope, the *General estoria* (1270–80), a history of the world. Menéndez
Pidal's edition of the *Crónica* is a quarto volume containing 774 densely printed pages, two columns to the page.
The preserved portion of the *General estoria* is several
times as long. Professor A. G. Solalinde began publishing
a critical text of the five *partes* in 1930, and his colleagues
at Wisconsin are continuing. The work is based chiefly
upon the Bible, with a curious blending of pagan mythology. World history is brought down to the birth of Jesus
Christ. While less valuable than the *Crónica,* it contains
several interesting prosifications of French romances, notably a prose version of the Alexander romance.

Other historians of the Middle Ages.—The impulse
given to history by *el rey sabio* bore fruit in the following
centuries in a series of chronicles devoted to the separate
reigns. Without having gained the critical spirit of the
modern historian, these chroniclers begin to show less
faith in legendary sources. The works of Pero López de
Ayala (1332–1407) stand out from those of a number of
obscure writers as having distinct literary merit. The
great chancellor's historic works are chronicles of the
reigns of Peter the Cruel, Henry II, John I, and Henry
III. Ayala writes as one who played a leading rôle in the

events he narrates, who knew the personages mentioned, who penetrated their designs and analyzed their motives. He paints recognizable likenesses, but externals interest him slightly. He seeks to reproduce the actor's soul, to understand the whys and wherefores of each event. There is a modernity of outlook which reminds one of a Philippe de Commines, or even of a Saint-Simon. Ayala also shows skill in marshaling his facts, and his prose is the best written in the fourteenth century. Ayala's nephew, Fernán Pérez de Guzmán (1376?–1460?), who wrote in the early fifteenth century, produced a curious collection of biographies, *Mar de istorias*. That portion dealing with the worthies of antiquity fails to interest; the author's fame rests upon the third part, *Generaciones y semblanzas*, in which he portrays his contemporaries. Though less psychological than Ayala, he is more vivid in his characterization of externals. Much good reading is provided by the *Crónica de Don Pedro Niño, o El victorial*, by Gutierre Díez de Games (1379?–1450), who narrates the fantastically adventurous career of his noble master. Pero Rodríguez de Lena, also of the fifteenth century, is chronicler of Spain's most famous exploit of chivalry. Suero de Quiñones, who had rashly vowed to wear a ring around his neck as a token of his abject servitude to his lady, sought release from the vow by undertaking to defend a bridgehead near León for a month during the summer of 1439, aided by nine companions. How successfully Quiñones executed this task is told by Rodríguez de Lena in the *Libro del passo honroso de Suero de Quiñones*. Another of the best chronicles is the *Crónica de Don Álvaro de Luna*, concerning the authorship of which we can only speculate. The writer was certainly a devoted adherent of the picturesque favorite whose fall and execution constitute one of the most dramatic episodes in Spanish history. With Pedro del Corral, the chronicle passes over into fiction. His *Crónica sarracina, o Crónica del Rey Don Rodrigo con la destruyción de España*, about 1443, is considered the oldest Spanish historical novel. Hernando del Pulgar (1436?–93?) produced a classic when he wrote *Claros varones de Castilla*, 1486. The men described are the chief figures of the reigns preceding that of the Catholic monarchs. Pulgar follows the tradition of Ayala and Pérez de Guzmán, but, living at the dawn of the Spanish Renaissance, he is more influenced by classic models.

THE NOVEL

The oriental apologue.—The Middle Ages were unoriginal. Few writers of the period show inventive power, but for the most part merely re-work old themes. The same stories recur, making the round of all the European literatures. Many of these fictional motives are oriental. Many are thousands of years old, traceable to the Sanscrit. A typical course of transmission was from the ancient languages of India, to the Persian, to the Arabic, to Latin or Spanish, and thence to the other European tongues. In the early Middle Ages, Spain was the chief intermediary between oriental culture and the rest of Europe, owing to her close contact with the Arabic races. Byzantium rendered the same service to a lesser extent. With the Crusades, all Western Europe came into direct contact with the Orient, and there resulted a new and abundant importation of fictional motives. Some of this oriental fiction was for mere amusement, but most of it was didactic. Christ taught in parables, but Buddha and many another Eastern teacher had long preceded him in this method. Such a moral fable, or story intended to convey a useful lesson, is called an "apologue." The characters are frequently talking animals. Æsop's *Fables* are typical apologues. Æsop did not invent them; he merely put into Greek, with slight variations, fables already current in the remote past of India. It was natural that such apologues should be gathered into collections. The framework binding together a series of short tales is also an invention of the East. Wheels within wheels was a favorite device. Every reader of the *Arabian Nights' Entertainment* is familiar with the tricks with which the artful Scheherazade, narrator of the tales, whetted the sultan's curiosity, and so kept gaining for herself an additional day of life. Boccaccio in his *Decamerone*, Chaucer in his *Canterbury Tales*, and many another occidental writer copied the framework device of the Orientals.

"*Calila e Dimna*," the oldest work of Spanish prose fiction, is a typical collection of apologues, set in a frame. It was translated into Castilian from the Arabic, by order of Alfonso el Sabio, in 1251, if we may accept Mr. Clifford G. Allen's arguments. Back of this Arabic version, made about 750 from a Pehlvi translation, lies an original Sanscrit narrative. Both the Pehlvi rendering and the Sanscrit original are lost, although there exists in the Sanscrit a work, called the *Panchatantra*, which is an extensive readaptation of the first books of the *Calila e Dimna*. Scholars are in doubt as to whether the whole compilation, as we have it in the Spanish version, derives faithfully from the Sanscrit, or whether Barzouyeh, physician to the king of Persia, author of the Pehlvi translation in the sixth century, added extraneous material to an original related to the *Panchatantra*. We cannot here go into the intricate questions of origins, or the history of the diffusion of this work throughout Europe. The apologues are accredited to a certain Bidpai, an Indian Æsop.

Contents.—The framework is simple. Two lynxes, Calila and Dimna, are the main characters. In ancient India the lynx or the jackal played the cunning rôle of the fox of European folklore. Dimna, envious of the fortune of Senceba, an ox who had become favorite of the lion, king of the beasts, plots against his rival for royal favor. He persuades the lion to kill Senceba, but is afterward brought to trial, found guilty, and starved to death. The interest lies in the many little stories introduced in the course of debate. Each point made by both parties in the suit is reinforced by an apposite anecdote. The tone is philosophical and edifying. The apologues resemble those of Æsop. The following one is characteristic:

A monk has by begging obtained a quantity of butter and honey which he places in a pot and hangs at the head of his bed. He lies down and builds castles in the air. With the proceeds of his honey and butter he will buy goats; later he will sell these and acquire cows. In time he will be a landowner, will marry a rich wife, will have a son who will be a great scholar. But if the boy refuses to study, he will beat him, thus. Suiting the action to the thought, he lets fly with his staff, breaks the pot, is smeared with its contents, and brought back to a sad reality. This is the earliest known form of the well-known story of the dreaming milkmaid. Many other stories in this collection have a familiar ring.

The animal epic, of which the *Roman de Renard* is typical, was an important medieval genre. The Indian

original of *Calila e Dimna* offers the earliest-known instance of a sustained narrative, having animal characters
which satirize the social categories. Compared with later
works of the sort, the satirical element in *Kalila et Digna*
is mild; yet it brings out forcibly the harm wrought by
evil counselors and credulous kings.

"*Libro de los engannos et los assayamientos de las
mugeres.*"—The *Book of the Deceits and Wiles of Women*
is the Spanish representative of another famous oriental
collection which achieved a remarkable European vogue.
In ancient times it was known as the *Dolopathos*, or the
Syntipas; in English literature it is called the *History of
the Seven Wise Masters*. The Spanish version was translated out of the Arabic into Castilian at the request of the
Infante Fadrique, Alfonso's younger brother, in 1253.
Again the framework is a trial. A king's son is accused by
his stepmother of offering her violence. He is brought to
trial. However, astrologers on consulting the prince's
horoscope learn that it will be fatal for him to open his
lips for a period of seven days. He therefore remains
dumb, intrusting his defense to seven wise masters, each
of whom holds the floor for a day. The defense is that
woman is naturally so deceitful that no words of hers may
be believed, and numerous stories are told illustrative of
feminine vices. The stepmother queen replies with stories
illustrative of the deceitfulness of false counselors. At
the end of the seven days, the prince speaks in his own
defense and wins his case. The wicked queen is burned
alive. Two dozen stories are told, amusing but licentious
in tone. They illustrate the low esteem in which woman
was held in the Orient; but they would scarcely have
gained such wide acceptance in Western Europe if the

medieval clergy had not entertained an opinion of woman almost as unfavorable.

"Barlaam and Josaphat."—This is another oriental collection, far nobler than the foregoing, though its framework is similar, which has made a profound impression upon Spanish literature. The ultimate source is a Sanscrit work called *Lalita Vistara,* now known to be a legendary account of the youth of Buddha. This was translated into Greek, in the seventh century, by a monk who gave it a Christian adaptation. A twelfth-century Latin version gave the story a general European currency, and it was speedily rendered into the various vernaculars. Josaphat (Buddha) and his mentor, Barlaam, were canonized in both the Greek and Roman churches. Their story may therefore be read in the *Golden Legend* and similar biographies of the saints. Spanish versions were numerous. Fragmentary ones, dating from the Middle Ages, and completer ones of the Renaissance have been preserved. Its influence is detected in Juan Manuel's *Libro de los estados,* and nearly every story-collection contains one or more tales originating in the *Barlaam.*

Contents.—A son, Josaphat, is born to an Indian king, whose astrologers predict that the prince will be either a great ruler or a noted religious teacher. To prevent the latter alternative, the father has the boy brought up in a palace filled with everything to delight the senses, and where he shall experience nothing to cause melancholy and reflection leading to a religious life. One day the boy escapes from his palace-prison and has four encounters (the four famous encounters of Buddha)—old age, sickness, poverty, and death. Barlaam explains the meanings of these things, whereupon Josaphat turns ascetic, and in

the end becomes a great religious teacher as the horoscope
had forecast. The stories, as usual, lend point to the
arguments between the characters. In the Christian
versions theological discussion replaces a trial resulting
from a false charge made by a woman of the harem, a situation similar to that in the *History of the Seven Wise Masters*
and the familiar story of Potiphar's wife. Many of the
most famous stories in the world's literature are traced
back to *Barlaam and Josaphat:* "The Trump of Doom,"
"Women as Devils," the story of the three rings symbolic
of three rival religions, made famous by Boccaccio and
used by Lessing in *Nathan der Weise,* and the tale of the
three caskets, familiar to readers of *The Merchant of
Venice.*

Other oriental collections.—Though written in Latin,
passing mention must be made of the *Disciplina clericalis*
of Petrus Alphonsi, an Aragonese converted Jew who
wrote in the early twelfth century. The framework is a
father's admonition to his son, teaching moral truths by
apologues. There are thirty-five excellent stories which
won wide acceptance in Spain and elsewhere in Europe.
The same form of a father instructing a son is found in
Castigos y documentos del rey don Sancho, perhaps of Sancho IV's time, perhaps later, by J. García de Castrojeriz.
It is partly oriental in inspiration, partly based on Egidio
Colonna's *De regimine principum. The Arabian Nights'
Entertainment,* or *The Thousand and One Nights,* as it is
variously styled, is the latest of the famous oriental compilations. It was given its actual form by the Arabs of the
late fifteenth or early sixteenth century, though much of
its matter had been known for centuries in the Far East.
It was unknown as a whole in Western Europe until Gal-
land published his translation in 1704. Nevertheless, an

occasional story found in this collection was already known in the medieval period.

The Christian exemplum.—While Buddhism, Mohammedanism, and Christianity differed as to theology, their ethical precepts often agreed; therefore oriental apologues were suited to Western pulpits. Many collections of moral stories (*exempla*) were made throughout Europe for the use of preachers. *El libro de los exemplos*, by Climente Sánchez de Vercial, is typical. It is a collection of more than 500 stories, alphabetically arranged according to the initial word of the Latin inscription which each fable bears. Under each Latin title there is a rhymed couplet of Castilian verse, summing up the content of the story. There is no framework. Some of the tales are pious legends from the lives of the saints, others are apologues. The whole *Disciplina clericalis* has been incorporated. A similar collection is the oddly named *Libro de los gatos*, where *gatos* seems a corruption of *quentos*, "stories." This suggestion, first made by the present writer, has found acceptance in the most recent histories of literature.[1] It is a translation of the *Narrationes* of Odo of Cheriton, an Anglo-Norman monk who wrote in Latin. The stories are mostly animal apologues. Odo was a master of satire and possessed of a stout democratic spirit. His pen was dipped in vitriol when he championed the commoner against rapacious baron and avaricious bishop; but the glory of this protesting voice belongs to England and not to Spain. Both the foregoing works are of the fourteenth century, and are representative of a host of similar compilations which have perished. It is well to read such crude productions, if only to appre-

[1] John E. Keller, "*Gatos*, not *quentos*," *Studies in Philology*, L (1953), No. 3, entirely rejects this suggestion.—N. B. A.

ciate the superiority of Juan Manuel in the domain of
the short story.

Juan Manuel (*1282–1349?*) was a powerful noble,
grandson of Fernando III and nephew of Alfonso el Sabio.
He played a leading rôle as statesman, warrior, and revolutionary. He continued the didactic movement inaugurated by his royal uncle and was himself a voluminous
encyclopedic writer. One regrets his lost *Libro de la
caballería*, the imitation of a like-named work by Raymond Lull, his *Libro de engeños*, a treatise on military
machines, but infinitely more his *ars poetica, Reglas de
como se debe trobar*, and a *Libro de los cantares*. Of his
preserved works there are the *Libro de la caza*, a treatise
on falconry, the *Crónica abreviada*, an epitome of *La
primera crónica general*, the *Libro del caballero et del
escudero*, in which a hermit instructs a squire in the virtues
of chivalry. This, too, was inspired by the above-men-
tioned work of Lull. Not to mention several other writings of slight importance, there is also the *Libro de los
estados*, already mentioned as an adaptation of *Barlaam
and Josaphat*.

"*El libro de los enxiemplos del conde Lucanor et de
Patronio*" is his masterpiece. Juan Manuel takes that
moral form, the *exemplum*, and gives it a worldly polish.
Count Lucanor is a ruler beset with cares, who propounds each dilemma to his counselor, Patronio. The
latter is inevitably reminded of a tale which he relates
together with the appropriate moral. Invariably Lucanor
accepts the advice as good, and the gist of each fable is
summed up in a line or two of rude verse. The awkward-
ness of this framework device—it is fifty times repeated—
is in contrast with the grace and suppleness of the stories

themselves. Juan Manuel had style. He is simple and un-
pedantic, vivacious and mildly satiric. His manner has
won praise from such a modern exquisite as Azorín. The
collection was compiled between 1323 and 1335, from
thirteen to twenty years previous to Boccaccio's *Decamerone*. Like Boccaccio, Juan Manuel stands as the earliest
cultivator of artistic prose fiction in a great modern literature. The fifty tales are varied in subject matter. Some
are oriental, some are pious legends, others belong to folklore, still others are anecdotes about notable personages
of the age, like Richard Cœur de Lion and Saladin. One
may single out for special mention *Exemplo XI*, the story
of the ungrateful dean of Santiago and Don Illán, the
magician of Toledo; *Exemplo XXXII*, how a stupid king
was taken in by swindlers who pretended to clothe his
nakedness with an alleged magic cloth—a theme familiar
to readers of Hans Christian Andersen, and recurring in
varied form in Cervantes' *Entremés del retablo de las
maravillas; Exemplo XXXV*, concerning the youth who
wed *una muger muy fuerte et muy brava*—an interesting
analogue of Shakespeare's *Taming of the Shrew*.

El Arcipreste de Talavera.—A good novelist was
wasted in Alfonso Martínez de Toledo, archpriest of
Talavera (1398?–1470?), who introduced in his *Corbacho,
o Reprobación del amor mundano* realistic material suitable for fiction. This curious work is one of numerous
satires directed against women, but it stands out among
the rest with a marked individuality. The word *corbacho*,
"whip," was suggested by Boccaccio's *Corbaccio*, the title
of a book of similar content. The archpriest's work is
divided into four parts: Part One is a condemnation of
carnal love; Part Two flays the foibles and vices of wom-

en; Parts Three and Four, of scant interest, contain curious medical and astrological lore. Part Two, then, is the most readable and important portion. Martínez de Toledo was strongly preoccupied with sex, possibly in a Freudian sense. He condemns woman unsparingly, with evident relish. He will allow her scarcely a redeeming virtue. His sweeping condemnations carry no conviction, yet his feminine portraits create the impression of drawings from living models. We feel convinced that women of the time looked, dressed, spoke, and acted precisely as he depicts them. We can imagine the author delivering these homilies from a pulpit, adding mimicry with telling effect. Every type of bad woman is introduced; only the good are lacking. There are the flirt, the gossip, the vain, overdressed beauty, the liar, the virago, the adulteress. All these are deceitful; none can keep a secret; all possess unbridled tongues. The archpriest tells stories to illustrate their perversities, some taken from French *fabliaux*. All these characters are made to paint their own portraits in self-revealing conversation. They converse in a popular idiom that is convincingly realistic, with the torrents of abuse and lamentation and the uncurbed loquacity which the angered woman of the people still employs. Martínez de Toledo is Spain's first master in the art of conversational narration. He learned much from Juan Ruiz, but he taught more to Rojas. The *Corbacho* is a great monument of realism. It is treated here among the novels on account of its important influence upon the future development of realistic fiction; for it is a forerunner of the picaresque novel.

Romances of chivalry.—By far the most popular form of fiction in the Middle Ages was the romance of chivalry.

The Spanish *Libros de caballerías* fall into two main divisions: first, those which are mere translations of foreign, chiefly French, romances; second, those composed in the peninsula in imitation of those of France, but which developed a new ideal of love and a new technique, so that when translated into French they were received by Frenchmen as an entirely new form of the novel. This second stage of development corresponds to the Renaissance. These were the books which Cervantes attacked. In the present chapter we shall deal merely with the origins of the genre.

The romance of chivalry in France.—French literature in the Middle Ages had the same universality of appeal as was the case in the seventeenth and eighteenth centuries. Narrative fiction was first cast in verse form. The three great *matières*, or subjects of medieval French fiction, have already been mentioned. Historians of French literature agree in calling the poems of the Carolingian Cycle epics, though the later, degenerate epic in its extravagance tends toward romance. The romance proper belongs to the Arthurian Cycle and the Cycle of Antiquity. It developed in the twelfth century when the old epic heroes and themes had begun to pall, when manners had become refined, when knight errantry with its noble ideals had developed, when woman had begun to exercise an influence unknown in the Dark Ages. Something new was demanded. The Celtic bards supplied themes, but the old Celtic heroes were pictured as embodying the ideals of twelfth-century knight errantry. Arthur's court became an idealized French court. Chrestien de Troyes is the outstanding poet of this courtly school. Like all writers of French romances, he employs an eight-syllable meter rhymed in couplets. In all these poems the historic foundation is slight or non-existent. Adventure and love are the main themes. Mere brutal fighting is no longer interesting, if unaccompanied with gallantry and courtesy. In many of them love is viewed as an all-consuming passion. It is extra-conjugal; that is to say, the woman courted is a married woman, like Guinevere and Iseult. The poetic form was essential when the story had to be memorized by a bard who sang the poem to his audience. Then came a time when chanting gave place to recitation, or reading aloud. As writing materials became cheaper and reading a more common accomplishment, less reliance was placed on memory. Most of the old verse romances were turned into prose. The story was retained, though the loss to art was considerable. Already in the thirteenth century this process began. In the following century prose romances became commoner; in the fifteenth they had practically replaced the metrical romance. Italy was the chief exception, where the French romances inspired the great romantic epics of Pulci, Boiardo, Ariosto, and others. In the early days of printing, prose romances were thrown off the presses in great numbers in every country of Europe.

Spanish translations of French romances.—At an early date French prose romances were turned into other languages and went the rounds of Europe. Many of those which entered Spain were not translated directly from French into Castilian; many were translations of translations. The Tristram romance came by way of Italy. Mr. Karl Pietsch has shown that the *Merlín*, the *Josep Abarimatia*, and the *Lanzarote* were first translated into a mixed dialect, partly Leonese and partly Galician-

Portuguese, thence into Castilian and Portuguese. Almost without exception these works were translated in the baldest possible fashion, were filled with error, and made not the slightest pretension to art. They were valued wholly for the story's sake; form was supposed not to matter. The Carolingian Cycle is represented in Spain by prose renderings of the *Maynete*, the *Reina Sevilla*, and the *Historia de Carlo Magno y de los doce pares*, which last harks back to the Fierabras epic. Belonging to the Arthurian Cycle are the *Tristán*, the *Lanzarote, Josep Abarimatia*, the *Demanda del Santo Grial, Tablante y Jofre*, and the *Baladro del Sabio Merlín* —this last is important as perpetuating a work whose French original has been lost. The Cycle of Antiquity is represented by various versions of the *Crónica troyana*, telling the story of Troy, not according to Homer, who was unknown to the Middle Ages, but following Dares, Dictys, Guido delle Colonne, and Bénoit de Sainte-More. There was also a Graeco-Oriental Cycle: *Partinuplés;* that ever delightful tale, *Flores y Blancaflor; Cleomedes y Clarimonda;* etc. Miscellaneous romances: *Oliveros de Castilla, Roberto el Diablo*, etc.

La gran conquista de Ultramar, belonging to the so-called Cycle of the Crusades, purports to be history. Its odd mingling of history and romance shows that its compiler adopted the identical procedure employed by the authors of Alfonso's vast chronicles; and this work, too, most probably came from the same scriptorium during the reign of Sancho el Bravo. It incorporates nearly the whole of William of Tyre's *Historia rerum in partibus transmarinis gestarum* but, instead of translating from the original, follows an Old French translation. Where William of Tyre ends, his various Old French continuators are followed. With this material are mingled long prosifications of many Old French Crusade epics; the *Helias* or Swan-knight legend, *Enfances Godefroi de Bouillon, La Chanson d'Antioche, Li Caitif, La Conquete de Jerusalem.* These works are incorporated almost entire. In addition we find the *Mainet, Berte aux grans pies*, the Provençal Antioch and lost epic fragments impossible to identify. This long work of eleven hundred chapters is a happy hunting ground for lovers of romance.

Before taking leave of this literature of translation, it should be stated that these stories have never ceased to charm certain portions of the population. They have been handed down through the centuries, so that even today they are read by the less cultured classes in the condensed form of chapbooks—*pliegos de cordel.*

"*El Caballero Çifar.*"—The oldest original Spanish romance of chivalry is the *Historia del Caballero de Dios que avia por nombre Çifar, el qual por sus virtuosas obras et hazañosas cosas fue rey de Menton.* The author was a cleric, as yet unidentified, who wrote between the dates 1299 and 1305, as may be deduced from internal evidence. It was first printed in 1512. Mr. C. P. Wagner's excellent critical text has made this work easily available. This is not a typical romance of chivalry, but a book of miscellaneous content. The first portion has for source a life of Saint Eustacius, a popular narrative in the Middle Ages. This is essentially a Greek romance with separations of husband from wife, children from father, piracies, shipwrecks, subsequent reunions and recognitions, and all the other features of the Milesian tale. After the first book, Çifar ceases to be the center of interest, and the adventures of his sons, Garfín and Roboan, are recounted. This portion is inspired by Arthurian romances. The episode of the Lady of the Lake occupies considerable space. Throughout there are many *exempla, cuentos*, and popular proverbs. The most important character is Roboan's peasant squire, El Ribaldo, crafty, shrewd, comic, materialistic. With him realism enters the Spanish romance of chivalry, not to reappear, except in *Tirant la Blanch,* until we reach the last of the series, *Don Quijote.* El Ribaldo has often been considered the prototype of Sancho Panza, though there is not the slightest evidence that Cervantes ever read the book. Menéndez y Pelayo is wrong in thinking El Ribaldo to be a new creation. One cannot insist too strongly upon the fact that the satire of romances of chivalry began in these romances themselves. For example, numerous realistic and comic traits occur in the prose *Tristram.* The anonymous author of the *Caballero Çifar,* Pulci, Folengo, and Cervantes were all continuing a tradition which began early in the history of the genre. This fact has been obscured by the prevailingly idealistic tone of the romances of the fifteenth and sixteenth centuries.

The medieval "Amadís."—The earliest redaction of *Amadís de Gaula* belongs to the fourteenth century. Pero Ferrús, a poet writing in 1379, alludes to an edition of it in three books. So does the chancellor Ayala in a work probably written earlier than the date mentioned. The earliest allusion to it dates from the year 1350. The *Amadís* may even be older than the *Çifar.* But the Montalvo re-working, the sole form in which we know it, was first printed in 1508. This great novel and the others to which it gave rise will be treated in the appropriate place.

*Early
Prose
Works*

BIBLIOGRAPHY

Alfonso X, el Sabio: Antología de sus obras, ed. A. G. SOLALINDE. 2 vols. Madrid, 1923.

——. *Siete partidas,* ed. ACADEMIA DE LA HISTORIA. 3 vols. Madrid, 1807.

——. *Libros del saber de astronomía,* ed. M. RICO Y SINOBAS. 5 vols. Madrid, 1863–67.

——. *Lapidario,* ed. J. FERNÁNDEZ MONTAÑA. Madrid, 1881.

——. *Libros de ajedrez, dados e tablas,* ed. A. STEIGER. Geneva and Zurich, 1941.

——. "Primera crónica general," ed. R. MENÉNDEZ PIDAL, *Nueva biblioteca de autores españoles.*[1] Madrid, 1906.

——. *General estoria,* Primera parte, ed. A. G. SOLALINDE. Madrid, 1930; Segunda parte, I, ed. A. G. SOLALINDE, LLOYD KASTEN, and VICTOR R. B. OELSCHLÄGER. Madrid, 1957.

PROCTOR, EVELYN S. *Alphonso X of Castile.* Oxford, 1951.

LÓPEZ DE AYALA, PERO. *Crónicas de los reyes de Castilla, Don Pedro, Don Enrique II, Don Juan I, Don Enrique III .* (Vols. I and II of *Crónicas españolas,* ed. LLAGUNO Y AMIROLA.) Madrid, 1799.

PÉREZ DE GUZMÁN, F. *Las generaciones, semblanzas y obras,* ed. R. FOULCHÉ-DELBOSC. Mâcon, 1907. Also *BAE,* Vol. LXVIII.

DÍEZ DE GAMES, G. *Crónica de Don Pedro Niño, Conde de Buelna.* (Vol. III of *Crónicas españolas,* ed. E. DE LLAGUNO Y AMIROLA. Madrid, 1782.) The French translation by CIRCOURT and PUYMAIGRE (Paris, 1867) is more complete.

RODRÍGUEZ DE LENA, P. *Libro del passo honroso de Suero de Quiñones.* Facsimile ed. by ARCHER M. HUNTINGTON. New York, 1902.

Crónica de Don Álvaro de Luna, ed. CARRIAZO. Madrid, 1940.

PULGAR, H. DEL. *Claros varones de Castilla,* ed. J. DOMÍNGUEZ BORDONA, *Clásicos castellanos.* Madrid, 1923.

MENÉNDEZ Y PELAYO, M. *Orígenes de la novela.* 2d ed.; 4 vols. Santander, 1943.

Calila e Dimna, ed. J. ALEMANY. Madrid, 1915.

---

[1] Henceforth this collection will be indicated by the initials *NBAE.*

El libro de los engaños, ed. J. E. KELLER. 2d ed. Chapel Hill and Valencia, 1959.

The Book of the Wiles of Women, trans. J. E. KELLER. Chapel Hill, 1956.

"Barlaam et Josaphat: La estoria del rey Anemur e de Iosaphat e de Barlaam," ed. F. LAUCHERT, *Romanische Forschungen*, Vol. VII (1893).

MOLDENHAUER, G. *Die Legende von Barlaam und Josaphat auf der iberischen Halbinsel*. Halle, 1929.

DE HAAN, F. "Barlaam and Josaphat in Spain," *Modern Language Notes*, Vol. X (1895).

PETRUS ALFONSI. *Die disciplina clericalis des Petrus Alfonsi*, ed. A. HILKA and W. SÖDERHJELM. Heidelberg, 1911.

———. *Ibid.*, ed. A. GONZÁLEZ PALENCIA. Madrid and Granada, 1948.

Castigos y documentos para bien vivir ordenados por el rey Don Sancho IV, ed. A. REY. Bloomington, 1952.

FOULCHÉ-DELBOSC, R. "Los Castigos e documentos de Sanche IV," *Revue hispanique*, Vol. XV (1916).

SÁNCHEZ DE VERCIAL, C. *El libro de los exenplos por a. b. c.*, ed. J. E. KELLER. Madrid, 1959.

"El libro de los gatos," ed. G. T. NORTHUP, *Modern Philology*, Vol. V (1908); ed. J. E. KELLER. Madrid, 1958.

GIMÉNEZ SOLER, A. *Don Juan Manuel: Biografía y estudio crítico.* Saragossa, 1932.

JUAN MANUEL. *Obras*, ed. P. DE GAYANGOS, *BAE*, Vol. LI (1857).

———. *El Conde Lucanor (Libro de Patronio)*, ed. F. G. SÁNCHEZ CANTÓN. Madrid, 1920; ed. JULIÁ MARTÍNEZ. Madrid, 1933.

———. "El libro del cauallero y del escudero," ed. S. GRÄFENBERG, *Romanische Forschungen*, Vol. VII (1893).

———. "La crónica complida," ed. G. BAIST, *Romanische Forschungen*, Vol. VII (1893).

———. *Libro de la caza*, ed. G. BAIST. Halle, 1880.

MARTÍNEZ DE TOLEDO, A. *El Arcipreste de Talavera o sea El Corvacho*, ed. L. B. SIMPSON. Berkeley and Los Angeles, 1939. Trans. L. B. SIMPSON as *Little Sermons on Sin*. Berkeley and

Los Angeles, 1959. Ed. (Spanish text) M. DE RIQUER. Barcelona, 1949.

ENTWISTLE, W. J. *The Arthurian Legend in the Literatures of the Spanish Peninsula.* London, 1925.

"Libros de Caballerías," ed. A. BONILLA Y SAN MARTÍN, *NBAE*, Vols. VI and XI; ed. (with Prologue and Bibliography) P. DE GAYANGOS, *BAE*, Vol. XL.

"La gran conquista de Ultramar," ed. P. DE GAYANGOS, *BAE*, Vol. XLIV.

MAZORRIAGA, E. *La leyenda del Cauallero del Cisne, transcripción del códice de la Biblioteca Nacional 2454, I. texto.* Madrid, 1914.

NORTHUP, G. T. "*La Gran Conquista de Ultramar* and Its Problems," *Hispanic Review*, II, 287–302.

Spanish Grail Fragments, ed. KARL PIETSCH. 2 vols. Chicago, 1924–25.

Libro del esforçado cauallero Don Tristán de Leonís y de sus grandes fechos en armas, ed. A. BONILLA Y SAN MARTÍN. Madrid, 1912.

El cuento de Tristan de Leonis, ed. G. T. NORTHUP. Chicago, 1928.

NORTHUP, G. T. "The Italian Origin of the Spanish Prose Tristram Versions," *Romanic Review*, III, 194–222.

El libro del Caballero Zifar, ed. C. P. WAGNER. Ann Arbor, 1929.

El caballero Zifar, ed. M. DE RIQUER. 2 vols. Barcelona, 1951. Based on the Wagner ed.

WAGNER, C. P. "The Sources of *El Caballero Cifar*," *Revue hispanique*, Vol. X (1903).

CHAPTER V

The Rise of the Courtly Lyric

The *kharjas* and the early lyric in Spain—The coming of the troubadours—The Galician-Portuguese lyric—Galician the supreme dialect for lyric poetry—Alfonso el Sabio's *Cantigas de Santa María*—Juan Ruiz, archpriest of Hita—Pero López de Ayala —La Escuela Trovadoresca Castellana—El Marqués de Santillana—Juan de Mena—Jorge Manrique.

The "kharjas" and the early lyric in Spain.—Probably some sort of primitive lyric existed early throughout all former Roman territory. The earliest body of lyrics yet discovered in medieval European Romance, about fifty in all, came from Moorish occupied Spain. They are called *kharjas* (*jarchas*) and are written in unpointed Hebrew characters. A *kharja* constitutes the last stanza or refrain of a popular type of Arabic poetry known as a *muwashshaha*. The earliest *kharjas* are supposed to date from about 1040 A.D., long before William of Acquitaine and a hundred years before the *Poema de Mio Cid*. The *kharjas* are delightful little *villancicos*, many of true and simple lyric freshness. Typically they are put in the mouth of an enamoured maiden—regretting the illness or the absence of her lover, inviting him to dance, or in general expressing her sentiments about him. The language is the Mozarabic dialect of Spanish.

There also existed among the mixed Christian and Moorish inhabitants of Andalusia a non-Classical, distinctly popular form of verse known as the *zéjel*, in Arabic, but containing many Spanish words, sometimes whole lines. Their structure is interesting: a *zéjel* normally begins with a refrain or *estribillo* of two, three, or four rhyming lines; then a stanza of four lines, three in a different rhyme but the fourth going back to the rhyme of the *estribillo*, a cue for the audience to repeat the *estribillo* in chorus. If that chorus was of two lines, the scheme would be thus: *aa/bbba/aa*. The form was later frequently used in popular Spanish and other verse.

Poems certainly existed too in connection with occupations and various occasions of the year, religious and secular: soldiers' and watchmen's songs (e.g., the "*Eya, velar,*" in Berceo's *Duelo de la Virgen*), songs for the grape or other harvests, *cantos de romería* ("religious picnic"), and notably songs of mountain girls known as *serranillas*. As Juan Ruiz presents them, these *serranas* were sturdy wenches capable of guiding less vigorous travelers over difficult mountain passes and more than capable of repulsing—or of accepting—the amorous advances of the less robust swain. Later on, the highly sophisticated Marquis of Santillana was to use the popular form most delicately in his famous ten *serranillas*. They also bear some resemblance to the French *pastourelles*.

In Galician-Portuguese territory the popular form seems not to have been the *zéjel*, but rather a four-line stanza rhyming *aabb*, with the *bb* lines repeating the same idea of the *aa* in different end-words. This parallelistic structure existed in many parts of the world, and reminds us of the poetic technique of the Psalms of David.

The coming of the troubadours.—French epic poetry was a product of Northern France. Southern France, especially Provence, was supreme in the lyric. In that joyous climate life was free and easy, manners were softened and refined. Long-continued peace brought the dawn of a new civilization. The Provençal courtly lyric starts with William IX, Duke of Aquitania (1088–1127), and flourished well into the thirteenth century. Provençal troubadours carried the prestige of their song to Northern France, thence to the Rhine, and over the Alps and Pyrenees into Italy and Spain. The airs to which these lyrics were set made them popular even when the words were incomprehensible. But many troubadours found it easy to adapt their verses to kindred Romance dialects. Some wrote new poems in acquired tongues. Nor did they lack imitators in the countries they visited. The Provençal lyric was highly artificial. Form mattered rather than content. Metrical forms were numerous and very complicated. The concept of love was artificial, too; a troubadour always courted in verse some lady of rank. This courtship was conventional and platonic.

The Galician-Portuguese lyric.—The troubadours made their influence most strongly felt in two regions, Catalonia and Galicia. In the former province the language was then almost identical with Provençal speech, and Catalan poetry may be considered an offshoot of that of Southern France. The early presence of large numbers of troubadours in Galicia may be explained by the importance of the pilgrimage to Santiago de Compostella. That their songs found such ready acceptance and imitation in Northwestern Spain was probably due to the racial sentimentality and lyric talent of the Galicians. In the early Middle Ages Galician differed little from Portuguese. King Dennis of Portugal (1259–1325), himself a noted troubadour, attracted many of the craft to his capital, and his reign marks the most brilliant period of the school. The work of these poets has been partially preserved in three *cancioneiros*. The oldest, the *Cancioneiro da Ajuda*, is wholly Provençal in tone, spirit, form. It is most interesting in the proof it affords of the wealth of new meters which had come in from France. The two later collections, *El Cancioneiro portuguez da Vaticana* and *Il canzoniere portoghese Colocci-Brancuti*, are anthologies giving the work of poets of the thirteenth and fourteenth centuries. They mark a new departure. The poets had partially broken away from Provençal models to imitate, artistically, the folk-song of their region. We find again the *cantiga de amigo* (so called from the frequent recurrence of the word *amigo*, "lover"), another form of love lyric, the *cantiga de ledino* (so called from the frequent use of *ledo*,"happy"), *serranillas*, *villanescas*, satiric *cantigas de escarnio*, and other popular forms. The folk-song of the peasants had revolutionized court poetry, making it less artificial. The dainty charm of many of these trifles is not lost to the modern reader.

Galician the supreme dialect for lyric poetry.—The literature above treated interests the student of Portuguese rather than of Spanish literature, but an understanding of it is essential to one who would trace the development of Castilian lyric verse. Just as Castilian was the dialect par excellence for epic poetry, so Galician for several centuries was the recognized medium for lyric expression. Galician was earlier molded to meet the demands of art. The prestige of Galician poets was such that for a time the court poets of Castile wrote in that dialect rather than in their own. In the latter half of the four-

teenth century there developed an *escuela trovadoresca*
which timidly began to substitute Castilian for Galician
in its lyrics. The increasing political dominance of Castile, together with the refinement of the language, gradually brought about a change, until, in the sixteenth and
seventeenth centuries, many of the greatest Portuguese
authors wrote wholly or partly in Castilian.

Alfonso el Sabio's "Cantigas de Santa María."—Alfonso X was a patron of troubadours, both French and Galician-Portuguese. He himself was one of the craft, if we
may accept as his personal effort the *Cantigas de Santa
María;* and though this attribution has been impugned,
there is nothing inherently improbable in the idea that a
man of his intellectual interests should dabble in the "gay
science," in an age when it was fashionable for kings to do
so. The *Cantigas* were written in Galician. They number
over four hundred, each recounting some miracle performed by the Virgin in behalf of some one of her devotees. Some of these pious legends belong to the general
fund of European tradition, like the story of how the
Virgin replaced an eloping nun, so that after the sinner's
return her absence was not noted—the theme of Zorrilla's
Margarita la tornera and Maeterlinck's *Sœur Béatrice.*
Others poetize motives more peculiarly Spanish, how one
of Alfonso's servants, who entered a river to secure a
heron brought down by a falcon, was saved from drown-
ing by the monarch's prayer to Our Lady; how a citizen
of Palencia was saved from a savage bull, etc. There
were many similar miracle collections in the Middle
Ages, notably Gautier de Coincy's *Miracles de la sainte
Vierge*, but none which equals that of the *rey sabio* in
artistry. In his hands the Galician speech is a supple

instrument; the formal execution all but perfect, the meters rich and varied. The themes are naïve; the versification is sophisticated. Each poem had its air, and this music has been preserved. Whether the effect of modernity which one notes on hearing it played is characteristic of the original, or due to the modern arranger, is a question for musicians to determine.

Juan Ruiz, archpriest of Hita.—In the first half of the fourteenth century there appeared a genius of first importance in the person of Juan Ruiz, archpriest in the little town of Hita. We know few of the facts of his life. He, the first of Spanish humorists, was born in Alcalá de Henares, the birthplace of the greatest of humorists, Cervantes. He flourished toward the end of the first half of the fourteenth century. For thirteen years, under the primacy of Gil de Albornoz, cardinal archbishop of Toledo (1337–67), he may have been in prison, during which period he composed his *Libro de buen amor*. We are ignorant of the reason for this imprisonment, which the victim considered unjust (*sin merescer*). The records of Hita show that in 1351 another incumbent occupied the archpriestship, so that it is supposed that Juan Ruiz had died before that date. But if we know few facts of the archpriest's biography, we know much about his appearance, tastes, accomplishments, and character. Few authors are more self-revealing. Like Cervantes, he has left us his verbal portrait. He describes himself as raw-boned, brawny, swarthy, with beady black eyes, and thick sensual lips. He was a merry wag (*doñeador alegre*), who could play various instruments and possessed the minstrel's craft (*sabe los estrumentos e todas juglarías*). His literary culture was considerable for one of his time and place.

His artistic range was wide. He could write the daintiest of hymns to the Virgin, full of the most genuine devotion, and then find relaxation in providing songs for blind beggars, students, and itinerant Moorish dancing-girls. His morals were pagan. Like Friar Tuck in *Ivanhoe*, he enjoyed the good things of life. Juan Ruiz was a type of dissolute priest all too common in the Middle Ages; but his is an interesting personality, and he stands out in refreshing contrast to a host of whining pietists.

Content of "El Libro de buen amor."—By *buen amor* Juan Ruiz meant the love of God and righteousness as opposed to *loco amor*, "sensual love." The title, then, promises an edifying work. Stories of carnal love are alleged to be introduced merely to point a moral and warn the unwary. But *loco amor* was what chiefly interested Juan Ruiz, and the most unhypocritical of men is here guilty of hypocrisy. He is laughing in his sleeve; a priest has to preserve appearances. *El libro de buen amor* is a work of miscellaneous content. There was an effort to bind together in a unified whole the most varied material; yet the only bond of union is the author's personality, just as the rogue's personality was later to serve the same purpose in the picaresque novel. Juan Ruiz narrates in the first person singular, a novel device in his day. The work begins with a quaint prayer and a medieval prose sermon, reminding one of "The Persones Tale" in *Canterbury Tales*. Then follow two charming poems on "The Joys of Holy Mary," when, the edifying preliminaries finished, the archpriest plunges with gusto into the picaresque account of his amours. The first lady of his heart is Cruz, *la panadera*, who prefers to him the rascally Fernand García, whom he had employed as go-between. Juan

Ruiz enjoys a laugh at his own expense. A more efficient pleader is found in the person of Trotaconventos, a hag realistically portrayed and ancestress of the whole brood of Celestinas so prominent in later literature. She serves him in a number of wooings, most of which prove to be fiascos. In this portion of his work Juan Ruiz is inspired by the *Pamphilus de amore*, a medieval adaptation of Ovid. In the discussions between characters, many short stories are told, *exempla* and animal apologues. Nobody has told better the familiar stories of "The Town Mouse and the Country Mouse," "The Frogs Who Wanted a King," etc. Such themes the author localizes in Spain and makes completely his own. He borrowed as freely as any writer of his time, but improved upon his sources and gave each theme the imprint of his rich personality. The love-story framework is interrupted in other ways. There is the famous *Enxiemplo de la propiedat que el dinero ha*, a common theme in all the literatures, but which has never been surpassed, unless, possibly, by Quevedo.

The first stanza of Mr. Elisha Kent Kane's clever rendering will give a good idea of the original:

Much power, indeed, Sir Money has and much for him we dabble,
He makes the dolt a man of worth and sets him o'er the rabble,
He makes the lame leap up and run, he makes the deaf-mute babble;
Why those who have no hands at all will after money scrabble!

Longfellow has been happy with the *Praise of Little Women*. I quote only the first and last stanzas:

I wish to make my sermon brief,—to shorten my oration,—
For a never-ending sermon is my utter detestation;
I like short women,—suits at law without procrastination,—
And am always most delighted with things of short duration.
. . . .

If as her size increases are woman's charms decreased,
Then surely it is good to be from all the great released.
Now of two evils choose the less—said a wise man of the East,
By consequence, of woman-kind be sure to choose the least.

Again, he tells some merry tale from the French, like the
story of *Don Pitas Payas, Pyntor de Bretaña*, evidently
based on some lost *fabliau* (a versified short story, usually
coarse in subject matter, which prevailed in medieval
France). There are also four *serranillas*, or *cantigas de
serrana*. Juan Ruiz's mountain-maids are not idealized
rustic beauties, but formidable creatures of the *hombruna*
type. He describes them with a comic naturalism which
is as irresistible as are the hussies themselves. Obviously,
he is parodying a favorite form of the Galician school.
Then, to make amends, this licentious verse is followed
by two exquisite hymns on "The Passion of Our Lord
Jesus Christ." The longest intermission is *La pelea que
ouo Don Carnal con la Quaresma*. At the beginning of
the forty-day period of her power, Lady Lent with her
army of fish, oysters, clams, lobsters, and crabs overcomes
Lord Flesh, who takes refuge among the Jews until he can
reform his army of beef, mutton, pork, fowls, etc. At
last, feeling secure, he sends Don Breakfast and Lady
Lunch to bear a challenge to the enemy. After a pitched
battle Flesh triumphs over Lent on Easter Day, and the
ensuing orgy is described with gusto, as is also the coming
of Don Amor. This episode is taken from the French
Bataille de Karesme et de Charnage, with the addition of
infinitely greater comic force. But, after such interrup-
tions, the archpriest always returns to the story of his
philanderings. Finally, Trotaconventos, otherwise known
as Urraca, dies, and the author writes her eulogy and

epitaph. She is replaced by Weasel (Don Furón), that paragon of servants except for the fourteen faults mentioned. Weasel is a poor substitute, and the work rapidly draws to a close with two poems on the *Gozos de Santa María, Del Ave María de Santa María,* and four *Cantigas de loores de Santa María.* In these last the archpriest reaches his highest point of achievement as a serious poet. Here the *Libro de buen amor* was doubtless intended to end, but some of the scribes have appended three short poems, the *Cantiga de los Clérigos de Talavera* and two *Cantares de ciegos.*

Influences and form.—Juan Ruiz was influenced by all the literary currents which affected his time and place. He was widely read in the Latin devotional literature of the church, and shows himself erudite in canon law. He had little opportunity to know the classics at first hand. Ovid he knew through the *Pamphilus de amore,* and Æsop and Phædrus through some of the numerous *exempla* collections then to be found in every religious establishment. He certainly knew French, as so many of his sources were in that language, and, what is not surprising, shows knowledge of more than a smattering of Arabic. He was close to the springs of folklore. His democratic leanings made him the boon companion of the vagrant bards who thronged every road in the Middle Ages. The aristocratic poetry of the Galician-Portuguese school of minstrelsy was familiar to him. What Provençal influence may be noted in his work probably came to him second hand through this last-named source. While he lacked the aristocratic temper which informed the poetry of the Galician school, he knew their meters and was able to apply them to his own ends. One of Juan Ruiz's chief claims to distinction is that he was a pioneer in the introduction into Castilian of new verse forms. More than any other poet, he proved that Castilian could be made a vehicle for lyric expression. The bulk of his narrative is written in *cuaderna vía*. He would have been a greater poet on the formal side if he had not adhered to this most ungrateful of meters; but he makes the old *mester de clerecía* throb with life. In his hands it acquired a vivacity which it elsewhere lacks. His lyrics are written in the most varied meters, with long lines and short, and intricate arrangements of rhyme, melodious and supple. Some authorities think that he occasionally lapses into popular ametric forms.

Juan Ruiz's aesthetic value.—Juan Ruiz is the first Spanish poet of distinct personality who expressed that personality in his verse. He is interested in himself and expects his readers to share that interest. This is a rare phenomenon in the Middle Ages, when writers, with few exceptions, lacked both originality and individuality. Juan Ruiz is one of those exceptions, hence his importance. Having personality, he also has style. He is the first great Spanish humorist, the first, too, who cultivated the picaresque in Spanish literature. He also interests through his wonderful faculty for painting the life of his times. There is no better source for knowing the details of fourteenth-century Spanish life: what the people ate and drank, the musical instruments they played, the songs they sang, the dances they danced, how they made love, the life of monastery, tavern, and the highway. We see displayed the whole medieval pageant, portrayed with realism and humor. Juan Ruiz envisages life from a democratic viewpoint. He possesses to a supreme degree

the national qualities of democracy, realism, and humor.
What he lacks is nobility of sentiment. He is a poet who
fascinates and interests, not one who exalts. Yet he is not
without religious fervor. The sincere devotion of his
hymns is distinctly felt; but one also feels that his devotion is formal and unrelated to ethics. If he had his
moments of contrition and devotion, he was no mystic.
He was an erring human being, and one can say of the
Libro de buen amor, as one can say of *Don Quijote*, that its
unfailing humanity constitutes its chief merit.

   Pero López de Ayala (1332–1407) was a nobleman
whose career extended over five chaotic reigns, and who
finally rose to be chancellor of Castile under Henry III.
He was the most intelligent courtier of his age, having
views far in advance of his time. He played a prominent
part in the troubled events of the fourteenth century, and
managed his private affairs so well that he triumphed over
every temporary reverse and rose to great wealth and
influence. As a youth he abandoned the falling fortunes
of Peter the Cruel most disloyally, and entered the service
of Henry of Trastamara. He was captured by Edward,
the Black Prince, in the battle of Nájera and forced to
pay a heavy ransom. When ambassador to the court of
Charles VI of France, he rendered important services
to that monarch. Under John I, Ayala's prudent counsel
to avoid war with Portugal went unheeded, and he paid
for his master's folly by falling into the hands of the enemy, who kept him prisoner in an iron cage for over a
year. There, it is said, he wrote a portion of his chief
poetic work, the *Rimado de palacio*. López de Ayala had
strength of body and was possessed of every knightly
accomplishment. He was one of those rounded charac-

ters, more suggestive of the Renaissance than of the
Middle Ages. He united the ideals of "arms and letters,"
like so many of his later compatriots. He was active as
translator, turning into Spanish portions of Livy,
Boethius' *De consolatione*, the *Morals* of Saint Gregory the
Great, Saint Isidore's *De summo bono*, and Boccaccio's
Fall of Princes. With this last work he initiated the current of Italian influence. He wrote an original treatise on
falconry, *Libro de cetrería, o de las aves de caza*. His most
important prose works were his chronicles, already considered.

"*El rimado de palacio*."—This, like the *Libro de buen
amor*, is a miscellaneous compilation, written chiefly in
cuaderna vía, broken by lyrics in varied meters. With
Ayala the *cuaderna vía* ends. There are disquisitions
on the Ten Commandments, the seven deadly sins, the
seven works of mercy, the five senses, the seven spiritual
works, hymns to the Virgin, and a long recital of the
story of Job. All this prosiness suggests the monk rather
than the courtier. Imprisonment had given the author
leisure to meditate on his sins. He weighs himself in the
balance of the Ten Commandments, finds that he has
broken them all, and, though he evidently exaggerates
his faults, displays a remorse of which the archpriest
was incapable. Having set his soul to rights, he proceeds
to show what is wrong with the world. His world is that
of the palace. He pictures rash young kings, heedless of
prudent counsel, turbulent feudal barons actuated by
self-interest to the detriment of the nation, the wiles of
lawyers and unscrupulous Jewish money-lenders, insolent
doorkeepers who admit to the royal presence only after a
bribe has been proffered. The merchants are just as bad.

They keep their shops dark so that bad merchandise may be palmed off on their customers. The church is in no better case. Ayala inveighs bitterly against the schism of Avignon.

Ayala and Juan Ruiz contrasted.—Ayala supplements marvelously Juan Ruiz's picture of fourteenth-century life. The latter looks upon sin indulgently, the former with bitterness. The one is democratic and optimistic; the other is aristocratic and pessimistic. Juan Ruiz is a forerunner of Rojas and Cervantes; Ayala anticipates the excoriating style of Quevedo. Ayala is the earliest of the great Spanish satirists. Though he knew how to feather his nest, he was undoubtedly a patriot. His pessimism springs from the fact that he was more intelligent than his contemporaries, more modern in his point of view. He knew what measures should be taken for his country's weal, and was easily discouraged at the spectacle of the almost universal ineptitude and corruption around him. His modernity is shown by his hatred of war and advocacy of pacifism. Speaking of the duty of a counselor to his king, he says:

> Quien bien le consejare, si lo puede fazer,
> en consejar la paz faga a su poder,
> ca esta puebla tierras e las finche de aver,
> e los pueblos muchigua con bien e con plazer.

Ayala lacks the archpriest's geniality and skill as a craftsman, but he evinces a capacity for righteous indignation which commands respect.

La escuela trovadoresca castellana.—In the year 1445, Juan Alfonso de Baena, a converted Jew, compiled for that patron of poets, John II, an anthology of the best productions of the preceding reigns. This collection, the

Cancionero de Baena, permits us to see the development of
Spanish poetry during the reigns of Henry II, John I,
Henry III, and the minority of John II, a period covering
the latter half of the fourteenth century and the beginning
of the fifteenth. There have thus been preserved 576 poems,
by fifty-four poets, in addition to thirty-five anonymous
works. All these writers belonged to the courtly, aristocratic school. They were struggling with novel metrical
forms and striving to adapt an unpolished speech to the
requirements of lyric expression. To such writers poetry
was purely a formal matter, a triumphing over difficulties. Genuine poetic inspiration is lacking. The *Cancionero de Baena* contains none of those dainty bits found in
the *Cancioneiro da Vaticana*. Hence its intrinsic value
is next to nothing; it is important solely to those interested in the historic evolution of a genre. As the lapse of
time represented is considerable, we are able to note a
change of literary fashion. The older poets in the collection are under the influence of the Galician-Portuguese
school, trying to do in Castilian what had been done in
Galician. The leader of this group was Alfonso Álvarez
de Villasandino (1350?–1428?), who in his day enjoyed a
reputation unsanctioned by posterity. Another member
is Macías, the Galician troubadour who died for his lady,
at the hands of a jealous husband, and whom tradition has
canonized as the martyr of devoted love. His preserved
work is commonplace. A later group, headed by Micer
Francisco Imperial, broke away from Galician models
and sought inspiration in the poetry of Italy, notably in
Dante. Imperial was a Genoese goldsmith, domiciled in
Seville. He was first to introduce into Spanish metrics
the noble hendecasyllable of Italy, thereby greatly enrich-

ing Spanish prosody. He also made popular the Dan-
tesque vision and allegory. In so doing he set a fashion
which found many imitators in the next generation. The
Galician and the Italian schools of poetry, as represented
in the *Cancionero de Baena*, were alike mannered and
artificial; but they aided in making Castilian Spanish a
poetic language.

El Marqués de Santillana (1398–1458).—These artistic gropings resulted in the formation of a real poet—
Íñigo López de Mendoza—better known by his title,
Marqués de Santillana. He was nephew of the chancellor
Ayala, and, like his uncle, a great feudal lord, who united
the ideals of arms and letters. Santillana was rich, accomplished, cultured, and brave. He fought valiantly against
the Moors, and engaged in more than one insurrection
against the weak John II and his powerful favorite,
Álvaro de Luna. Santillana had too much of an aristocrat's disdain to appreciate Luna's statesmanship; for
Luna was a *parvenu* who saw the necessity for curbing
the turbulent class to which Santillana belonged. But if
unable to rise above class prejudice, Santillana's career
was creditable for the time. His fame is marred by no
act of perfidy. He was a faithful friend and devoted in his
domestic relationships. His writings reveal him as a man
of refinement.

"Proemio e carta."—Santillana is the earliest historian
and critic of Spanish poetry, if we except Villena's *Arte
de trovar*, a mere re-echoing of Provençal precepts. The
Marqués presents his views in a brief prose work, called
Proemio e carta, addressed to Pedro, constable of Portugal, and intended to serve as introduction to a number of
his *decires* and *canciones*. He affects to make light of

these trifles, the fruits of "the new age of youth." He defines poetry as *un fingimiento de cosas útiles, cubiertas o veladas con muy fermosa cobertura, compuestas, distinguidas e scandidas por cierto cuento, passo e medida.* Thus he is Horatian in his demand for the *utile dulci*, and insists upon form. He does not perceive wherein he himself surpassed his immediate predecessors who had been equally insistent upon form—the possession of genuine poetic feeling. Poetry is divided into three categories: the sublime, the poetry of the ancients; the mediocre, the artistic verse of modern peoples; the low—*ínfimos son aquellos que sin ningún orden, regla nin cuento façen estos romances e cantares, de que las gentes de baxa e servil condición se alegran.* It is thus that he scorns the popular genres, and yet he often turned to the people for his inspiration, handling artistically their simple themes. Precisely this crossing of the popular and the artistic constituted Santillana's genius, elevating his work above the tiresome insipidities of the *Cancionero de Baena.* Tracing the history of poetry, he finds that it was first cultivated by the Hebrews, carried to perfection by the Greeks and Romans, and rediscovered by the Provençals. He admits that he is unacquainted with the Provençal poets, but shows familiarity with those of Northern France and the Galician-Portuguese school. He rightly considers the Italians leaders in the poetry of his age, and his favorite Spanish poet is their imitator, Imperial. The two chief influences in his work are therefore the Italian and the Galician-Portuguese schools. His poems contain many reminiscences of Dante, Petrarch, and Boccaccio.

His other works.—Dante was the inspiration of his

two longer poems, *La comedieta de Ponza* and the *Infierno de los enamorados*. These are cast in the form of allegoric visions. His forty-two sonnets contain many direct imitations of Petrarch. They lack that perfection which sonnets should have, and are chiefly interesting as the first ever written in Spanish. Santillana is therefore a herald of the Renaissance and a forerunner of Boscán. But his fame rests principally on his *canciones y decires*, and, above all, on his *serranillas*. These last lack the archpriest's spirit of comic realism. They are dainty trifles with just a dash of cynical mischief. Lightness of touch is Santillana's distinguishing trait. He is a writer of exquisite society verse. Reared in an artificial school of poetry, he succeeded in adding simplicity, sentiment, grace, and taste, without departing from the formality of his predecessors. Santillana and Jorge Manrique are the two poets of the time who can most easily be appreciated by moderns. These few lines from his famous *Serranilla sexta*—no translation does them justice—will serve as a sample of his airy lightness:

> Moça tan fermosa
> non vi en la frontera
> como una vaquera
> de la Finojosa.
>
> Faziendo la vía
> del Calatraveño
> a Santa María
> vencido del sueño,
> por tierra fragosa,
> perdí la carrera,
> do ví la vaquera
> de la Finojosa.

Juan de Mena (*1411–56*) was not an aristocrat like most of the poets of his age, but a scholar who won success through native talent. He was a Cordovan, educated in Salamanca, and resided for a time in Rome—a circumstance of supreme importance for his intellectual development. He became Latin secretary to John II, whom he served with never failing loyalty. Menéndez y Pelayo considers him the first professional man of letters in Spanish history.

"*El laberinto.*"—Mena's fame rests upon a single work written in 1444, entitled *El laberinto de Fortuna*, though frequently designated *Las trescientas*, because it consisted of three hundred octave *coplas*. Later, twenty-four additional stanzas were added at the king's request. This is an allegorical work, inspired by Dante's *Paradiso*. The poet is transported by Providence, his Beatrice, to the palace of Fortune, where he sees three great wheels, two motionless, one in motion. The moving wheel represents the present, the others the past and the future. On each wheel there are seven circles: that of Diana, the abode of the chaste; of Mercury, where the wicked are housed; of Venus, where the sensual reside; of Phoebus, the retreat of philosophers; of Mars, where warriors linger; of Jupiter, seat of kings; of Saturn, elysium of just governors. In each of these circles the poet meets the shades of ancient worthies and the persons of the mighty ones of his own time. This framework is tedious, but the reader is rewarded by many interesting episodes, the most famous of which is the tender description of the death of the Conde de Niebla. Mena displays a national, patriotic spirit in advance of his time.

Verso de arte mayor.—Mena made famous a meter of

116

*The Rise
of the
Courtly
Lyric*

obscure, probably Galician origin, called *verso de arte mayor*. The striking feature of this meter is that it is rhythmic rather than syllabic. Each line has four beats, and, though most lines are of twelve syllables, eleven-syllable verses are frequently substituted, and ten-syllable lines are not unknown. The strongest beats regularly fall on the fifth syllable of each hemistich, though in the first hemistich it frequently falls on the fourth. The usual rhyme-scheme is: *abbaacca*. English readers feel the rhythm of *arte mayor* better than they do that of most Spanish measures—it is so like our own metrical structure; but its regularity of stress renders it intolerable to the modern Spanish ear. Mena doubtless considered this meter the closest approach to the classic hexameter which his language afforded. For a century *arte mayor* remained the Spanish meter par excellence, as *cuaderna vía* had been in the preceding generation.

Mena's importance.—Mena was first to feel that Spanish had an impoverished vocabulary, inadequate to express subtle shades of thought. He determined to supply this want by borrowing copiously from the Latin. He introduced numerous neologisms, many of which retained a permanent place in the language. It was a common Renaissance idea that the modern tongues should be enriched by the spoils of the ancients. Mena must have acquired this idea in Italy; but it is striking that he should anticipate by so many years the pronouncements of Sperone Speroni and Joachim du Bellay. The enrichment of the language and the creation of a poetic vocabulary wholly distinct from that of prose are Mena's most important contributions. In these tendencies he anticipates Góngora, his fellow-townsman, whom he undoubtedly

influenced. He anticipated the *cultistas* also in his wealth
of classic allusion and in the calculated obscurity of much
of his verse. He was chief of a school of learned poets,
and his affectation of erudition endeared him to the
humanists of the next generation. Though he makes
slight appeal to modern taste, he is historically important
as the poet most representative of the transition from
the Middle Ages to the Renaissance.

"Coplas de Mingo Revulgo" (*1464*).—The popular
note evident in this anonymous satire contrasts sharply
with the aristocratic and erudite tendencies of the period.
The poem is a dialogue in dialect between two peasants
who discuss the anarchic conditions of the times. One
character, Mingo Revulgo, symbolizes the Spanish
nation. He blames incompetent rulers for chaotic conditions. The other, Gil Arribato, points out the shortcomings of the people, who must assume their share of
responsibility for national evils. This work exerted a
decisive influence upon Juan del Encina and other early
dramatists.

Jorge Manrique (*1440?-1479*).—The troubled reign of
Henry IV (1454–75), produced three outstanding poets,
Álvarez Gato, Gómez Manrique, and the latter's nephew,
Jorge Manrique. The first two continued the tradition
of courtly poetry, producing the usual graceful trifles.
Jorge Manrique is famous for a single work in which he
surpassed not only himself but every other poet of his
age. The *Coplas a la muerte del Maestre de Santiago, Don
Rodrigo Manrique, su padre* remains the best-known and
most perfect specimen of Spanish medieval poetry. This
father, Grand Master of the military order of Santiago
and Conde de Paredes, was the most famous general of his

time, a feudal chieftain possessed of all the virtues of a great noble. The poem was written immediately after the Conde de Paredes' death, in 1476. The son died a soldier's death beneath the walls of Garci Muñoz three years later.

The "Coplas."—Manrique's masterpiece is an elegy of forty stanzas. In it the bereaved son, after recounting his father's virtues, generalizes upon the briefness of life and the transitoriness of all things human. This sinking of individual grief in the common woe of humanity is, according to Menéndez y Pelayo, one of the author's chief merits. *Memento mori* was the motto of the Middle Ages. Preachers and writers throughout Europe kept harping on the theme that "in the midst of life we are in death," and asking what has become of the great men and fair ladies of the past. *"Ubi sunt qui ante nos in mundo fuere?"* The *"ubi sunt?"* motive," as it is called, is a commonplace in European literature. From beginning to end there is not an original thought in the *Coplas*, nothing but commonplaces, but, as Fitzmaurice-Kelly observes, they are "the sublime commonplaces of death." Jorge Manrique's merit is that he said what everybody else was saying and said it better. He excels in the mastery of artistic form. In all literature he has only one equal in the handling of the *ubi sunt?* motive, François Villon, in the *Ballade des dames du temps jadis*, with its haunting refrain, *"Mais où sont les neiges d'antan?"* By virtue of Longfellow's translation, so literal, and faithful as to meter and spirit, this poem has become an English classic. A few of Longfellow's stanzas will suffice to convey an idea of Manrique's style:

Where is the king Don Juan? Where
Each royal prince and noble heir
    Of Aragon?
Where are the courtly gallantries?
The deeds of love and high emprise,
    In battle done?
Tourney and just that charmed the eye,
And scarf, and gorgeous panoply,
    And nodding plume—
What are they but a pageant scene?
What but the garlands, gay and green,
    That deck the tomb?
Where are the high born dames, and where
Their gay attire, and jewelled hair,
    And odours sweet?
Where are the gentle knights that came
To kneel, and breathe love's ardent flame,
    Low at their feet?
Where is the song of Troubadour?
Where are the lute and gay tambour
    They loved of yore?
Where is the mazy dance of old?
The flowing robes, inwrought with gold
    The dancers wore?

.   .   .   .

The noble steeds, and harness bright
And gallant lord, and stalwart knight,
    In rich array,—
Where shall we seek them now? Alas!
Like the bright dewdrops on the grass,
    They passed away.

The modern reader can note scarcely an archaism in
Manrique's verse. He was no scholar, and avoided
Mena's pedantic tendencies. All is simplicity, clarity.

The *Coplas* proves that toward the end of the fifteenth century the language was becoming fixed.

BIBLIOGRAPHY

MENÉNDEZ PIDAL, R. *La primitiva poesía lírica española.* (In *Estudios literarios.* Madrid, 1920).

———. *Poesía árabe y poesía europea.* Buenos Aires, 1942.

———. *Poesía juglaresca y juglares.* Madrid, 1924.

STERN, S. M. *Les chansons mozarabes.* Palermo, 1953.

ALONSO, D. "Cancionillos 'de amigo' mozárabes," *Revista de filología española,* Vol. XXXIII (1949).

NYKL, A. R. *Hispano-Arabic Poetry.* Baltimore, 1946.

Cancioneiro da Ajuda, ed. CAROLINA MICHAELIS DE VASCONCELLOS. 2 vols. Halle, 1904.

Cancionero da Ajuda, ed. H. H. CARTER. New York and London, 1941. A diplomatic ed.

Canzoniere portoghese Colocci-Brancuti, ed. E. MOLTENI. Halle, 1880.

Cancioneiro portuguez da Vaticana, ed. TH. BRAGA. Lisbon, 1878.

MENÉNDEZ Y PELAYO, M. *Antología de poetas líricos castellanos.* New ed.; 10 vols. Santander, 1944–45. Good biographies and criticism of early Spanish poets through Garcilaso.

ALONSO, D. *Poesía española. Antología. Poesías de la Edad Media y poesía de tipo tradicional.* 2d ed. Buenos Aires, 1942.

POST, C. R. *Mediaeval Spanish Allegory.* Cambridge, 1915.

ALFONSO X, EL SABIO. *Cantigas de Santa María,* ed. REAL ACADEMIA ESPAÑOLA. 2 vols. Madrid, 1889.

JUAN RUIZ. *Libro de buen amor,* ed. JEAN DUCAMIN. Toulouse, 1901; ed. J. CEJADOR Y FRAUCA. (In *Clásicos castellanos.* 2 vols. Madrid, 1913). Readable ed. with notes.

———. *The Book of Good Love of the Archpriest of Hita, Juan Ruiz.* Trans. into English verse by ELISHA KENT KANE. Privately printed, 1933. A rendering amazing for its virtuosity.

PUYOL Y ALONSO, J. *El Arcipriste de Hita.* Madrid, 1906.

ULRICH, LEO. *Zur dichterischen Originalität des Arcipreste de Hita.* Frankfurt, 1958.

LECOY, F. *Recherches sur le "Libro de Buen Amor."* Paris, 1938.

LÓPEZ DE AYALA, PERO. *Poesías*, ed. A. F. KUERSTEINER. New York, 1920.

DÍAZ DE ARCAYA, M. *El gran canciller D. Pero López de Ayala.* Vitoria, 1900.

PUYMAIGRE, COMTE DE. *La Cour littéraire de don Juan II, roi de Castille.* 2 vols. Paris, 1873.

AMADOR DE LOS RÍOS, J. *Historia crítica de la literatura española.* 7 vols. Madrid, 1861–65. Through the fifteenth century only.

MILLARES CARLO, A. *Literatura española hasta fines del siglo XV.* Mexico, 1950.

Cancionero del siglo XV, ed. R. FOULCHÉ-DELBOSC, *NBAE*, Vols. XIX, XXII.

Cancionero de Baena, ed. P. J. PIDAL. Madrid, 1851; Facsimile ed., Hispanic Society of America. New York, 1926.

BONILLA Y SAN MARTÍN, A. *Antología de poetas de los siglos XIII al XV.* Madrid, 1917.

SANTILLANA, MARQUÉS DE. *Obras*, ed. J. AMADOR DE LOS RÍOS. Madrid, 1852.

———. *Canciones e decires*, ed. V. GARCÍA DE DIEGO, *Clásicos castellanos.* Madrid, 1913.

MENA, JUAN DE. *El laberinto de Fortuna*, ed. R. FOULCHÉ-DELBOSC. Macon, 1904; ed. J. M. BLECUA, *Clásicos castellanos.* Madrid, 1943.

LIDA DE MALQUIEL, ROSA. *Juan de Mena: Poeta prerrenacentista español.* Mexico, 1950.

MANRIQUE, JORGE. *Coplas*, ed. R. FOULCHÉ-DELBOSC. Madrid, 1912.

———. *Cancionero*, ed. CORTINA, *Clásicos castellanos.* Madrid, 1929.

———. *Obras completas*, ed. J. GARCÍA LÓPEZ. Barcelona, 1942.

CHAPTER VI

The Renaissance
and Humanism

General characteristics of the European Renaissance—Contacts between Spain and Italy—General characteristics of the Renaissance in Spain—The Inquisition—Patronage—Isabella as patron—Printing—Humanism—The Complutensian Polyglot Bible —The Reformation—Luis Vives.

General characteristics of the European Renaissance.— The term "Renaissance," applied to the quickening of life and thought in Europe at the end of the Middle Ages, is only partially descriptive. The movement was not exclusively a "rebirth"; it was to a very considerable extent a "new life." Classic antiquity was, to be sure, rediscovered and its interrupted tasks resumed; but, in addition, human civilization embarked upon new enterprises of which the ancients had never dreamed.

The motto of the Middle Ages had been *memento mori*, "remember to die." All life was but a preparation for eternity. Earthly existence was contemptible; the human body was mortified, not developed; the mind was held in fetters. Speculation was discouraged, submission to dogma encouraged. The important studies were theology and dialectics. The deductive, not the inductive, method was employed. A few Latin authors were studied, mainly for the purpose of acquiring the language of the Church. These texts afforded a sinful, surreptitious pleasure to the few who were capable of enjoying them, but in the main they were misunderstood. After the early years of the Dark Ages, first-hand acquaintance with the Greek perished in Western Europe.

This was the prevailing philosophy against which only a few superior minds reacted. But, not to paint too dark a picture, it must be remembered that a few arts flourished during this period, notably cathedral architecture during the twelfth and thirteenth centuries. There was an admirable spirit of craftsmanship. A few great works of literature were produced in spite of a prevailing lack of individuality. A few joyous pagans, like Juan Ruiz, rebelled against churchly asceticism; but these were exceptional.

Petrarch (1304–74) was the precursor of the Renaissance in Italy. The encouraging advance which civilization took in Europe during the thirteenth century had received a setback during the fourteenth. Petrarch, "the first modern man," saw the light when most of Europe was still struggling with feudalism. But the Renaissance really begins in the fifteenth century. Its finest period of flowering was the sixteenth. Many scholars have attached excessive importance to the date 1453, when Byzantium fell into the power of the Turks, and Greek scholars, bringing their precious libraries, began to teach in Italy; but Greek studies had been well under way before that year.

The fifteenth century was the period when ancient life and letters first began to be understood. Many works in Latin were recovered. To these finds was added Greek literature. Greek became an important study, and translations made available many works inaccessible to the many who did not possess that tongue. The philosophy of Plato was added to that of Aristotle, and this last was now known at first hand. Those were the great days of philology, the science which unlocked the many others known to the Classic authors. The ancient languages then had a practical importance which they now lack; for they provided a fund of information upon which the inquiring minds of the Renaissance erected new intellectual structures. Thus, back of Columbus' voyages lies ancient astronomy which had proved that the world is round. Ancient science inspired Galileo to discoveries of his own.

The term "humanism," applied to the scholarship of that time, emphasizes the fact that learning served humanity. The bonds of theological dogma were relaxed. The intellect was freed. Life became joyous, pagan. The Renaissance was an age of intense individualism. Personality developed with fewer restraints than at any other period of human history. Genius was commoner than at any other time, except, perhaps, at Athens under Pericles. Life was enriched in every conceivable direction, both practical and idealistic.

The Renaissance was a time of great inventions. Banking and credit revolutionized business. Gunpowder, which had come into use in the late Middle Ages, together with improved firearms, killed chivalry. The mariner's compass, probably introduced into Europe from China by some traveler, made possible ambitious enterprises of exploration culminating in Columbus' discovery of the West Indies in 1492 and Vasco da Gama's opening of the Cape of Good Hope route to India in 1497. But the greatest invention was that of printing. This originated in the Netherlands, or Germany, about the middle of the fifteenth century. There is evidence that Gutenberg was probably not the first practitioner of the art, so it is impossible to assign date, place, or inventor for the most revolutionary of all the new arts. It was providential that at the precise moment when so many new manuscripts were being found a new means was discovered for perpetuating and vulgarizing them.

The development of the fine arts during this period is a matter of common knowledge. In painting, sculpture, and music, the Italians equaled, if they did not surpass, the ancients. Architecture produced nothing to surpass the Gothic cathedrals of the Middle Ages, but reverted to the Roman types. Literature sought to imitate the writings of Greece and Rome. The Aristotelian doctrine of imitation was interpreted to mean not only the imitation of nature, but that of the ancient writers as well. Everywhere there was the desire to enrich the vernacular literatures with the spoils of the ancients. A poet was not considered unoriginal who treated some Classic theme in his own tongue. New literary forms appeared. Italy produced a school of literary critics whose interpretations and misinterpretations of Aristotle and Horace were law in Europe. Her many brilliant writers were everywhere imitated. Throughout the fifteenth and sixteenth centuries, Italy stood foremost in most of the manifestations of civilization.

The Renaissance was not without its faults. Italy's supremacy in intellectual matters was coincident with political and military weakness. Her joyous, pagan spirit degenerated into shocking immorality. Love of learning often manifested itself in stupid pedantry. Unrestrained individuality begot lawlessness. Renaissance authors are often overexuberant, as chaotic as they are richly imagi-

native and individualistic. It became the task of the
Catholic Reaction and the Protestant Reformation to
correct morals. Critics of the seventeenth and eighteenth
centuries fought pedantry and chaos, and restored Classic
simplicity.

Contacts between Spain and Italy were many. The
crown of Aragon had long been established in Sicily,
Naples, and Sardinia. When Aragon and Castile were
united under Ferdinand and Isabella, Castilian troops,
too, found their way thither. While the Renaissance was
at its height, Spain and France were disputing the possession of Italy. Spain's hold was the more enduring. The
rich northern state of Milan became a Spanish possession.
Thousands of soldiers and administrators were profoundly influenced by residence in Italian cities. The papal
court attracted numerous visitors, like Encina and Torres
Naharro. Italian universities drew large numbers. The
many Italian merchants and bankers who flooded Spain
brought something of their native culture. The first of
these, as we have seen, was Messer Francisco Imperial.
Italian actors, touring Spain, exerted some influence upon
the Spanish drama. Even closet students were influenced
by Italian books.

The Spanish Renaissance had long been ripening. The
commonly assigned date for its beginning is 1469, when
Ferdinand of Aragon married Isabella of Castile; but
the uniting of the two great *reinos* merely lent impetus to
a movement already under way. A less artificial choice of
date would be 1444, the year when Mena's *Laberinto* was
published. Yet how can one attempt to determine precisely the start of a movement of such complexity? Under
the Catholic monarchs, Spanish holdings in Italy were

made more secure and greatly extended by a succession of victories won by Gonzalo de Córdoba in the early years of the sixteenth century. When, in 1525, Francis I lost the battle of Pavia to Charles V, Italy was completely dominated by Spain. The most civilized nation of the age was unable to withstand the most virile. One is reminded, though, of that cultural victory of Greece over Rome which caused Horace to write: *"Græcia capta ferum victorem cepit."* Italy too, though captured, captured the fierce victor.

General characteristics of the Renaissance in Spain.— But while it is true that the Renaissance profoundly stirred Spain, the intellectual revolution was not so thoroughgoing as in other countries. The reasons are not far to seek. First, two national traits already mentioned, *españolismo*, that stubborn resistance to foreign influence which continued to act as a deterrent upon many writers, and, second, the spirit of individualism and democratic independence which rebelled against the rules of critics and scholars. The writers most affected by the Renaissance are those least in touch with the people. A single illustration will suffice to show the difference between France and Spain in this respect. When the poets of the Pléiade introduced into France the Classic and Italian verse forms, the traditional French meters were abandoned. Spanish poets, while accepting the new verse forms, clung tenaciously to the old, national ones. More of the Middle Ages lingered on in Spain, as one would expect of that conservative nation.

The Inquisition.—Though Ferdinand and Isabella encouraged most of the Renaissance movements, in one respect their influence was repressive. The Inquisition, introduced into Spain in 1478, was a new form of tyranny, half-spiritual, half-temporal, which made freedom of thought dangerous. The Catholic Reaction which in Italy came only at the end of the Renaissance, in Spain was almost coexistent with its beginnings. While many of the Italian rulers and even a few popes were pagan in spirit, Spain, rulers and people alike, remained narrowly orthodox. To the Inquisition's censorship may be ascribed the fact that Spanish literature of this period is less obscene than that of any other nation.

Patronage.—Another important difference is the relatively small amount of patronage which letters and the arts enjoyed in Spain, and that, too, in an age when most men interested in the finer things could only live when subsidized by a wealthy patron. Charles V and Philip II were too engrossed with wars and statecraft to interest themselves much in letters and arts. In Italy, each petty despot became a Mæcenas. The papal court, Milan, Florence, and Ferrara were brilliant centers of idealistic endeavor. In France, Francis I and his sister, Marguerite of Navarre, were generous patrons of letters and the arts. In Spain, Isabella the Catholic encouraged scholarship, art, and letters when these did not clash with her pious standards. If her immediate successors had shown equal zeal and intelligence, the course of the Renaissance in Spain would have been different. The patronage of Cardinal Ximénez belongs to this reign. Later, it is true, there were many petty patrons, and nearly every book written in the Golden Age is dedicated to some noble nonentity in return for a handful of ducats; but it is equally true that patronage, by and large, was neither liberal minded, intelligent, nor generous in Spain. It was not the same vital force as elsewhere. Hence it is that most Spanish writers sought to please a wider audience than that afforded by an aristocratic group. Criticism exerted only a feeble force. Definite literary schools were slow to form. Spanish literature of the Renaissance continued largely democratic, whereas in Italy and France it was almost exclusively aristocratic.

Isabella as patron.—Isabella the Catholic displayed an intelligent interest in intellectual enterprises. In her girlhood she learned several modern languages. On coming to the throne, she took up the study of Latin and made sufficient progress to understand it when spoken, and even to speak it reasonably well. She owned a considerable library for the time. The catalogue of this shows that she was interested in the ancient writers, theology, and contemporary Spanish literature. As the daughter of John II, she might be expected to favor poets; but, though she encouraged them, her reign produced few poets of merit. She was solicitous that the members of her court should be well educated. Under her example the noble classes began to devote themselves to humanistic studies. The ladies, too, followed her lead. The reign produced several feminine Latinists of note, two of whom lectured on the Latin classics at Salamanca and Alcalá. Her patronage of Columbus is her most famous deed in the furtherance of science; but throughout her life she consistently encouraged science, the arts, and letters when they seemed not to militate against the faith. Her orthodoxy, which at times amounted to bigotry, was her chief limitation as an intelligent patron. Furthermore, the vast enterprises which filled her reign failed to afford the leisure suitable for a fine artistic flowering. Nevertheless, much was accomplished, and Isabella did more for the intellectual well-being of her subjects than any Spanish sovereign, with the exception of Alfonso el Sabio, has ever done.

Printing.—The first book printed in Spain is a collection of hymns to the Virgin Mary, *Les trobes en lahors de la Verge Marie*, Valencia, 1474. Serrano y Sanz has unearthed a license to establish a press in Saragossa, dated the year before, but we have no knowledge that any book was there published so early. Barcelona had its press in 1475. Printing was therefore introduced into Spain through the eastern provinces. Before the end of the century nearly every provincial capital of importance had its publishing-house conducted by German workmen, who, in the early days of the art, possessed something like a monopoly in the printing trade. The works published were diverse: Bibles, books of devotion, theological treatises, editions of the Classics, romances of chivalry, and other works of popular literature. The sociological importance of the new invention speedily manifested itself. It was now possible to accumulate libraries at little cost and to disseminate learning and culture more widely than ever before in the history of the world. Propaganda was more feasible, and public opinion became a force more difficult to oppose.

Humanism.—During the reign of Ferdinand and Isabella began the influx of humanists from Italy to Spain—men like Marineo Sículo and Pedro Mártir. The latter is noted for two Latin works, *Opus epistolarum*, a history of contemporary happenings in Spain from 1488 to 1525, and *Decades de orbe novo*, one of the most important sources for our knowledge of the early voyages of discovery in America. Mártir's intelligence, lively curiosity, and prominent position at court made him an invaluable chronicler. The learning of the humanists was encyclopedic. Specialization was undreamed of. The science par excellence was philology, because all worth knowing was thought to be locked up in the literatures of Greece and Rome. Philology supplied the key. Though the humanists were primarily grammarians, it is nevertheless true that they were not grammatical specialists, because they took all knowledge for their field. Nevertheless, their knowledge of other branches, such as philosophy and science, was a by-product. Their aim was a restoration of the superior civilization of the ancients. Restoration was for them synonymous with progress.

Elio Antonio de Nebrija (or Lebrija, 1441–1522) was the greatest of Spanish humanists. After a course at Salamanca, disgusted with the barbarous Latinity of his professors, he resolved to drink humanism at the fountainhead. He passed to Italy at the age of nineteen and returned ten years later. He was almost immediately recognized as Spain's greatest scholar, and filled various chairs at Salamanca and Alcalá de Henares, where his personal influence was tremendous. The publication of his *Introductiones latinæ*, 1481, provided Spain with its first good Latin grammar. Henceforth the quality of Spanish Latinity was much improved. Other important works were his Latin-Spanish and Spanish-Latin dictionary of 1492, and his *Gramática sobre la lengua castellana*, Salamanca, 1492. This is the first scientific grammar of any modern language. To compose such a work was an original idea for the time. Humanists, as a rule, scorned the modern tongues. It is characteristic of the democracy of the Spanish race that even her humanists did not disdain contacts with the people. A later humanist, Gonzalo Correas, did not feel that he was misapplying his learning when he compiled his *Vocabulario de refranes*.

The Complutensian Polyglot Bible.—The great Cardinal Ximénez de Cisneros was another enlightened patron of learning under the Catholic monarchs. Out of his revenues he founded the University of Alcalá de Henares, which opened its doors to students in 1508. Less hidebound than the older University of Salamanca, humanism could be freely imparted at Alcalá. Under the auspices of Alcalá, Ximénez caused to be edited the Polyglot Bible, the most considerable scholarly enterprise which Spain achieved during the Renaissance. Ximénez was liberal minded enough to see that the official Latin Vulgate was not infallible. His plan was to publish an edition of the original texts side by side with the accepted rendering. Europe was ransacked for ancient manuscripts. A corps of learned linguists were assembled to collaborate. After fifteen years of work, their labors were printed in six folio volumes, in 1514–20. The first four volumes contain the Old Testament in Hebrew and Chaldaic, together with the Latin Vulgate. Volume V contains the New Testament in Greek and Latin. Volume VI is a Hebrew and Chaldaic glossary. Nebrija was prominent among the collaborators. Whatever its defects, this was the first attempt to publish a critical edition of the Bible. It is significant that whereas Italy was chiefly concerned with issuing critical editions of Greek and Latin authors, Spain made the new learning serve religion. In general, Spanish humanism was more democratic, practical, and religious than that of Italy.

The Reformation.—Ximénez' liberal attitude would have been impossible a few years later when the Protestant Reformation of the north had made men bigoted and suspicious. The Dutch scholar, Erasmus of Rotterdam (1465–1536), who was pensioned by Charles V, influenced many Spaniards with his reforming ideas. He maintained close personal relations with all the leading scholars of Spain, particularly Luis Vives. In the middle of the sixteenth century there existed a wide group of *erasmistas*, most of whom, like their leader, never broke with the church, but advocated reform from within. A few, like Antonio and Juan de Valdés, were more heterodox and are usually classed as Protestants. But the Inquisition became active and Protestantism was short-lived in Spain. The influence of the Reformation was therefore almost wholly negative in that country. Repression grew more severe; *autos de fe* were frequent; the reactionaries were completely successful. At no period of Spanish history was religious intolerance so great as in the latter sixteenth century. In Italy, the Catholic Reaction ended the Renaissance. In Spain, the Renaissance began later and the Reaction started earlier. This is perhaps the chief reason why the movement never developed so magnificently in the latter country.

Luis Vives (1492–1540) is termed by Menéndez y Pelayo "the loftiest embodiment of scientific Spain." He was certainly Spain's greatest philosopher. A cosmopolitan, he taught at Oxford and was Erasmus' colleague at Louvain. His numerous works were written in Latin of the purest. He was an eclectic philosopher who "combined the gold extracted from decadent scholasticism with the most refined elements extracted from the other systems" (Menéndez y Pelayo). He was neither exclusively Platonist nor Aristotelian. His views were liberal and original. His contributions to pedagogics, sociology, and philosophy were important. In many respects he foreshadowed Descartes, Locke, and Kant, and anticipated Bacon's inductive method. His fame would be greater if he had developed his thought in a logical system; but he furnished hints which were to make the reputations of several of the greatest thinkers of the ensuing generations.

BIBLIOGRAPHY

BURCKHARDT, J. *Die Cultur der Renaissance in Italien.* Basle, 1860. Trans. S. G. C. MIDDLEMORE as *The Civilization of the Renaissance in Italy.* London, 1887.

SYMONDS, J. A. *The Renaissance in Italy.* 5 vols. London, 1875–86.

On Spanish-Italian relations:

CROCE, B. *I primi contatti fra Spagna e Italia.* Naples, 1893.

———. *La Spagna nella vita italiana durante la Rinascenza.* Bari, 1917.

———. *Ricerche ispano-italiane.* Naples, 1898.

FARINELLI, A. *Italia e Spagna.* Turin, 1929.

A good specific work on the Spanish Renaissance is lacking; the following will prove helpful:

MENÉNDEZ Y PELAYO, M. *Historia de las ideas estéticas en España.* New ed.; 5 vols. Santander, 1940.

LEMUS Y RUBIO, P. "El Maestro Elio Antonio de Lebrija," *Revue hispanique*, Vols. XXII, XXXIX.

NEBRIJA, E. A. *Gramática castellana*, ed. ROGERIO SÁNCHEZ. Madrid, 1931.

VALDÉS, JUAN DE. *Diálogo de la lengua*, ed. J. F. MONTESINOS. (In *Clásicos castellanos.* Madrid, 1928.)

BONILLA Y SAN MARTÍN, A. *Luis Vives y la filosofía del Renacimiento.* Madrid, 1903, 1929.

BATAILLON, M. *Érasme et l'Espagne.* Paris, 1937. Trans. A. ALA-
TORRE as *Erasmo en España.* 2 vols. Mexico, 1950.

———. *Historia de los heterodoxos españoles.* New ed.; 8 vols.
Santander, 1946–48.

———. *La ciencia española.* New ed.; 3 vols. Santander, 1953–54.

RADET, G. "La Renaissance en Espagne et au Portugal," *Revue
hispanique,* Vol. XIV.

BELL, A. F. G. "Notes on the Spanish Renaissance," *Revue hispanique,* Vol. XXX (1930).

GREEN, O. H. "A Critical Survey of Scholarship in the Field of
Spanish Renaissance Literature, 1914–1944," *Studies in Philology,* Vol. XLIV (1947).

MOREL-FATIO, A. *L'Espagne au XVIᵉ et au XVIIᵉ siècles.* Heilbronn, 1878.

———. *Études sur l'Espagne.* 3 vols. Paris, 1888–1904.

SCHEVILL, R. *Ovid and the Renascence in Spain.* Berkeley, 1913.

LEA, H. C. *History of the Inquisition in Spain.* 4 vols. New York
and London, 1906–7.

HAEBLER, C. *Bibliografía ibérica del siglo XV.* The Hague and
Leipzig, 1904.

———. *Typographie ibérique du quinzième siècle.* The Hague,
1901–2.

———. *Geschichte der spanischen Frühdrucker in Stammbäumen.*
Leipzig, 1923.

Lyric Poetry
of the Renaissance

Boscán—The new meters—Garcilaso de la Vega—Castillejo—
Luis de León—Herrera.

Juan Boscán Almogáver (d. 1542), initiated the
poetic revolution of the Spanish Renaissance. He was a
Catalonian aristocrat, educated in Castile. Menéndez
y Pelayo has effectually dispelled the legend that his
relative clumsiness as a versifier was due to the fact that
he wrote in a foreign idiom. Castilian was familiar to him
from childhood; his mediocrity as a poet must be ascribed
to lack of genius. In 1526, an important date, took place
his momentous interview with Navagero, Venetian ambassador and one of Italy's most distinguished humanists. Navagero urged the superiority of the Italian
meters and besought Boscán to employ them in writing
Spanish verse. "It is rare," writes Ticknor, "that any one
individual has been able to exercise such an influence on
the literature of a foreign nation as was exercised by
Navagero." For Boscán followed Navagero's advice and
produced verse which pleased by its novelty. The friendly praise and rivalry of Garcilaso de la Vega led him to
persevere.

The new meters.—Boscán's chief metrical innovation
was the acclimatization of the Italian hendecasyllable in
Spain. Sporadic attempts to employ this meter had been
made before his time, but never with much success.
Boscán thus gave Spanish verse a more dignified line

than the tripping *verso de romance*. Since his day every
poet has used the eleven-syllable verse. Santillana had
written successful sonnets, but his premature attempt
had found few imitators. Boscán naturalized the form.
He is beyond dispute the first to introduce the Italian
octave (*octava real*), the epic meter of Ariosto and Tasso,
and this became the meter of all Spanish epic poets of
the Renaissance. He also wrote *canciones* and handled
Dante's *terza rima* (*tercetos*). Mr. R. H. Keniston argues
that Garcilaso may have anticipated Boscán in a few
of these meters. With all these new verses and strophes at
command, the poet of the time found himself immeasur-
ably enriched. But the old native verse forms continued
to be used.

Boscán's place in literature.—Boscán was a mediocre
poet whose work has slight intrinsic value. Yet he occupies an important place in the history of Spanish culture
as the initiator of a metrical revolution. Every succeeding
poet owed much to him; even those of the present are his
debtors. His close relations with the Alba family and his
intimacy in court circles made him a person of influence
His works circulated in manuscript until printed by his
widow in 1543. But it may be doubted whether Boscán's
experiment would have been so generally taken up by
others, if there had not appeared a more gifted poet to
continue his work. Possibly Boscán's forte was prose.
His translation of Castiglione's *Cortegiano* is considered
by some the best Spanish prose of the reign of Charles V.

Boscán's gifted successor was *Garcilaso de la Vega*
(*1501–36*), the most representative Renaissance gentleman whom Spain produced. Born of a noble family, he
received a good education in Latin, Greek, French, and

Italian. He was cultured without being erudite. He was
handsome in appearance and possessed all the arts and
graces—could fence and play the lute as well as turn a
sonnet. Garcilaso seems to have made Castiglione's perfect courtier his pattern. He it was who persuaded his
friend Boscán to translate the *Cortegiano*, which more
than any other book, with the possible exception of
Amadís de Gaula, was influential in determining the
manners and standards of the aristocracy. Garcilaso was
early attached to the emperor's household; but the life of
a court parasite was not enough to satisfy one so imbued
with the Renaissance ideal of glory. His brief existence
was crowded. We find him serving his emperor in the
most remote regions, fighting in Austria and Africa, and
intrusted with delicate diplomatic missions. There may
be exaggeration in the accounts of those contemporaries
who depict him as a reckless dare-devil; but that he was
something of a D'Artagnan is evident from the manner
of his death. He perished attacking a fortified mill in
Southern France, after having removed cuirass and hel-
met in a spirit of bravado. This end must have pleased
the poet who had written complainingly:

> Y esta muerte no permitió mi dura suerte
> que me sobreviniese peleando,
> de hierro traspasado agudo y fuerte.

Garcilaso, the faultless poet.—Garcilaso's literary
production was slight. Aside from a few early verses in
the old Castilian manner, there survive only three eclogues, two elegies, one epistle, five odes, and thirty-
eight sonnets. These were first published by Boscán's
widow, in 1543, in connection with those of her husband,

a fitting memorial to a literary friendship. If Garcilaso wrote little, it was because he had an artistic conscience. Each poem left his hands filed, polished, perfect. On reading Boscán one gets an impression of effort; with Garcilaso all is ease and fluidity. Scarcely a word is antiquated or difficult. His ideas and images are seldom original. They are taken from the Latin and Italian poets, above all from Petrarch. His originality consists in expressing for the first time in Spanish concepts which had charmed in other tongues. Love is the principal theme. The poet was deeply in love with a Portuguese lady of high rank named Isabel Freyre. Upon her death, Garcilaso penned three of the loveliest and most poignant poems in Spanish, perhaps in any language: the first eclogue and the tenth and sixteenth sonnets. Possibly they are too intensely felt to fulfil Wordsworth's ideal of "emotion recollected in tranquillity." At any rate, grief has seldom been more beautifully expressed. One can readily understand the continuing admiration for such a poet. It was in our own times that a poetry magazine was founded in Spain called *Garcilaso*.

The noble artist also had lighter strings on his lyre. In fact, the name *lira* for the graceful five-line stanza (7- and 11-syllable lines, rhyming *ababb*) is taken from Garcilaso's lightsome *canción* for his friend Mario Galeota, called *A la Flor de Gnido*. The first line runs: "*Si de mi baja lira.*"

Garcilaso de la Vega should be remembered as that Spanish poet most typical of the spirit of the Renaissance, who possessed the most complete mastery of form.

Cristóbal de Castillejo (1490?–1550) was chief of a school of traditionalists. In his tract, *Contra los que dejan*

140

Lyric
Poetry
of the
Renaissance

los metros castellanos y siguen los italianos, he makes a plea
for the native meters. Castillejo, a priest of the Juan
Ruiz type, wrote both devotional and erotic verse. His
crusade failed to make the Italian meters less popular,
but may have aided to conserve the old. Most poets of
the latter half of the century use both.

Fray Luis de León (1527-91), except for one unpleasant episode, led the uneventful life of scholar, professor, and priest. He professed in the Augustinian order
at seventeen, studied under the greatest masters of his
time, and soon won recognition as one of the most learned
men in Spain. In 1561, he won a chair at Salamanca, and
continued actively connected with that university for the
greater part of his life. His most stirring experience was
imprisonment and trial for heresy by the Inquisition.
Luis de León was learned in Hebrew, which was of itself
sufficient to arouse suspicion among the bigoted. His
enemies used to his disadvantage the fact that he had
translated Solomon's "Song of Songs," and various other
charges of heresy were added to the indictment. Petty
university jealousies complicated the controversy. After
four years of incarceration, he was acquitted, and, according to a doubtful story, resumed his lecturing with the
words: *"Dicebamus hesterna die . . . . "* ("As we were
saying yesterday. . . . "). Luis de León was one of
those rare Renaissance scholars who wore his learning
lightly. To him erudition was the handmaid of religion.
He was devoid of personal vanity, which meant that as a
scholar he was free from pedantry, as a writer from affectation. His greatness as a prose writer will be treated in
the chapter on the mystics. He is Spain's greatest lyric
poet, and ranks high among the foremost poets of the
world.

Fray Luis, as poet.—Fray Luis is greater than Garcilaso de la Vega, because, while almost the latter's equal as to form, he is not content with form alone. He has a message: the doctrine of plain living and high thinking, the charms of nature as a refuge from human pettiness, the strength derived from solitude. Fray Luis, with complete lack of literary vanity, attached slight importance to his verse. This does not mean that he wrote carelessly. On the contrary, his artistic conscience was exacting. No poet filed and polished more carefully. Poetry was a loved diversion, but an avocation not comparable in importance to his priestly vocation. Horace was his master, and Horace has seldom if ever found a happier imitator. What was the bond of union between the pagan poet and the Christian mystic? Fray Luis shared Horace's love of simplicity, nature, and art, his hatred of the *profanum vulgus*. There the analogy ends. Horace was an Epicurean who sought country life to cultivate more refined forms of enjoyment than were accessible to the common herd. Luis de León sought nature for prayer and meditation, for the cultivation of a beautiful soul. He is a christianized Horace. Though his feeling for nature was so fine, nature was not an end in itself. To him as to Kant, later, the beauties and grandeurs of nature suggested the superior beauties and grandeurs of the moral law. It must not be thought that Luis de León's range is as restricted as the foregoing would indicate; I have merely stressed his most important message to humanity, the philosophy found in his two masterpieces, *Noche serena* and *Vida retirada*. It is the ideal epitomized in the famous verses written on his prison wall:

> Aquí la envidia y mentira,
> me tuvieron encerrado.

> ¡Dichoso el humilde estado
> del sabio que se retira
> de aqueste mundo malvado!
>
> Y con pobre mesa y casa
> en el campo deleitoso
> con solo Dios se compasa,
> y a solas la vida pasa
> ni envidiado ni envidioso.

This last verse is, perhaps, the one most frequently quoted in all Spanish literature.

Fernando de Herrera (1534–97), termed by admiring contemporaries El Divino, continued in a way the tradition of Garcilaso, *"Lasso, gloria immortal de toda España."* Herrera's admiration for Garcilaso appears in his *Anotaciones a las obras de Garcilasso de la Vega*, 1580, and everywhere in his writings. But if Garcilaso stands for simple grace, Herrera stands for vigor. His forceful personality kept him from being a mere imitator. The Castilian's verbal parsimony is replaced with Andalusian rhetoric and exuberance. In many respects he anticipates *culteranismo*. Herrera's rugged nature and brusque manner made him enemies; but he was honest, disinterested, and independent toward the rich and powerful. He never stooped to flatter these. Having taken a priest's minor orders, he received a small benefice, the income of which completely satisfied his needs, leaving him free to enjoy a life of study and authorship. Doubtless Herrera thought that his fame would rest upon such ambitious undertakings as his burlesque epic, the *Gigantomachia*, and a serious epic based upon the *Amadís*. Was there any connection between this last and Bernardo Tasso's *Amadigi?* It is impossible to say, as both of Herrera's epics are lost. His general history of the world and a treatise on the poetic art met with a like fate. An interesting sketch of the English humanist and statesman. Thomas More, and a *Relación de la guerra de Cipre, y sucesso de la batalla naual de Lepanto* alone survive as examples of his historical style.

Herrera's love lyrics.—Among his contemporaries Herrera's reputation rested mainly upon his love lyrics. The object of his devotion was a certain lady of elevated rank, Doña Leonor, Condesa de Gelves. Such verse, directed by a humble priest to an exalted personage should occasion no scandal. Herrera plays the game of love according to the rules laid down by the Italian neo-Platonists. With him, as with these, the lady is the embodiment of all that is beautiful and excellent. More than that, she leads her lover along the path of perfection to heaven itself:

> Que yo en essa belleza que contemplo,
> aunq'a mi flaca vista ofende i cubre,
> la immensa busco, i voi siguiendo al cielo.

These poems, in spite of their manifest artistic qualities, are monotonous and tiresome to all modern readers save those interested in the subtleties of neo-Platonism; but they remain a characteristic manifestation of Renaissance art.

Patriotic pieces.—It is not as a sublimated lover, but as a patriot, that Herrera makes his lasting appeal. His fame rests upon two occasional poems, well worthy of the occasions which inspired them. *La canción por la victoria de Lepanto* is a hymn of triumph inspired by the crushing defeat of the Turk by Christian arms. In *La canción por la pérdida del rey Don Sebastián*, the poet wonders at the inscrutable ways of Providence, but with unabated faith. Both these works are majestic and inspired. Their beauty is that of strength. The poet casts aside his usual guides, Petrarch and the platonizing Italians, and takes as his model the Book of Psalms. If the style be, as alleged, a trifle too emphatic, that is the penalty of an effort to achieve vigor. Herrera was one of the first critics in literature to proclaim that the poem should express the poet's individuality. His strong personality found vent in verse more vigorous than had been required to express the gentler emotions of Garcilaso and Luis de León.

BIBLIOGRAPHY

Boscán, J. *Obras*, ed. W. I. Knapp. Madrid, 1875.

————. "El cortesano," ed. A. M. Fabié, *Libros de antaño*, Vol. III. Madrid, 1873.

Menéndez y Pelayo, M. *Antología*. See Vol. X for biography and criticism of Boscán.

Garcilaso de la Vega. *Obras*, ed. Navarro Tomás, *Clásicos castellanos*. Madrid, 1924.

Garcilaso and Boscán. *Obras poéticas*, ed. E. Díez-Canedo. Madrid, 1917.

Keniston, H. *Garcilaso de la Vega: Works, A Critical Text with a Bibliography*. New York, 1925.

————. *Garcilaso de la Vega: A Critical Study of His Life and Works*. New York, 1922.

Castillejo, C. de. *Obras*, ed. J. Domínguez Bordona, *Clásicos castellanos*. Madrid, 1925–28.

León, Luis de. *Obras*, ed. A. Merino and C. Muiños. 4 vols. Madrid, 1885.

————. *Poésies originales*, ed. A. Coster. Chartres, 1923.

Coster, A. "Luis de León," *Revue hispanique*, LIII, 1–468; LIV, 1–346.

Vossler, K. *Fray Luis de León*. Buenos Aires, 1946.

Herrera, F. de. *Poesías*, ed. V. García de Diego, *Clásicos castellanos*. Madrid, 1914.

Coster, A. *Fernando de Herrera (El Divino)*. Paris, 1908.

CHAPTER VIII

Forms of Idealistic
Fiction during
the Renaissance

The romance of chivalry—The *Amadís* question—The Montalvo redaction—Characteristics of the romances of chivalry—*Las sergas de Esplandián*—The *Amadís* Cycle—*Palmerín de Ingalaterra* and the *Palmerín Cycle*—*Tirant lo Blanch*—Other romances of chivalry—The decline—The pastoral romance—Jorge de Montemayor—The *Diana*—Sequels and imitations—The sentimental novel—*Historia del Abencerrage y de la hermosa Jarifa*—Ginés Pérez de Hita and the historical novel—The Milesian tale, or Greek novel—*Persiles y Sigismunda.*

The romance of chivalry.—We have seen that the Spanish romance of chivalry, as cultivated during the Middle Ages, consisted chiefly of mere translations from the French, but that two works of marked originality belong to the fourteenth century, the *Caballero Çifar* and *Amadís de Gaula.* The romance of chivalry was a medieval form refined upon and re-created by Renaissance writers. The sixteenth century was the period of its greatest popularity. The number of these works published in the early days of printing is amazing.

The "Amadís" question.—Three theories have been proposed regarding the genesis of this celebrated novel. The first theory, that it is a translation of a work originally French, is now universally rejected. The *Amadís* is French merely in the sense that it is drawn from the *Tristram,* the *Launcelot,* and other French romances;

but the work of imitation, arrangement, and invention was plainly due to some peninsular novelist.

The case for Spain is better. Spain has preserved the one version of the novel known to us—that printed by Garci Rodríguez de Montalvo, *Los quatro libros del virtuoso cauallero Amadís de Gaula*, Saragossa, 1508. Montalvo wrote in so pure a Castilian that not a single lusitanianism has been noted in his work, a remarkable fact if the original be indeed Portuguese. Furthermore, Spain provides the earliest-known allusion to the romance, found by Foulché-Delbosc in a work called *Regimento de los príncipes*, Seville, 1350. Hence it appears that some form of the *Amadís* was circulating in Spain in the first half of the fourteenth century. But in what language? We cannot be sure that this was Castilian, at a time when the influence of the Portuguese-Galician school was so strong. The poet, Pero Ferrús, writing in 1379, adds the information that the work was divided into three books. Most scholars believe that Montalvo reworked the first three books of a primitive redaction, as crude as the existing manuscript versions of other medieval romances, and is the original author of the fourth.

Portugal's claim rests upon the earliest attribution of authorship. In dealing with the Briolanja episode,[1] Montalvo hesitates between three distinct variants of that incident found in his sources. He states that the original form was altered by express command of the Infante Alfonso of Portugal, who ascended the throne in 1325. This is earlier than any date discovered in connection with the Spanish versions; but we cannot be certain that the version changed by royal order was Portuguese and

[1] See Book I, chap. xl.

not Spanish. Furthermore, a fifteenth-century chronicler, Azurara, states that a certain Vasco de Lobeira,
who flourished in the reign of Don Fernando I (1367–83),
wrote the *Amadís,* "all things in the said book being feigned
by the author." As the date assigned is later than the
time when the *Amadís* is known to have been in existence,
little attention was paid to this attribution until the publication of the *Canzionere Colocci-Brancuti* in 1880. In that
collection was found a little Portuguese song, *Leonoreta
fin roseta,* ascribed to Juan Lobeira. Now this same song,
in Spanish translation, occurs in the Montalvo version.[1]
Juan Lobeira was a gentleman-poet of the court of King
Dennis (1257–85) and may conceivably have been the
author. Professor Edwin B. Place suggests, in the excellent introduction to his edition of the Montalvo 1508 redaction:

> Aunque no se sabe nada concluyente acerca de la identidad del
> autor del Amadís primitivo, en nuestro concepto la teoría de
> orígenes más atrayente es que sería compuesto en la corte de Al-
> fonso XI de Castilla por algún escritor profesional no español pero
> domiciliado en Castilla, bajo el patrocinio del Rey, el que du-
> rante la primera parte de su reinado se esforzó a popularizar la
> caballería y los procedimientos caballerescos.[2]

The Montalvo redaction.—The prose romances of the
fourteenth century reflect in their crudity the decline
which civilization had taken after the fine flowering of
the thirteenth. Montalvo's book, however, shows the
artistic spirit of the Renaissance asserting itself in prose—
a prose clear and beautiful, if somewhat florid. It was immediately recognized as one of the best-written prose
works of Spanish literature, and, as such, influenced
other writings. Similarly, Herberay's French version of

[1] See Book II, chap. xi.

[2] *Amadís de Gaula* (Madrid, 1959), p. x.

1540 was the best example of French prose known to that date. As editions and translations multiplied throughout Europe, the book was received as a guide to gentlemanly conduct and a treasury of elegant diction. *Amadis of Gaul* is one of the world's great novels, one of Spain's most important gifts to civilization.

Characteristics of the romances of chivalry.—The vogue of this remarkable work set a fashion in literature. One may readily gain the idea, on reading certain modern critics, that little can be said in favor of a ridiculous genre which Cervantes did well to laugh out of existence. The contrary is the case. The admirable features of the best of these romances outweigh the silly ones. Montalvo published his redaction at a moment when the noble ideals of chivalry were threatened with extinction. Gunpowder had revolutionized warfare. Capitalism had developed, creating a powerful middle class, many of whose members were elevated to the aristocracy, often to the detriment of good manners. But this new form of literature, an aristocratic form, appeared just in time to give the chivalric ideals a new lease of life. The romances of chivalry inculcated bravery, modesty, self-sacrifice, fair play, the protection of the weak against the strong. Their value in the history of culture is immense. Who can say how much of the modern gentleman's spirit of sportsmanship and fair play is due to the resurrection of chivalric ideals during the Renaissance? Above all else, these books emphasized constancy in love. The extra-conjugal love of the old French romances was superseded by a new form, half-chivalric and half-bourgeois. The object of the knight's affection was no longer a married woman, but a marriageable young person of rank. Both parties looked forward to an honorable marriage, the realization of which was an indispensable feature of the dénouement. Meanwhile, whatever the vicissitudes through which they passed, both parties were constant and true. Glorification of constancy as an ideal is the chief message of the *Amadís* and others of its kind.

The defects of this work, and still more of its sequels and imitations, are many. The plots are as unreal as those of fairy tales: combats with giants, wild beasts, dragons; innumerable duels with other knights, resulting in the hero's inevitable victory; abuse of the marvelous. The modern reader finds much that is puerile and prosy. Such a form of literature could only have won favor in an age which offered few distractions. But the country gentleman of the time, passing his days in some castle remote from the busy centers, without newspapers, regular mail service, and the thousand-and-one advantages and amusements of our more complex civilization, found in them a solace and a delight—the more so as there existed then so few works of imaginative literature in the modern tongues.

"Las sergas de Esplandián."—This was the first of the many sequels to the *Amadís*. It was probably written by Montalvo, who appended it to the *Amadís* as the fifth book. Foulché-Delbosc[1] offers the most plausible explanation of this curious title. *Sergas* means "canvasses," "tapestries," referring to those series of scenes from favorite romances painted upon cloth with which the aristocracy decorated their mansions. "Scenes from the life of Esplandián" is a free but exact rendering. This work has a curious interest to the American reader. The

[1] *Revue hispanique*, XXIII, 591–93.

fantastic adventures of the *conquistadores* in the new world constantly reminded them of incidents described in romances of chivalry, just as, contrariwise, readers of these felt that nothing recounted therein was stranger than the reports brought home from overseas. Bernal Díaz del Castillo relates how, when Cortés and his followers caught their first glimpse of the city of Mexico, "we remained astonished and said that it resembled the things of enchantment which they relate in the book of *Amadís*, by reason of the great turrets, temples, and edifices which they had within the water." So, too, when the early explorers set foot in Lower California they were reminded of an island of that name, "mentioned in *Las sergas de Esplandián*, on the right hand of the Indies, and very near to the Earthly Paradise." Thus it came that a fictitious place-name, found in a romance of chivalry, was bestowed upon our third largest state. Such incidents show how fiction influenced adventure during that age of high achievement. The reverse was also true.

The "Amadís Cycle."—Renaissance fiction was of loose construction. The romance of chivalry, the pastoral romance, and the picaresque novel had this in common: they seldom if ever came to a clearly defined end. The author left it possible to write a sequel. If he neglected to do so, it was not held dishonorable for another to supply the continuation. An immense series of sequels to the *Amadís* were written, prolix, tedious, absurd to the last degree. The continuators lacked originality and contributed little that was novel, though Feliciano de Silva, with his *entricadas razones*, added bombast and affectation. A certain Bachiller Juan Díaz thought this process had gone far enough, and caused Amadís to die of old

age, turned his sweetheart, Oriana, into an abbess, and
Galaor and Agrajes into friars. These favorite characters
were so real to the naïve readers of the time that the
latter could not bear such a summary disposition of them.
Díaz was branded as an impostor and a falsifier. So,
succeeding novelists revived Amadís, who became an
immortal upon earth, witnessing the glorious deeds of
his progeny, sons, grandsons, great-great-grandsons.
Gayangos thought it interesting to construct the family
tree of the Amadís family. All told, there were twenty-
four *partes* in this cycle.

"*Palmerín de Ingalaterra*" *and the* "*Palmerín Cycle*."—
Almost simultaneously with the "*Amadís Cycle*" another
flourished. The first of the "Palmerín Cycle" is *Palmerín
de Oliva*, 1511, the second, *Primaleón*, 1516. Both are the
work of a woman, of name unknown, written in imitation
of the *Amadís*, and deserving of Cervantes' harsh criticism. But the third of the series is one of the greatest of
its kind. *Palmerín de Ingalaterra* was first printed in
Spanish, Toledo, 1547–48, accompanied by an acrostic
attributing it to Luis Hurtado. But Mr. W. E. Purser
has conclusively demonstrated this to be a Portuguese
work, corroborating a view first advanced by Robert
Southey. The author was Francisco de Morões, an
attaché of the Portuguese embassy in Paris from 1541 to
1543, who incorporated into the romance some of his own
love passages. The Portuguese edition did not appear in
print until 1567. This, the original, is one of the noblest
monuments of early Portuguese prose. Some consider
the book superior to *Amadís*, and, in fact, it does display
more unity and deftness in the handling of plot. Southey's
English translation was published in 1807.

"*Tirant lo Blanch*."—This, the third great romance of chivalry, belongs to Catalonian literature. It was the first of these novels to be printed (Valencia, 1490). The first three parts were by Mossén Johanot Martorell, who began writing in 1460. A fourth was added by Mossén Martí Johán de Galba. The Preface states that the work was translated out of English into Portuguese, thence into Catalan. The only basis for the first assertion is that the Guy of Warwick romance is the source of certain episodes. The adventures of the great admiral, Roger de Flor, also incorporated, can obviously hark back to no English original. Menéndez y Pelayo and Givanel y Mas take seriously the alleged Portuguese original. They would reduce Galba to the rôle of a mere translator of the first three books. But have we not to do with the typical lying preface which was a stock device with the writers of these romances, one of those many conventions which Cervantes burlesques? This romance is unlike any other in tone, with the possible exception of *El caballero Çifar*. It is less aristocratic, reflecting the middle-class spirit of Barcelona and Valencia. It is realistic, obscene, and contains not a few burlesque elements. Tirant, like Don Quijote, makes a will and dies in bed. Martorell's undoubted influence upon Cervantes remains to be studied. *Tirant lo Blanch* enjoyed a considerable vogue in Spanish, French, and Italian translations, but is *sui generis* and untypical.

Other romances of chivalry.—Other romances were written wholly detached from the two great cycles. The vogue lasted throughout the whole sixteenth century. Luis Zapata tells of a "*caballero muy manso, muy cuerdo y muy honrado,*" who set forth from the court *furioso*

committed the follies of Orlando, threw off his clothing,
killed a donkey, assailed peasants with a club, etc. Evidently the Don Quijote type existed in real life. Saints
like Ignatius Loyola and Santa Teresa caught the contagion. The latter even wrote one, it is said. Sour,
women-hating priests attacked the genre on account of
certain licentious passages, but the Inquisition was leni-
ent. However, an order of the year 1531 forbade the ex-
portation of such books to the New World. Other priests
saw in them possibilities for propaganda. Hence the silly
libros de caballerías a lo divino. The allegorized romance of
chivalry started in France with the *Pélerinage de la vie
humaine,* 1490. The most celebrated Spanish example was
Hojas de la rosa fragante, in which Christ, the Knight of
the Lion, aided by twelve paladins, the disciples, won
victories over the devil, alias the Knight of the Serpent.
Only the English Protestant, John Bunyan, achieved
success in this peculiar genre.

The decline.—In the closing years of the sixteenth
century the public had begun to weary of these romances.
New forms of the novel were gaining favor. The drama
was developing. *Lazarillo de Tormes* killed the genre
quite as much as did *Don Quijote.* The romance of chivalry had run its course. Cervantes merely dealt the coup
de grâce. After 1605 new works of this sort ceased to be
written, though new editions of the old have occasionally
been printed. Sporadic readers opened the old quartos,
but with the seventeenth century the great vogue was
past.

The pastoral romance.—The second great form of
idealistic fiction, also an aristocratic genre, was the
pastoral romance. Pastoral poetry's most famous ex-

ponent in ancient times was Theocritus, a Sicilian Greek.
He, a tired and disillusioned city-dweller, idealized country life. His *Idyls* are an artificial but very pleasing
genre which Vergil carried over to Latin poetry in his
Eclogues. During the Renaissance, when the ancient
writers were so freely imitated, pastoral verse was prominent in all the European literatures. Boccaccio was first
to combine prose and verse in a pastoral novel, the
Ameto. This was the model for Sannazaro's *Arcadia*,
which first appeared in complete and authorized form in
1504. Sannazaro is the true father of the pastoral romance, a literary form which took Europe by storm and
was the delight of the cultured readers of all civilized
nations during the sixteenth century. The *Arcadia* is a
series of twelve eclogues, bound together by artistic
prose. Clearly the verse is of chief importance, but the
prose carries the thread of the story and provides a setting
and a relief. This exquisite work still delights the modern
reader. It lacks, perhaps, the charm of Tasso's *Aminta*,
more dramatic and wholly in verse; but it stands as one
of the most delightful idealizations of the simple life
ever conceived. It has the merit of brevity, is never
prosy, never lacking in the artistic touch.

As the genre developed, it tended to become conventionalized. The prose passages became longer, and the
modern reader finds them tedious. But the authors
strove to write artistic prose at a time when good prose
was in its infancy. No slight part of their former appeal
was due to the fact that they provided models of courtly
address at a time when conversation was a fine art and its
cultivation part of a successful courtier's equipment.
Like the romances of chivalry, the pastoral romances be-

came monotonously similar in plot. There is always the
same game of love at cross-purposes. The shepherd A
loves the shepherdess B, who bestows her affections upon
C, who scorns B for another shepherdess D. D, of course,
is madly in love with A. Thus the vicious circle of love is
completed. Numerous episodes and descriptions are interspersed, most of which produce an effect of insipidity.
Another source of interest, now lost, was the fact that
each of these novels was a *roman à clef*. The characters
were always real personages in disguise. The Anas became Dianas; the Isabels, Belisas, etc. These aristocrats,
thinly disguised as shepherds and shepherdesses, were
recognized at the time. We can still identify some of
them.

Jorge de Montemayor (d. 1561).—Professor Rennert
has pointed out that the beginnings of the Spanish pastoral romance may be noted in the ninth book of *Amadís
de Grecia*, Burgos, 1553; but the first real work of the sort
is Montemayor's *Diana*, Valencia, not dated (probably
1559). The author was a Portuguese of humble, possibly
Jewish, extraction, a native of the town of Montemôr.
As he wrote in Spanish and is identified with Spain rather
than his native country, the hispanicized form of the name,
Montemayor, is usually preferred. The date of Montemayor's birth is unknown. His education was limited to
the modern tongues, but he appears well versed in the
poetry of Portugal, Spain, Catalonia, and Italy. By profession he was a musician. He became attached to the
chapel of the Infanta Juana, Spanish wife of Prince John
of Portugal. When his patroness became a widow, he
accompanied her to Spain in 1554. He is said to have
followed Philip II to England and the Netherlands in the

same year. That he visited the latter country is certain. He was killed in a duel in Italy. Montemayor always moved in court circles, where his musical and literary talents won him favor. The audience addressed was exclusively aristocratic.

The Diana was not only the first of the Spanish pastoral romances but one of the best. It had all the characteristics of the genre already noted. Far inferior to its model, Sannazaro's *Arcadia*, it won a success second only to the *Amadís*. Its plot is slight, and unskilfully handled, its general effect monotonous; but its delicate verse and artistic prose charmed contemporaries. Its fame spread abroad, and Sir Philip Sidney drew from it for *The Countess of Pembroke's Arcadia*. Whatever its intrinsic merit, the *Diana* is an important landmark in the history of Spanish culture at home and abroad.

Sequels and imitations.—Montemayor had projected a second part, but, dying without achieving his purpose, the task was assumed by others, with that fine disregard for literary property characteristic of the age. Alonso Pérez' *Diana*, 1564, was justly consigned to the flames by the curate in the episode of the scrutiny of Don Quijote's library. On the other hand, Gil Polo's *Diana enamorada*, 1564, has been held to equal the work of Montemayor. It remains one of the most successful works of its kind. It is needless to mention each of the twenty-two pastoral romances which Professor Rennert analyzes in detail. Cervantes' *Galatea*, 1585, was the first important work which that author published. To his dying day he thought that his fame would rest largely upon that romance. He promised a continuation no less than five different times. He expended upon it a painstaking care

bestowed upon none of his more famous works. The
style is academic, ornate, diffuse, affected—a style which
readers of *Don Quijote* would not recognize. The plot
is complex. Cervantes' forte was the simple, the natural,
an idealized realism. We witness an interesting failure
on the part of a genius who has followed false gods. Lope
de Vega, though he failed to produce a masterpiece, was
somewhat more successful with his *Arcadia*, 1598, for
Lope was a poet. The pastoral romance in Spain enjoyed a vogue of nearly a century.

The sentimental novel.—Another form of idealistic
fiction was the *novela sentimental*. Juan Rodríguez del
Padrón (de la Cámara), who lived in the times of John II,
wrote *El siervo libre de amor*, inspired by the tragic death
of Inés de Castro. The influence of Boccaccio's *Fiammetta* is heavy on Juan de Flores. Probably in the 1480's
he wrote a continuation called *Grimalte y Gradissa*. His
Historia de Grisel y Mirabella had great success and influence in Spain and abroad.

A highly popular allegory of love is Diego de San
Pedro's *Cárcel de Amor*, 1492. The hero pines and dies
because his beloved no longer favors him. This little book
was unbelievably successful. The first full-fledged
epistolary novel in Europe was Juan de Segura's *Processo
de cartas de amores*, 1548, which stands almost unmatched
for highly elaborated lachrymosity.

"*Historia del Abencerrage y de la hermosa Jarifa*," the
first artistic short story of Spanish literature, has come
down to us in two forms. The first, the more artistic, and,
according to Menéndez y Pelayo, distinguished for its
"sublime simplicity," was published by Antonio de
Villegas in his *Inventario*, 1565. A second version, more

affected and rhetorical, was inserted in the fourth book of Montemayor's *Diana*, in the edition of 1561 and later. Clearly Montemayor is not the author, and the same holds true for Villegas. Some anonymous genius is responsible for this artistic gem. It relates how the Moor Abindarráez was captured by Rodrigo de Narváez, *alcaide* of Antequera, on the eve of the former's marriage to Jarifa. Abindarráez is condemned to death, but demands liberty on parole that he may enjoy a few days of wedded happiness. Rodrigo grants the favor. At the end of the time specified, the Moor surrenders himself, accompanied by his bride. Rodrigo, not to be outdone in magnanimity, grants the pair their liberty. As Rodrigo de Narváez is a historic personage, Spaniards have liked to believe the incident authentic. But one who knows what use the Italian novelists of the Renaissance made of the motive of magnanimity will suspect that a literary plot has been attached to the name of Narváez, a man noted for nobility of character. Mr. J. P. W. Crawford has recently indicated an Italian source for one episode. With the story of Abindarráez a new literary form appears— the *novela*. Short stories of the *cuento*, *exemplum*, and *patraña* types existed in abundance. While these are interesting, they are crude in style and belong to folklore rather than to literature. The artistic short story was something different. Cervantes was destined to develop it.

Ginés Pérez de Hita and the historical novel.—Far more readable than the chivalric and pastoral romances is the historical novel, the invention of which is often credited to Ginés Pérez de Hita (1544?–1619?), though Menéndez y Pelayo would accord the honor to Pedro del Corral, author of *La crónica del rey Don Rodrigo*. Pérez de Hita's book is called *Historia de los bandos de los Zegríes y Abencerrajes*. For this cumbrous title is commonly substituted the unauthorized *Guerras civiles de Granada*. It appeared in two parts. The first, dealing with the inner dissensions of Granada just previous to its fall in 1492, was published in 1595. The second, printed in 1604, describes the Alpujarra insurrection of the Moriscos under Philip II, events in which the author participated. Pérez de Hita is happier when he lets his fancy play than when he narrates fact. Hence the first part is vastly superior to the second. The author paints a brilliant picture of Moorish society in its last days feasts, tournaments, effeminate luxury, and bloody inter necine feuds. Interspersed are many beautiful border bal· lads which would have perished but for their preservation here. Sir Walter Scott fell under the spell of this book in his latter years, and regretted that he had not known it earlier so that he might have made Spain the scene of one of his Waverley novels. Chateaubriand was also influenced by it. Washington Irving copied it in *A Chronicle of the Conquest of Granada*. Pérez de Hita was the first to experience and convey the romantic charm of the Alhambra.

The Milesian tale, or Greek novel.—This form of fiction has already been characterized in treating the *Libro de Apolonio*. During the Renaissance many of these ancient works were circulating in prose. The most typical was *Teágenes y Cariclea*, translated into Castilian several times during the sixteenth century. Next appeared original romances of adventure, constructed after the same formula: adventures with bandits, shipwrecks, separations of kinsmen and lovers, fantastic geography.

Jerónimo de Contreras' *Selva de aventuras*, 1565, was constructed according to this pattern and enjoyed popularity; but let it suffice to consider a single representative of the class, Cervantes' *Persiles y Sigismunda*.

"*Persiles y Sigismunda.*"—With delightful inconsistency, Cervantes' last work was as preposterously impossible as any of the romances of chivalry which he had satirized. This was *Los trabajos de Persiles y Sigismunda, historia septentrional*, published posthumously in 1617. In the early books the scene lies in a fantastic world verging upon the Arctic zone. In the latter portion, where the pilgrims journey through Spain, Southern France, and Italy, one is closer to the world of reality. Cervantes predicted that this would be either the best or worst work of entertainment in Spanish. It is neither. Critics have dealt harshly with it. It is all too evident that the author has mistaken his proper field. But many recent critics (Schevill, Bonilla, Azorín) have initiated a reaction in its favor. There are obvious merits. The style is polished —far more so than in *Don Quijote*. There are none of those evidences of carelessness in which the latter work abounds, and for which, after all, the printer may be responsible. The complex plot is skilfully handled, and was evidently worked out to a nicety beforehand. The fantastic geography is pardonable in an age of discovery when the most amazing stories, many of them true, were coming in from the newly discovered portions of the globe. Many of the intercalated episodes are charmingly done. There are many autobiographical details, scores of pages in the master's best manner, much of his homely philosophy and serene common sense. It should be stressed that, unlike the *Galatea*, the *Persiles* is readable.

BIBLIOGRAPHY

MENÉNDEZ Y PELAYO, M. "Orígines de la novela," *NBAE*, Vol. I (chap. v, "Romances of Chivalry"; chap. vi, "The Sentimental Novel"; chap. vii, "The Historical Novel"; chap. viii, "The Pastoral Novel").

THOMAS, H. *Spanish and Portuguese Romances of Chivalry.* London, 1920.

ENTWISTLE, W. J. *The Arthurian Legend in the Literature of the Spanish Peninsula.* London, 1925.

"Amadís de Gaula" and "Las sergas de Esplandián," ed. P. DE GAYANGOS, *BAE*, Vol. XL.

WILLIAMS, GRACE S. "The 'Amadís' Question," *Revue hispanique*, XXI, 1–167.

PLACE, E. B. *Manual de novelística española.* Madrid, 1926.

―――. *Amadís de Gaula.* Edición y anotación por EDWIN B. PLACE. Tomo I, Madrid, 1959.

―――. "Amadís of Gaul, Wales or What," *Hispanic Review*, XXIII (1955), 99–107.

―――. "Pictorial Evolution: The Old French Romances and the Primitive Amadís Reworked by Montalvo," *PMLA*, LXXI (1956), 521–29.

GIVANEL Y MAS, J. *La novela caballeresca: Estudio crítico de "Tirant lo Blanch."* Madrid, 1912.

AVALLE ARCE, J. B. *La novela pastoril española.* Madrid, 1959.

RENNERT, H. A. *The Spanish Pastoral Romances.* Philadelphia, 1912.

MONTEMAYOR, J. DE. "Los siete libros de la Diana," ed. M. MENÉNDEZ Y PELAYO, *NBAE*, Vol. VII.

SAN PEDRO, D. DE. "Cárcel de amor," ed. R. FOULCHÉ-DELBOSC, *Bibliotheca hispanica*, Vol. XV.

MATULKA, BARBARA. *The Novels of Juan de Flores and Their European Diffusion.* New York, 1931.

SEGURA, PEDRO DE. *Processo de cartas de amores . . . ,* ed. E. B. PLACE. Evanston, 1950.

El Abencerraje, ed. C. PÉREZ PASTOR, *La Imprenta en Medina del Campo*, pp. 209 ff.; ed. N. B. ADAMS and GRETCHEN TODD STARCK. School ed. Chicago, 1927.

DEFERRARI, H. A. *The Sentimental Moor in Spanish Literature.* Philadelphia, 1927.

CARRASCO URGOITI, MARÍA. *El moro de Granada en la literatura.* Madrid, 1957.

PÉREZ DE HITA, G. *Guerras civiles de Granada*, ed. PAULA BLAN-CHARD-DEMOUGE. 2 vols. Madrid, 1913–15.

CERVANTES, M. DE. *Persiles y Sigismunda*, ed. R. SCHEVILL and A. BONILLA Y SAN MARTÍN. 2 vols. Madrid, 1914.

LEONARD, I. *Books of the Brave.* Cambridge, Mass., 1949.

CHAPTER IX

Realistic Types of Fiction—The Celestina and the Picaresque Novel

The *Celestina*—*Celestina* problems—The plot—The characters—Sources and vogue—Defects and merits—The picaresque novel—The *pícaro*—Definitions of *novela picaresca*—Further characteristics of the genre—Literary forerunners of the picaresque novel—*Till Eulenspiegel*—*Pedro de Urdemalas*—Early Spanish realistic forerunners—*La Loçana Andaluza*—*Lazarillo de Tormes*—Sequels to *Lazarillo*—Mateo Alemán and his *Guzmán de Alfarache*—*La pícara Justina*—Salas Barbadillo—Cervantes and the picaresque novel—Vicente Espinel and his *Marcos de Obregón*—*La desordenada codicia de los bienes agenos*—*Alonso mozo de muchos amos*—*Varia fortuna del Soldado Píndaro*—Quevedo and his *Buscón*—Alonso de Castillo y Solórzano—Antonio Enríquez Gómez—*Estevanillo González*—Agustín de Rojas and *El viaje entretenido*—Luis Vélez de Guevara and *El diablo cojuelo*—The decline—The European vogue.

The "*Celestina.*"—Menéndez y Pelayo rates the three most important works of Spanish literature as, first, *Don Quijote;* second, *Celestina;* and third, *El libro de buen amor.* The second of these, which we shall now consider, inaugurated a new fictional form—the dramatized novel. In the later, completer redactions the *Celestina* consists of twenty-one long acts and bears the title *Tragicomedia de Calisto y Melibea,* in the three earliest editions known there are sixteen acts and the title is *Comedia de Calisto y Melibea.* These long titles have never found favor, and the work is commonly designated *Celestina*, from the name of its most important character. Obviously it was never written for the stage, and should be treated under the novel rather than under the drama. It is a landmark in the development of European realism, though, like all of the greatest imaginative works, it is not exclusively realistic; but its realism is so powerful as to overshadow the idealistic elements. The *Celestina* is important intrinsically, for its influence on the subsequent drama and novel of Spain, and lastly for its influence on the literatures of other countries.

"Celestina" problems.—The world knew only the later, twenty-one act versions until, in 1900, Foulché-Delbosc republished in the *Bibliotheca hispanica* the edition of 1501, now regarded as the third of preserved editions. This proved the existence of an earlier redaction of sixteen acts, originally called *cenas*, "scenes." There is also in this edition a *Carta de un autor a su amigo*, in which it is stated that the author, finding time hanging heavy on his hands during a fifteen-day vacation, supposedly at Salamanca, happens upon an unfinished story written to warn the indiscreet against the perils of foolish love. On each of the fifteen days he completes an act, making sixteen all told. The first author, he tells us, had remained anonymous, fearing detractors. He, too, begs leave to conceal his name lest people form the opinion that he is neglecting his vocation, the law. Then follow eleven *coplas de arte mayor*, containing the following acrostic: *"El Bachiller Fernando de Royas acabo la comedia de Calysto y Melybea, y fue nascido en la Puebla de Montalvan."* Then comes an *argumento general.* Next in order follow the sixteen acts, each accompanied with its individual *argumento*. These brief synopses are stated on the

title-page to be "newly added." At the end are six more *coplas de arte mayor* by a printer's corrector, Alonso de Proaza, who in them reveals the secret of the previous acrostic. It is generally thought that Proaza wrote the first *coplas* also, and possibly the *carta*.

Two years later Foulché-Delbosc gained access to a still earlier edition, Burgos, 1499, and republished it.[1] This also contains the sixteen detailed *argumentos*, proving that a still earlier edition must have existed, if we are to believe the words "newly added." (The first ten preserved editions are represented each by a single copy, including the fairly recently discovered edition of Toledo, 1500, and several editions of the *Celestina* must have perished utterly.) The first and last pages of Burgos, 1499, are unhappily lost, and one can only conjecture what they contained; but there was no room for the *coplas*, and the *carta*, if it existed at all, must have been shorter and different from that in the edition of 1501.

Who was Fernando de Rojas? Cañete had previously found in a manuscript history of Talavera the statement that Fernando de Rojas lived, died, and was buried in that city. He was a learned lawyer who at one time acted as *alcalde mayor* of Talavera. Both this statement and that of the acrostic were confirmed by a brilliant discovery made in 1902 by Serrano y Sanz, who brought to light the proceedings in a trial instituted in the years 1525–26 by the Inquisition against a converted Jew, Álvaro de Montalbán, accused of practicing Judaism. The defendant deposed that he had a daughter who was "wife of the Bachelor Rojas who composed 'Melibea,' an inhabitant of Talavera." He asked that this son-in-law defend him, but the court denied this prayer, preferring

[1] *Bibliotheca hispanica*, 1902.

una persona sin sospecha. It is now established that Rojas
wrote at least a portion of the *Celestina*, that he was still
alive at the time of the trial, that the work was written in
his youth, that he was a converted Jew. This last fact explains many heretical statements and covert allusions.

All scholars agree that Rojas wrote Acts II–XVI,
but are disagreed as to the authorship of the rest. Did
he merely continue work begun by another as stated in
the *carta?* Possibly, but Renaissance prefaces are often
deceitful, and the *carta* may be the work of another. The
Jews who refused conversion were expelled from Spain
in 1492. Members of the race who lingered on resorted
to any means to mystify their persecutors and avoid
notice. Rojas' desire for anonymity is understandable.
Three English translations and numerous books and
articles concerning the *Celestina*, published or in preparation in the 1950's, attest to the increasing admiration of
this great masterpiece of the late fifteenth century. A
summary of scholarly opinion with regard to the many
difficult problems concerning the book and its author (or
authors?) made in any particular year might be inaccurate the next, for opinions have veered, and very seriously, and may well continue to do so in the future. Opinions
based solely on the reading of the text by any one
scholar or critic are likely to be subjective and not neces-
sarily valid. The critical edition and study based on
eighteen early editions—and other serious studies
promised as this is written—may help to solve problems.
All who are interested (what savorer of Spanish art is
not?) wish that further documentary evidence might be
discovered which would put an end to speculation by
establishing the definite facts. Meanwhile the *Celestina*
itself is here to delight and enrich us all.

The time when the *Celestina* was written has also been warmly debated. One can only be sure that it was some time in the last decade of the fifteenth century. In localizing the action the author seems to have had no one Spanish city in mind.

The plot.—The basis of the plot is the love-story of Calisto and Melibea. The former, a young aristocrat, wanders into Melibea's garden in pursuit of a stray falcon. Calisto experiences love at first sight. As the parties are equal in wealth and station, a commonplace marriage might be expected to ensue, but Melibea is cold, and Calisto resorts to indirect means. Following the advice of a rascally servant, he enlists the services of Celestina, a crone, half-witch, half-pander. Assuming the rôle of peddler, Celestina gains entrance into Melibea's house, and, by her wheedling arts gradually persuades the girl to respond to her lover's advances. The lovers meet. On leaving Melibea's garden, Calisto falls from a ladder and is killed. Melibea, after a long, tragic lament, commits suicide by hurling herself from a tower. This dénouement is imitated from Boccaccio. Fiammetta contemplated but did not accomplish suicide by the same method.

The characters.—Plot is secondary to character delineation as a source of interest. To the aristocratic group belong the two lovers and Melibea's parents, Pleberio and Alisa. They correspond to the *barbas* of the later comedy. All these speak in high-flown rhetoric, in bookish fashion. They produce an impression of unreality. Yet their diction may not be so untrue to the courtly standards of the time as the modern reader imagines. They talked at least as courtiers would have liked to talk. Calisto is a lover of the Petrarchian type. He grovels in the presence of the loved one with a sense of his own unworthiness. One can only understand his motives by first becoming familiar with that conventional form of love popular among the disciples of Petrarch. Of these Rojas was not the least.

Far more understandable and interesting are the proletarian characters. The hag Celestina is the supreme creation of the work. She possesses the gift of blarney, a sagacity born of the devil, a love of evil for evil's sake. She is a satanic figure, heartless intelligence devoted to evil. The two prostitutes, Elicia and Areusa, who flourish under her wing, are perfect models of the type. Calisto's two picaresque servants, Pármeno and Sempronio, are likewise finished portraits. So is Centurión, the braggart soldier. Rojas, like Shakespeare, fully develops even the minor personages, such as the little pages, Tristán and Sosia. These creatures of the underworld intrigue, make love, and quarrel among themselves, hold bacchic orgies. They converse in a picturesque language full of proverbs and slang. One is convinced of the reality of it all. Just so the low-life people of the Spain of Christopher Columbus must have talked. A similar remark has been made of the archpriest of Talavera's realistic dialogue; but Rojas is an infinitely greater master. With him realism took an advance surpassing anything of the sort yet achieved in the world's literature. He does not move in an unreal world of fantastic knights and conventionalized shepherds, but observed accurately "a slice of life" and perpetuated it for us. Rojas was one of the first to show the interest which lies in the sayings and doings of common people.

Sources and vogue.—The main sources indicated for the *Celestina* are the works of Petrarch, the Latin works in particular, Ovid (according to Schevill indirectly through the *Pamphilus de amore*), Juan Ruiz, Martínez de Toledo, Diego de San Pedro, Plautus, and Terence. The word *tragicomedia* in the later title is apparently taken from the *Amphitryo*, but this may well have been substituted for the original *comedia* by a later reviser.

The large number of editions which have continued to be printed in Spain through the centuries prove the *Celestina's* popularity and influence. So, too, the many imitations. In his *Orígenes de la novela*, Menéndez y Pelayo studies in detail the *Celestina*-inspired dramatized novels. Lope de Vega tried his hand at the genre in his *Dorotea*. Ordóñez' translation into Italian appeared in 1506. Wirsing turned this into German in 1520. The first French translation dates from 1527. The *Celestina* was the first Spanish book ever rendered into English. This was a partial verse translation, of the first four acts, published in London about 1530. James Mabbe's *The Spanish Bawd*, 1631, remains an English classic. In Spain sixty-odd sixteenth-century editions have been listed, whereas only twenty-seven printings of *Don Quijote* were made in the century following its appearance. These figures show that the vogue of Rojas was of long duration and widely spread. His influence upon the development of realism in Europe can scarcely be over-estimated.

Defects and merits.—The *Celestina* has a reputation for obscenity. There is much coarse speech offensive to modern taste. A spade is called a spade. *Pan, pan; vino, vino.* Nevertheless, no more moral book was ever written. It teaches the lesson of the retribution of sin. Not only do the lovers suffer for their sin, but Celestina and the whole band of criminal parasites meet bad ends. Rojas' plot is simple, and this is good art, but without much theatric effect. It may be unreasonable to expect this in a work properly to be classified as a novel.[1] His wonderful gift of characterization has been mentioned. The chief defect of style is a heaping up of pedantic allusions and citations. But these affectations are only occasional and do not occur in the more realistic passages. Modern critics accept with only slight reservations the opinion of Juan de Valdés: "No book has been written in Castilian in which the language is more natural, fitting, and elegant."

The picaresque novel.—The most characteristic form which Spanish realistic fiction took during the sixteenth and seventeenth centuries was the picaresque novel, or romance of roguery. This, like the romance of chivalry and the pastoral romance, was an international genre. But Spain, in a sense, inaugurated it, crystallized it, and furnished the model. The picaresque is by no means limited to the novel. There were picaresque memoirs, plays, ballads, poems of various sorts. But the picaresque found its best expression in the novel.

The picaro.—The adjective *picaresco* is derived from the noun *picaro*, the first appearance of which is found in a work of the year 1548. It does not occur in *Lazarillo de Tormes*. No one of the etymologies proposed is wholly convincing. The term was first applied to a ragged street gamin, and meant "tatterdemalion." Covarrubias in his dictionary of 1611 defined *picaño*, which he regarded as synonymous: *el que es andrajoso y despedazado*. As these boys usually fell into crime, the meaning soon

---

[1] Some scholars and critics might disagree with the preceding opinions.—N. B. A.

changed to "sharper," "rogue." Sometimes *picaros*
served as scullions, sometimes as *esportilleros*, "bearers
of light burdens," opposed to the *ganapanes*, "porters
who carried heavy loads." Such pursuits were convenient
covers to a life of petty crime. Recognizing the *picaros*
as a pest, various municipalities limited their numbers,
compelling them to wear a special costume of green or
red. As the protagonist of a novel, the *picaro* is neither
hero nor villain. Mr. Chandler has invented the term
"anti-hero" as a fitting designation. The *picaro* deserves
condemnation for his refusal to accept useful employment, but merits sympathy as the victim of a pernicious
social organization.

Definitions of novela picaresca.—Many definitions
of the term "picaresque novel" have been attempted,
most of which are too narrow and exclude works which
should properly be classified under this head. This is
because, while attempting to define the genre, critics are
really defining only its most typical form. The definition should be simple and inclusive: The picaresque
novel is a realistic portrayal of criminal life in which
criminals and their tricks constitute the chief source
of interest. I agree with Chandler that "the true test
of the genre is the rogue's preponderance." Novels
which introduce crime and criminals incidentally are
not picaresque novels. Neither are detective stories,
where the interest consists in the unraveling of mysteries.
The typical picaresque novel is the biography, usually
the autobiography of a peripatetic rogue, recounting his
adventures in the service of a series of masters, whose
trades and professions are satirized. It is humorous,
satiric, and a salutary reaction against the absurdities of

the idealistic fiction of the time. Its tone is hard, cynical, and, in some cases, heartless.

Further characteristics of the genre.—The story may sometimes be told in the third person, e.g., *La hija de Celestina*. Often a *pícara* replaces the *pícaro*, in which case there is a series of lovers in place of the series of masters. But there is no concern with sex; the interest lies in the tricks by which the *pícara* deceives her lovers. Sometimes an animal replaces the anti-hero (*El coloquio de los perros*). Or, later, we may have to do with an inanimate object, as the adventures of a coin in passing from hand to hand. The service of masters is not indispensable. In *El siglo pitagórico* are described the adventures of a soul incarnated successively in a series of social types. As with the other forms of fiction, the structure was always loose. The personality of the anti-hero is the only bond of unity. All other characters come and go; he alone continues through the book. His adventures never really end; there is always room for a sequel. There is no well-knit plot, only a series of disconnected adventures. One may begin or cease reading anywhere. Satire is always present. The amount of moralizing varies. The author of *Lazarillo* offers it in discreet doses. Mateo Alemán preaches tiresomely, at such length that his narrative moves slowly. Some authors are sincere social reformers with a message; others moralize hypocritically and obligingly set off their preachments so that the reader may skip them. Cervantes is an exception to the rule that the genre is devoid of pity; Quevedo stands at the opposite pole. The picaresque novel constantly reacts against, and often parodies, the idealistic fiction of the time, as when the anti-hero's family-tree is elaborated to ridicule the heroic genealogies in the romances of chivalry. If the authors of this type of fiction revel in the seamy side of life, it is by way of protest against the absurd unrealities of their rivals. The picaresque novel is a faithful reflection of social conditions at a time when Spain, though still powerful, was already showing signs of decadence. The nation was spent after centuries of heroic endeavor. Economic conditions were unsound. Beggars and parasites abounded, but the whole nation lived in the clouds, victims of false pride. Reluctance to engage in manual labor, trade, and commerce was general. Large portions of the populace were on the verge of starvation. The picaresque novel has been called the "epic of hunger."

Literary forerunners of the picaresque novel.—The picaresque novel inherited from a venerable tradition of realism and satire. The picaresque occurs already in the *Satyricon* of Petronius Arbiter. Apuleius' *Metamorphoses*, with its donkey-hero serving various owners, offered a model for the service of masters device. Its direct influence may occasionally be noted.

European medieval literature afforded many models of realistic cynicism and the satire of the social classes. One might mention the various "Dance of Death" poems, the animal epic, best represented by the *Roman de Renard*, the *Fabliaux*, those coarse productions of the French bourgeoisie, the works of such satirists as Rutebeuf and Villon. The latter was himself a finished *picaro*, but with a capacity for tenderness lacking in his Spanish counterpart. A closer model is offered, as Mr. Ford has indicated, in Italy by Pulci's *Morgante maggiore*. In this epic, burlesque and realistic passages abound. One of the

characters, Margutte, tells the story of his life in an
episode which may be considered a picaresque novel in
miniature. Folengo in his *Baldus* and *Orlandino* deals
largely with the picaresque. So do the *novellieri* and the
compilers of jokebooks, *facezie*. The Spanish novelists
drew many an incident from such sources. In Germany,
too, there was a rich manifestation of bourgeois realism.
"Here," says Kuno Francke, "lie the roots of the modern
realistic novel." Typical works are Stricker's *Der Pfaffe
Amis*, Wernher's *Meier Helmbrecht*, Ulrich Boner's
Edelstein, Hugo von Trimberg's *Der Renner*, with its
satire of *die Stände*, or social classes. More important
was Sebastian Brant's *Narrenschiff*, 1494, a work which
achieved a European vogue. The ship of fools contained
a cargo of one-hundred varieties of the species, whose
foibles are hit off wittily. A work in Latin, *Liber vaga-
torum*, 1510–16, according to Chandler the first pure
example of German rogue realism, did much to create
throughout Europe an interest in the ways of criminals. Luther honored it with a German translation, in
1528.

"*Till Eulenspiegel.*"—This most famous of jestbooks
was first written in Low German, in 1483. The collection
contains ninety-two authentic and nine unauthentic droll
stories dealing with the witticisms and pranks (*Schwänke*)
of a wag whose name provides the title. Till may have
existed in the flesh. An epitaph on an alleged tomb states
that he died in 1350. While he may have originated some
of the drolleries associated with his name, many more of
them belong to the fund of international folklore. Fitzmaurice-Kelly considers *Till Eulenspiegel* first of the
world's distinctively picaresque novels. Here is a series

of detached episodes bound together solely by the protagonist's personality. It is a novel of the road. Change of residence is motivated by the fact that Till is one of those itinerant journeymen apprentices who went the rounds of the old German *Reich* practicing their craft, also by the fact that each new prank makes the town too hot to hold him. Till differs from a Spanish *pícaro* in that his motive is always incorrigible waggery. The joke is its own justification; whereas the Spanish rogue plays tricks to satisfy hunger. *Till Eulenspiegel* is characterized by coarse robustness; Spanish picaresque novels are more cynical.

"*Pedro de Urdemalas.*"—Spanish folklore contains almost the exact counterpart of Till Eulenspiegel. Pedro de Urdemalas, too, was a wag who played tricks along the highways and byways. Like Till's, many of his adventures are coarse and obscene. There is no evidence that they were ever collected in a book, but they are still orally transmitted wherever Spanish is spoken. Some have been collected and published. When a thorough monograph on the subject is available, we shall know more about the origins of the *novela picaresca*. Cervantes in his comedy, *Pedro de Urdemalas*, makes Pedro recite his adventures with various masters. Allusions to him are so frequent in the literature of the Golden Age that one may conclude that the influence of this folklore material was important.

Early Spanish realistic forerunners.—While foreign works exerted their influence, Spain had a strong native tradition of realism, satire of the classes, and roguish types. In Juan Ruiz' vast gallery of rogues the closest approach to a *pícaro* is his lackey Furón:

> Era mintroso, beodo, ladron e mesturero,
> tahur, peleador, goloso, rrefertero,
> rreñidor, adevino, susio e aguero,
> neçio e pereçoso: tal es mi escudero.

We have seen the social classes flagellated in *La danza de la muerte*, and how López de Ayala, Martínez de Toledo, and Rojas, with less sympathy than the archpriest of Hita, nevertheless manifest an interest in low life. The novelists of the sixteenth and seventeenth centuries had merely to hit upon a formula for the picaresque novel, in its narrower and more characteristic form, to appear.

"*La loçana Andaluza.*"—The first of the picaresque novels was the *Retrato de la loçana Andaluza*, Venice, 1528, written by an expatriate and Italianate priest, Francisco Delicado. It is composed in prose dialogue, like the *Celestina*, is peripatetic, lacks plot-structure, has an anti-heroine, and one hundred and twenty-five incidental characters, "who pass by making grimaces and cutting capers in incoherent dialogue" (Menéndez y Pelayo). The style is crude but very colloquial, and is therefore a happy hunting-ground for lexicographers. The work interests by its description of Roman corruption under the pontificate of Julius II. It is the most obscene book in Spanish literature, and the natural prejudice which many critics entertain toward it has blinded them to the fact that it deserves mention as the first of a series. It influenced subsequent writers little, and happily is unique of its kind.

"*Lazarillo de Tormes.*"—But the first truly important rogue romance, and in many respects the greatest of the series, was *La vida de Lazarillo de Tormes: y de sus for-*

tunas y adversidades, three editions of which (Alcalá, Burgos, Antwerp) appeared in 1554. These presuppose an earlier edition, now lost, and our best modern text (Foulché-Delbosc's) is a collation of all three. Nothing positive is known as to authorship. The attribution to Hurtado de Mendoza and other equally improbable guesses have all been exploded. One can only infer that the author was a man of scant culture and considerable common sense, a sincere reformer, keenly alive to abuses within church and state. He seems to have lived in Toledo and to have sympathized with a group of Erasmists who strove to reform the church from within.

Lazarillo, like Pedro de Urdemalas, was a folklore personage. He is already mentioned in *La loçana Andaluza*, and was the hero of various anecdotes circulated orally. In the proverbs the name Lázaro stood for a victim of chronic starvation and one who served many masters. Several anecdotes in the novel are drawn from folklore. To these the anonymous author added from his own invention, creating living character types and interesting situations. Before its printing, *Lazarillo* doubtless circulated in manuscript. It seems certain that before publication the text underwent censorship and condensation. The four final *tratados* are suspiciously short and betray the hand of the pruner. The Alcalá version contains several long passages missing in the others, clumsily fitted into the text, but which may, for all that, go back to an authentic manuscript.

Plot and characters.—The story is divided into seven *tratados*. The reader is first introduced to Lazarillo's criminal family. This is not done, as the modern novelist would do it, to explain and justify Lazarillo by reason of heredity and environment. It is rather a parody on the illustrious lines of descent with which the heroes of idealistic fiction were provided. For the picaresque novel is always a reaction against the novels in vogue. Next follow the adventures with the blind man to whom the *pícaro* is apprenticed. His initiation into a life of low cunning and crime opens Lazarillo's eyes to the necessity of providing for number one. The world is against him. Hunger is his justification for rascality. In the first chapter the author does not tread upon dangerous ground. In the second begins the satire on the clergy. Lazarillo's next master is an avaricious priest under whom he fares worse than under the blind man, but whom he contrives to deceive by many ingenious devices. The third *tratado* is the gem of the whole novel. The character of the proud, starving hidalgo, so susceptible on the point of honor, but willing to live on the alms of an unpaid servant, is one of the supremely great creations of fiction. The portrait is not overdone. This *escudero* is a true representative of thousands of his kind who swarmed in sixteenth-century Spain. He symbolizes the nation—impractical and vainglorious, contemptuous of the true sources of individual and national prosperity, riding for a fall. The anonymous author clearly saw that the two greatest evils from which Spain suffered were starvation, due to economic mismanagement and parasitism, and that false pride on the part of all classes of society which prevented recourse to the proper remedies—industry and thrift. The fifth "treatise" shows Lazarillo serving an indulgence-seller, and describes the tricks by which the populace was duped. After reading it, one better understands Luther's indignation against Tetzel. The next two divisions of the story, suspiciously short, deal with other clerical vices. Lazarillo finally attains prosperity as an auctioneer of wines in Toledo, where he becomes the complaisant husband of a canon's mistress.

Its importance in literature.—The popularity of this little work was immense. It was short; the tale was unfolded in the first person singular, then a novel device; it dealt with easily recognizable types; it expressed truths which many were thinking, but which few dared utter. With the appearance of such a work, the unrealities of the romance of chivalry and the pastoral romance were doomed. Authorities became alarmed. The book was placed on the index; but pirated editions came in from other lands so that it was thought wiser to sanction an expurgated edition, *El Lazarillo castigado*, of 1573. Translations were circulated in other lands, where they did much to spread a taste for realism. One cannot accept Chandler's view that *Lazarillo de Tormes* is a crude form of the genre and that this, as it developed, showed increasing artistic excellence. Crude it is, but in the sense that Michel Angelo's work is crude. The style is clumsy and often obscure. But if he lacked polish, the author possessed to a supreme degree the gift of creating character. His personages live and convey an impression of reality unequaled in any Spanish novels other than the *Celestina* and *Don Quijote*. *Lazarillo de Tormes* is a rough, but great masterpiece.

Sequels to the "Lazarillo."—Almost immediately there appeared an anonymous sequel, Antwerp, 1555. The unknown continuator had the unhappy idea of resorting to the fantastic. Lazarillo is shipwrecked, but being so full of wine that he cannot drown, resides among the tunny-fish, marries a female tunny, becomes their leader. The descriptions of the intrigues of the water-world and the campaigns of the tunnies against the other finny tribes may contain political satire, after the fashion of Gulliver. Finally the man-fish is caught in a net and liberated. The book ends with a number of amusing riddles.

A happier effort was that of Juan de Luna, an Aragonese of liberal tendencies and teacher of Spanish at the Parisian court, who made a puristic revision of the first part, clarifying the language, and substituting for the silly anonymous sequel one of his own. Luna, too, follows Lazarillo in his submarine adventures, though the space devoted to this episode is restricted. One need not believe Luna's statement that his work is taken from certain *cartapacios* found in Toledo. But when he states that he had heard Lazarillo's adventures related at the fireside by his grandmother and aunt, he is probably telling the truth. There is other evidence that the tunny-fish episode was a widely disseminated folklore tale. Luna regarded it as an essential feature in the story. But aside from this unhappy start Luna's sequel is almost worthy of the original. He soon abandons the fantastic for the realistic. The style is simple, the narrative interesting. From the safe vantage-ground of Paris it was possible to attack the clergy vigorously. Luna's is one of the most readable of the *novelas picarescas*.

"*Guzmán de Alfarache.*"—In spite of the popularity of *Lazarillo*, nearly a half-century elapsed before the next picaresque novel appeared. The risk was too great under Philip II. Mateo Alemán (1547–1614?) published the first part of *Guzmán de Alfarache* in 1599. A second part appeared in 1605, and a third part, said to have been completed, was never printed. Alemán, a doctor's son, got his first acquaintance with criminal life by accompanying his father on professional visits to the *cárcel de Sevilla*. After some years of harum-scarum student life and a long and checkered career as a government clerk, probably interrupted by a brief sojourn in Italy, Alemán's affairs became involved and he emigrated to Mexico in his old age, where he died. His *Guzmán* continues the *Lazarillo* on a far more extensive scale. There is the same service of masters, the same wandering over the highways and byways of Spain, though a portion of the action takes place in Italy. It required some courage to revive a literary form frowned upon by the authorities. To satisfy clerical censors and to lend an air of serious purpose Alemán indulged in excessive moralizing. The story advances so slowly in consequence that the modern reader is bored; yet there can be no doubt that formerly this pietism contributed to the book's success. Alemán's style was highly individualistic, his experience of life rich. In view of his own picaresque career his moral sincerity is sometimes open to question. Between the publication of the first and second parts, a pseudo-continuation was printed, 1602, by an individual alleged to be Juan José Martí, a Valencian lawyer. Alemán's attitude toward this production was on the whole good natured, though he revenged himself by turning Martí into a ridiculous character in the genuine second part. The authentic parts of *Guzmán de Alfarache* met with a reception so favorable that it became the most popular novel of the day. The editions printed exceeded in number the early printings of *Don Quijote*. Its success abroad was remarkable. Some critics consider *Guzmán* the greatest of Spanish picaresque novels.

"*La pícara Justina.*"—This work, published in Medina del Campo, 1605, is ascribed to a Francisco López de Úbeda. Whether the name is that of a real person, or a pseudonym, is open to question. There is reason to suppose that this novel was written much earlier than the date of publication and retouched before going to press. Justina is a female rogue who tricks her admirers, and in the end bestows her hand upon no less a personage than Guzmán de Alfarache himself. The studied obscurity of style and the forced word-play make this one of the most difficult of Spanish works of fiction. The many whimsical devices by which the action is interrupted just as it promises to begin may have influenced Laurence Sterne in the introductory chapters of *Tristram Shandy*. *La pícara Justina* enjoyed more foreign translations than its merit justified.

Alonso Jerónimo de Salas Barbadillo (1581–1635), friend of Cervantes, was a prolific writer of novels, short stories, plays, farces, comic and satiric verse. Some of his novels are constructed on the narrow picaresque formula; all contain picaresque elements. His greatest work, *La hija de Celestina, o La ingeniosa Elena*, is admirable for the clarity and purity of its style. As usual in the *novela picaresca*, there is no stress laid upon sex. Elena is merely a rogue who happens to be female, and tricks lovers instead of masters. This novel was re-worked by Scarron in his *Hypocrites*, and indirectly from Salas Barbadillo, Molière drew his famous unmasking scene in *Tartuffe*. *El subtil Cordovés, Pedro de Urdemalas*, 1620, is a picaresque novel until the characters organize themselves into

an academy, tell tales, sing songs, and even act a play
for mutual entertainment. Salas Barbadillo made his
novels receptacles for his contributions to the programs
of the literary academies of Madrid; hence their lack of
form and miscellaneous content. *La sabia Flora Malsa-
bidilla*, 1621, is a dialogued novel with a gypsy anti-
heroine. *El necio bien afortunado*, 1621, is also picaresque.
Its protagonist, Dr. Ceñudo, is lucky so long as thought
to be a fool, unfortunate as soon as his intelligence is
manifest. *Don Diego de noche*, 1623, is an account of nine
successive nocturnal adventures experienced by Don
Diego. Here the author employs the device, already used
by Juan de Segura in *Proceso de cartas*, of telling a story
in the form of letters. In *El curioso y sabio Alexandro*
five social types are satirized. A short story, *La peregrinación sabia*, 1635, describes the adventures of two
foxes, and suggests the influence of *El coloquio de los
perros*.

Cervantes and the picaresque novel.—Menéndez y
Pelayo has denied that Cervantes, in his *Novelas Ejemplares*, followed the picaresque formula. This may be
true in the narrow sense, for Cervantes was gifted with
too much power of invention to adhere willingly to a
cut-and-dried literary procedure. But his interest in
roguery was intense, and the picaresque abounds in his
work. According to the wider definition proposed, he
deserves to rank among the great producers of rogue fiction. In one instance, the passage from *Pedro de Urdemalas* already alluded to, he follows the formula of *Lazarillo;*
and it seems absurd to deny *El coloquio de los perros* the
classification of picaresque novel, no matter how narrow
the definition adopted. In this masterpiece, a dog, en-

dowed for one night with a miraculous power of speech, relates to another dog his adventures in the service of various masters. Cervantes has harked back to Apuleius in choosing an animal protagonist. He sought to revive a formula, fast wearing threadbare, by the use of dialogue and the introduction of the fantastic. There is the same satire of the social classes, with the added piquancy gained by the fact that it is a dog who reads humans much-needed lessons. Where Cervantes most differs from other writers of this fiction is in his never failing humanity. He was wholly incapable of the cynical tone common to most of them. His satire is good natured and mild.

"*Rinconete y Cortadillo*" is the most graphic description of criminal life in Seville ever written. Two youths from the north journey to the picaresque paradise, Seville, where they undergo the demoralization common to sojourners in that delightful but immoral city. They are instructed in the ways of vagabondage and crime at the thieves' school of Monipodio. The latter was a real person; the other characters in the story are probably no less real. The story is a genre picture, faithfully drawn from life. The ordinary devices of the picaresque novel are lacking, but, applying Chandler's criterion, that in a novel of roguery, the *pícaros* and their tricks should constitute the main interest, one is constrained to consider this story one of the most brilliant examples of the picaresque genre. Others of the *Novelas ejemplares* are romantic in tone and only incidentally concerned with roguery. The charms of the *pícaro's* life are so feelingly described in *La ilustre fregona*, and with such apparent nostalgia that one is tempted to infer that in his youth Cervantes had tasted the delights of that carefree existence. The chapter on the galley-slaves in *Don Quijote* is another picaresque novel in miniature.

Vicente Espinel (1550–1624), soldier, priest, musician, poet, *pícaro*, produced, in 1618, one of the most readable of the series, *Relaciones de la vida del escudero Marcos de Obregón*. It contains more of adventure than others of its kind and is the most autobiographical. Espinel led an adventurous life in his youth, and personal experiences are retailed with a mixture of truth and fiction now difficult to define. He avoids tedious moralizing and enlivens his narration with witticism and good stories. In writing *Gil Blas*, Lesage drew more heavily from Espinel than from any other of his many Spanish sources. Espinel is also famous in Spanish literature for inventing the *décima*, or *espinela*, a ten-line stanza of eight-syllable verses with the rhyme scheme, *abbaaccddc*. Espinel shows more intellectual curiosity than any other Spanish writer of his century. Everywhere he betrays his interest in nature and natural phenomena and evinces a real passion for music.

"La desordenada codicia de los bienes agenos" was published in Paris, 1619, by a Dr. Carlos García, about whom we know nothing except that he was a Spanish expatriate resident in France, a traveled man of an inquiring and open mind who loved both France and Spain and strove to bring them into closer harmony. His book suggests the influence of *Rinconete y Cortadillo* in its detailed description of organized crime and the interest shown in *germanía*, "thieves' slang." The action takes place in France, but the characters and conditions satirized are Spanish, just as conversely, though the scene of *Gil Blas* is Spanish, many of the conditions attacked are French. García interests by his quaint philosophical dissertations on miscellaneous subjects.

186

*Realistic
Types of
Fiction*

"*Alonso mozo de muchos amos.*"—The first part of
this work appeared in 1624, the second in 1626. A secondary title was *El donado hablador*, or *The Garrulous Lay-
Brother*. The protagonist's propensity for tiresome speech
motivates his frequent dismissals by a long series of masters. Of all *pícaros* he is the least roguish. The author,
Gerónimo de Alcalá Yáñez, was a medical man, which
explains why this is the one book of the class in which
doctors are not attacked. The moralizing is set off from
the rest of the text, making it easy for the reader to avoid
edification. This novel contains interesting descriptions
of the life of actors on the road.

"*Varia fortuna del soldado Píndaro.*"—The hero of
this novel, written in 1626 by Gonzalo de Céspedes y
Meneses, is a soldier-adventurer rather than a finished
pícaro. There is a strong admixture of the romantic, and
interspersed are short stories, imitated from the Italian.

Francisco de Quevedo y Villegas (1580–1645), philosopher, critic, wit, satiric poet, produced one of the greatest
picaresque novels, *Historia de la vida del Buscón, llamado
Don Pablos, ejemplo de vagamundos y espejo de tacaños*,
Saragossa, 1626. Quevedo's wit is the antithesis of Cervantes' genial humor. It is keen, cynical, vitriolic. The
Buscón is one of the most heartlessly cruel books ever
written. Its author neither loved humanity nor believed
in it. Furthermore, Quevedo was not a squeamish person,
and reveled in repulsive descriptions. For all that, the
Buscón is a great work. Its brilliancy fascinates even if
its coarseness offends. One of the character-types in this
novel has become world-famous, Domine Cabra, keeper
of a Salamanca student boarding-house, from whom
Dickens probably took a hint for Squeers. Cabra, Pablo's
hangman uncle, the fencing-master, the poet, are all cari-

catures of the most exaggerated sort. Unexaggerated
realism is a comparatively recent invention. Early Spanish realism contains much caricature, but in Quevedo
the tendency is carried to the extreme. His influence upon
the world-literature in this respect and others is enormous. Scarron used the same technique in France, as did
Smollett in England. The cultivation of the grotesque
lasts well into the Victorian period.

"*Los sueños.*"—Far less repulsive than the *Buscón* are
the *Sueños y discursos de verdades y engaños en todos los
oficios y estados del mundo*, Valencia, 1627. The "visions"
are imaginary dreams in which the author fancies himself
a visitor to the nether regions, where he meets representatives of the various trades and social classes undergoing
punishment for their sins. The conception is not sublime,
like Dante's, but irresistibly witty. No other writer has
so successfully mastered the possibilities offered by Spanish for punning. His verbal dexterity is marvelous. But
one feels a serious purpose beneath this raillery. Quevedo's scathing indictment of the institutions of his time
was as justified as it was severe. Doubtless it would have
been more effective if less bitter. The *Sueños* enjoyed an
immense European vogue and were frequently imitated.
They have nothing in common with the picaresque novel
except the satire of the classes.

Alonso de Castillo y Solórzano (1584–1648?), an author
distinguished for story-telling gifts, has to his credit a
picaresque trilogy. Of these the most famous is *La
niña de los embustes, Teresa del Manzanares*, 1631. Some
years later, 1637, was published the work which should
have been the first of the series, *Aventuras del Bachiller
Trapaza*. This precious pair marry and have a daughter

worthy of them, whose career is recounted in *La garduña de Sevilla y Anzuelo de bolsas*, 1642. *Las Harpías en Madrid y coche de las estafas*, 1631, relates the ruses of four feminine sharpers who affect wealth and position by means of a borrowed coach. All four of these books are pleasant reading, though somewhat lacking in vigor.

Antonio Enríquez Gómez (1600–1669?), a converted Jew who sought refuge in France for reasons connected with the Inquisition, enriched the picaresque novel with a new device. Borrowing a hint from Lucian and the latter's imitators, he imagines a soul undergoing successive incarnations in the souls of a miser, a hypocrite, a doctor, a thief, a backbiter, etc. His book is entitled *El siglo pitagórico y vida de D. Gregorio Guadaña*, Rouen, 1644. All is in verse with the exception of the life of Don Gregorio Guadaña, a short picaresque novel complete in itself. This work, published in France, was presumably known to many French writers. It deserves study as a possible source of Molière.

"Estevanillo González."—*La vida y hechos de Estevanillo González, hombre de buen humor, compuesto de él mesmo*, Antwerp, 1646, is a work of intriguing interest which still awaits a monograph. The anonymous author may have been a court jester as he alleges; at all events, he was one who had exceptional opportunities to observe life in Italy, Flanders, and the Germany of the Thirty Years' War. Historic personages and events are freely introduced, and the author speaks with the authority of an eye-witness. This is one of the most autobiographical of the whole series. By no means a masterpiece, it interests by its curious subject matter.

Agustín de Rojas (1572–1611?), himself a *pícaro*, has

related some of his extraordinary experiences in *El viaje entretenido*, Madrid, 1603. Rojas was long a strolling player, and won celebrity as the cleverest writer of theatrical prologues (*loas*) of his time. His narrative serves to bind together a number of the best of these, and is not a typical picaresque novel. The interest lies in Rojas' descriptions of the shifts and devices of barn-stormers on the road in the early days of the Spanish drama. Scarron, in writing *Le roman comique*, may have drawn from Rojas his central idea, but certainly took nothing else. As Goethe, in his Wilhelm Meister series, was influenced by 'Scarron, Rojas' unassuming little book may have started a literary tradition.

Luis Vélez de Guevara (1579–1644), better known as dramatist than novelist, produced one famous work of satiric fiction in *El diablo cojuelo, novela de la otra vida*, Madrid, 1641. This is a picaresque novel with a new device, and owes much to Quevedo's *Sueños*. A student, evading the watch, enters an astrologer's apartment, where he releases an imp from a bottle, the famous "limping devil." The imp takes Cleofás, the student, on an aerial journey, making the roofs transparent. The secret lives of the citizens are thus revealed with rich opportunity for satire. The chapters are called *trancos*, "strides." Guevara's idea was novel, and the story began well but was poorly sustained. His strained, equivocal style renders reading difficult. Lesage, appreciating both the merits and defects of *The Limping Devil*, re-wrote it and won for its French version a European vogue.

Juan de Zabaleta (1610?–70?), though a satirist of social types, forsook the picaresque formula to become the first of the *costumbristas*. *El día de fiesta por la mañana*, 1654, and its sequel, *El día de fiesta por la tarde*, 1660, describe the holiday employment of various individuals, the gallant, the hypocrite, the sluggard, the gambler, the poet, etc. With Zabaleta the reader assists at the theater, witnesses *la fiesta del Corpus*, strolls along the *paseos*, participates in popular sports and diversions. His works remain the best fictional source from which to reconstruct the life of the period.

The decline.—Many other picaresque novels must pass unmentioned. Under favorable conditions the genre might have developed into the novel of manners, but after the middle of the seventeenth century it entered upon a decline, as did every other genre, every institution of Spain. Francisco Santos' *Periquillo, el de las gallineras*, 1668, is commonly mentioned as the last of the series. But vagabondage did not cease in Spain, and the eighteenth century shows some literary survivals. Padre Isla translated Lesage's *Gil Blas* so successfully as to make it a Spanish classic. That interesting impostor, Diego de Torres Villarroel, charlatan and professor at Salamanca, wrote an autobiography which is one of the most entertaining rogue stories in existence. The Mexican, Lizardi, in his *Pedro Sarniento*, produced a picaresque novel of the new world, admirable for its advanced and liberal ideas. Modern authors no longer follow narrow formulas, but such works as Pereda's *Pedro Sánchez* and many a novel of Pío Baroja prove that the rogue still interests.

The European vogue.—Nearly every one of the books mentioned in this chapter was translated into Italian, French, German, English, and other tongues. Many went through numerous foreign editions. Their influence was incalculable. They diminished the popularity of the chivalric and pastoral romances. They suggested new literary fields. They determined the style of many authors. In England their influence is to be noted as late as Dickens and Thackeray. Modified, they gave rise to new forms of fiction. When it was discovered that all "low life" was not criminal, authors, turning their attention to the everyday existence of peasants and the middle class, evolved the modern novel of manners. The picaresque novel democratized the fiction of the world.

BIBLIOGRAPHY

Studies of the *Celestina* were made a generation or more ago by numerous scholars, such as Menéndez y Pelayo, Foulché-Delbosc, Conrad Haebler, R. E. House, and many others. Excellent in their day, they have been now mainly superseded.

ROJAS, F. DE. "Comedia de Calisto y Melibea," ed. R. FOULCHÉ-DELBOSC, *Biblioteca hispanica*, Vol. I (1900); Vol. XII (1902). Texts of two of the three earliest known editions.

———. "La Celestina," ed. J. CEJADOR Y FRAUCA, *Clásicos castellanos*. 2 vols. Madrid, 1913. Contains full text and highly opinionated introduction and annotations.

MCPHEETERS, D. W. "The Present Status of *Celestina* Studies," *Symposium*, XII (1958), 196–205. Excellent survey through 1958.

CASTRO GUISASOLA, F. *Observaciones sobre las fuentes literarias de "La Celestina."* Madrid, 1924.

MENÉNDEZ PIDAL, R. "La lengua en tiempos de los Reyes Católicos," *Cuadernos Hispanoamericanos*, XIII (1950), 9–24. The great scholar thinks that Act I was continued by a different author through Acts II–XXI.

SIMONÁ, CARMELO. *Aspetti del retoricismo nella "Celestina."* Rome, 1953.

PENNEY, CLARA L. *The Book Called Celestina.* New York, 1954. Supersedes all previous lists of editions.

CRIADO DE VAL, M. *Indice verbal de la Celestina.* Madrid, 1955.

GILMAN, STEPHEN. *The Art of La Celestina.* Madison, 1956. Stimulating, controversial. Violently attacked by Leo Spitzer in *Hispanic Review*, XXV (1957), 5–10. Later defended by Gilman and others.

Three new English translations of the *Celestina* appeared in the 1950's. The translators were L. B. Simpson, Mack Singleton, and Phyllis Hartnoll.

CHANDLER, F. W. *Romances of Roguery.* New York, 1899.

———. *The Literature of Roguery.* 2 vols. New York, 1907. A comprehensive study of the literature of roguery in other lands, unlike the preceding work, which is concerned chiefly with Spain.

REYNIER, G. *Le Roman réaliste au XVIIᵉ siècle.* Paris, 1914.

BATAILLON, M. *Le Roman picaresque.* Paris, 1931.

DE HAAN, F. *An Outline of the History of the "Novela Picaresca" in Spain.* New York and The Hague, 1903.

———. "Pícaros y ganapanes," *Homenaje a Menéndez y Pelayo*, II, 149–90. Madrid, 1899.

DELICADO, F. *La lozana andaluza.* Madrid, 1916. For criticism, see MENÉNDEZ Y PELAYO. *Orígenes de la novela*, Vol. III, chap. xi.

"Vida de Lazarillo de Tormes," ed. R. FOULCHÉ-DELBOSC, *Bibliotheca hispanica*, Vol. III. Best text.

"Vida de Lazarillo de Tormes," ed. J. CEJADOR Y FRAUCA, *Clásicos castellanos.* Madrid, 1914. A convenient annotated copy.

"Vida de Lazarillo de Tormes," ed. A. BONILLA Y SAN MARTÍN, *Clásicos de la literatura española.* Madrid, 1915. Notes and good introduction.

The Life of Lazarillo de Tormes, trans. LOUIS HOW. New York, 1917. Best English trans. with an excellent introductory study by C. P. Wagner.

MOREL-FATIO, A. "Recherches sur Lazarille de Tormes," *Études sur l'Espagne*, I, 109–66. Paris, 1895.

"Novelistas anteriores a Cervantes," *BAE*, contains the following works mentioned in this chapter: *La Celestina, Lazarillo de Tormes* (including the two sequels), *Guzmán de Alfarache* (also Luján's pseudo-Guzmán).

"Novelistas posteriores a Cervantes," two volumes in *BAE*, contains the following works mentioned in this chapter: *Fortuna varia del Soldado Píndaro, Marcos de Obregón, El donado hablador Alonso, Mozo de muchos amos, El diablo cojuelo, La pícara Justina, La Garduña de Sevilla, Vida de Gregorio Guadaña, Vida y hechos de Estebanillo González.*

Discursos leídos ante la Real Academia española en la recepción del excmo. señor Dn. Francisco Rodríguez Marín. Madrid, 1907. Marín's address is the best biography of Mateo Alemán.

Lopez de Ubeda, F. "La pícara Justina," ed. J. Puyol y Alonso, *Bibliófilos madrileños.* 3 vols. Madrid, 1912. The glossary is most useful.

Obras de Alonso Jerónimo de Salas Barbadillo, ed. E. Cotarelo y Mori. 2 vols. Madrid, 1907–9. The introduction is the best biographical and bibliographical study made of this author.

Salas Barbadillo. "La hija de Celestina," ed. Holle, *Bibliotheca romanica,* Nos. 149, 150. Strassburg, n.d.

Dos novelas de D. Alonso Jerónimo de Salas Barbadillo reimpresas por la Sociedad de Bibliófilos Españoles. Madrid, 1914. (*El cortesano descortés* and *El necio bien afortunado.*)

Salas Barbadillo. "La peregrinación sabia y El sagaz Estacio, Marido examinado," ed. F. A. de Icaza, *Clásicos castellanos.* Madrid, 1924.

———. *La casa del plácer honesto,* ed. E. B. Place. Boulder, 1927.

Cervantes Saavedra, Miguel de. *Novelas exemplares,* ed. R. Schevill and A. Bonilla y San Martín. 3 vols. Madrid, 1922–25.

———. *Rinconete y Cortadillo,* ed. F. Rodríguez Marín. Madrid, 1905.

———. *El casamiento engañoso y El coloquio de los perros,* ed. Amezúa y Mayo. Madrid, 1912.

Espinel, V. *Vida del escudero Marcos de Obregón,* ed. Pérez de Guzmán. Barcelona, 1881. Also, ed. Gilí Goya, *Clásicos castellanos.* 2 vols. Madrid, 1922–23.

García, Carlos. "La desordenada codicia de los bienes agenos," *Libros de antaño,* Vol. VII. Madrid, 1877.

Quevedo y Villegas, F. G. de. *Obras completas,* ed. M. Menén-

DEZ Y PELAYO. 3 vols. Madrid. *Sociedad de bibliófilos andaluces*, 1897–1907.

———. *La vida del Buscón*, ed. R. FOULCHÉ-DELBOSC. New York, 1917. Best text.

———. "La vida del Buscón," ed. A. CASTRO, *Clásicos castellanos*. Madrid, 1927.

———. "Los Suenos," ed. J. CEJADOR Y FRAUCA, *Clasicos castellanos*. 2 vols. Madrid, 1916–17.

CASTILLO Y SOLÓRZANO. *La niña de los embustes*, ed. E. COTARELO Y MORI. Madrid, 1906.

———. "La Garduña de Sevilla," *Clásicos castellanos*. Madrid, 1922.

———. *Noches de placer*, ed. E. COTARELO Y MORI. Madrid, 1907.

———. *Tardes entretenidas*, ed. E. COTARELO Y MORI. Madrid, 1908.

———. *Jornadas alegres*, ed. E. COTARELO Y MORI. Madrid, 1909.

ROJAS VILLANDRANDO, A. DE. *El viaje entretenido*, ed. M. CAÑETE. 2 vols. Madrid, 1901.

VÉLEZ DE GUEVARA, L. *El diablo conjuelo*, ed. A. BONILLA Y SAN MARTÍN. Madrid, 1910.

SPELL, J. R. *The Life and Works of José Joaquín Fernández de Lizardi*. Philadelphia, 1931.

CHAPTER X

The Mystics

Mysticism—Luis de Granada—Santa Teresa de Jesús—Her letters and autobiography—*Las moradas*—Luis de Léon—*La perfecta casada*—*De los nombres de Cristo*—San Juan de la Cruz—*Soneto a Cristo crucificado.*

Mysticism.—So devout a nation as Spain could not fail to produce its saints. If certain of the *conquistadores* were devils incarnate, they carried in their train philanthropists like Las Casas. If much of the literature of the Siglo de Oro is realistic, there were nobler natures who revolted against the paganism of the Renaissance and looked to higher things. The Spanish mystics of this period differ mainly from those of the Middle Ages in their superiority of culture and their application to religion of the platonic philosophy. We have seen that mysticism is one of the great departments of Spanish literature. Only Germany with her three fourteenth-century mystics, Master Eckhart, Heinrich Suso, and Johannes Tauler, has anything comparable to offer.

A mystic has been defined as "one who professes direct divine illumination, or relies chiefly upon meditation in acquiring truth." The Spanish mystics wrote some of the best prose of their day. They were devoid of vanity, pedantry, and literary affectation. Their works are simple, except where their raptures become too ethereal for ordinary comprehension. This literature of devotion is best appreciated by Roman Catholics, but all except those lacking in religious feeling may enjoy it.

Luis de Granada (1504–88), the son of a washer-woman, achieved such fame as a pulpit orator that he was offered bishoprics. These he refused, preferring a simple life of piety and devotion. He wrote voluminously in Latin, Spanish, and Portuguese. His most famous work is the *Guía de pecadores*, a practical guide to right-eousness. The style is Ciceronian. On its first publica-tion in 1567, the Inquisition objected to certain passages. These were corrected in the edition of 1570, and the book became famous throughout the Catholic world, even threatening to exceed in popularity Thomas à Kempis' *Imitation of Christ*.

Santa Teresa de Jesús, the religious name of Teresa de Cepeda y Ahumada (1515–82), is the most human of saints and the greatest female writer in Spanish litera-ture. Even those who do not revere her as a saint honor her as a great woman. A recent Protestant biographer, who attributes her visions to catalepsy, portrays her as a great feminist. Teresa was born in the ascetic city of Ávila, a fitting home for heroes and mystics. As a child she displayed a devout and romantic nature. She enjoyed romances of chivalry, and at the age of seven ran away with a brother to seek martyrdom. As an adolescent, she was sickly. Her period of religious ecstasy began at this time, and at nineteen she professed in the order of the Discalced Carmelites. In time she became mother-superior of the order, founded seventeen new convents, and governed her little communities with never failing intelligence and tact. Teresa was beatified in 1614 and canonized in 1622.

Letters and autobiography.—Santa Teresa united the most divergent qualities, mystic idealism with executive acumen, piety with a strong sense of humor. Her interest in ideas did not dull her affection for people. She never lost sight of her relatives and lay friends, sharing their joys, sorrows, and smallest interests, always favoring them with good counsel. Her *Cartas*, of which more than four hundred are preserved, are self-revealing. So is her autobiography, the *Libro de su vida*. These are her most personal writings in which she shows herself, turn by turn, friendly, confidential, admonitory, jocular. Nothing is too trivial or too exalted to elicit her interest: the jams and sweetmeats manufactured by her nuns, the fine-spun speculations of theology. She wrote without thought of fame, only at the behest of her confessor. Hence the simplicity with which she imparts her message. Her colloquial style gives the best possible idea of the state of spoken Castilian during the sixteenth century. It is vigorous, colorful, simple, racy. There is one great fault, lack of clarity. But so distinguished a writer as Luis de León recognized the merit of this style, became Teresa's editor, and preserved many of her manuscripts from destruction.

"Las moradas."—Santa Teresa's mystic masterpiece is *El castillo interior, o las moradas*. The human soul is described allegorically as a castle containing seven "abodes," or "apartments." In the innermost dwells God, the Lord of the castle. The radiance of his presence fills in varying degree each of the rooms and extends to the castle moat. These seven *moradas* correspond to seven degrees of prayer. The saint tries to instruct her reader how to attain to the most perfect form of prayer.

that which will lead to the innermost chamber, where human personality will be all but annihilated, absorbed into the divine essence. Teresa's *summum bonum* was a sort of Christian Nirvana.

Luis de León (*1528?–91*) has already been called Spain's greatest lyric poet. One cannot be quite so confident in saying that he was also the greatest *prosista* of the period, but such a statement would not fall far short of the truth. He was one of those rare beings of the Renaissance, a scholar without pedantry. His simplicity is not the artless simplicity of the Saint of Ávila, but reasoned. He has left us a statement of his theory of good prose style, ideas wholly sound and modern. First, Castilian is not to be despised. The writer should cultivate his Spanish style with the same care which he devotes to his Latin prose. He should avoid slovenly improvisation, strive for precision, clarity, and energy. He should seek the one inevitable word necessary to express his shade of meaning. Slovenliness, on the one hand, affectation, on the other, were the two evil extremes to be avoided. Spanish literature would be the richer if these ideas had found more ready acceptance.

"*La perfecta casada.*"—In the same year, 1583, appeared Luis de León's two prose masterpieces, *La perfecta casada* and *De los nombres de Cristo*. The first is a sixteenth-century priest's conception of the perfect married woman, pious, subservient to her husband, a model housewife content to fill a humble sphere. The portrait is old fashioned. Patient Griseldas are no longer in fashion. Few modern women would accept Fray Luis as a guide; all might profit by his sane wholesomeness. Whether or not one accepts all of its ideas, the simple charm of this little tract is undeniable.

"*De los nombres de Cristo.*"—Luis de León, as a poet, is one of Horace's happiest imitators. His prose masterpiece is the most successful imitation of a platonic dialogue ever made. Of the three interlocutors, Sabino, Juliano, and Marcelo, the latter represents Fray Luis himself, the former, two of his friends. The topic of conversation is the mystic significance of the various appellations applied to Christ in the New Testament: Beloved, Son of Man, Prince of Peace, and the like. The loftiness of conception, the fine feeling for nature, the exquisite beauty of style make this work the prose masterpiece of mysticism.

San Juan de la Cruz (*1542–91*), the "ecstatic Doctor," attains to rhapsodic heights where few can follow him. Fitzmaurice-Kelly considers his *Obras espirituales* the supreme expression of Spanish mysticism. The *Subida del Monte Carmelo* consists of eight *canciones* with three books of prose commentary. It is as the poet of mysticism that he stands supreme. Finding his chief source of inspiration in Solomon's "Song of Songs," he describes the union of the soul with God in terms of human passion. Thus, in his masterpiece, *En una noche oscura*, the Amada is the soul; the Esposo, God; the "dark night," faith, etc. This short poem is found in all anthologies. It will always live, while his prose rhapsodies will appeal to but few.

The last three stanzas from Mr. Arthur Symons' inspired translation:

> Upon my flowery breast
> Wholly for Him, and save Himself for none,

There did I give sweet rest
To my belovèd one;
The fanning of the cedars breathed thereon.

When the first moving air
Blew from the tower and waved his locks aside,
His hand, with gentle care,
Did wound me in the side,
And in my body all my senses died.

All things I then forgot,
My cheek on Him who for my coming came;
All ceased, and I was not,
Leaving my cares and shame
Among the lilies, and forgetting them.

"*Soneto a Cristo crucificado.*"—Spain is said to have
produced over three thousand mystic writers. Some are
distinguished by homely common sense, others by scholarship, still others by divine intoxication. Those simpler efforts which require no strain on the intelligence and
the emotions will doubtless find most permanent favor.
Of these the anonymous *Soneto a Cristo crucificado* may
stand as the perfect example of Christian poetry:

TO CHRIST CRUCIFIED

I am not moved to love Thee, O my Lord,
By any longing for Thy Promised Land;
Nor by the fear of hell am I unmanned
To cease from my transgressing deed or word.
 'Tis Thou Thyself dost move me,—Thy blood poured
Upon the cross from nailèd foot and hand;
And all the wounds that did Thy body brand;
And all Thy shame and bitter death's award.
 Yea, to Thy heart am I so deeply stirred
That I would love Thee were no heaven on high,—

That I would fear, were hell a tale absurd!
Such my desire, all questioning grows vain;
Though hope deny me hope I still would sigh,
And as my love is now, it should remain.

—Thomas Walsh

BIBLIOGRAPHY

Peers, E. A. *Spanish Mysticism: A Preliminary Survey*. London, 1926.
———. *Studies of the Spanish Mystics*. New York and Toronto, 1927.
Rousselot, P. *Les Mystiques espagnols*. Paris, 1867.
Granada, Luis de. *Obras*, ed. R. Cuervo. 14 vols. Madrid, 1906. Also *BAE*, Vols. VI, VIII, XI.
Cuervo, R. J. *Biografía de Fray Luis de Granada*. Madrid, 1906.
Teresa de Jesús. *Obras*, ed. De la Fuente. 6 vols. Madrid, 1881. Also *BAE*, Vols. LIII, LV.
———. "Las moradas," ed. Navarro Tomás, *Clásicos castellanos.* Madrid, 1910.
Wilkens. "Zur Geschichte der spanischen Mystik, Teresa de Jesús," *Zeitschrift für wissenschaftliche Theologie*, V, 111–80.
Cunninghame-Graham, G. *Santa Teresa: Her Life and Times*. London, 1894.
Bell, A. F. G. *Luis de León: A Study of the Spanish Renaissance*. Oxford, 1925.
León, Luis de. *Obras*, ed. A. Merino. 6 vols. Madrid, 1816. Also *BAE*, Vols. XXXV, LIII, LXI, LXII.
———. *La perfecta casada*, ed. A. Bonilla. Madrid, 1917.
———. "De los nombres de Cristo," ed. F. de Onís, *Clásicos castellanos*. 2 vols. Madrid, 1914.
Coster, A. "Luis de León," *Revue hispanique*, XIII, 1–468; LIV, 1–346. The fullest and best biography.
Fitzmaurice-Kelly, J. *Fray Luis de León: A Biographical Fragment*. Oxford, 1921.
Vossler, K. *Fray Luis de León*. Buenos Aires, 1946.

SAN JUAN DE LA CRUZ. *Obras, BAE,* Vols. XXVII, XXXV.
BARUZI, JEAN. *St. Jean de la Croix.* Paris, 1924, 1930.
PEERS, E. A. *Saint John of the Cross.* Cambridge, 1932.
MENÉNDEZ Y PELAYO, M. "De la poesía mística," *Estudios de crítica literaria,* pp. 1–72. Madrid, 1884.
"Soneto a Cristo crucificado." See R. FOULCHÉ-DELBOSC, *Revue hispanique,* II, 120; VI, 56.

CHAPTER XI

The Historians

A new spirit in the writing of history—Diego Hurtado de Mendoza—Juan de Mariana—The historians of the Indies—Bernal Díaz del Castillo—Bartolomé de las Casas—Álvar Núñez Cabeza de Vaca—Antonio de Herrera y Tordesillas—El Inca Garcilaso de la Vega—Antonio de Solís.

A new spirit in the writing of history.—It was natural that the learning of the Renaissance should influence the writing of history. The production of chronicles was continued in a more scientific spirit, and efforts were made to imitate the great historians of antiquity, particularly Livy, Sallust, and Tacitus. The age was not one to encourage detached judgment, yet there were a few who rose above the prevailing bigotry and viewed history philosophically. But, in general, Spanish historians interest for their picturesqueness and color. Jerónimo Zurita's *Anales de la corona de Aragón* (1562–80) is Spain's first scientific history. It is based on original documents collected by the author. Ambrosio de Morales continued Ocampo and wrote *Las antigüedades de las ciudades de España*, 1575. Morales was first to utilize inscriptions, epitaphs, and coins as sources. Prudencio de Sandoval wrote the *Historia de la vida y hechos del emperador Carlos V*, 1604–6, and the *Historia de los Reyes de Castilla y de León*. These three wrote without distinction and belong to science rather than to literature. Suffice it to say that they came nearer to satisfying the rigid standards of modern research than did any of the more famous **writers** about to be mentioned.

Diego Hurtado de Mendoza (1503–75) is Spain's greatest philosophical historian. A grandee, diplomat, humanist, collector of pictures and of books, he is one of the outstanding figures of the Spanish Renaissance. Between the years 1568 and 1574 he was banished to Granada where he resided during the campaign against the rebellious Moriscos of the Alpujarras. The result was the *Guerra de Granada,* first published posthumously in 1627. The theme was slight, but one permitting the author to speak with the authority of first-hand knowledge. Mendoza is modern in his unbiased analysis of the causes of the uprising and surprisingly fair to a hated race. His criticism of muddling officials is merciless. This spirit of fair play, involving a willingness to condemn wrong done by his countrymen and to get the enemy's point of view, is admirable. The style is concise and antithetic. The model was Sallust's *Conspiracy of Catiline.* In addition one notes much of Tacitus' epigrammatic quality.

Juan de Mariana (1535–1624) was a learned Jesuit, who, after lecturing in the universities of Italy, France, and Flanders, settled down in Toledo to lead a life of letters. He was an original thinker in the fields of government and political economy. In his *De monetæ mutatione* he assails the prevalent custom of debasing the currency. In *De rege et regis institutione* he shocked the world by denying the divine right of kings and even justifying tyrannicide in certain cases. Clearly, Mariana was a thinker impossible to muzzle. The first twenty-five books of the Latin edition of his *Historia de España* were published in 1592; the remaining five in 1605. He chose Latin in order to acquaint all Europe with Spain's past. Then, appealing to a home public, he translated the whole into Castilian in 1601. The last five books, therefore, first appeared in Castilian.

Mariana's history is less critical than one would expect of a scholar of his ability. He rarely draws from original sources. Like his master, Livy, he considered history an art, not a science; and like Livy he was unwilling to subject a good story to critical analysis. His leading characters indulge in set orations, after the manner of the ancient historians. He draws from the old *cronicones* whatever seems picturesque, occasionally expressing his private disbelief. One reads Mariana, as one reads Froissart, for the colorful pageantry of his pages. His book is important culturally, because for many generations it was the world's almost unique source of knowledge for Spanish history from the origins to the death of Ferdinand the Catholic.

The historians of the Indies.—To the American reader Spanish literature offers no more interesting field than the thrilling narratives of the discovery, conquest, and colonization of the New World. Christopher Columbus may be considered the first historian of the Indies, although we possess only a few of his letters. Humanity regrets that he never published his projected annals. Hernán Cortés (1485–1547), the conqueror of Mexico, was an educated man and a polished writer. Brief as are his *Cartas y relaciones*, directed to Charles V, they constitute a vivid setting forth of the thoughts and observations of the chief actor in the Mexican drama. Gonzalo Fernández de Oviedo y Valdés (1478–1557) took part in various campaigns in the New World. His *Historia general y na-*

tural de las Indias was not printed until the middle of the
nineteenth century. Written by a veteran, unskilled in the
use of the pen, its value lies in the author's first-hand
experience. It is interesting to observe the impressions
made upon an average intelligence by the flora, fauna,
races, and customs of the newly discovered regions. A
more polished work is *Hispania victrix, Historia general
de las Indias,* 1552, from the pen of Cortés' private chaplain, Francisco López de Gómara (1511–57?). This may
be regarded as the great conquistador's official history.
As might be expected, Gómara is strongly biased in favor
of his hero.

    Bernal Díaz del Castillo (1492–1581?), a staunch
henchman of Cortés, felt that Gómara had minimized the
services of Cortés' companions. His graphic *Verdadera
historia de los sucesos de la conquista de la Nueva España,*
first printed in 1632, is the work of a veteran who carried
on his body the scars of one hundred and nineteen battles.
The style is crude to the point of illiteracy, yet the old soldier, artlessly spinning his yarn, offers the most authentic
account of the conquest of Mexico. In addition to the
authority which results from being an eyewitness, Bernal Díaz possessed a remarkable memory and a spirit of
fairness. He supplies precisely those details which make
for vividness and interest, details which academic historians are prone to omit. He is a principal source of
Prescott.

    Bartolomé de las Casas (1470–1566), priest and mis-
sionary, is author of a monumental *Historia de las Indias*
from the discovery to 1520. Las Casas is an ardent partisan of Columbus and a detractor of Americus Vespucci.
To him is largely due the idealized conception of Colum-

bus which the world has since held. We now know that
Columbus was shifty in his dealings and that his enemies
had a case. One must constantly guard against Las Casas' prejudices even when these are inspired by noble
motives. He is most noted as a humanitarian. His *Bre-
vísima relación de la destruyción de las Indias* is the eloquent protest of a noble soul against a heartless exploita-
tion of the aborigines which he thought with reason was
resulting in race murder. We may admit that the Spaniards were no more brutal in their dealings with the natives than were other Europeans of the time. The chief
cause of depopulation was doubtless the spread of new
diseases contracted from the civilized races. Furthermore, Las Casas idealized the red man, being the first to
disseminate in Europe the romantic conception of "the
noble savage." But the evils he denounced were real,
even if his enthusiasm for a good cause led him to exaggerate. Foreign writers armed themselves with citations
from Las Casas to foster the belief that Spaniards were a
race of devils. Hence there is now a tendency on the part
of some Spaniards to consider Las Casas an enemy to
his country and to hold him largely responsible for the
century-old tradition regarding Spanish cruelty. But
criticism of one's country and race, love of fair play, and
crusading zeal in behalf of the lowly and oppressed are
qualities more likely to give the world a good idea of
Spanish character than all that can be accomplished by
such works of propaganda as Juderías' *La leyenda negra*,
with its unfair attack upon one of the noblest Spaniards
ever born.

    Álvar Núñez Cabeza de Vaca (1490?–1564?) is less a
historian than a writer of memoirs. His *Naufragios* de-

scribes his various voyages, shipwrecks, pioneer explorations in the Gulf states, and long captivity among the Indians. It would be difficult to find a more thrilling narrative of adventure.

Antonio de Herrera y Tordesillas (1549–1625) wrote one of the famous histories of discovery and exploration, *Décadas, o Historia general de los hechos de los castellanos en las islas y tierra firme del Mar Océano,* 1601. The period embraced is between 1492 and 1554. Herrera drew from Las Casas and other sources not available in print until much later. He lacks the authority of an eyewitness, and is a historian of the literary type.

El Inca Garcilaso de la Vega (1540–1615) is the most picturesque historian of Peru. As the offspring of a cousin of the poet, Garcilaso de la Vega, and a princess of the Inca line, he had every reason to be impartial in his story of the warring relations of the two races from which he derived. His *Florida del Inca, o Historia del adelantado Hernando de Soto* is the chief source of our knowledge of the romantic wanderings of the discoverer of the Mississippi. More important are his *Comentarios reales que tratan del origen de los Incas* and the *Historia general del Perú.* Though he mingles fable with fact, the Inca paints, on the whole, a very reliable picture of the curious civilization of the ancient Peruvians, their despotic state socialism, their wonderful system of roads and inns and postal service, their method of writing by tying knots in strings called *quipus,* their sun-worship, architecture, methods of agriculture, and similar interesting facts. The Inca wrote late in life, a retired soldier living in Cordova. One detects in his writings a nostalgia for the Andes and a gentleness of nature suggestive of his aboriginal strain.

Fitzmaurice-Kelly points out that he was the first South American to make a name in Spanish letters.

Antonio de Solís y Rivadeneyra (1610–86) undertook the task of writing the definitive history of the conquest of Mexico. Solís was a poet of mediocre reputation, also a minor dramatist of the school of Calderón. Appointed *cronista mayor de Indias*, he made his history his life-work. He lived sufficiently remote from the events to attain a historical perspective lacking in the accounts of eyewitnesses. He digested and treated critically the narratives of his predecessors. Solis' style is clear and elegant, and his book is as readable today as when first written, though superseded for the American reader by Prescott's admirable *Conquest of Mexico*.

BIBLIOGRAPHY

HURTADO DE MENDOZA, D. "Guerra de Granada," *BAE*, Vol. XXI.

FOULCHÉ-DELBOSC, R. Various important studies on Hurtado de Mendoza, *Revue hispanique*, I, 338; II, 208; VII, 247; XXXII, 1; XXXV, 476.

MARIANA, J. DE. "Obras," ed. PI Y MARGALL, *BAE*, Vols. XXX, XXXI.

CIROT, G. *Mariana historien*. Bordeaux, 1905.

Historiadores de los siglos XVI y XVII and *Exploradores y conquistadores de Indias. Relatos geográficos, Biblioteca literaria del estudiante*, ed. J. DANTIN CERECEDA. Madrid, 1922. An excellent choice of extracts from the historians and explorers.

"Historiadores de Indias," ed. M. SERRANO Y SANZ, *NBAE*, Vols. XIII, XV.

FERNÁNDEZ DE OVIEDO, G. *Historia natural de las Indias*, trans. STERLING A. STOUDEMIRE. Chapel Hill, 1959.

Díaz del Castillo, B. *Historia verdadera de la conquista de la Nueva España*, ed. G. García. 8 vols. Mexico, 1904–5. Also *BAE*, Vol. XLIX.

Las Casas, B. de. *Colección de obras*, ed. Llorente. Paris, 1822. Also *NBAE*, Vol. XIII.

MacNutt. *Bartholomew de las Casas*. New York and London, 1909.

Núñez Cabeza de Vaca, A. "Naufragios," *BAE*, Vol. XXII.

Fitzmaurice-Kelly, J. *El Inca Garcilasso de la Vega*. Oxford, 1921.

Solís, A. de. "Historia de la conquista de Méjico," *BAE*, Vol. XXVIII.

Lummis, C. F. The Spanish Pioneers. 2d ed. Chicago, 1929. Spanish trans. A. Cuyás. Barcelona, 1922.

Bourne, E. G. *Spain in America*. New York and London, 1904.

CHAPTER XII

Balladry

The ballad genre—The ballad meter—Stylistic peculiarities of early ballads—The fragmentation theory—Objections to the fragmentation theory—The long precedes the short—A classification of ballads—How ballads were transmitted—Modern collections—The aesthetic value of the ballads.

The ballad genre.—At the very moment when humanism and art were exerting their influence, the popular genius also asserted itself, so that the sixteenth century became the great century of Spanish folk-song. Curiously enough, the ballad won the favor of artistic poets at the very time when the Italian meters were in vogue, exerting a powerful counter-influence. Balladry began at some uncertain time in the Middle Ages, and was long viewed askance by sophisticated court-poets like the Marqués de Santillana; but with the Renaissance it becomes the possession of a whole nation. It appealed alike to peasant and prince. The most gifted poets cultivated it. Originally epic, the ballad form now lent itself to lyric expression and to the treatment of every variety of subject. There are therefore many kinds of ballads which one must carefully distinguish. We have seen that balladry is one of Spain's greatest genres. In fact, no other nation, with the possible exception of England, boasts anything comparable to it in richness and interest.

The ballad meter.—All ballads are written in the so-called *verso de romance.* In this meter all verses have eight syllables, when the penult of the last word is stressed (*verso llano*); seven actual syllables, when the last word is stressed on the ultima (*verso agudo*); and nine actual syllables when the final word is stressed on the antepenult (*verso esdrújulo*). In every verse the verse stress falls on the seventh syllable. All types described above count theoretically as eight-syllable verses. The odd verses are blank, the even assonate. Assonance neglects the rhyming correspondence of consonants, vowels alone being considered. It may be single (*asonante agudo*), where only the last stressed vowel of seven-syllable verses is identical, or double (*asonante llano*), where any combination of two vowels, the first under stress, is repeated through the even lines. In this case a consonant or a consonant group may or may not separate the two vowels. Ballad lines were originally not grouped into stanzas. A *romance* might consist of any number of even lines. Late in the sixteenth century it became common to group them into quatrains.

Verso de romance was probably first written in sixteen-syllable lines, with assonance at the end of each, divided into two hemistichs separated by a caesura. This is the view of as old an authority as Nebrija, and is maintained by most modern scholars. Many of these sixteen-syllable lines occur in *The Cid*. Lines of this sort are parallel to the Spanish Alexandrines, also a favorite epic measure, there being eight syllables in each hemistich instead of the seven of the Alexandrine. Mr. H. L. Lang would, on the contrary, derive *verso de romance* from a lyric measure of eight-syllable verse in which every line enters into assonance, the odd verses having one, the even another. Menéndez Pidal, who defends the commoner theory, in order to account for the difference between epic metrical irregularity and the regularity of the ballads, is forced to assume that lyric verses exerted a regularizing influence upon narrative poetry.

Stylistic peculiarities of early ballads.—The oldest-preserved ballads date from the fifteenth century; and there are only a few of these. Foulché-Delbosc's effort to prove that none existed previous to that century has convinced few. Short works are less likely to be preserved than long, and this was a form of literature memorized more frequently than written. The oldest ballads display marked stylistic features. They plunge boldly into the midst of things. They are vigorous, fragmentary, dramatic. They imply familiarity on the part of the listener with the hero's life-story. Hence there is no need for character delineation or completeness of exposition. Much may be taken for granted. Each old ballad portrays some culminating moment of the hero's career. There are also the usual epic formulas and the direct address to an audience characteristic of the primitive epic.

The fragmentation theory.—Such stylistic features led Bello and Milá y Fontanals to believe that the oldest ballads are merely epic débris; that they were "purple patches" torn from their context and lingering in the memory while the prosier wastes had passed into oblivion. This theory has found many adherents, the most vigorous of whom is Menéndez Pidal. It has been attacked by Lang and doubted by Pio Rajna; but it explains most of the stylistic features mentioned. Professional bards carried in their memories long epic compositions. These they recited at length in the castles. In the market-place, where the pecuniary reward would be smaller and the temptation to pass the hat quickly and seek a new audience would be strong, these entertainers may have limited themselves to a recitation of the most striking passages. In any case the human mind best retains such verses as are most forceful and which give most pleasure. The principle of memory fatigue explains much; incompleteness, contaminations, mnemonic devices such as epic formulas, limitation to the striking.

Objections to the fragmentation theory.—Lang's theory of a lyric origin for the *romances* can hardly be demonstrated, though the regularizing influence exerted by lyric poetry on epic narration cannot be denied. Rajna has objected that the fragmentation theory lacks analogy. Nowhere else has a folk-epic broken down into a folk-ballad. To this the reply is that Spanish is the most democratic of literatures and that it is possible to indicate many developments in Spanish literature which are unique. Rajna also finds a difference in tone between the *cantares* and certain *romances*. Leaving out of consideration all but the oldest ballads, for to these alone does the fragmentation theory apply, this objection is sound. Menéndez Pidal admits such difference and is forced to own that in the long course of oral transmission there has been an intrusion of lyric influences. Rajna further puts the question: How reconcile the remarkable accuracy with which ballads have been orally transmitted during the last four centuries with the earlier sweeping changes which the fragmentation theory assumes? Menéndez Pidal's answer to this is interesting, and to the present writer convincing. He posits two periods of ballad evolution: first, a bardic period of active creation when

all was plastic and change was frequent; second, a rhapsodic period, when the ballad stock was rich and mechanical repetition became the rule. Biological evolutionists,
too, have been forced to posit a greater plasticity at
the beginning of things. Now, the populace resents
change in a ballad, just as a child objects to alteration
in a favorite story. When a ballad has become common
property this conservative check is powerful. But at
the outset, when the same ballad was the possession of
only a few, no such check operated against drastic change.

The long precedes the short.—A study of many individual ballads, notably the famous *Conde Arnaldos*, proves
that the commonly accepted variants are frequently not
the completest versions in existence. But the shortened
form usually has the advantage aesthetically. The complete form explains vague allusions in the shorter and
often tells a well-rounded little tale; but in the case of
Conde Arnaldos we regret that the mystic vagueness of the
common version has been rationalized and reduced to
the commonplace. To illustrate, the English ballad which
begins, "That Turk he had a lovely daughter," must derive from a completer version of less startling abruptness.
Menéndez Pidal has made a series of studies bearing on
this point. Where a ballad has seemed far removed from
a passage in a *cantar*, or the prosification of a *cantar*, recounting the same anecdote, he has often been able to indicate a missing link in the form of an earlier version of
the same ballad or a prosification of a degenerate form of
the same *cantar*. Thus the connection of many ballads
with the *cantares de gesta* seems less forced than it used to,
and the case for the epic origin of the genre is strength-
ened. Having proved that many of the stock of ballads

are contracted versions of works originally longer and complete, Menéndez Pidal argues that this was the general rule. But oral transmission beautified while it mangled.

A classification of ballads.—*El Romance Viejo,* or *histórico,* is supposed to be a detached fragment of an old *cantar* which has undergone certain alterations and acquired a distinctive style in the manner described above. It is national and historic, austere in tone. The heroes are the same as those listed in the chapter on the epic. Some seem to hark back to the best epic period, others to more degenerate epic forms.

The *romance juglaresco,* or minstrel ballad, seems to come from Spanish adaptations of French epic material. The heroes are often not national. The tone is romantic. Woman and the marvelous play a large part. The fragmentation theory applies to these two ballad forms. When a distinctive ballad style had once developed, it is supposed that that style was imitated in other ballads which had no relation to the *cantares.*

The *romance fronterizo,* or border ballad, is national like the *romance viejo.* It deals with the fighting between Christians and Moors in the fifteenth century. The authors seem to have been soldiers or camp followers. They do not deal with the larger aspects of the campaigns, but with trivial incidents such as would appear important to an eyewitness but which never would have occurred to a stay-at-home writer. Yet some of these incidents have been shown to be historic. We assume that all had some basis of fact. The border ballads offer vivid pictures of the raids and sieges which took place in the three generations preceding the fall of Granada.

The romance erudito.—When Ocampo's edition of the *Crónica general* was published in 1541, a vast amount of legendary lore became common property. Many poets based ballads on the stories found in the chronicles. They did not know that their prose models were often a rewriting of old epic material and that they were merely restoring to poetry what was poetry's own. By this time there had developed a recognized ballad style which all poets tried to imitate. Few sophisticated poets did so with success. They missed the haunting vigor of the introductory lines of the genuine old ballads, frequently beginning with a date or some prosy statement of fact. Erudite ballads are easy to detect. Most of the ballads in the extensive *romancero del Cid* are erudite.

The *romance artístico* is a term applied to ballads written by recognized literary artists. Cervantes, Lope de Vega, and nearly every poet of the sixteenth and seventeenth centuries used the ballad form. Every sort of theme was treated, and the ballad became lyric as well as narrative. The "artistic ballad" had many special forms.

The *romance pastoril* is an artificial form in which love passages between society people are discreetly veiled by turning the characters into shepherds and shepherdesses. Its relation to other forms of the pastoral is obvious.

The *romance morisco* is a still more popular form in which Christian characters pose as *moros* and *moras*. There is much description of Moorish dress, customs, and manners, but the personages are masqueraders. Though written with art, these ballads are tiring to modern taste.

Romances a lo divino treated sacred themes, and at the opposite pole stood the *jácara*, or *romance picaresco*.

These last were written in *germanía*, thieves' slang, and recounted the careers of famous criminals.

The *romance vulgar* is a coarse form of ballad cultivated by the proletariat. Many are jocose, others relate crimes or the exploits of notorious highwaymen or bullfighters. These ballads show a greater present-day vitality than any others. With the fall of Granada, spontaneous ballad production all but ceased. Except for a few sporadic instances in the early sixteenth century, military events were no longer celebrated in ballad song. Yet these were the days of the Great Captain's exploits in Italy and the epic achievements of the *conquistadores* in America. The stock of *romances* of a heroic sort was sufficiently large; the masses preferred to re-sing the old ones. Artistic balladists were producing work of a different sort. But even today the illiterate writers of vulgar ballads find inspiration in sensational happenings, even though it be the criminal that they celebrate, not the hero.

How ballads were transmitted.—Those ballads we now possess come from various sources: (1) Manuscript compilations and printed broadsides. (2) Printed collections. The earliest is the famous *Cancionero sin año*, a publication printed at Antwerp previous to 1550. The *Silva de varios romances*, the second printed collection, appeared in 1550. The popularity of these works was such that many others were offered the public. These early balladbooks are accurately listed by Wolf in his *Studien*. (3) Oral transmission. Ballads have been orally transmitted by the peasantry of Spain for hundreds of years. The traveler may today hear them sung by farmers on their way to work, by washerwomen at the river's edge. They may still be collected from the lips of the illiterate, not only on Spanish soil, but everywhere that the race has wandered: South America, Mexico, New Mexico, Colorado, California, the Caribbean Isles, the Philippines. In recent years, thousands of ballads, some new, some variants of known ones, have been garnered by diligent folklorists. It is often found that these versions, despite hundreds of years of oral transmission, are more faithful than versions printed in the sixteenth century. They supply gaps, missing beginnings and endings, and often furnish better readings. A great task still remains to be done—that which Child did for English balladry: to collate all available variants of each ballad and restore the authentic text. The Spanish-speaking Jews of the Levant have provided many interesting ballad variants. They are descendants of Jews exiled in 1492, and though they have preserved their tongue and folklore traditions, they have had no contact with Spain for over four centuries. Any ballad recovered from them is certainly older than the date of their exile. The ballad, like the epic, is most intimately associated with the province of Castile; but many appeared in other dialects. Many more were transliterated or re-written in Catalan and Portuguese, languages which often preserve a *romance* whose Spanish original is lost.

Modern collections.—Ballads fell into disfavor during the eighteenth century when neo-Classicism prevailed. With the rise of Romanticism they came into their own again. Percy's *Reliques* showed Englishmen the beauties of their native balladry, and Percy gives one Spanish ballad in translation, *Río verde.* In Germany, Herder did not overlook Spain in his *Voices of the Peoples.* Jacob

Grimm, who, like his brother, was interested in the folk-antiquities of all races, published a tasteful anthology of sixty-nine of the best Spanish ballads, *Silva de romances viejos*, Vienna, 1815. Depping's more extensive collection appeared in 1817. This was the basis of Lockhart's *Ancient Spanish Ballads*, 1823, still the most extensive translation of Spanish ballads in English. Only after the *romance* had won the admiration of the rest of Europe did it return to favor in its native land. Durán's monumental *Romancero general* was first published in five volumes between 1828 and 1849. It was subsequently republished with additions as two volumes, X and XVI, of the *Biblioteca de autores españoles*. Durán's is to date the most extensive Spanish ballad-book, but the least discriminating. The arrangement is by subject, and ballads of all periods are lumped together uncritically. The most scholarly collection, including only the oldest and best, is Wolf's *Primavera y flor de romances*, Berlin, 1856. This was reproduced by Menéndez y Pelayo in his *Antología de poetas líricos castellanos* (Vols. VIII, IX, X), with additional material and notes. One who reads these three volumes has skimmed the cream of Spanish balladry.

The aesthetic value of the ballads.—The pleasure derived from the reading of ballads differs from that obtained from the perusal of a carefully planned work of art; but the naïve effects of popular song have a charm appealing to the best taste. They are artless, but not without art. This form of literature is communal, in the sense that each ballad in its existing form represents the work of a number of authors. It is no longer believed that communal production means the joint work of a synchronous group. Each song was originally written by a

poet, in close touch with the multitude, but superior to
the common crowd in creative ability. Then in the course
of centuries of oral transmission, one reciter has omitted,
another has added, another has changed. Only in this
sense are ballads communal. Such changes improved
the original work more frequently than the reverse, evolv-
ing a distinct style, vigorous and haunting.

Ballad language is full of solecisms and grammatical
errors. This is particularly noticeable in the use of tenses.
Such traits are the stamp of popular origin and no longer
offend. Ballads please by their infinite variety of subject
and tone. The Castilian dignity of the heroic *romance* is
illustrated by such pieces as *Las huestes de Don Rodrigo;
Con cartas y mensajeros; Castellanos y leoneses; Buen conde
Fernán González; ¡Ay Dios, qué buen caballero!; A cazar
va Don Rodrigo; Por el val de las Estacas; Rey don Sancho,
rey don Sancho;* and many another work related to the
old epic material. Everybody is familiar with Lockhart's
spirited rendering of the first of these, with the concluding
lines:

Last night I was the King of Spain—today no king am I;
Last night fair castles held my train,—today where shall I lie?
Last night a hundred pages did serve me on the knee,—
Tonight not one I call mine own:—not one pertains to me.

One encounters a similar tone in many of the border-
ballad group: *Abenámar, Abenámar; Álora, la bien cer-
cada; Ya se salen de Jaén;* and others of the sort. Robert
Southey has caught something of the charm of *Abenámar*,
which Menéndez Pidal has shown derives from a historic
incident:

O thou Moor of *Morería,*
There were mighty signs and aspects
On the day when thou wert born,

Calm and lovely was the ocean,
Bright and full the moon above.
Moor, the child of such an aspect
Never ought to answer falsely.
Then replied the Moorish captive,
(You shall hear the Moor's reply):

Nor will I untruly answer,
Though I died for saying truth.
I am son of Moorish sire.
My mother was a Christian slave.
Often would my mother bid me
Never know the liar's shame.
Ask, thou, therefore, King, thy question.
Truly will I answer thee.

Thank thee, thank thee, Abenamar,
For thy gentle answer, thanks.
What are yonder lofty castles,
Those that shine so bright on high?

That, O King, is the Alhambra,
Yonder is the Mosque of God.
There you see the Alixares,
Works of skill and wonder they;
Ten times ten doubloons the builder
Daily for his hire received;
If an idle day he wasted
Ten times ten doubloons he paid.
Farther is the Generalife,
Peerless are its garden groves.
Those are the Vermilion Towers,
Far and wide their fame is known.

Then spake up the King Don Juan
(You shall hear the Monarch's speech):
Wouldst thou marry me, Granada,
Gladly would I for thy dowry
Cordoba and Seville give.

> I am married, King Don Juan.
> King, I am not yet a widow.
> Well I love my noble husband.
> Well my wedded Lord loves me.

The delicate lyricism of the artistic ballads makes a wholly different appeal in such works as *Rosa fresca, rosa fresca; Fonte-frida, fonte-frida;* and the incomparable *Conde Arnaldos.* Mr. James Elroy Flecker bases his translation of this last upon the current and more artistic version:

> The strangest of adventures
> That happen by the sea,
> Befell to Lord Arnaldos
> On the evening of Saint John;
> For he was out a-hunting—
> A huntsman bold was he!—
> When he beheld a little ship
> And close to land was she.
> Her cords were all of silver,
> Her sails of cramasy;
> And he who sailed the little ship
> Was singing at the helm;
> The waves stood still to hear him,
> The wind was soft and low;
> The fish who dwell in darkness
> Ascended through the sea,
> And all the birds in heaven
> Flew down to his mast-tree.
> Then spake the Lord Arnaldos,—
> (Well shall you hear his words!)—
> "Tell me, for God's sake, sailor,
> What song may that song be?"
> The sailor spake in answer,
> And answer thus made he:
> "I only tell the song to those
> Who sail away with me."

The fate of this ballad is typical of that of others. In its complete form it tells how a king, captured by Moorish pirates, happily encounters a ship equipped for his rescue by faithful vassals. Arnaldos recognizes his countrymen through the helmsman's song, is taken on board and restored to his kingdom. How preferable is the vagueness of the artistically mutilated popular version! Some critics have thought the poem written to celebrate the spell of music, others say it sings the mystery of the sea. The original poet sought merely to tell a commonplace story; but the genius of the people, in this case as in many others, transmuted the baser metal into fine gold.

Turning to the ballads gleaned in the northern provinces, one finds one's self in a land of Celtic romance, a world of fairies and of mystery: *Gerineldo, Don Bueso, El Conde Olinos,* and *Delgadina.* Nearly all classes of ballads have charm, except such artificial forms as the *romance morisco* and the clumsy erudite attempts at imitation of the genuine. As compared with the hothouse productions of many artistic poets, the ballads afford the same aesthetic delight as that afforded by a field of wild flowers. The *romancero* is a never failing source of pleasure. Azorín, than whom we know few more discriminating critics, calls it "Castile's most inspired literary work."

BIBLIOGRAPHY

REAL ACADEMIA ESPAÑOLA. *El romancero,* ed. A. Rodríguez Moñino. 12 vols.; Madrid, 1957.

MENÉNDEZ PIDAL, R. *El romancero español.* New York, 1910. Two popular lectures which provide a succinct and clear introduction to the subject.

MILÁ Y FONTANALS, M. *De la poesía heroico-popular castellana.*

Barcelona, 1874. A later ed., 1896, appears as Vol. VII of Milá's *Obras completas*.

WOLF, F. "Über die Romanzen-Poesie der Spanier," *Studien*, pp. 303–554. Berlin, 1859.

MENÉNDEZ Y PELAYO, M. *Antología de poetas líricos castellanos*, Vols. VIII–XII. Madrid, 1899–1916. Contains reprinting of Wolf's "Primavera y flor de romances" and Menéndez' own critical treatise, "Tratado de los romances viejos."

MENÉNDEZ PIDAL, R. *L'Épopée castillane à travers la littérature espagnole*. Paris, 1910.

LANG, H. L. "Notes on the Meter of the Poem of the Cid," *Romanic Review*, V, 1–30, 295–349; VIII, 241–78, 401–33; IX, 48–95. A questioning of many of Menéndez Pidal's theories of the epic and ballad, far wider in scope than the title indicates.

RAJNA, PIO. "Osservazioni e dubbi concernenti la storia delle romanze spagnuole," *Romanic Review*, VI, 1–42.

MENÉNDEZ PIDAL, R. "Poesía popular y romancero," *Revista de filología española*, I, 357–77; II, 1–20, 105–36, 329–38; III, 233–89. Studies on individual ballads followed by general conclusions. A reply to the two foregoing attacks and the best statement of the author's theories concerning the ballad.

FOULCHÉ-DELBOSC, R. *Essai sur les origines du* Romancero, Prélude. Paris, 1914.

MENÉNDEZ PIDAL, R. "Sobre Foulché-Delbosc: Essai sur les origines du *Romancero*, Prélude," *Revista de libros*, II, 3–14. A reply to the foregoing.

———. *Poesía popular y poesía tradicional en la literatura española*. Oxford, 1922.

MORLEY, S. G. "Are the Spanish Romances Written in Quatrains?" *Romanic Review*, VII, 42–82.

DURÁN, A. "Romancero general," *BAE*, Vols. X, XVI.

LOCKHART, J. G. *Ancient Spanish Ballads, Historical and Romantic*. London, 1823. 2d ed. London, 1840.

MENÉNDEZ PIDAL, R. "Algunos caracteres primordiales de la literatura española," *Bulletin hispanique*, XX, 205–31.

———. Relatos poéticos en las crónicas medievales," *Revista de filología española*, X, 324–72.

ENTWISTLE, WM. J. *European Balladry*. Oxford, 1939. Long section on Spanish ballads, with translations.

CHAPTER XIII

Miscellaneous
Authors of the
Sixteenth Century

The dialogue—Juan de Valdés—Alfonso de Valdés—Cristóbal de Villalón—Pero Mexía—Diego de Saavedra Fajardo—Antonio de Guevara—Antonio Pérez—The artificial epic—Alonso de Ercilla y Zúniga and *La Araucana*.

The dialogue.—One of the important genres in Spain, as elsewhere during this period, was the dialogue. The development of this form was a direct result of the newly awakened interest in Plato, not merely his philosophy but also the artistic method employed by him to convey his thought. Most dialogues of a serious nature are imitations of those of Plato. Those of a lighter sort adopt the manner of the witty skeptic, Lucian. Such universally read contemporary dialogues as Erasmus' *Colloquies* and Castiglione's *Courtier* also influenced the writers who used this form. At a time when newspapers and periodicals were still undreamed of, the dialogue was a happy form for the presentation of information, criticism, and propaganda. Renaissance didacticism is therefore far more artistic than that of the Middle Ages. Usually there are several interlocutors, one of whom may be the author himself. Each character represents a different point of view, and the debate proceeds with points scored by each speaker, but with the author's views triumphant in the end. The subject debated might be grammar, literary criticism, natural science, platonic love, political economy, government, mystic philosophy, or what-not. We have seen that Luis de León's *De los nombres de Cristo* is the greatest imitation of the platonic dialogue in Spanish. A comprehensive study of this genre has never been made.

Juan de Valdés (1503?-41) has already been mentioned as one of the Erasmist group. *El diálogo de la lengua* has been ascribed to Valdés on good authority. It is the first important treatise on the Spanish language ever written. For a pioneer Valdés' judgments are singularly sound, and the modern philologist can take exception to but little. Never has grammar been made more fascinating. *Ciento diez consideraciones divinas* offers a complete statement of Valdés' theological system. As a stylist Valdés shares with Boscán the honor of writing the best prose produced in the reign of Charles V. He wrote as he talked, without affectation, but always seeking the inevitable word. His views on style are almost the same as those later advanced by Luis de León.

Alfonso de Valdés (d. 1532), twin brother of Juan and secretary of Charles V, essayed the difficult task of defending the sack of Rome, for which his royal master was indirectly, if not directly, responsible. The *Diálogo en que particularmente se tratan las cosas acaecidas en Roma en el año de 1527* is a trenchant political pamphlet in which the author's anticlerical bias is apparent. The vivacious *Diálogo de Mercurio y Carón*, 1528, long erroneously attributed to Juan de Valdés, satirizes European politics after the manner of Lucian. The ideas expressed are chiefly those of Erasmus.

Cristóbal de Villalón, who died subsequent to 1558,

was another brilliant disciple of Lucian. A much-traveled Hellenist, he narrates his adventurous youth in the *Viaje de Turquía*—his captivity in Constantinople, his escape and tribulations on the long journey overland to home and safety. The touching description of how the supposedly dead son takes his aged parents by surprise has been imitated by Cervantes in an episode of *Persiles y Sigismunda*. *El Scholástico* is a dialogue debating the requirements of the ideal university. His masterpiece is the *Crotalón*, based closely upon Lucian, containing *novelas* and a long episode from *Orlando furioso*, is unoriginal in subject matter but very original in manner of presentation. It is a caustic satire of contemporary life.

Pero Mexía (1497–1551) made his *Diálogos*, 1547, a catch-all for miscellaneous information. As a disseminator of popular science, especially in that much-read hodgepodge, *Silva de varia lección*, 1540, his work was useful. But he yielded to a fondness for paradox, making his interlocutors praise things and institutions commonly condemned, and in this respect he exerted a pernicious influence upon the succeeding generations who were too prone to exalt mere ingenuity.

Diego de Saavedra Fajardo (1584–1648), statesman and diplomat, was a man of serious purpose and original ideas. His *Idea de un príncipe político-cristiano representada en cien empresas*, 1640, is an attempt to counteract Machiavelianism by painting the portrait of a ruler at once able and ethical. The *Locuras de Europa*, 1748, a Lucianesque dialogue, interests the modern reader by its anticipation of the philosophy of pacificism. The *República literaria*, also printed posthumously, in 1665, is one of the most important works of literary criticism of its time.

Antonio de Guevara (1480?–1545), who died a bishop and who occupied a prominent position at court for the greater part of his lifetime, is author of a didactic novel entitled *Libro llamado relox de príncipes en el qual va encorporado el muy famoso libro de Marco Aurelio*, 1529. This work, long so popular throughout Europe, today irritates by its sermonizing, in spite of occasional interesting passages. Lord Berners' translation, *The Dial of Princes*, was long held to be a source of English euphuism, though this view is today scouted. All Guevara's voluminous writings are neglected after two centuries of popularity, with the exception of *Menosprecio de corte y alabanza de aldea*, 1539. This modest little work is a courtier's sigh for the simple life which is denied him. The charms of rural existence have seldom been portrayed more happily.

Antonio Pérez (1540–1611), the notorious secretary of Philip II, is one of the few exponents of the epistolary genre, a literary form in which Spanish literature is weak. His *Cartas* show a lightness of touch rare among his countrymen at that time, and are vivacious and interesting, even though marred by affectation. In his *Relaciones*, the rascal tries to justify past misconduct, and here as well as in his *Norte de príncipes* advances his theories of statecraft.

The artificial epic.—While the *romancero* remains the supreme expression of the Spanish epic genius throughout the sixteenth century, more sophisticated forms of heroic song could hardly be neglected in the age of learning. Homer and Vergil did not provide the models; one turned for inspiration rather to the great Italian writers of epic romances then in the ascendant, Boiardo, Ariosto, and later Tasso. Spanish imitators of these followed closely the precepts of Italian critical theorists concerning the epic, whereas the rules laid down by the same authorities for the drama were almost universally neglected. The meter employed was invariably the Italian octave, *octava real*. A certain Alonso Hernández was early in the field with an epic devoted to the deeds of the Great Captain. Luis Zapata celebrated Charles V in *Carlo famoso*, 1566, and Juan Rufo pleased with his *Austríada*, 1584. Luis Barahona de Soto wrote a sequel to Ariosto's work in his *Lágrimas de Angélica*, 1586. This effort was soon to be imitated by Lope de Vega in his *Hermosura de Angélica*. All these works and countless others of the same sort possess little merit. Spain produced no Camoens. But if she did not achieve the epic of geographical discovery, she did bring forth the epic of colonial conquest.

Alonso de Ercilla y Zúñiga (1533–94), a gentleman who started life as page to Philip II when the latter was a prince, yielded to the lure of the New World and enlisted in the army of Don García Hurtado de Mendoza, mustering for the conquest of Chile. Chile was the province of America which cost Spain most trouble to conquer. The Araucanos, who held the temperate and cold regions of the south, were of hardier stuff than the Aztecs and Peruvians. They yielded only after many desperate campaigns.

Ercilla's *La Araucana* is the poetic narrative of these struggles. It is a mixture of fact and fancy, with a slight infusion of the marvelous. The first of its three parts was written, the author tells us, in the intervals between fighting, by bivouac fires, on odd scraps of paper. *La*

Araucana is the first literary work of importance written in the Western Hemisphere and inspired by an American theme. Like all the epics of the time it is written in octaves. There is little unity. Extraneous episodes, such as the descriptions of the battles of San Quentín and Lepanto, break the thread of narration; yet these are admirable in themselves and serve to make this one of the most patriotic of Spanish poems. There is no one outstanding hero. On the Christian side all the gallant leaders are praised, except that the *generalissimo* Don García is reduced to a secondary rôle. The general had all but hanged Ercilla for an infringement of discipline, and this was the poet's revenge. The closest approach to an epic hero is Caupolicán, the Araucanian chief. Ercilla respected the Indians as brave and noble foemen and in his idealization of them anticipated Cooper. Caupolicán and Colocolo, an Indian Nestor, indulge in many eloquent harangues, and in these declamatory passages Ercilla is at his best. The poem interests also for its exotic flavor, its descriptions of strange scenes and manners. We must omit mention of many other artificial epics. Let *La Araucana*, with all its faults, stand as the example of the best work of the sort produced in Spain, of a genre which in the main was a failure.

BIBLIOGRAPHY

ALFONSO DE VALDÉS. "Diálogo de Mercurio y Caron," ed. G. F. MONTESINOS, *Clásicos castellanos*. Madrid, 1928.

JUAN DE VALDÉS. "Diálogo de la lengua," ed. G. F. MONTESINOS, *Clásicos castellanos*. Madrid, 1928.

WIFFEN, B. *Life and Writings of Juan Valdés, Otherwise Valdessio*. London, 1865.

*Authors
of the
Sixteenth
Century*

BOEHMER, E. *Spanish Reformers.* Strassburg and London, 1874–83.

VILLALÓN, C. DE. *"El Crótalon, etc.," NBAE*, Vol. VII.

———. "El Scholástico," *Bibliófilos madrileños*, Vol. V. Madrid, 1911.

COSTER, A. "Pedro Mexía, chroniste de Charles-Quint," *Bulletin hispanique*, XXII, 1–36.

MEJÍA, PEDRO. *Diálogos o coloquios*, ed. MARGARET MULRANEY. Iowa City, Iowa, 1930.

SAAVEDRA FAJARDO, DIEGO DE. "Obras," *BAE*, Vol. XXV.

———. *República literaria*, ed. M. SERRANO Y SANZ. Madrid, 1907.

GUEVARA, ANTONIO DE. "Menosprecio de corte y alabanza de aldea," ed. MARTÍNEZ DE BUGOS, *Clásicos castellanos*. Madrid, 1915.

PÉREZ, ANTONIO. "Cartas," *BAE*, Vol. XIII.

FITZMAURICE-KELLY, JULIA. *Antonio Pérez.* Oxford, 1922.

ERCILLA Y ZÚÑIGA, ALONSO DE. "La Araucana," *BAE*, Vol. XVII.

———. "La Araucana," ed. V. MEDINA. Santiago de Chile, 1911–13. (Facsimile of first edition, printed by Huntington, New York, 1902–3.)

CHAPTER XIV

The Drama Previous
to Lope de Vega

The silent centuries—Juan del Encina—His *Églogas*—His later manner—*Aucto del repelón*—Torres Naharro—*Propaladia*—Gil Vicente—Lope de Rueda—Lope's *Pasos*—Juan de la Cueva—*La ingeniosa fábula de España*—Cueva's school—Cervantes as dramatist—His farces.

The silent centuries.—More than three hundred years elapse between the *Auto de los reyes magos* and the next preserved dramatic piece, Gómez Manrique's *Representación del nacimiento de nuestro Señor*. We cannot suppose that this interval was a dramatic blank; rather must we assume the complete loss of an extensive literature. The liturgical drama must have developed along the lines it followed in other European countries, though without such elaborate productions as the guild representations in France. In addition there were pageants, mimes, or crude itinerant entertainers, mummeries, and the like. Clergy and jurists legislated against certain plays called *"juegos de escarnios,"* which offended by their burlesque of the mass and other sacred things. The *farsas* of Diego Sánchez de Badajoz, a provincial cleric who wrote between 1525 and 1547, serve to give some idea of this vanished drama.

Juan del Encina (1469?–1529?), "father of the Spanish drama," was not so lonely a figure as was once supposed. He inherited a tradition which he diverted into new channels; he was surrounded by a group of imitators whose names and works we are just beginning to know; but it is correct to state that he is the first outstanding personage appearing in the history of Spanish dramatic art. Encina, though of humble birth, was educated at Salamanca. He early took minor orders and adopted music as a profession. With music he combined verse. Sixty-eight of his musical compositions have been preserved. He was a political priest with an eye to ecclesiastical sinecures. We find him attached to the households of the Duke of Alba and other magnates, serving in the pope's chapel in Rome, where he resided many years. Not until the age of fifty did he take final orders. In 1519 he said his first mass at Jerusalem, which he visited as a pilgrim to atone for past frivolities. He probably died in León.

His "Églogas."—Encina was a composer of note in his time and one of the best lyric poets of the fifteenth century. He excelled in a refinement upon a peasant verse form called the *villancico*, with one of which most of his plays end. But his dramatic achievement constitutes his chief fame. Shepherds played a prominent part in the Christ-child story and hence entered largely into the liturgical drama. Encina, who knew Vergil's *Eclogues*, translated them crudely into Spanish, and drew many a hint from the Latin author. But his shepherds are far removed from those of Vergil. As a good Spaniard, Encina gave them realistic treatment. They become comic characters, designed to amuse aristocratic audiences, stupid *bobos* who raise a laugh by their naïveté and misuse of big words. They speak a peasant dialect, already used in the *Coplas de Mingo Revulgo*, and which with Encina's successors becomes a stock device. The serious part of each play is made up of the old religious motives. There are Christmas, Good Friday, and Easter plays. The first *Égloga* was acted at the Alba palace in Alba de Tormes, in 1492 or earlier. Eight were printed in Encina's *Cancionero,* 1496.

His later manner.—After residence in Rome, where he served in the musical chapel of Leo X, Encina came more under the influence of Italian pastoral poetry. Few dramatic models in Italian were available—Machiavelli's *Mandragora* dates from about 1504; but pastoral verse contained dialogue. Poliziano's *Orfeo* was first of a series of mythological and allegorical plays. Encina's three Italianate plays, *Égloga de Plácida y Vitoriano, Égloga de tres pastores,* and *Égloga de Cristino y Febea,* show progress toward refinement. They are less crudely realistic than the earlier attempts at the pastoral manner written in Spain. The second of these was taken from an eclogue by Tebaldeo. At least one of them was produced before a brilliant audience at Leo's court. Doubtless all were written for noble patrons. Encina employed an octosyllabic meter with a variety of strophe forms.

The *Aucto del repelón,* his one farce, if one may accept the common attribution, represents a return to the realistic. The story has to do with tricks played by Salamanca students upon peasants who have come to market. It all ends with a scuffle and a general pulling of hair, whence the title. This is the first example in Spanish literature of a farce-genre soon to develop into the *entremés.*

Encina did not bring the drama to the people, but secularized it and made it popular with the aristocracy. His work shows the old liturgical drama revivified by the influence of the Renaissance pastoral. Encina's innovations are hesitating and slight, but if we could compare his plays with the lost ones of the antecedent generation, we should doubtless note a considerable artistic progress.

Bartolomé de Torres Naharro (*d. about 1531*) was more original than his predecessor. Born near Badajoz, he seems to have started life a soldier. He suffered captivity in Algiers, was ransomed, and soon after appeared in Rome a priest and man of letters. There and in Naples he was patronized by popes, cardinals, and the famous banker, Chigi. He possessed far more moral earnestness than Encina, if we may judge by his scathing satire on the immorality of sixteenth-century Rome. His impression of the holy city differed but slightly from Luther's— *"una escuela de pecar"* ... *"un mercado do se vende lo que nunca tuvo precio."* Most of Torres' writings are collected in a book bearing one of those pedantic titles so dear to the Renaissance, *Propaladia*, 1517. This signifies, according to the author, *primeras cosas de Pallas*, that is to say, the first-fruits of a muse from which riper products may be expected later.

The *Propaladia* contains short verse, all but two of Torres' extant plays, and an interesting *prohemio*, the first bit of dramatic criticism ever attempted in Spain. Torres distinguishes sharply between comedy and tragedy, a distinction later lost. He follows Horace in advocating five acts, which he is the first to call *jornadas*, because, as he explains, they are *descansaderos*, "resting-places." The personages should number between twelve and twenty, unless the nature of the subject requires more. He divides plays into *comedias a noticia* (realistic works based on observation) and *comedias a fantasía* (imaginative productions). His earliest play, *Comedia Trofea*, was produced before Leo X in 1512. It is a pageant-play written to honor a Portuguese embassy to the Vatican, a mixture of allegorical and pastoral elements, ending in a *villancico*. If this shows the influence of Encina, Torres came into his own with *Comedia tinellaria*, which may be rendered *Servants' Hall*. This is a brilliant satire on the waste, corruption, and intrigue going on in the palace of a Roman cardinal. The pope and cardinals before whom it was acted were not merely intended to enjoy a laugh at their own expense, but were also admonished to set their houses in order. *Comedia tinellaria* is therefore the first play with a serious purpose in Spanish literature. Six different languages are spoken in this play, indicative of the cosmopolitan character of the audience addressed. *Comedia soldadesca* is a realistic picture of the brutal soldiery who ravaged Italy in the days of the *condottieri*. These two plays are *comedias a noticia*. In *Comedia Serafina* we find for the first time a romantic love intrigue, based on the *Conde Alarcos* ballad, but with a happy ending contrived. Lope de Vega was to essay the same theme in *La fuerza lastimosa*. *La Ymenea* is the first cape-and-sword play in Spanish literature, with window love-making and a compromised lady.

La Calamita and *La Acquilana* were printed, separately, in 1520. The first is in the cynical, licentious Italian manner. The latter, another romantic drama, is the most modern in manner of all that Torres wrote. Torres was incomparably richer in ideas than Encina, and foreshadowed much more clearly the future course of the *comedia*. During the first half of the sixteenth century, the many minor dramatists whom we are forced to omit range themselves in two schools: the followers of Encina and the disciples of Torres Naharro. Here and there, too, the influence of *Celestina* is apparent.

Gil Vicente (1470?–1539?), founder of the Portuguese drama, wrote eleven of his forty-three plays in Castilian. He was a goldsmith-banker and financial adviser of the court of Lisbon. Later, when he had won success through his poetic avocation, he was charged with providing amusements for the royal circle. He flourished in the reigns of Manuel the Great and John III, the time when Portugal was a great nation, famous for geographical exploration and colonization. Vicente's dramatic career began in 1502, when, with a few courtiers dressed as shepherds, he entered the apartments of Queen Maria and enacted a playlet of the Encina sort. The participants in this little scene had no idea that they were engaged in the founding of a national drama. Vicente speedily freed himself of the Encina leading-strings, proving himself both copious and versatile. He wrote pageants, comedies, tragicomedies, and farces. Many of these were produced with much scenic elaborateness. He wrote always for the court, never for the people. His poetry is distinguished by lyric grace and is enriched by folk-elements. In his trilogy of the three ships (*Barca do inferno, Barca do purgatorio,* and *Barca de la gloria,* the last in Spanish) he displays himself a keen satirist of the social classes and a religious liberal of the school of Erasmus. The *Comedia de Rubena* is the oldest comedy of magic and contains a *bobo* clown. *La comedia del viudo* (in Spanish) shows an admirable lightness of touch. *Don Duardos* and *Amadís de Gaula* (both in Spanish) are the first plays based upon romances of chivalry. The modern reader takes most delight in Vicente's farces. Collectively, they provide a picture of most of the social types who thronged Lisbon in the days of its glory. His masterpiece, *Ignez Pereira*, tells the story of the peasant heroine's two marriages: first, with a knight, an ornamental husband but a poor provider; secondly, with an honest fellow of her own class. Gil Vicente excelled all his dramatic predecessors as a poet and in stagecraft as well. Lope de Vega was not above taking hints from him.

Lope de Rueda (*1510?–65*) democratized the drama. He was a gold-beater by trade and a native of Seville. There is no evidence that he ever visited Italy, but there is reason to think that in his youth he came into contact with Italian actors who had now begun to tour Spain. Certainly of all Spanish playwrights he was most under Italian influence. He organized a troupe of players and began to tour the provinces, acting adaptations and original works. Later the term *autor* came to mean "manager." In Lope de Rueda's time "author" and "manager" were synonymous. Sometimes he played in mansions— he even acted before Philip II; but usually he found audiences at inns and market-places. In like manner, the *juglares* had left the castle to entertain the populace. Lope de Rueda was the first "barnstormer." He created that passion among the people for things theatrical to which his successors were to cater so lavishly. Cervantes has described the primitiveness of Lope's equipment, the planks stretched on trestles, the costumes consisting of shepherds' fleece coats, the orchestra composed of an aged guitarist crooning ballads. Most of Lope's plays were in prose, a tendency confined to his school, and which did not reappear until modern times. But he was also famous for his verse pastorals, now lost except for a chance quotation by Cervantes. A. L. Stiefel has shown that Lope's longer plays are re-writings, almost translations, of Italian originals easy to identify.

Lope's pasos.—More original are his brief prose farces, termed *pasos*, "incidents." The plot is of the slightest: A stupid servant is cheated out of a meal, a doctor's servant impersonates his master, husband and wife dispute about the future price of olives to be borne by a tree just planted. The characters are the *bobo*, the barber, the sacristan, the negro, the Biscayan, etc. These are native types similar to those in the plays of Diego Sánchez de Badajoz. Yet many *pasos* have features in common with the Italian comedy of masks. Lope states that they are to be used as a *divertissement* between acts, or inside the main play as a bit of extraneous comic action. There is a tendency to use conventional names for certain types. Thus, Alameda seems to be a stock name for the *simple*, Salcedo for the "master," etc. Lope probably took jokes and incidents from the Italian masked comedy but substituted native types for the well-known Italian characters. Lope's style is vigorous and racy, an admirable record of contemporary popular diction. His influence upon Cervantes was important. He interests by his humanity and simple directness. To his school belong Alonso de la Vega and Juan de Timoneda, who wrote plays and *pasos* of the same sort.

Juan de la Cueva (1550?–1620?) did much to shape the future *comedia*. He reduced the number of acts to four and enriched dramatic versification by the employment of a variety of meters, some native, some foreign: *redondillas, octavas, tercetos,* etc. He did not use ballad meter as has been erroneously stated. Most countries have adopted distinctive dramatic meters which incline toward epic narration rather than toward lyricism. Critics find fault with the *comedia* for the excess of lyricism in its metrical scheme, though it is granted that the Spanish system pleases by its variety. For better or for worse Juan de la Cueva initiated this tendency. At the outset of his career Lope de Vega accepted Cueva's ideas and developed them.

Exempar poético.—Late in life, 1606, some thirty years after his most active period as a dramatist, Cueva wrote an *ars poetica* in which he boldly takes issue with ancient criticism as it was then interpreted by the Italians. He finds the ancient drama tiresome, unsuited to modern conditions. He brushes aside the unities of time, place, and action, and by precept and example determines that disregard for hampering restrictions which was to be adopted by all his successors. One of his phrases, *la ingeniosa fábula de España*, has been misunderstood by critics. It is not a plea that national subjects be used, but a complimentary reference to the Spaniard's skill in inventing interesting plots of all sorts. But by example, if not by precept, Cueva did more than anyone else to make the Spanish drama a national drama. By national drama we mean one which has its roots in native history and tradition and appeals to a whole nation rather than to a social class. It is the expression of a race. The great national dramas are those of Greece, England, and Spain. French classicists, on the contrary, avoided national subjects and appealed to an aristocratic group. Cueva was first to sense the dramatic possibilities of the chronicles and the *romancero*. His *Cerco de Zamora, Bernardo del Carpio,* and *Los siete infantes de Lara* are the first historic

plays written in Spain, if one except Palau's *Santa Orosia*,
which is primarily a saint play. Rojas Villandrando
credits Cueva, too, with the introduction of royal personages on the boards, "*figuras graves, como son reyes y
reinas.*" We find also enchantments, ghosts, metamorphoses, murders, disguises, gods, furies, devils. He ex-
hibits a strong tendency toward sensationalism. *El infa-
mador*, an allegorical play, is his best-known drama.
Cueva's plays are of slight intrinsic merit, but he had an
original mind, and the importance of his innovations in
shaping future developments is increasingly recognized.

Cueva's school.—The Valencian, Andrés Rey de Artieda, continued Cueva, though sometimes observing the
unities. *Los Amantes*, his one preserved play, is important as the first work based on the legend of the lovers of
Teruel. Cristóbal de Virués outdid Cueva in sensationalism, carrying this tendency to the point of absurdity.

Cervantes as dramatist.—One of the disappointments
of Cervantes' life was his inability to win fame as a dramatist. His chief period of productivity as a writer for
the stage lies between the years 1583–87, when he staged
some twenty plays with relative success—"*sin que se les
ofreciese ofrenda de pepinos ni de otra cosa arrojadiza.*"
But with the dramatic début of the "monster of nature."
Lope de Vega, Cervantes' old-fashioned methods no
longer pleased, and managers refused him a hearing.
Later in life he made several ineffectual efforts to get
plays staged, until, in a fit of disgust, he published his
*Ocho comedias y ocho entremeses nuevos, nunca represen-
tados*, Madrid, 1615. Some of these plays were new,
others revampings of old ones. Schevill and Bonilla, who
have spoken the last word on the subject, plausibly conjecture that *El laberinto de amor* is a new redaction of *La*

confusa, that supposedly lost work which the author regarded as his dramatic masterpiece.

His plays.—If Cervantes expected to convince an admiring world that he was a misunderstood genius of the stage, his book tended to justify the theatrical managers. He possessed power to create character and to write sparkling dialogue, but little sense of dramatic situation or skill to conduct a plot. His acts end when he has covered the requisite number of pages. Everywhere there is lack of planning and logical development. The verse is mediocre or worse. Most famous is his patriotic play, *Numancia*, celebrating one of the most famous sieges of history. The style is noble and elevated, if somewhat too stilted. Cervantes considered the allegorical characters in this play something new in dramatic art; but they had had a long tradition in the churchly drama. The novelty consisted in introducing them into a secular play. Equally unfounded is his claim to have been the first Spaniard to divide plays into three acts; yet he should be granted credit for having brought about the definite acceptance of the three-act division. The modern reader may find some slight enjoyment in *Pedro de Urdemalas*, with its gypsy life and strong picaresque element. His two Moorish plays. *Los baños de Argel* and *El trato de Argel*, interest for the autobiographical material they present and their descriptions of the life of Christian captives in Algiers. Cervantes, like Torres Naharro, found dramatic material in his own experiences. His romantic plays are frankly tedious. Some, like *La casa de los celos*, interested at the time by their elaborate use of *tramoyas*, "stage machinery."

His farces.—The foregoing remarks apply solely to his plays. Cervantes' *entremeses* are not only good, but probably the best ever written. In this minor genre the humorist had full scope. There was little question of plot. Character was more important. Laying aside all academic pretensions, the author followed his proper bent, that of comic realism. The influence of Lope de Rueda is apparent, even if the model is surpassed. There is the same gallery of conventionalized comic types. But the humor, the humanity are Cervantes' own. Like Lope de Rueda, Cervantes wrote by preference his farces in prose. Most famous is *La guarda cuidadosa*, in which a sacristan and a picaresque soldier are rivals for the favors of a *fregona*. *La cueva de Salamanca* gives a humorous turn to an old legend and relates how a Salamanca student hoodwinks a credulous husband. *El juez de los divorcios* treats the question of unhappy marriage with kindly philosophy. *La elección de los alcaldes de Daganzo*, in verse, deals with a type of rural official with whom Cervantes had had unhappy bickerings. These and others of his farces stand out from the *entremeses* of other writers, because their humor does not depend upon verbal ingenuity, but springs from human nature. Criticism has not yet done Cervantes full justice as an *entremesista*. Next to *Don Quijote* and the *Novelas ejemplares*, his *entremeses* constitute his best work.

BIBLIOGRAPHY

[See bibliography to chap. iii]

CRAWFORD, J. P. W. *The Spanish Drama before Lope de Vega.* Philadelphia, 1922.

SCHAEFFER, A. *Geschichte des spanischen Nationaldramas.* Leipzig, 1890.

SCHACK, A. F. VON. *Geschichte der dramatischen Literatur und Kunst in Spanien.* 2d ed.; 2 vols. Frankfurt a. M., 1854; trans. E. DE MIER. 5 vols. Madrid, 1885–87.

BONILLA Y SAN MARTÍN, A. *Los Bacantes o del origen del teatro.* Madrid, 1921.

ENCINA, JUAN DEL. *Teatro completo,* ed. M. CAÑETE and F. A. BARBIERI. Madrid, 1913.

———. *El aucto del repelón,* ed. A. ALVAREZ DE LA VILLA. Paris, 1910.

Cancionero musical de los siglos XV y XVI, ed. F. A. BARBIERI. Madrid, 1904.

ESPINOSA MASEO, R. "Nuevos datos biográficos de Juan del Encina," *Boletín de la Real Academia Española,* VIII, 640–56. Madrid, 1914.

MENÉNDEZ Y PELAYO, M. *Antología,* VII, i–c. Best literary criticism on Encina.

MITJANA, P. *Sobre Juan del Encina: Músico y poeta.* Málaga, 1895.

TORRES NAHARRO, BARTOLOMÉ DE. "Propaladia," ed. M. CAÑETE and M. MENÉNDEZ Y PELAYO, *Libros de Antaño,* Vols. IX, X. Madrid, 1880 and 1900. Second volume contains Menéndez y Pelayo's invaluable critical study.

———. *Propalladia and Other Works . . . ,* ed. J. E. GILLET. 3 vols. Bryn Mawr, 1943–52. The authoritative edition and study.

GILLET, J. E. "Une Édition inconnue de la Propaladia," *Romanic Review,* XI, 26–36.

———. "The Original Version of Torres Naharro's *Comedia Tinellaria,*" *Romanic Review,* XIV, 265–75.

VICENTE, GIL. *Obras,* ed. BARRETON FEIO and GOMES MONTEIRO. 3 vols. Hamburg, 1834.

———. *Obras,* ed. MENDES DOS REMEDIOS. 2 vols. Coimbra, 1907–12.

FREIRE, A. B. *Vida e obras de Gil Vicente.* Oporto, 1920.

BELL, A. F. G. *Gil Vicente.* Oxford, 1921.

RUEDA, LOPE DE. *Obras,* ed. E. COTARELO Y MORI. 2 vols. Madrid, 1908.

————. *Teatro,* ed. G. Moreno Villa, *Clásicos castellanos.* Madrid, 1924.

Cotarelo y Mori, E. *Lope de Rueda y el teatro español de su tiempo.* Madrid, 1901.

Cueva, Juan de la. "Tragedias y comedias," ed. F. A. de Icaza, *Bibliófilos españoles.* Madrid, 1917.

Walberg, M. "Juan de la Cueva et son *Exemplar poético*," *Acta Universitatis Lundensis,* Vol. XXXIX. Lund, 1904.

Sargent, C. V. *A Study of the Dramatic Works of Cristóbal de Virués.* New York, 1930.

Cervantes Saavedra, Miguel de. *Obras completas, Comedias y entremeses,* ed. R. Schevill and A. Bonilla y San Martín. 6 vols. Madrid, 1915–22. Best text. Vol. VI contains the best criticism of Cervantes' dramatic work.

CHAPTER XV

Cervantes

Miguel de Cervantes Saavedra—Biography—*Don Quijote*—
Sancho and Don Quijote—The minor characters—Plot construction—Style—Avellaneda's *Don Quijote*—Part II—*Don Quijote*,
the world's great novel—The *Novelas ejemplares*—Cervantes as
poet—The Dedication and Prologue to *Persiles y Sigismunda*.

Miguel de Cervantes Saavedra (1547–1616) is the outstanding figure in Spanish literature. More important
still, he is one of the greatest personages in the literature
of the world. No other of his countrymen approached
him in this quality of universality. He is to Spanish
literature what Shakespeare is to English, Molière and
Racine to French, Dante to Italian, and Goethe to German. No author is more racial, yet no author is less
bound by race. He wrote for all times and all peoples.
As thinker, Américo Castro has shown that he was more
cosmopolitan than most Spaniards, most touched by
Renaissance thought. He is a great humorist, but this is
not the quality which makes him stand pre-eminent.
What chiefly distinguishes him is humanity. With his
advent there is more of the milk of human kindness in
literature. He made the world more democratic, kindlier,
better.

Biography.—Miguel de Cervantes was born into a
family on the down-grade of worldly prosperity. His
grandfather, Juan de Cervantes, was a lawyer who held
many important administrative posts under the crown

and maintained a costly establishment. The father, Rodrigo de Cervantes, followed the then less highly esteemed profession of medicine. His deafness may have contributed to his failure, for his frequent changes of residence indicate an inability to get on in the world. It was mere chance that Miguel, the fourth of Rodrigo's children, was born in Alcalá de Henares, where the family had taken up their temporary residence. For the Cervantes family came from Cordova. Their possessions and family connections lay in the south. This newly established fact is important. Cervantes never displays the austere spirit of Castile. His works are penetrated by the sun of Andalusia.

Education.—Little is known of Cervantes' education. Rodríguez Marín thinks that the author's references to the Jesuit school of Seville betray the fond regard of an alumnus. He shows familiarity with Salamanca, but there is no evidence that he studied there or in the equally famous university of his birthplace. We know positively that around the years 1568 and 1569 he studied under the Madrid humanist, Juan López de Hoyos, and contributed verses to a work which that master and his students published on the occasion of the obsequies of Queen Isabelle of Valois. Certain it is that he enjoyed little formal schooling. To his contemporaries he was *el ingenio lego*, "the lay genius," a phrase which reminds of Ben Jonson's patronizing remark concerning Shakespeare, that he had "little Latin and less Greek." Cervantes had, however, intellectual curiosity and a fondness for reading. Though this was desultory, it was wide. He knew the classics mainly through translation and was familiar with the best Spanish and Italian writers. Those romances of chivalry which he was later to burlesque he devoured eagerly. But the school of life was Cervantes' university, travel and experience his best teachers. Hence he remained human and democratic. Learning might have made him a literary pedant, as happened in the case of so many of his contemporaries.

The years in Italy.—In the episode of the *cautivo* (*Don Quijote*), an impoverished gentleman calls his sons into his presence, bids them choose professions, and sends them into the world with his blessing and some slight pecuniary aid. Something similar must have happened in the Cervantes household when Miguel set out for Italy in 1569. Whether, as there is some reason to suppose, his departure was hastened by an affair of honor, which had involved him with the authorities, is unimportant. The important fact is that a boy of spirit and alert mind set forth to visit the most civilized land in the world. As an old man he reverted to this time with evident enjoyment. In *El licenciado Vidriera* we get an inkling of the impression made upon him by the great cities of Italy, bustling with manufacture and trade, ornamented with all the refinements of art. He delighted to recall the excellence of the Italian inns, the foods and wines he had enjoyed there as a youth. There, too, he became acquainted with the masterpieces of Italian literature. Sannazaro, Pulci, and Ariosto were the authors who influenced him most. This Italian experience was epoch making in his life. New horizons were extended before him.

Military life.—He first served in the household of Cardinal Acquaviva at Rome, but soon forsook the semi-servile employment of a gentleman-in-waiting for a soldier's life. His military service lies between 1570 and 1575. There was much garrison duty in Italy and several campaigns against the Turks and Moors. Cervantes' most important engagement was the naval battle of Lepanto, 1571, in which he conducted himself with conspicuous gallantry. Besides a gunshot wound in the chest, his left hand was permanently crippled, winning for him the sobriquet, *"el manco de Lepanto."* His merits were appreciated by the commander-in-chief, Don Juan de Austria, who made him a *soldado aventajado;* that is to say, his pay was advanced beyond that of the rank and file, and he was in line for a commission. But Philip II, that master of detail, kept such matters in his own hands. A visit to Madrid seemed necessary. Therefore Miguel and his brother, Rodrigo, who had been serving with him, embarked for Spain on the galley "Sol."

Captivity in Algiers.—Six days later, September 26, 1575, the "Sol" was captured by the renegade pirate, Arnaute Mami, and the Cervantes brothers sold into slavery at Algiers. The five years which followed are the most romantic of the novelist's career. Letters of recommendation which Miguel bore on his person proved his undoing. The importance of the bearer was exaggerated in the eyes of the Moors, and the ransom demanded too heavy for the slender resources of the family at home. The thirty thousand Christian captives of Algiers enjoyed considerable liberty. Miguel, on account of his rank, was never forced to do menial labor. He soon became a recognized leader among the Christians. Space forbids a detailed account of his five conspiracies to escape: a desperate attempt to reach Orán across the desert, a ship chartered to appear off the coast at an appointed time, and similar expedients. Invariably there was a traitor in the ring who betrayed the plot. In each case Cervantes assumed the blame and refused to reveal his associates. Later he made literary use of his experiences during these years. The full account of them, set forth in a narrative to the government when seeking employment, was confirmed by many witnesses. The contemporary historian, Diego de Haedo, author of the *Topografía e historia general de Argel*, 1612, confirms the same facts. All agree that during these years Cervantes was gallant and magnanimous. He was finally ransomed for the sum of 500 ducats, paid in part by his family and the rest by the philanthropic order of Trinitarians. Rodrigo had been ransomed earlier.

A hero of the prosaic.—Thus far Cervantes had been a hero of romance, he next became a hero of the prosaic. His first joy at the recovery of liberty was tempered by the impoverished condition of his family and a realization that the government was indisposed to reward his services. He must contribute to the support of parents and sisters who had ruined themselves to raise his ransom. In 1584 he married Catalina de Salazar y Palacios, who brought him a slight dowry. The union remained childless. The following year was marked by the publication of the *Galatea*, a work which brought him a "success of esteem" but little financial prosperity. No wealthy patron appeared with a generous pension. For years he had been striving to win a place as a dramatist, but when routed by Lope de Vega he became convinced of his inability to earn a living by his pen and entered the world of affairs. In 1587 he became a naval purchasing agent, touring the south to collect stores for the "Invincible Armada." In this and similar capacities he served nearly six years, undergoing various vicissitudes. There were bickerings with peasants angered at the expropriation of their crops, excommunications from the clergy, tangled accounts difficult to explain to fussy auditors, losses due to bank failures, imprisonments for debt. During one of these incarcerations, probably at Seville, he conceived or began to write *Don Quijote*, which was, he tells us, "engendered in a prison."

The last years.—In 1603 the Cervantes family was resident in Valladolid, then the capital. The manuscript of *Don Quijote* was nearly, if not wholly, completed. Cervantes' attendance at court appears to have been partly due to the necessity for explaining his tangled accounts to the government auditors, partly to find a patron for the forthcoming work. While in Valladolid certain members of the Cervantes family were arrested, charged with being concerned in the death of a Gaspar de Ezpeleta, who had been mortally wounded in a duel fought before the novelist's residence. While the accused were acquitted of this charge, the evidence in the case indicates the slight esteem in which the family, especially its female members, were held. Part I of *Don Quijote* was published by the slovenly and undeservedly famous printer, Juan de la Cuesta, in 1605. Its success was instantaneous. Editions, authorized and pirated, were published at home and abroad in rapid succession. Translations soon followed. Cervantes had failed in poetry and the drama, and had won only a qualified success with his pastoral novel. His success in a lighter genre, which the taste of the time could scarcely consider serious literature, must have seemed to him ironic. But his name was now a household word. Publishers sought his work; patrons lent support. Cervantes followed the court to Madrid, re-established as capital, and devoted his last years to writing. The *Novelas ejemplares* appeared in 1613; the *Viaje del Parnaso* in 1614; Part II of *Don Quijote* and *Ocho comedias y ocho entremeses nuevos, nunca representados* in 1615. His last years were embittered by the wayward conduct of an illegitimate daughter, Isabel de Saavedra. He died on the twenty-third of April, 1616, the same date as that given for Shakespeare's death, though there was a discrepancy between the calendars of the two countries.

"Don Quijote."—A great book must be written by a great man. Cervantes' life was, if possible, greater than his literary creation. All that research has discovered reveals a man brave, chivalrous, unselfish, loving a joke, but with a heart full of pity. These noble qualities appear throughout his writings. In his case it is especially true that the style is the man. Few great novels are the work of young men. Cervantes began his in the maturity of his powers, sometime in the last years of the sixteenth century. He had had a rich experience of life, had rubbed elbows with all sorts and conditions of men. His life was a failure judged by worldly standards, but his spirit was unsubdued, his disposition unsoured. He had attempted those serious genres most esteemed by the taste of his age, and had come to a realization that he could never be a Garcilaso, a Sannazaro, or even a dramatic writer like Lope de Vega. At last he found his true path. To beguile the tedium of a prison cell he conceived the idea of a satire on the romances of chivalry.

Cervantes' attitude toward the romances of chivalry.—
These same romances had been Cervantes' favorite reading. He knew most of them thoroughly. It must not be
supposed that his attitude is one of sweeping condemnation. The good that was in them appealed to him strongly. He accepted their lofty idealism, their standards of
bravery, loyalty, constancy, generosity, and fair play.
Don Quijote is not rendered ridiculous by his practice of
these ideals; on the contrary, he is ennobled. In his clash
with a world incapable of rising to so lofty a conception,
he ceases to be a comic and becomes a tragic figure. Cervantes quarrels with the romances of chivalry only when
they fail to reconcile idealism with reality, when they are
silly, puerile, and affected. He spares from condemnation
Amadís de Gaula and *Palmerín de Ingalaterra*, and directs
his shafts at their unworthy sequels. The picaresque
novel had made manifest the absurdities of the older
forms of fiction; but its cynicism must have been dis-
tasteful to Cervantes. *Don Quijote* has been called the
last of the series of romances of chivalry. It represents
rather the emergence of a wholly new fictional form, for
it is a synthesis of the best of the *libros de caballerías* with
the best of the *novela picaresca*. This happy blend of the
ideal with the real marks the book's essential greatness.
Those writers who wallow in realism perceive only
one side of the shield; the same is true of those
others whose thoughts are in the clouds, retaining little
contact with mother-earth. Their message strikes men
as unpractical. Human life is compounded of noble and
ignoble elements. The greatest writers envisage both
aspects of life. And the very greatest are those who
like Shakespeare, Molière, and Cervantes, while recog-

nizing the existence of the real, incline by preference toward the ideal.

Sancho Panza and Don Quijote.—These two sides of life are eternally symbolized by the characters Sancho Panza and Don Quijote—the servant who can see things only as they are, the master who sees everything glorified. If the author's first intent was to make Sancho a rogue, his kindly nature was unequal to the task. Sancho is a half-baked figure when first introduced. It is uncertain whether he is to have long shanks or short ones. His propensity to speak in proverbs develops late in the book. His sagacity also increases. When the portrait is completed we behold a typical Spanish peasant with faults due to the limitations of environment, ignorant, fond of the creature comforts, tricky, self-seeking, an odd mixture of craft and naïveté, but loyal to his master and capable of generous action. Admittedly the character is inconsistent. It illustrates the difficulty always encountered by Cervantes in creating characters less noble than himself. Some of his own sentiments inevitably come to their lips. Because Sancho contains so much of his creator, he is loved in spite of his faults. Don Quijote may first have been intended to serve as a mere butt for practical jokes; but horseplay is less frequent as the farce of Part I develops into the comedy of Part II. The author had come to love his character, who constantly gains in dignity. Cervantes had had predecessors in the burlesquing of the institutions of chivalry. If, like Folengo's Baldus, Don Quijote had been a merely comic figure, the conception would have failed. Cervantes' achievement is loftier, because he made the Manchegan knight a tragic figure. Don Quijote is dignified

in the most undignified situations, always the gentleman, never wavering in the faith; and the tragedy is
that he is a conservative reformer, seeking to bring
into a materialistic present the finer ideals of a vanished
past. Heinrich Heine, speaking with the bitterness of a
disillusioned reformer, said that life offered only one
greater tragedy, that of the radical reformer seeking to
bring the future to a present unprepared. Tourgenieff,
in what is perhaps the most brilliant piece of criticism
written upon Cervantes, compares Don Quijote with
Hamlet. Hamlet is the man of inhibitions, who weighs,
doubts, and never acts except where his own interests
are concerned. Don Quijote has the faith in humanity
which the Dane lacks. He never thinks of self. Misdirected philanthropy has never been more pleasantly
satirized than in the Andrés episode; but in spite of the
fact that Don Quijote here as elsewhere plays a ridiculous
rôle, he wins rather than forfeits respect. He portrays
the nobility of unselfish devotion, no matter how misdirected. Sancho and Don Quijote are the eternal sym-
bols of humanity's two ways of viewing life, viewpoints
which can and should be reconciled.

The minor characters.—As in the picaresque novel, the
minor characters are passing figures, but so admirably
drawn with a few deft strokes that they produce indelible
impressions. Their variety is infinite: the priest and the
barber, the niece and the housekeeper with their feminine prejudices, the wench Maritornes, inn-keepers,
drovers, carriers, shepherds, *pícaros*, students, priests,
country gentlemen like the Knight of the Green Over-
coat, nobles—all the motley society of sixteenth-century
Spain as Cervantes had come to know it in a wayfaring

life. Then there are the romantic types: the love-lorn student Grisóstomo, Marcela (something new in the pastoral, a shepherdess who pleads for woman's rights), the charming Dorotea, Camila, Fernando, Anselmo, Lotario (conventionalized aristocrats appearing in the episodic portions), Zorayda the converted Mooress. And over all hovers the shadowy figure of Dulcinea del Toboso.

Plot construction.—Cervantes began to write with a few of the episodes thought out. The crazed hidalgo was to be dubbed "knight," undergo several of the adventures of the early chapters, and the scrutiny and burning of the mischievous books, with Don Quijote's restoration to sanity, may or may not have been the first ending planned. Sancho Panza was probably an afterthought. But the subject grew upon the author. The idea expanded into a volume divided into four parts, now called Part I. The structure was as loose as that of other Renaissance forms of fiction. Like the picaresque novel, *Don Quijote* is a peripatetic romance, only slightly more complicated as to plot. Those who think Cervantes incapable of plot construction have never read *Persiles y Sigismunda,* a work as intricate as a Chinese puzzle. In *Don Quijote* the nature of the subject did not demand a well-knit intrigue. The thing sought was variety of character, incident, and style. The adventures are of many sorts, but fearing that the reader would be bored by a narrative devoted exclusively to the doings and sayings of Don Quijote and Sancho, Cervantes introduced several extraneous episodes more or less artfully adjusted to the main story. The tale of Grisóstomo and Marcela is a *novela pastoril* in miniature; the story of the captive, a novel of adventure; *El curioso impertinente,* a *novela* in the Italian manner. The chapter on the galley-slaves, though less episodic, may be considered a *novela picaresca;* and chapter xxi, Part I, contains a miniature *libro de caballerías*. Thus *Don Quijote* is a synthesis of all the fictional forms of the time. The device of intercalating short stories in a novel was imitated by many. Lesage and Scarron used it in France; in England we find it in *Tom Jones* and *Pickwick Papers*. Cervantes all but abandoned it in Part II, in response to criticism. The public demanded more of Don Quijote's adventures and Sancho's jokes.

Style.—Cervantes possessed not one style, but several. He was a master at suiting his diction to the narrative. Most of *Don Quijote* is written in *estilo llano*, simple, realistic, racy. Then there is the archaic style of those passages imitating the stilted verbiage of the romances of chivalry. The famous apostrophe to the Golden Age is in that same carefully polished, but overrhetorical, manner which he had earlier employed in his *Galatea*. *El curioso impertinente* is a painstaking imitation of the best models of Italian prose. The "Captive's Tale" is plain, unvarnished narration. There is a current misconception that Cervantes was a slovenly, careless writer. It was his misfortune that his best and most widely read book was the worst printed. A study of his other writings reveals no such large number of slips and grammatical errors. We may conclude that his publisher, Juan de la Cuesta, was responsible for most of the blunders which have caused *Don Quijote* to be considered the most carelessly written of the world's great masterpieces. The first drafts (*borradores*) of two of his *novelas* have been preserved, though copied by another hand. These, compared with the printed versions, reveal painstaking revision. Cervantes, therefore, was a conscientious workman and a master of Spanish prose.

Avellaneda's "Don Quijote."—Between the first and second parts of *Don Quijote* appeared the so-called *pseudo-Quijote*, written by a certain Alonso Fernández de Avellaneda, and published in Tarragona, in 1614. The name is probably a pseudonym, and the many attempts to solve the mystery surrounding this author are not worth repeating. It is a false, modern viewpoint that would criticize Avellaneda's free use of Cervantes' literary rights. During the Renaissance everybody felt free to write sequels to the books of others. Ariosto had continued Boiardo; Gil Polo, Montemayor; Luna wrote a sequel to *Lazarillo;* Mateo Alemán had received similar treatment from Mateo Luján de Sayavedra. What Cervantes and others had cause to resent was Avellaneda's insulting Preface. The latter was evidently some hack offended by something in Part I, and who sought financial gain. Cervantes had reached chapter lix of Part II when the publication of the pseudo-Part II came to his notice. He immediately altered his hero's route, sending him to Barcelona instead of to Saragossa, where it had been announced that Don Quijote was to participate in a joust. Avellaneda spurred Cervantes to a speedy completion of his work. The latter chapters contain several playful allusions to the rival work. The abusive Preface was answered in his own *prólogo* with dignified restraint. Avellaneda's work is not without merit. Some of the incidents and episodic *novelas* are interesting; but, of course, the imitation cannot stand comparison with the genuine.

Part II.—The early scheme by which the 1605 edition was divided into four parts was eventually abandoned. By Part II we now mean the second half of the whole work, that published in 1615, one year before the author's death. Few sequels or continuations equal the original. This is an exception. Cervantes had mellowed with age; adversity had brought out the sweetness of his character; infirmities served only to increase his zest. The humor of Part II is richer, the philosophy riper, the touch surer. The parody and satire of the romances of chivalry, boresome to moderns, though the delight of contemporaries, is less insisted on. Horseplay is not altogether wanting, but less conspicuous than in the earlier part. Don Quijote becomes a more majestic figure; Sancho Panza, as governor of the Isle of Baratraria, blossoms out into a sage. By describing Don Quijote's death the author indicated that he had brought his story to its conclusion. He sought to make it difficult for another Avellaneda to take liberties with his ideas.

"Don Quijote," the world's great novel.—The vast majority of critics have considered *Don Quijote* the greatest novel ever written. What are the qualities which give it this pre-eminence? Other novels show more carefully constructed plots, greater perfection of technique, characters more perfectly drawn, a deeper philosophy, a style more polished. These very limitations contribute to its universality. It appeals both to the cultured and the uncultured. It was addressed to no narrow group. No novel was ever more national. It is racy of the soil of Spain, and the product of the age when it was written—so much so that elaborate commentaries are necessary if all allusions are to be understood. What makes it appeal to

all countries, to all ages, and to all classes is that it taps the well-springs of human nature, and human nature is the same everywhere. Cervantes knew humanity and loved it, and with all its failings viewed it optimistically. Perhaps no other author has possessed so fully that "sweetness and light" which Matthew Arnold demanded of great writers. Cervantes loved humanity, and the world in consequence loves Cervantes and the creatures of his fancy. It is impossible to estimate the benefit to civilization wrought by this new note of kindliness in literature. What would Sterne, Fielding, Dickens, and the long line of British novelists have been without Cervantes as a teacher? And the expression of pity was not confined to one country or to the novel alone. The book in time began to affect politics and sociology. Its influence can never be traced even approximately, but one can confidently say that no other novel has so served to make the world better.

The novel of humanity.—Don Quijote everywhere evidences the democratic spirit of Spanish society. Its philosophy, like that of Poor Richard, is homely, of the people, most frequently embodied in the form of proverbs. Cervantes was no original thinker, no revolutionary. He accepts, in the main, the beliefs of his time, literary, political, religious. When he does rebel, it is a revolt of the heart rather than of the mind. He lived in a brutal age, but himself incapable of hatred or petty meanness, reacted against much that was cruel. This attitude is strikingly manifest in his opposition to the honor code of his day. While Lope de Vega and Calderón strove to justify an abhorrent standard of conduct, Cervantes recognized that dueling and the "religion" of honor were national evils of the first importance. His remedy was the practical application of Christian forgiveness, avoiding all metaphysical subtleties. And this is his remedy for all other human ills. Not greatness of technique but greatness of heart makes *Don Quijote* the world's greatest novel.

"*Novelas ejemplares.*"—But for the superior fame of *Don Quijote*, Cervantes, through his short stories, would have won the position of first writer of his time. The *Novelas ejemplares* were published in Madrid, in 1613. *Rinconete y Cortadillo* is mentioned already in Part I of *Don Quijote*, so it is probable that some of the tales had formed part of his literary baggage for many years. The word "*novela*" had only recently been naturalized into Spanish. It still had an Italian flavor, and meant to Cervantes and his contemporaries, not "novel," but a short story in the Italian manner, artistically handled. The word "*ejemplares*" was appended as a safeguard, to indicate that the author shunned the licentiousness of the Italian *novella*. Not that these *Exemplary Tales* were written for the straight laced. The scabrous details of *El casamiento engañoso* are strong for the modern taste; but for a plain-spoken age Cervantes' standard of decency was high. "I am the first," wrote Cervantes, "to write *novelas* in the Castilian tongue, for the many which here circulate in print are all translated from foreign tongues." This claim to be an innovator in a new genre was accepted by contemporaries. Only moderns have misunderstood Cervantes' words. He was not unaware of the many long novels and crude *cuentos* and *patrañas* written by his predecessors. The only possible exception to the contention that he was the first to write artistic short stories in Spanish is the *Historia del Abencerrage y de la hermosa*

Jarifa, and this, as we have seen, is now shown to be influenced by the Italian. Cervantes boasted also of originality: "They are my own, neither imitated, nor stolen; my wit begot them, my pen bore them." This contention may be questioned in part, for the main plot of *El celoso Extremeño* is drawn from an episode in Boiardo; but, in the main, his inventiveness made him independent of sources. When invention failed, he drew from observation. His enemy, Suárez de Figueroa, testifies that Cervantes *"ha historiado sus propios sucesos,"* imagining that he has launched a damning accusation. As if it were a fault that a work of fiction should contain the author's experiences and emotions!

Their varied interest.—Not all the stories are cut to the same pattern. As in *Don Quijote*, Cervantes sought to please by variety. They range from the crude naturalism of *El casamiento engañoso* to the most delicate flights of fancy. *Rinconete y Cortadillo* and *El coloquio de los perros*, already discussed in chapter ix, interest by the photographic accuracy of their realism. In the latter Cervantes is more satirical than elsewhere; but his satire is so just and good natured that it scarcely deserves the name. *El celoso Extremeño* and *La ilustre fregona* combine picaresque realism with romantic plot. Romance is still more evident in *La gitanilla*, where the description of gypsy life is inaccurate; for Cervantes lacked first-hand acquaintance with these nomads. Others, *El amante liberal*, *La fuerza de la sangre*, *Las dos doncellas*, and *La Señora Cornelia*, are still more romantic. Their interest lies in plot and stylistic charm. Cervantes is least happy, when, as in *La Española inglesa*, he relies wholly upon imagination rather than upon observation. His descrip-

264

Cervantes

tions of English ways raise a smile; but it is worth noting
that, unlike Lope de Vega, he directs no word of hate
against the archenemies of his nation. *El licenciado
Vidriera* stands apart. It is a collection of aphorisms, put
in the mouth of the wisest of madmen, and imitated from
Lucian's *Demorax*. Little need be said of *La tía fingida*, a
scabrous tale, not included in the *Novelas*, and never
attributed to Cervantes until Arrieta published it in
1814. The only reasons for supposing that Cervantes
wrote it are the style and its occurrence in an old manuscript, which, besides other miscellaneous material, contained *Rinconete y Cortadillo* and *El celoso Extremeño*.
While the style appears Cervantine to many authorities,
others are strongly convinced to the contrary. The controversy still rages, with an increasing tendency to reject
the attribution.

Cervantes as poet.—Cervantes himself deplores his
lack of the poetic gift, a judgment shared by contemporaries and since confirmed by posterity. His many
sonnets, lyrics, and occasional poems of all sorts may be
dismissed as mediocre or worse. Aside from his plays
(see chap. xiv), his most ambitious work in verse is the
Viaje del Parnaso, Madrid, 1614. This was an imitation
of Cesare Caporali di Perugia's *Viaggio in Parnaso*, 1582.
Caporali, like Cervantes, had served the Cardinal Acquaviva, and the two authors were probably acquainted.
The framework is the story of the author's visit to Mount
Parnassus, the battle between Apollo's cohort of good
poets and the poetasters, his translation to Naples while
sleeping, and other adventures. He passes in review the
poets of the day, with little discrimination and much
good nature. Many unimportant names are thus saved

from oblivion. The device is similar to that already employed in the "Canto de Caliope" (in *La Galatea*, see
chap. viii), and the famous scrutiny of the books in *Don
Quijote*. Lope de Vega's *Laurel de Apolo* is a later work of
the same sort. The *Viaje* ends with an Appendix,
"Adjunta al Parnaso," with which, abandoning lame
tercets for vivacious prose, Cervantes rewards the patient
reader with several of his characteristic, gossipy pages.

Dedication and Prologue to "Persiles y Sigismunda."—
If one were asked to single out the best half-dozen pages
written by Cervantes, one could do no better than indicate the last he ever wrote. *Persiles y Sigismunda* has
been treated in chapter viii; but the Dedication and the
Prologue which accompany this posthumous novel are
worth many times over the book which they introduce.
The Dedication is addressed to the Conde de Lemos, that
grandee whom Cervantes elsewhere calls his Maecenas.
It was written one day after the administration of extreme
unction and four days before the end. The dying author
quotes plaintively the old ballad, *Puesto ya el pie en el
estribo*, and takes leave of his benefactor, regretting only
his inability to complete such projected works as *Semanas
del jardín*, *El famoso Bernardo*, and the long-promised
second part of the *Galatea*. The Prologue, written simultaneously or about the same time, recounts a meeting on
the road with an *estudiante pardal*, a grotesque but sincere
admirer of the great author. The flattering tokens of
admiration received from this stranger must have been
one of the last cheering experiences of Cervantes' life.
With a few deft strokes the student's portrait is painted.
We witness his awkward horsemanship, his portmanteau
falling to the ground as he hastily dismounts, his Walloon

collar all awry, to clasp his idol's crippled hand. The whole is a vivid "snapshot" which can never leave the reader's memory. But this trifling episode, so comic and so human, is preparatory to the author's farewell to the world: *"Adiós, gracias, adiós, donaires: adiós, regocijados amigos, que yo me voy muriendo y deseando veros presto contentos en la otra vida."* In both Dedication and Prologue there is the same gallantry, cheerfulness, and sweetness found throughout his other writings. The dying Sir Walter Scott requested Lockhart to read aloud these passages; for he knew that in all literature there is no finer example than this of a brave man meeting death with a smile.

BIBLIOGRAPHY

SCHEVILL, R. *Cervantes.* ("Master Spirits of Literature.") New York, 1919. As many new biographical data have come to light in the last two decades, the earlier studies on Cervantes are obsolete. Mr. Schevill's book is abreast of the new discoveries up to date of publication.

FITZMAURICE-KELLY, J. *Miguel de Cervantes Saavedra: A Memoir.* Oxford, 1913.

"Obras completas de Miguel de Cervantes Saavedra," ed. R. SCHEVILL and A. BONILLA Y SAN MARTÍN. Madrid, 1914–41. This series replaced the old edition of Rosell and provides the best text of Cervantes' minor works.

Don Quijote, ed. F. RODRÍGUEZ MARÍN. 6 vols. Madrid, 1916–17. The best and most exhaustive of the modern commentaries, However, the editions and commentaries of Bowle, Pellicer, Clemencín, and Cortejón are of almost equal value. Rodríguez Marín's abridged edition (8 vols.) in the *Clásicos castellanos* series, is the best of the cheaper editions to own, and provides a sufficiently ample commentary.

ICAZA, F. A. DE. *Las novelas ejemplares de Cervantes.* Madrid, 1915·

BOURLAND, CAROLINE B. *The Short Story in Spain in the Seventeenth Century*. Northampton, 1927.

RÍUS, L. *Bibliografía crítica de las obras de Miguel de Cervantes Saavedra*. 3 vols. Madrid, 1895–1904.

FORD, J. D. M., and LANSING, RUTH. *Cervantes: A Tentative Bibliography*. Cambridge, Mass., 1931.

GRISMER, R. L. *Cervantes: A Bibliography*. New York, 1946.

CASTRO, A. *El pensamiento de Cervantes*. Madrid, 1925. A fundamental study. Indispensable.

ENTWISTLE, WM. J. *Cervantes*. Oxford, 1940.

BELL, A. F. G. *Cervantes*. Norman, Okla., 1947.

HAZARD, P. *Don Quichotte de Cervantes: Étude et analyse*. Paris, 1931.

HATZFELD, H. *"Don Quijote" als Wortkunstwerk*. Leipzig, 1927.

SAVJ-LÓPEZ, P. *Cervantes*, trans. A. G. SOLALINDE. Madrid, 1917.

MADARIAGA, S. DE. *Guía del lector del Quijote*. Madrid, 1926.

English translations of *Don Quixote* since about 1612 (Thomas Skelton) are too numerous to list. Among the more recent are those of Samuel Putnam, J. M. Cohen, and Walter Starkie (abridged).

CHAPTER XVI

Lope de Vega and His Dramatic School

Lope Félix de Vega Carpio—Biography—His non-dramatic writings—*El arte nuevo de hacer comedias*—Types of plays—The corrales—How plays were staged—The players—The plays and their transmission—Lope's fecundity—His dramatic achievement—Gabriel Téllez (Tirso de Molina)—The Don Juan Tenorio legend—Mira de Amescua—Guillén de Castro—Ruiz de Alarcón—The comedy of character—Vélez de Guevara—Jiménez de Enciso—Pérez de Montalbán—Rojas Zorilla—Moreto.

Lope Félix de Vega Carpio (1562–1635), after Cervantes the greatest literary figure of the Golden Age, essayed every genre. His ambitious epics and novels, on which he supposed his fame would rest, are now forgotten. He lives as a writer of short lyrics and dramas. Like Shakespeare, he undervalued his plays. They were potboilers, and his attitude toward them was almost contemptuous. He seems to have taken pride in their number and the ease with which he turned them out, but did not consider them artistic. Lope was a genius of the first order who never achieved the best of which he was capable. He falls short of the highest attainment, but remains a unique and stupendous figure.

Biography.—Lope's life was one long scandal, and will be recounted only briefly. Born in humble circumstances and early orphaned, his education was desultory. But he picked up some Latin, various social accomplish-

ments, such as fencing, dancing, singing, and a knowledge
of Italian, all of which stood him in good stead. There
is nothing remarkable in Montalbán's statement that
Lope composed verse before he could write. His precoc-
ity won him recognition while still in his "teens." Various
patrons were glad to aid so promising a youth. Many of
his early experiences, some distinctly unedifying, are
contained in *La Dorotea*, a dialogued novel in imitation of
Celestina. His earliest play, *El verdadero amante*, preserved
in revised form, was written at the age of twelve. *Los
hechos de Garcilaso de la Vega y moro Tarfe* is the one boy-
ish production which has survived without change. It
is the only one of his plays divided into four acts. Lope
becomes an active purveyor of plays a few years previous
to 1587, when we find him in difficulties with the manager
Jerónimo Velázquez, whose family he had savagely lam-
pooned. Velázquez's daughter, Elena, was one of Lope's
early flames, the Filis who figures in much amatory verse.
For satirizing this family Lope was deservedly sentenced
to two years of banishment from Castile and eight from
Madrid. We find him next a prominent figure in the Valencian circle of dramatic poets. Then comes a proxy marriage, followed by an elopement with Isabel de Urbina, a
lady of good family. Lope is thought to have returned
to Madrid in disguise during this affair, which brought
upon him additional suits from the lady's family. The
poet soon parted from his bride to embark with the "Invincible Armada," when it sailed forth from Lisbon to
conquer England, 1588. In the intervals of fighting he
worked on *La hermosura de Angélica* the epic in which he
sought to rival Ariosto. Lope's galley, the San Juan, was
one of the few to survive the disaster. The poet disem-

barked in La Coruña and soon after accepted the patronage of the Duque de Alba. He resided at Alba de Tormes
in the capacity of entertainer of the Alba family just as
Encina had done under a previous duke. There, in
1595, his young wife, Isabel, died. She figures as Belisa
in many of Lope's writings. The poet never ceased to
cherish the endearing whimsicalities of this child-wife.
Las bizarrías de Belisa was written in 1634 shortly before
his death. We prefer to linger upon this early romance
rather than to relate his marriage of convenience with a
butcher's daughter and the amours with Lucinda, Amari-
lis, and the rest. When free to return to Madrid, Lope
bought a house there and settled down to feverish literary
productivity. The drama was the only lucrative form of
literature, and to secure a livelihood in those days of short
"runs" ceaseless productivity was necessary. Hence that
astounding prolificness which won for Lope the record of
the world's most voluminous writer and led Cervantes
to dub him *"el monstruo de la naturaleza."* Late in life
Lope took priestly orders without ceasing to write for the
stage or otherwise mending his ways. His most attractive
side appears in his love for flowers and children. The last
years were embittered by the elopement of a daughter
and the death of a favorite son. His funeral was a vast
public affair. All classes, high and low, seemed delighted
to pay honor to his genius.

   His non-dramatic works.—Passing mention has already been accorded several of Lope's most ambitious
performances. In addition one should cite *La Dragontea,*
1598, a vitriolic, patriotic epic directed against his old
foe, Sir Francis Drake, who to Spaniards of the time was
a "dragon" both in name and deed. *Los pastores de Belén,*

1612, still pleases by its idyllic charm. *La corona trágica*,
1627, takes Mary Stuart for a heroine and paints an un-
flattering portrait of Elizabeth. This is a literary curiosity rather than a work of art. Lope is at his best in the
genre of the verse epistle, the ballad, and all forms of lyric
verse. He will always rank as one of the greatest of Spanish lyricists. These short pieces possess the charm of
spontaneity and simple directness. It is true that Lope
is not always free from desire to impress by display of ingenuity. *Discreteo* is not wanting in his work. But this was
a universal fault of the age. As compared with the generation which followed, Lope shines by his comparative
lack of affectation. The sonnet would seem, of all literary
forms, that least adapted to an improviser; but in his best
sonnets Lope is impeccable. It may serve as a useful corrective to the harsh comments on Lope's private character made above to quote Longfellow's rendering of a
sonnet, the sincere piety of which cannot be questioned:

TOMORROW

Lord, what am I, that with unceasing care
Thou did'st seek after me, that Thou did'st wait
Wet with unhealthy dews before my gate
And pass the gloomy nights of winter there?
Oh, strange delusion, that I did not greet
Thy blest approach, and oh, to heaven how lost
If my ingratitude's unkindly frost
Has chilled the bleeding wounds upon Thy feet.
How oft my guardian angel gently cried,
"Soul, from thy casement look, and thou shalt see
How He persists to knock and wait for thee!"
And oh, how often to that Voice of sorrow,
"Tomorrow we will open," I replied,
And when the morrow came I answered still "Tomorrow."

"*El arte nuevo de hacer comedias en este tiempo.*"—
This critical document by Lope appeared in 1609. It is
a poetical composition, written for recitation before a
literary academy. The nature of the audience addressed
explains the author's lack of courage; for Lope piqued
himself on being held an educated man. Juan de la Cueva
previously and Tirso de Molina subsequently attacked
the theories of the ancients, holding that new times demand novel methods. Lope in hangdog and cynical fashion admits himself a money-making sinner. The *vulgo*
pay him, and the rabble are incapable of appreciating
art. Fools must be addressed in the language of folly.
El arte nuevo is a plea of confession and avoidance.

Nevertheless, the new style of play (*comedia nueva*),
is not without its rules. Tragedy and comedy are mingled, for the mob delights in variety. The variety of
nature is infinite, and such a mingling of the genres is an
imitation of nature. Of the unities, that of action alone
should be preserved. Lapses of time, however, should be
made to take place between acts. Lope insists upon appropriateness of diction. The clown should talk like a
clown, ladies like ladies; kings should discourse in grave
style. Rhetoric should not be wasted upon simple scenes
of domestic life. Verisimilitude is insisted upon.

Lope derives his ideas of imitation, verisimilitude, and
appropriateness of dialogue from the Italians who then
held the lead in critical theory. Robortello was his most
immediate source. But he has original, purely Spanish
ideas to offer. The number of acts should be three. The
first act should contain exposition. Then the plot should
be thickened until the middle of the third act, where, and
not before, the dénouement should begin. Lope insists

upon complexity of intrigue and the necessity of holding the audience in suspense, lest seats be vacated and disorder begin. He further recommends a number of subtle devices, such as "deceiving with the truth" and "equivocal speech." Metrical variety is urged. *Décimas* are good for complaints, sonnets for soliloquies, octaves and tercets for grave thoughts, quatrains (*redondillas*) for love passages, ballad meter for ordinary narration. (There is no mention of other common dramatic meters such as the *lira, silva,* and *versos sueltos.*) Honor and virtuous actions are instanced as themes which never fail to stir the heart. This insistence on the point of honor is Lope's principal critical contribution. In an age of dueling when the demands of honor frequently resulted in tragedy, honor came to be almost as important a dramatic motive as fate had been in Grecian tragedy. An act should be *cuatro pliegos* in length. In practice each averaged about one thousand lines of verse. But an act must not end anyhow. Both acts and scenes should end with maxims or elegant verses. An effective "curtain" was a part of Lope's technique.

The modern reaction toward all this is that the neglect of the unities of time and place was not the unpardonable offense which Lope thought it. Admirers of Shakespeare may even pardon the mingling of tragedy and comedy. Lope's great mistake was in subordinating character to mere plot, making the *comedia* so largely a drama of intrigue. He possessed the power of creating character, and here and there has drawn living figures; but such results were subordinate to his real intent and largely accidental. Hence the lack of universality of Lope and his school as compared to masters like Shake-

speare and Molière. Juan Ruiz de Alarcón is the one outstanding exception. Insistence upon elaborateness of intrigue, mere ingenuity, and pomposity of rhetoric are the
cardinal vices of the *comedia nueva*.

Types of plays.—The types of plays developed by
Lope and continued by his school are varied. First, and
most interesting to us, are the *comedias históricas*, or
heroicas, springing from the chronicles and ballads, and
celebrating national themes and events. Lope was king
of this genre, though Tirso once or twice equaled his best.
Here the gravity, valor, and courtesy of the Castilian
appear at their best. The gallery of ancient worthies of a
race which Lope has painted in these plays is unique in
literature except for Livy's portraits of the heroic ancestors of Rome. More sensational plays of this sort were
termed *comedias de teatro*, or *ruido*. Cape and sword
plays, *comedias de capa y espada*, deal with the upper
bourgeoisie or lower aristocracy. They are so called from
the typical street costume of these classes. They are not
realistic, but highly romanticized. The plot is most complex, often difficult to follow: duels, disguises, mistaken
identities, cross-purposes, and mutual misunderstand-
ings. Love and honor are the dramatic motives. They
end happily with the marriages of two or three pairs of
lovers. Calderón excelled in this type of play. More rhetorical and poetic were the *comedias palaciegas*, "palace
plays," so called because the principal characters are
reigning monarchs or high aristocratic personages. These
plays, too, are intricate as to plot and deal with love and
honor. The scene is some remote region, Bohemia, Po-
land, Russia, or an Italian court. The nearest approach
to a comedy of manners is the *comedia de carácter*, de-

veloped principally by Ruiz de Alarcón. A play of this sort portrays some social type, the liar, the slanderer, etc. All the other characters are conventional. When the social type is caricatured, the play is termed a *comedia de figurón*. There were besides *comedias pastoriles, comedias picarescas, comedias de santos,* dealing with the lives of saints, and later *comedias mitológicas,* the first operettas, based on some theme of classic mythology. These are libretti with the music lost. A wholly Spanish form is the *auto sacramental,* a descendant of the medieval mystery play, treating the sacrament of the Eucharist in allegorical fashion. The *autos* were acted in the open air on floats and especially constructed platforms. The story could be anything, but somewhere the miracle of transubstantiation must be dragged in, for *autos* were acted only during the Corpus Christi festivities. The characters were mostly allegorical personages. The *autos* contain magnificent lyric passages, but are for the most part an odd mixture of the sublime with the naïvely ridiculous. Calderón was the greatest writer of *autos.*

Plays usually began with a prologue, or *loa,* so called because it praised somebody or something. In an endeavor to be wittily ingenious, *loas* were written in praise of flies, fleas, a given day of the week, or what-not. After the *loa* came the first act of the play, then an *entremés* (the short farce already characterized), then the second act, next some minor form such as the *baile,* or the *baile cantado,* next the third act, the whole ending with the *fin de fiesta,* a spirited revel of song and dance.

The corrales.—The first permanent theatrical establishments were *corrales,* "courtyards." The earliest recorded for Madrid is the *Corral de la Pacheca,* situated in the *Calle del Príncipe*. Performances were given there as early as 1568. Later this became the *Corral del Príncipe*, much later the *Teatro del Príncipe*, and the nationally subventioned *Teatro Español*, standing on the same site, has the oldest uninterrupted tradition of all playhouses in the world. The rival establishment, the *Corral de la Cruz*, dated from 1579. For more than two centuries and a half these were, with few intermissions, the only playhouses in Madrid. Other dramatic centers, such as Valencia and Seville, had similar *corrales* and *coliseos*. The stage was set up at one end of the yard. The aristocracy looked down upon it, seated at the windows of surrounding houses. In front of the stage, and laterally around the buildings, were benches. At the opposite end, directly facing the stage, was a cage termed the *cazuela*, "stewpan," in which women of the lower class were cooped. In front of this was standing-room for the groundlings, *mosqueteros*, always a turbulent element.

Stage devices.—There was no drop-curtain. A momentary vacation of the stage was a convention indicating change of scene, though sometimes the shift was indicated in dialogue. At the rear was a raised partition, *lo alto del teatro*, which served to represent a house, a wall, a mountain, etc. In this was sunk an alcove, covered by a curtain, which when drawn revealed a tableau. The stage could be divided at will by sheets, *paños*. Forests were represented by painted canvas or small trees set on the stage. There was little scenery and much appeal to the imagination. Some of Cervantes' plays demand elaborateness of stage machinery. This may be one reason why managers thought him impractical, for little use was made of stage machinery until the second third of the seventeenth century, when Italian stage-carpenters introduced many novelties. Lope thought this appeal to the eye a sign of degeneracy. Like Shakespeare's, his appeal was to the ear. Costumes, on the other hand, were elaborate. Leading actresses or their admirers squandered small fortunes on dress. There was little sense of local color. Roman worthies dressed like Spaniards of the time, but Moorish characters wore the distinctive garb of the race. Plays were acted in daylight, beginning at 2:00 or 3:00 P.M. Hence effects of light and darkness were wanting. An awning, stretched over the adjoining roofs, protected the audience from sun and rain. During Lent and periods of royal mourning, and while the Corpus Christi *autos* were being played, there were cessations of public performances in the *corrales*. Actors were also at the beck and call of the king, who frequently had plays acted at court.

The players.—Not long after the time of Lope de Rueda players swarmed on every highway and byway of Spain. In 1600 an attempt was made to regulate them. Eight royal troupes, *compañías de título*, were organized; but many aggregations of lesser fame supplied the wants of smaller cities. Under Philip II there was much opposition to play-acting. Churchly bigots were always endeavoring to suppress the drama entirely. But the two succeeding pleasure-loving Philips were the actors' friends, and the church was bribed by allowing certain religious charities to share in the proceeds. Actors were looked down upon as a disreputable crew, yet such was the passion for the stage at this time that many youths of education and birth adopted the profession. Female parts were originally acted by boys. Actresses appear on the boards toward the end of the sixteenth century—earlier than was the case in England and France. A typical company was composed of three pairs of lovers (three *galanes* and as many *damas*), a *barba* who played old-man parts, a *gracioso* and a *graciosa*. The *gracioso*, "clown," was first introduced by Lope, he tells us, in *La Francesilla*, a play certainly written previous to 1602, and probably about a decade before that date. Henceforth no play was written without a comic part. There were utility players intrusted with minor parts. This organization discouraged versatility. When new plays had to be produced every few days, it was necessary that actors should be playing almost identical parts. The lines varied; the character remained the same. This system hampered authors, and explains why the Spanish drama lacks plays containing a large variety of interesting characters. With insufficient time for preparation, many plays were badly performed. The prompter was a busy man. The dreaded *silbo*, "whistle," of the "musketeers" served a useful purpose in making actors careful. The audience, flatteringly called "illustrious senate," was constantly implored to excuse the errors of the reciters. Everything leads to the conclusion that the acting of plays at this time was as much a matter of improvisation as their writing.

The plays and their transmission.—Of all the thousands of *comedias* preserved only a few have reached posterity in authentic form. Only when the author's manuscript original is preserved are we sure of the real text. Even these are carelessly scrawled and wholly devoid of punctuation and a rational system of capitalization. Copies of the original, made for the actors, were still more careless, with additions, suppressions, and introduction

of gross errors. Then one of these copies would be printed
as a *suelta*, "broadside." *Sueltas* seem to have been printed with almost no proofreading, and are proverbially
worse than the manuscript copies. There were often pirated editions taken down by shorthand or from memory
In self-defense leading dramatists began the publication
of authorized play-collections. The number of these, extending to many volumes and frequently reprinted, shows
that a large play-reading public had sprung up. Though
better than the *sueltas*, these editions were far from carefully edited. Almost invariably there was shortening
and change of text. Most Spanish plays, therefore, in
their present form, are as truly communal as the ballads,
if by communal we mean that a series of revisers have
participated in the work. The Spanish drama is the most
democratic of all dramas. Like no other it is the expression of a race.

Lope's fecundity.—It has been necessary to digress in
order to indicate the conditions which determined Lope's
work. Even today rapid production is necessary if a
Spanish man of letters may hope to live by his pen. Lope
was harassed by weekly, almost daily, demands for new
plays. He was equal to the task. No other writer in the
world's history even remotely approaches his record for
productivity. Of the other great producers, Hans Sachs
wrote in a crude doggerel as compared to Lope's graceful
verse; Voltaire wrote mainly in prose; Alexandre Dumas
directed a bureau of literary hacks. But with the exception of a few plays written in partnership (*de consuno*),
Lope did his own writing, which was mostly in verse.
The novel, *El peregrino en su patria*, 1604, lists over 200
plays then written; the 1618 edition of the same work con-

tains a much extended catalogue. These two lists are invaluable for dating approximately his early plays. In the *Arte nuevo*, 1609, he mentions 483 comedies. Henceforth he reckons, suspiciously, in round numbers. In 1618 he counts 800 (Parte XI); in 1620, 900 (Parte XIV); in 1625, 1,070 (Parte XX); in 1632, 1,500 (*Égloga a Claudio* and *Moza de cántaro*). Montalbán, his biographer, writing in 1636, foots up a grand total of 1,800 *comedias*, 400 *autos*, without counting the lesser dramatic forms. Neither Lope nor Montalbán is a reliable witness. One may safely discount the final figures by 50 per cent without ceasing to be amazed. Of these plays there exist nearly 400 of unquestioned authenticity. This would mean a total of about 1,500,000 lines of verse. And this amazing output was almost equaled by his non-dramatic writings, only a few of which have been mentioned. We may well believe his statement that he wrote many plays in the space of twenty-four hours; for Lope could write verse almost as fast as a business man can dictate letters to a stenographer. And each of these plays has its complicated plot, a rich variety of metrical forms, its brilliant situations, its clownish humor. Montalbán relates how he and Lope were writing a play in partnership. The poets, each having written one act, were to divide the remaining one. Montalbán arose at two in the morning and finished his task at eleven. Descending to the garden, he found Lope watering a frozen orange tree. Lope had arisen at five, completed his half of the act, written fifty tercets of lyric verse, breakfasted on a rasher of bacon, and had been engaged for an hour or more in gardening. Lope de Vega is the greatest exemplar of Spanish copiousness and facility. He is the greatest improviser of all time.

His dramatic achievement.—During Lope's lifetime there arose a proverb, "*Es de Lope*," to signify superlative excellence. Does posterity accept the same view? No one of his plays is wholly bad, no one a finished masterpiece. All show signs of haste. Repetition of situations, incidents, jokes, and rhetorical figures inevitably occurs. One easily sees how deliberate care could have improved this or that situation or play. Lope fails to extract the utmost dramatic effect from his most brilliant conceptions. His is not a drama of character or ideas. He shines through native ability, and belies the saying that genius is an infinite capacity for taking pains. First must be noticed his fertility in devising dramatic situations. He has anticipated nearly every dramatic situation since employed. He took his plots from every conceivable source: chronicles, ballads, the Bible, lives of the saints, novels, especially the Italian *novelle*, etc. Often he invents. He did not plagiarize the plays of rival authors. His own dramatic output became a huge quarry from which playwrights of every nation drew; but for Lope it was easier to create than to revamp. Though character delineation was incidental to plot, he did at times draw charming portraits. He was especially successful with his female types. Every one of his plays contains lyric passages which charm by their facile simplicity. In short, he was a wide-ranging, untamed genius, who, in spite of many faults, affords aesthetic delight by the many incidental beauties in his work. Historically, he is important as the dramatist who found the formula which prevailed in Spain until the neo-Classic reaction of the eighteenth century.

It is difficult to single out for special mention a few

plays where so much is admirable. Each of the lesser dramatists has his outstanding plays. Lope produced scores which may be said to illustrate his best manner. Characteristic of his historical plays may be mentioned *El mejor alcalde el rey; Las paces de los reyes y judía de Toledo; El rey Don Pedro en Madrid, o el infanzón de Illescas; Peribáñez y el comendador de Ocaña; Los Tellos de Meneses; El caballero de Olmedo; Porfiar hasta morir; Fuente Ovejuna.* Practically all agree now that the former attribution to Lope of *La estrella de Sevilla* is extremely doubtful. These breathe the very spirit of old Spain. They show a democratic feeling lurking beneath a political autocracy, and are distinguished by a strong sense of human dignity. The following are typical light comedies: *El acero de Madrid, La moza de cántaro, Amar sin saber a quién, El perro del hortelano, La hermosa fea, Milagros del desprecio, La dama boba, Las bizarrías de Belisa, El anzuelo de Fenisa.* These will give the reader an idea of Lope at his best, but a far more extensive course of reading is necessary before one can appreciate his incomparable variety and richness.

Gabriel Téllez (Tirso de Molina) (1583?–1648).—It is commonly stated that, whereas the English drama possesses one star of the first magnitude, Shakespeare, the Spanish drama has four: Lope de Vega, Gabriel Téllez, Ruiz de Alarcón, and Calderón de la Barca. We turn now to the second of this galaxy who is more commonly known by his pseudonym, Tirso de Molina. Tirso was born in Madrid, educated at Alcalá de Henares, and professed in the Order of Mercy in 1601. He is often called "El Mercenario." His life was uneventful. He traveled much, even to the West Indies, on errands connected with his order, was historiographer of his brotherhood, and superior of several of its most important establishments. His worldly contacts were many, and his association with the stage surprising. It was a government agency, not his religious order, that stopped him from writing plays after 1625, because they caused *"escándalos."* Of more than four hundred plays he presumably wrote, eighty-six survive.

Non-dramatic works.—Besides plays he wrote two long books of miscellaneous content: *Los cigarrales de Toledo,* 1624, and *Deleitar aprovechando,* 1635. In these he imitates Boccaccio and Cervantes' *Novelas ejemplares.* A group of aristocrats exchange visits in their respective villas, *cigarrales,* each contributing to the entertainment. They tell stories, recite verse, act plays, and indulge in philosophical disquisition. Tirso excels as a writer of the short story. Several of his best plays were first edited in these collections. The first-named work is notable for a criticism of the "new comedy," in which, with greater boldness than Lope de Vega, he justifies the mingling of the tragic with the comic and the disregard for the unities of time and place. These restrictions he regards as hampering and leading to absurdities which sin against verisimilitude. Tirso anticipates many of the arguments later used by the Romantic school, notably those of Hugo in the Preface to *Cromwell.*

Tirso's plays.—Tirso excelled in the palace play, *comedia palaciega.* Like Lope, his feminine characters are best. His men are often weaklings, his women virile. His *graciosos* are the wittiest of any, for Tirso possessed much comic force. Priest though he was, he sometimes showed a fondness for the risqué situation. He came nearer to being immoral than any other dramatist of his time.

One suspects that being a priest he was less hampered by the censor. Humanity, wit, and lightness of touch are the dominant traits of his work. Of his lighter comedies, *Marta la piadosa* (one of the first hypocrite plays), *El vergonzoso en palacio*, *Palabras y plumas*, *La villana de Vallecas*, and *Don Gil de las calzas verdes* never fail to please. In *Los amantes de Teruel*, Tirso follows Artieda in staging the tragic loves of Diego de Marsilla and Isabel de Segura, who, thwarted in love, die in each other's arms. This famous legend seems to be one of Boccaccio's tales which has passed into folklore and become localized in the Aragonese village of Teruel. *La prudencia en la mujer* is a historical play rivaling Lope's best. Some even consider it the finest historical play in Spanish. Its heroine is the dowager queen, Doña María, mother of the child-king, Fernando IV. By tact and womanly virtues Doña María thwarts the designs of conspiring vassals and maintains her son on his tottering throne. She is a character worthy of Shakespeare. The finest of all Spanish religious plays, *El condenado por desconfiado*, is commonly assigned to Tirso, though the attribution has been questioned. Of the two chief characters, one is a hermit famous for good works, though weak of faith, the other a criminal strong in faith. The former is damned, the latter saved. The theme is therefore justification through faith. Whether or not one favor such a tenet, the power of this drama cannot be denied. It is one of the first "thesis plays" of modern times.

The Don Juan Tenorio legend.—*El burlador de Sevilla y convidado de piedra* is the first dramatization of the famous Don Juan legend. Don Juan Tenorio is the most universal fictional type, after Don Quijote, which Spain

has given the world. Tirso's immediate sources are unknown. They were probably ballads and folklore. There
are existing ballads older than this play dealing with parts
of the legend. Tirso's version is, in part, as follows: Don
Juan Tenorio is a dissolute young noble, a rake, a reckless
gambler, and, worst of all in the eyes of the Spaniards of
the time, a cynical blasphemer. One of his many victims
is the daughter of Don Gonzalo de Ulloa, comendador de
Calatrava. The commander challenges Don Juan to a
duel and falls mortally wounded. Later Don Juan enters
the church where the commander lies buried, pulls the
beard of his stone effigy, and invites the statue to dinner.
At midnight Don Juan and his friends are making merry.
There is a knock at the door. The statue enters. Don
Juan, not in the least abashed, entertains his guest with
perfect courtesy. At the end of the supper the statue de-
parts, offering return hospitalities at his tomb the following midnight. Juan's friends seek to dissuade him. All
know that if he accepts he is doomed. But Don Juan is
undaunted as ever. He visits the church, flames emerge
from the tomb, the statue strangles him, thus restoring
the family honor, and devils carry off the profligate's soul
to hell.

The Spanish conception of Don Juan.—Tirso's conception of Don Juan is nobler than that of most of his
imitators. Don Juan is commonly taken to be a symbol
of libertinism and nothing more. With Tirso his rakish-
ness is incidental, though figuring largely in the plot.
What interests is the superhuman bravery of this titanic
character. He is not merely gallant in all those human
situations where a gentleman was obliged to be brave,
but he is unafraid in the presence of the supernatural.

He defies alike the powers of darkness and of light. He is a weak mortal measuring swords with God. Such blasphemy resulted in the loss of his soul, but his superhuman bravery redeemed him in popular esteem. Don Juan is the embodiment of the many vices and the one redeeming virtue of the typical nobleman of the sixteenth and seventeenth centuries. He lacks that hypocrisy which makes Molière's Don Juan doubly odious.

Don Juan's world-vogue.—Tirso's play was soon imitated by a host of Italian dramatic writers, who were in turn copied by French authors. By such roundabout means the story reached Molière, who, in the *Festin de pierre*, produced one of his masterpieces. Mozart, Byron, Mérimée, Zorrilla, Bernard Shaw, and Rostand are only a few of the others who have treated the Don Juan subject tragically, humorously, cynically, paradoxically, in plays, operas, novels, and verse. Bibliographers have listed by the thousands the works in which this theme occurs. Few authors had any direct knowledge of Tirso's play, from which the whole movement springs, and which in nobility of concept surpasses all other versions.

Antonio Mira de Amescua (1577?–1644) was a literary priest, a fertile and original poet, inclined toward the fantastic. His most celebrated play is *El esclavo del demonio*, in which the hero makes a compact with the devil. It interests through its resemblance to the Faust legend and its connection with Calderón's *Mágico prodigioso*.

Guillén de Castro (1569–1631) was a soldier turned man of letters. His aristocratic connections gave him early advantages which he forfeited because of a temperamental disposition. He wrote good dramas. As friend and disciple of Lope de Vega, he wrote numerous successful plays in the master's manner. His is a famous name in literature, because he was first to dramatize the Cid legend. The *Mocedades del Cid* deals with the early portion of Rodrigo's story; the *Hazañas del Cid* takes up the tale of the siege of Zamora. Castro's sources are the ballads in the *Romancero del Cid*. His material was known to all; there was no freedom to change it materially. But he did develop the famous conflict between love and honor waged in Jimena's heart. As everybody knows, Castro's *Mocedades* inspired the first great French Classic tragedy, Corneille's *Cid*. Corneille puts the material into the strait jacket of the unities, lops off extraneous episodes, substitutes taste for picturesque crudity. But many of his most telling lines are lifted direct from his source. Castro, if unable to produce a masterpiece, at least inspired one.

Juan Ruiz de Alarcón (1580 ?–1639) is the most modern in spirit of any dramatist of his time. He is also the least prolific. His plays barely exceed twenty. Alarcón was a Mexican who studied at Salamanca and held high business and administrative positions. Physically he was ill favored and a hunchback. This business man who wrote plays for amusement rather than for gain became unpopular with his rivals, who were almost unanimous in their hatred, and mocked his deformities brutally. These attacks led Alarcón to defend himself, and out of this self-defense came the development of the thesis play. Alarcón had a noble nature. The best of his plays aim higher than at mere entertainment. They drive home moral truths.

Alarcón's moral comedies.—From the standpoint of seriousness of purpose, the greatest of all Spanish plays are

Las paredes oyen and *La verdad sospechosa*. The first is an attack upon slander. Don Mendo, a rich and handsome courtier, is unable to speak good of anybody. Don Juan, ugly but a true gentleman, is Mendo's rival for the hand of Doña Ana. All goes well with Mendo until his lady, suspecting his loyalty, lays a trap for him. She and two others to whom he has been attentive hide behind a screen, where they hear themselves traduced by Mendo and defended by Juan. Mendo later makes three successive proposals and is as many times confounded by the statement that walls have ears. The second of these plays makes odious the vice of lying. The protagonist is a young aristocrat who cultivates lying as a fine art. How the first lie necessitates a long series of untruths and leads to the liar's undoing is skilfully unfolded as the plot develops. *Mudarse por mejorarse* attacks inconstancy in love. *La prueba de las promesas* assails ingratitude. Alarcón is the greatest dramatic moralist Spain has ever produced.

Alarcón's formula.—His method was to introduce into a play a character type and through this type to develop a moral thesis. This formula he passed on to France. Just as Castro inspired the first great French tragedy, Alarcón suggested the first important French comedy, Corneille's *Le menteur*. This piece is an adaptation, or rather a free translation, of *La verdad sospechosa*. Now, Molière was familiar with Alarcón's work and besides that based his comedy on *Le menteur*. Hence the direct and indirect influence of Alarcón upon Molière was very great. Molière, too, selects a character type, the misanthrope, the miser, the hypocrite, and makes some vice ridiculous and odious. And yet some critics still assert that the thesis play originated in the nineteenth century with Alexandre Dumas fils. What the development of comedy the world over owes to Ruiz de Alarcón is only beginning to be appreciated.

Luis Vélez de Guevara (1570–1644) was an Andalusian lawyer whose merry disposition caused Cervantes to nickname him *"quitapesares."* We have already considered him as author of the novel *El diablo cojuelo*. His specialty as a dramatist was the sensational *teatro de ruido*. To him is due the best dramatic version of the Guzmán el Bueno story, *Más pesa el rey que la sangre*. Guzmán, governor of the city of Tarifa, besieged by the Moors, sends his son on a foray without the walls. The son is captured and a message sent to the father that only immediate surrender will save the captive's life. The answer of the Spanish Brutus is to throw his dagger over the wall to the captors. Loyalty weighs more than paternal love. Guevara's second famous play is *Reinar después de morir*, the best of a long series of plays on the Inés de Castro legend. Inés was a Spanish *infanta* married to a Portuguese prince. She was murdered by a band of conspirators. Later, according to the story, when the prince came to the throne, his first act was to exhume the body of his loved bride and crown her queen in death.

Diego Jiménez de Enciso (1585–1624) may indeed have been a minor dramatist, but he at least deserves mention. He is noteworthy as the first to write a play on the tragic legend of Philip II's son, Don Carlos. The mysterious death of this prince, after altercations with his father, had caused gossip. Carlos was supposed to have Protestant leanings, to have conspired with the revolting Netherlanders, to have conceived a mad passion for his royal stepmother, who had first been intended as his own bride. Research has dispelled all these picturesque imaginings. Carlos was a weakling and died a natural death. Philip was not a murderer. But in *El príncipe Don Carlos* Enciso follows rumor. He achieved an effective play, since eclipsed by the masterpieces of Alfieri, Schiller, and Núñez de Arce, based on the same theme.

Juan Pérez de Montalbán (1602–38), Lope's disciple and first biographer, can be accorded only passing mention. He lost his mind and died young, but not before achieving nearly one hundred plays. His outstanding piece is *Los amantes de Teruel*, a theme, which we have seen, was also treated by Tirso.

Francisco de Rojas Zorrilla (1607–48) wrote tragedies and a new form of play, *la comedia de figurón*, in which an eccentric is the chief personage. His style wavers between simplicity and the affectations of *culteranismo* which were now beginning to invade the stage. *Del rey abajo, ninguno, o García de Castañar*, usually attributed to Rojas, is one of the greatest of Spanish plays. García is living in retirement with his young wife, Blanca. He is under a cloud through no fault of his own. The king resolves to visit incognito this vassal of whom he has received good reports. A friend forewarns García of the impending visit, stating that the king may be recognized as the wearer of a red ribbon. The king, however, exchanges favors with Don Mendo. García entertains the royal party in his forest lodge. Mendo falls in love with Blanca. Later García surprises him forcing an entrance into the house. Mendo still wears the red ribbon and is mistaken for the king. In a scene of singular dignity García rebukes the intruder for his act, professes loyalty,

and allows him to depart. Mendo, unaware of the true
state of things, imagines García a coward. There is much
dramatic force in this double misunderstanding. Later
García goes to court, discovers his mistake, kills Mendo
in a duel, and is restored to royal favor. The king can do
no wrong. No act of his should shake a subject's loyalty.
But the slightest infringement of a gentleman's personal
dignity, coming from another, must be washed out in
blood. Such was the code of honor.

Agustín Moreto y Cabaña (1618–69) was the least original inventor of plots of any Spanish dramatist. As the
drama developed, it was less easy to find good subjects.
There came a time of re-working old plays. All the later
playwrights did this more or less, but Moreto is the chief
exponent of the tendency. This is not to say that he was
wholly lacking in originality. He possessed a happy
knack of improving upon his sources. Many a half-
worked idea of Lope's Moreto took over and made complete. He was a good theatrical carpenter, and made up in
improved technique for his deficiencies as a creator.
His style is simple, his verse facile. Next to Ruiz de
Alarcón he is the best writer of comedies of character,
and *de figurón*. His *Lindo Don Diego* is an irresistible portrait of a fop. He insists less than Alarcón on the lesson
to be taught, but the moral is not lacking. His masterpiece is *El desdén con el desdén*. This is a patchwork of
three or four of Lope's plays, but the seams are not visible. A haughty beauty scorns the suits of several illustrious aspirants, only to fall to the wiles of a victim who
treats her to a liberal dose of her own medicine. The
sparkling vivacity, the dainty grace, with which this
hackneyed theme is worked out have made this play a

favorite. It is today as living a work as when first written. Molière sought to imitate it in his *Princesse d'Élide*, and scored a failure. An imitator himself, Moreto sometimes achieved results which were inimitable.

BIBLIOGRAPHY

[For the histories of the drama by Creizenach and Schack, see bibliography to chap. iii.]

LA BARRERA Y LEIRADO, C. DE. *Catálogo bibliográfico y biográfico del teatro antiguo español, desde sus orígenes hasta mediados del siglo XVIII*. Madrid, 1860. The invaluable bibliographic guide for the student of the Spanish drama. Many of the biographies of the lesser writers have not since been improved upon.

RENNERT, H. A., and CASTRO, A. *Vida de Lope de Vega*. Madrid, 1919.

VOSSLER, KARL. *Lope de Vega und sein Zeitalter*. Munich, 1932. Trans. as *Lope de Vega y su tiempo*. Madrid, 1940.

MONTESINOS, J. F. *Estudios sobre Lope de Vega*. Mexico, 1940.

LOPE DE VEGA. *Colección de las obras sueltas, assí en prosa como en verso*. 21 vols. Madrid, 1776–79. For Lope's non-dramatic writing.

———. "Arte Nuevo de hacer comedias en este tiempo," ed. A. MOREL-FATIO, *Bulletin hispanique*, III, 364–405. Best text and commentary.

———. *La Dorotéa*, ed. E. MORBY. Berkeley, 1958.

———. *Obras de Lope de Vega publicadas por la Real Academia Española*, ed. M. MENÉNDEZ Y PELAYO. 13 vols. Madrid, 1890–1902. Only dramatic works included. The first volume contains La Barrera's extensive biography of the author. The texts offered are unsatisfactory. The editor's critical studies of each play are admirable.

———. *Obras*. 13 vols. New ed. by E. COTARELO and others for the *Real Academia Española*, Madrid, 1916–30.

———. *Non-dramatic works*, ed. F. CERDÁ Y RICO. 21 vols. Madrid, 1776–79.

———. *Poesías líricas*, ed. J. F. Montesinos. 2 vols. Madrid, 1925–26. (*Clásicos castellanos*, Vols. LXVIII and LXXV.)

SCHEVILL, R. *The Dramatic Art of Lope de Vega*. Berkeley, 1918.

VOSSLER, K. *Lope de Vega y su tiempo*. Madrid, 1932.

RENNERT, H. A. *The Spanish Stage*. New York, 1909.

TÉLLEZ, GABRIEL. "Comedias," *BAE*, Vol. II, and *NBAE*, Vols. IV, IX (Vol. IV contains the best biography, by E. Cotarelo y Mori).

MENÉNDEZ PIDAL, R. (ed.). *El condenado por desconfiado*. Madrid, 1902. Also *Bulletin hispanique*, VI, 38–43.

MOREL-FATIO. "La Prudence chez la femme, drame historique de Tirso de Molina," *Études sur l'Espagne*, III, 27–72. Paris, 1904.

GENDARME DE BÉVOTTE, G. *La Légende de Don Juan*. Paris, 1906; 2 vols. Paris, 1911.

FARINELLI, A. "Don Giovanni," *Giornale storico della letteratura italiana* (1896), pp. 1–77, 254–326.

MIRA DE AMESCUA, A. *BAE*, Vol. XLV.

———. *El esclavo del demonio*, ed. M. A. BUCHANAN. Baltimore, 1905.

CASTRO, GUILLÉN DE. *BAE*, Vol. XLIII.

———. *Première partie des Mocedades del Cid*, ed. E. MÉRIMÉE. Toulouse, 1890.

RUIZ DE ALARCÓN, JUAN. *BAE*, Vol. XX.

FERNÁNDEZ-GUERRA Y ORBE, A. *Don Ruiz de Alarcón*. Madrid, 1871.

HENRÍQUEZ UREÑA, PEDRO. *Don Juan Ruiz de Alarcón*. Havana, 1915.

SCHONS, DOROTHY. "Apuntes y documentos nuevos para la biografía de Juan Ruiz de Alarcón y Mendoza," *Boletín de la Academia de la Historia* (1921).

VÉLEZ DE GUEVARA, L. *BAE*, Vol. XLV.

COTARELO Y MORI, E. "Don Diego Jiménez de Enciso y su teatro," *Boletín de la Real Academia Española*, I, 209–48, 385–415, 510–50.

JIMÉNEZ DE ENCISO, D., *BAE*, Vol. XLV.

———. "Luis Vélez de Guevara y sus obras dramáticas," *Boletín de la Real Academia Española*, III, 621–52; IV, 137–71, 269–308, 414–44.

294

LEVI, E. *Il principe don Carlos nella legenda e nella poesia.* Rome, 1924.

PÉREZ DE MONTALBÁN, J. *BAE*, Vol. XLV.

ROJAS ZORRILLA, F. DE. *BAE*, Vol. LV.

COTARELO Y MORI, E. *Francisco de Rojas Zorrilla, noticias biográficas y bibliográficas.* Madrid, 1911.

MACCURDY, R. R. *Francisco de Rojas Zorrilla and the Tragedy.* Albuquerque, 1958.

MORETO, A. "Comedias escogidas," *BAE*, Vol. XXXIX.

———. *Teatro*, ed. N. ALONSO CORTÉS, *El lindo don Diego* and *El desdén con el desdén, Clásicos castellanos*, Vol. XXXII. Madrid, 1916.

KENNEDY, RUTH LEE. *The Dramatic Art of Moreto.* Philadelphia, 1932.

MARTINENCHE, E. *La Comedia espagnole en France de Hardy à Racine.* Paris, 1900.

———. *Molière et le théâtre espagnol.* Paris, 1906.

HUSZÁR, P. *Corneille et le théâtre espagnol.* Paris, 1903.

MORLEY, S. G., and BRUERTON, C. *The Chronology of Lope de Vega's "comedias."* New York, 1940.

CHAPTER XVII

The Age of
Affectation

Political and literary decline—Literature becomes affected—
Conceptismo—Culteranismo—Reforms misdirected and beneficial
—Luis de Carrillo y Sotomayor—Luis de Argote y Góngora—"The
angel of light"—"The angel of darkness"—Baltasar Gracián—His
works—Francisco Gómez de Quevedo—His Works—Pedro Calderón de la Barca—Characteristics of Calderón's art—His plays—
The autos—Calderón's vogue.

Political and literary decline.—Most of the authors
writing in the early seventeenth century possessed something of the generous spirit of the Renaissance. As the
century progresses a meaner spirit prevails. The reaction
succeeded in stifling intellectual inquiry, and the only
way in which originality could express itself was in affectation of the singular. The degeneracy of art during this
period is exactly parallel with the decline of Spain as
a power. Four rulers, not merely great, but geniuses,
Ferdinand, Isabella, Charles V, and Philip II, had raised
Spain out of feudal anarchy to greatness. There followed
a series of incompetents, Philip III (1598–1621), Philip
IV (1621–55), and Charles II (1655–1700), each worse
than his predecessor. The decline had begun, without
being visible to the nation, under Philip II with the defeat of the "Invincible Armada," 1588. Under Philip III,
Spain began to reap the harvest of bad financial administration, its meddlesome foreign policy, and the banish-

ment of its two most productive classes, the Jews and the Moriscos. In this and the following reigns, government was intrusted to favorites, who ruled corruptly and unwisely. Spanish arms were now seldom victorious. Important portions of the empire were lost. Taxes rose; trade, education, and the mechanical arts languished. Parasitism and beggary flourished. Such a régime was more fit to inspire satire than any other form of literature. Charles II, the last of the House of Hapsburg, was a physical and mental degenerate. He symbolizes the end of a dynasty and the collapse of a nation. At his death Spain had sunk as low as a nation can well decline and survive. It required many generations to recover. As with the nation, so with literature. From the death of Calderón in 1681 it was one hundred fifty years before another really vital movement manifested itself in Spanish literature. Philip III and Philip IV deserve some credit as patrons of literature, even though their patronage was unintelligent. The reign of Philip IV was distinguished in art by Velázquez, that wonderful exponent of Spanish realism. But Velázquez was a conspicuous exception. More characteristic of the age was its tasteless church architecture and the euphuistic poetry of Góngora and Calderón: two aspects of baroque art.

Literature becomes affected in the first decade of the seventeenth century. Two opposing tendencies are manifest: *conceptismo*, "cultivated subtlety," and *culteranismo*, "the cultivation of the obscure." These two tendencies go together. The former had long existed in Spanish literature, but at this period they unite. The resultant form of literary affectation was not confined to Spain, but was world wide. It was called "Marinism" in Italy, *"préciosité"* in France, "euphuism" in England, *"Schwulst"* in Germany. In Spain the term "Gongorism" was also used in honor of *culteranismo's* most famous poet.

Conceptismo is a legacy of the Middle Ages, a product of the hair-splitting dialectics of the scholastics. Schoolmen trained to theological debate applied their method to the discussion of questions of love and honor. Finespun reasoning was a note of Provençal poetry. From the Provençal it spread to the Italian and Spanish. Few of the poets already considered were wholly devoid of it. Conceptism garbed itself in a wealth of rhetoric. The most used figures were antithesis, parallelism, chiasmus, metaphor, and the "conceit." The "conceit" (*concepto*) is, of course, the characteristic figure of *conceptismo*. It differs from an ordinary metaphor in that it is strained and tasteless to the point of being comic. The *equívoco*, or "play upon words," was cultivated as a display, not of wit, but of ingenuity. Another favorite figure was oxymoron, or joining to the noun an impossible adjective, as "living corpse," "warm tomb." Back of all these rhetorical devices is the desire to shine by a cheap display of ingenuity.

Culteranismo is cultivated obscurity of style. The obscurity comes from abundance of allusions, enigmatic to all but the erudite, violations of the usual rules of syntax, and neologisms. Spanish literature is in general democratic. Here is a movement aristocratic to the point of snobbishness. The poet is to scorn the ordinary reader and appeal to a limited audience of the learned. The verbal coinages and syntactical innovations were part of a movement to make Spanish conform more nearly

to **Latin.** Everywhere throughout Europe, during the
Renaissance, scholars were impressed with the inferiority
of the vernacular languages to the Latin. The ancient
tongue was richer in vocabulary, more elegant in syntax.
Romance languages were held to be "corrupted" forms
of Latin. To enrich these tongues with borrowings, to
reform their grammatical lawlessness, was considered a
patriotic endeavor. These ideas were sound in the main,
though some of the procedure of the reformers was silly.
We have seen that Juan de Mena started such a reform
in the fifteenth century; the *cultistas* resumed the effort
in the seventeenth. Many of their ideas coincided with
the more fruitful movement championed in France by
the Pléiade.

Reforms misdirected and beneficial.—The syntactical
reforms brought into poetry were contrary to the genius
of Spanish, and hence destined to perish. The frequent
omission of the definite article, in imitation of Latin
usage, was absurd; for the lack of articles is a manifest
weakness of the Latin language. Other affectations were
forced inversions and the use of a construction analogous
to the "accusative of specification" in a language which
had lost case. The chief service rendered by the *cultistas*
was the enrichment of the vocabulary. The author of the
Diálogo de la lengua is forced to define an unfamiliar word
—*excepción.* Lope, in *Amar sin saber a quién*, ridicules a
neologism employed by the affected—*acción. Conducir*
and many other words of everyday use today were introduced by the *cultistas.* High-sounding words like *canoro,
luciente, ilustrar, aplauso, celestial,* etc., received naturali-
zation. The *cultistas,* therefore, enriched the language
and renovated a threadbare poetic vocabulary. They

also registered an effective protest against facile improvisation in poetry. Artistry, they thought, lay in the
imitation of the Classic poets. Their rhetorical affectations are all drawn from ancient writers. What they
lacked was the taste and tact of their models. In so far as
the *cultistas* reacted against the careless writing of their
contemporaries, their influence was wholesome. They
were right in demanding higher artistic standards; but
they did not discern that true art is simple. They cultivated the ornate, the pompous, the mannered. Hence, as
a whole, the movement was pernicious.

Luis de Carrillo y Sotomayor (*1583–1610*).—The *cultistas* had many precursors in Spanish literature: Juan de
Mena, Herrera, and the poets represented in Pedro
Espinosa's *Flores de poetas ilustres de España*, 1605.
Everywhere there was a tendency toward inflation,
bombast, neologisms, and the use of hyperbaton. But
culteranismo absorbs the older tendency of *conceptismo*
and becomes a full-fledged, self-conscious, literary movement only in the first decade of the seventeenth century.
Its doctrinaire was Luis de Carrillo, aristocrat, soldier,
scholar, poet, who had frequented the Italian-Spanish
literary circle of Naples. There he became familiar with
the poetry of the Italian poet, Marino. It is often stated
that this literary contagion was caught from Marino,
but *Adone*, the latter's most characteristic work, was not
published until 1623, and Marino appears to have bene-
fited quite as much from Carrillo and Góngora as the
latter did from him. Probably both Marino and Carrillo
were subjected to the same influences at the Neapolitan
court. In 1607 Carrillo circulated in manuscript his *Libro
de la erudición poética*, a document whose importance Lu-

cien-Paul Thomas was the first to recognize, and which,
in a small way, may be compared to Du Bellay's *Défense
et illustration de la langue française.* Spanish is held to
be a degenerate form of Latin; it should be improved
by latinization both as to vocabulary and syntax. Only
the erudite deserve the name of poet. The poet should
scorn all readers but the learned. His work should demand the closest study on the reader's part, who, if unable to understand, should blame, not the poet, but his
own ignorance. Obscurity is not to be avoided, but rather
to be sought, if introduced with a reasonable amount of
discretion. As for clarity, "in the poet it will have the
character of a vice." Thus was set forth the whole mistaken doctrine of *culteranismo.* Carrillo also exemplified
his views in a series of poems which prove that his idea
of "discretion" was a liberal one. For latinization, obscurity, and subtlety are cultivated to a degree hitherto unknown. His language can scarcely be called Spanish.
Both his verse and prose writings were published in his
Obras of 1611 and reprinted in 1613. Carrillo inaugurated
a movement. It remained for a greater poet to give it
vogue.

   Luis de Argote y Góngora (1561–1627).—Born in Cordova, Góngora displays the exaggeration, *agudeza,* and
Epicureanism of his native Andalusia. A sojourn in the
austere university of Salamanca failed to modify his
pleasure-loving disposition. While still in his "teens,"
poetry had distracted his attention from the study of
the law. In order to indulge the poetic urge he took
orders and secured a clerical sinecure. It is on record that
his bishop rebuked him for neglecting the choir to attend
bull-fights. It is apparent that he was a worldly priest,
wholly without vocation. If late in life he rose to be
private chaplain to Philip IV, he owed that preferment

to literary and social gifts rather than to piety. It may or
may not be significant to the student of his second manner
that his latter years were marked by mental decadence
ending in insanity. There were two Góngoras, "the angel
of light" and "the angel of darkness." His early poetic
manner won him wide popular recognition. This work
lives and will never cease to be enjoyed. By a strange
paradox, however, one associates chiefly with his name
those works which were read by the few and which nobody longer reads.[1]

"*The angel of light.*"—The Góngora of the first manner is distinguished by exuberance, wit, elegance, charm,
grace. He excelled in the ballad form. Such poems as
Amarrado a un duro banco, Servía en Orán el rey, and
the like, form part of every anthology. Others like
Dineros son calidad are cynically satirical. Still others
are merely jocular without the note of bitterness. Most
charming of all are the *romancillos* like *La más bella niña
de nuestro lugar*, and *Lloraba la niña*. To say that the
poems written in the first manner are simple is to use the
word in a very relative sense. On the contrary, there is
constant striving for subtlety, with queer tricks of language. Góngora was a *conceptista* before he was a *cultista*.
The ballad, *Angélica y Medoro*, is as good an example of
conceptismo as the literature affords. Its details can be
comprehended only after the most searching study. Góngora excelled in the *letrilla*, and became the most popular
song-writer of his day. Certain songs like *Aprended,
flores, de mí* and *Clarín que rompe el alba* took the country
by storm. All the poet's works were collected and pub-

[1] Góngora wrote simple lyrics throughout his career. His more difficult poems are now widely read and admired. Dámaso Alonso disproved
the light-darkness dichotomy.—N. B. A.

lished in 1627 by a devoted friend, López de Vicuña, who spent twenty years collecting Góngora's poetic waifs. Churton's happy renderings have made many of his lyrics familiar to the English reader. The following stanzas from his translation of *Ande yo caliente, / y ríase la gente* illustrate Góngora's waggish Epicureanism:

GIVE ME WARM LIFE AND SPIRITS FREE

> Give me warm life, and spirits free,
> To mock the world that mocks at me.
>
> Let those, who climb on Glory's wings,
> Rule the wide earth and all its kings:
> For me, upon a lowlier throne,
> I'll rule a kingdom all my own;
> Each morn on simple table spread
> Fresh butter and sweet household bread;
> And while, in Winter's driving storms
> Mild lemon-punch my heart's blood warms,
> Ensconced beneath a safe roof-tree
> I'll mock the world that mocks at me.
>
> Let lordlings feast in envied state
> At boards that groan with gorgeous plate:
> A sad physician, spectral Care,
> Stands waiting on that golden fare,
> Embittering all its lavish cost:
> For me, whene'er I play the host,
> The savoury sausage, neatly dress'd
> By glowing fire, shall cheer my guest,
> Poor as myself, but fancy-free
> To mock the mocking world with me.
>
> And when white-bearded Janivere
> With silvery snow hangs bush and briar,
> And ice is on the mountain-brow,
> In chafing-dish good store I'll throw
> Of beech or chestnut-fruits, nor fail
> To win some neighbor's merry tale,—

Still merry, though the theme be sad,—
Of kings, who in old days went mad,
Who now are dead, and leave me free
To mock the world that mocks at me.

"The angel of darkness."—Whether or not Góngora enjoyed the reputation he had won as the foremost song-writer of his nation is uncertain; but about 1609 he executes a volte-face. Henceforth he despises the plaudits of the *vulgo* and poses as a literary snob. Following the ideas of Carrillo, he will write only for the *cultos*. The first work in the new manner was the *Panegyrico al duque de Lerma*, 1609. There followed the *Fábula de Polifemo y Galatea* and *Soledades*, circulated in manuscript as early as 1613, but not printed until 1627. These are the most characteristic monuments of *culteranismo*. They are purely descriptive, possess all the previously mentioned peculiarities of *estilo culto*, and largely incomprehensible, stand as examples of literary insanity.[1] At the time they created a furor. There was much sham in the way these poems were acclaimed. Few were willing to admit that they did not understand and enjoy them, for fear of being excluded from the charmed circle of the *cultos*. But the movement did not prevail without opposition, in spite of the approbation of Philip IV and his literary clique. Wits like Lope de Vega and Quevedo made the most of their opportunity. There were polemics, serious and comic, between the "swans," as the new bards termed themselves, and the "geese," or advocates of simple style, *estilo llano*. But in spite of satires almost as brilliant as Molière's *Précieuses ridicules*, common

[1] These opinions might be widely disagreed with. The same Góngora wrote all his poems. Great poets like Guillén, Salinas, Lorca, Alberti, and Gerardo Diego acclaim Góngora as a master.—N. B. A.

sense did not assert itself against euphuism so quickly in Spain as was the case in France and England. Paravicino, the court preacher, carried the manner into sacred oratory. Calderón transferred some of it to the stage. Imitators of Góngora seldom went to the extreme of utter unintelligibility. The movement lasted well into the eighteenth century.

Baltasar Gracián (1601–58), an Aragonese Jesuit, is the outstanding prose writer among the *cultistas*. He is the greatest of Spanish moral philosophers since Luis Vives. His style is the most condensed to be found in Spanish, much of it suggesting that of Bacon's *Essays*. This striving for concision was wholesome in a land where diffuseness was the rule, but Gracián's mania for verbal ingenuity and his contempt for clarity constitute a veil difficult to penetrate. Nevertheless, he is a great and original thinker who rewards the effort he demands of the reader. His mind naturally expressed itself in epigram. His thought, while not subversive, is always stimulating. Humanity and its foibles are this author's chief concern. Gracián's trend of mind is pessimistic—so much so that Schopenhauer found in him a kindred spirit.

His works.—In the *Héroe*, 1637, Gracián depicts his ideal of the Christian hero. The *Discreto*, 1646, is the portrait of the perfect type of educated gentleman, a sort of Spanish counterpart to the Italian *cortegiano* and the French *honnête homme*. The twenty-five *realces*, "adornments," which this paragon must possess are discussed in detail. The *Oráculo manual y arte de prudencia*, 1647, is a collection of three hundred elegantly turned maxims from which La Rochefoucauld and La Bruyère borrowed freely. In his *Arte de ingenio*, 1642, expanded and repub-

lished as *Agudeza y arte de ingenio*, 1648, Gracián provided a rhetorical treatise for the practitioners of conceptism. His masterpiece is the philosophical novel, *El
criticón*, 1651–53–57. This has to do with the travels of
Critilo, symbolic of the man of judgment, and Andrenio,
the man of nature. The three divisions correspond to the
periods of adolescence, maturity, and old age. It is
stretching the definition of the word to call this work a
novel. Of action there is little. Allegory is abundant.
The whole interest consists in the author's philosophic
observations. Andrenio, marooned from childhood on a
desert island, has suggested Robinson Crusoe to some.
It is perhaps more pertinent to inquire whether Gracián
by stressing the blessedness of a primitive state of nature
may not have influenced Rousseau. One cannot open a
page of the *Criticón* without reward; but a whole novel of
epigrams is cloying.

Francisco Gómez de Quevedo y Villegas (1580–1645),
brilliant and cynical, is Spain's greatest satirist and wit.
A gentleman of wealth and education, he served his
country in administrative and diplomatic capacities in
Italy, under the Viceroy Osuna, until forced to share his
patron's disgrace. Later he enjoyed a brief restoration
to royal favor, but, never a courtier, preferred a life of
letters to the service of an ungrateful country. Quevedo,
shortsighted and lame, but for all that a noted duelist, has
become a legendary character who figures in many a
play and novel. He paid the penalty of plain speech. The
story goes that one morning, at breakfast, Philip IV
found in his napkin the satiric memorial, *"Católica, sacra,
real Magestad."* A sovereign accustomed to adulation
punished the author with four years of imprisonment in

the monastery of San Marcos, León. Quevedo was released, a broken man, to die.

His works.—Quevedo was a voluminous writer of wide range. His many theological and philosophical writings are little read. His literary criticism possessed only passing interest. He who played so many tricks with language fought *culteranismo* in behalf of a simplicity of style of which he was himself incapable. The world is his debtor for editing the poems of Luis de León and Francisco de la Torre—models whom he would have his countrymen imitate rather than follow the false gods of Gongorism. A few of his historical writings are valuable documents for an understanding of the time. We have already considered the great picaresque novel, *El Buscón*, and his ever enjoyable *Sueños*. As a poet, Quevedo was copious. Most of his verse, not all, was collected after his death in *El Parnaso español*, 1648, where the poems are roughly classified, according to their nature, in nine divisions, each headed by the name of one of the Muses. Quevedo achieved a few lyrics, serious and pure of style; but most of his work is marred by conceptism, which he failed to see, in spite of his admiration for Luis de León, is a vice of style almost as pernicious as *culteranismo*. But Quevedo's satiric verse is most characteristic and important. The times were rotten, and, he thought, called for plain speech.

> ¿No ha de haber un espíritu valiente?
> ¿siempre se ha de sentir lo que se dice?
> ¿nunca se ha de decir lo que se siente?

The work in which these lines occur, *Epístola satírica y censoria escrita al Conde-duque de Olivares*, is Quevedo's noblest satire. An intelligent observer is attacking

existing abuses with patriotic purpose. National evils
are accurately diagnosed. Quevedo assails the false pride
of vainglorious Spain, the cruel honor code, the prejudice
against useful employment, parasitism, luxury, incapac-
ity, and moral corruption. He writes in a white heat of
righteous indignation. He was indeed a "valiant spirit,"
but he took all too evident a relish in the saying and writing of cruel things. Of all Spanish writers he is the most
heartless. He has none of the humor of his countrymen,
but surpasses them all in wit. His models are Juvenal,
Martial, and the Italian, Berni. He has little faith in
humanity, or love for it. He is always caustically brilliant, but for the most part a repulsive writer.

Pedro Calderón de la Barca (1600–1681) is the fourth
great dramatic luminary, the last glorious figure of the
Golden Age. With him the drama virtually ceases until
the late eighteenth century. He sprang from a prosperous
family of the lower aristocracy. His father, who was
employed in the department of the treasury, had contact
with the court. Pedro received an excellent education at a
Jesuit school and later at Salamanca. His training was
not such as to give him broadly humanistic interests. The
hair-splitting subjects of logic, law, and theology claimed
his attention. He emerged from the schools with a mind
that was scholastic, legalistic, and theologic. Hence the
tendency toward meticulous distinction everywhere apparent in his writings, as when he debates questions of
love and honor with the subtlety of the Schoolmen. He
seemed eminently fitted for either a theological or a legal
career. Instead he chose to be a poet-courtier. His début
as a poet dates from about 1620. He went bag and baggage over to the new school of Gongorism, then the latest

literary fad. The chance to develop a new form of play
was to bring Gongorism to the stage. This he clearly
saw, but he saw no less clearly that Góngora's obscurity
would not serve upon the boards. He therefore eschewed
obscurity and developed his drama in the direction of
subtlety. Like Gracián and Quevedo he is more *conceptista* than *cultista*. Calderón in his youth suggests Aramis
of *Les trois mousquetaires*. His interests were divided
between theology, dueling, and petticoats. He was involved in several scrapes which prove that his knowledge
of dueling was not wholly theoretical. What saved him
was his shrewd business sense, a trait possibly derived
from a Flemish strain in his ancestry. An ability to
feather his nest, to advance the interests of himself and
family manifested itself early. His poetic gift and conversational ability gained him a position at court which
he exploited to the utmost. Calderón is first and foremost a courtier. To understand that explains much in his
writings. Spain was in an advanced state of degeneration,
but this adulatory poet showed no appreciation of the
fact that anything was wrong in the world. His ideas fail
to interest today. As he advanced in age he grew staid
and religious. In 1650 he took priestly orders, and apparently would gladly have devoted his life to works of
charity. Unlike Lope he took his priesthood seriously
and ceased to write for the *corrales*. But requests to provide palace-plays and the two annual *autos* required for
the Corpus Christi festivities of Madrid could not be
refused. For these he received rich stipends, and the
income derived from several ecclesiastical sinecures rendered his circumstances easy. He died a respected octo-
genarian, leaving an unfinished manuscript.

Characteristics of Calderón's art.—Calderón has been
called "the first of mannered poets." He is also the poet
of the reaction. The Renaissance liberated; the reaction
enslaved. This period was an era of bad taste in other
arts. One can compare Calderón's poetry to the baroque
church architecture then coming in. Everywhere in his
work there is lavishness of rhetoric insufficiently con-
trolled by taste. His imagination ran riot. Other poets
have found in his work a mine from which to dig metaphors and similes. But the most sublime effects are often
followed by bathos. Nevertheless, at his best he attains
lofty flights of which Lope was incapable. And it is fair
to judge him by his best. On such occasions he is truly
inspired. Affectation is cast aside like a discarded gar-
ment. In general, the characteristics of his style are
subtlety, a nice sense of balance, abundant use of rhetorical figures, with conceits, bombast, and an oriental pro-
fusion of imagery.

His plays.—Calderón did not excel in the historical
drama. His attempts in this field were mediocre. He
was supreme as a writer of cape-and-sword plays. Typical of these are *La dama duende, Casa con dos puertas
mala es de guardar,* and *Mañanas de abril y mayo.* These
contain as elaborate plots as ever were devised. They are
triumphs of ingenuity. Unlike Lope's hasty improvisa-
tions, they evince the most exact carpentry, the completion of a plan worked out previously to the last detail.
Their fault is that they are too ingenious. They offend
the sense of realism. Nevertheless, the reader finds enjoyment in threading their mazes. Goethe complained
that the characters of such plays were as like as so
many bullets cast in the same mold. The *enredo* was

everything; there was no room for the creation of character.

That he could create flesh-and-blood characters when he chose, Calderón proved by writing *El alcalde de Zalamea*. Pedro Crespo, the self-respecting rustic, and the gouty old soldier, Lope de Figueroa, are fine portraits. This is an honor tragedy, re-worked from a like-named play formerly attributed to Lope de Vega. Calderón has improved upon his source. So, too, the hero of his *Príncipe constante* is a lofty conception of the ideal ruler, to whom patriotism and religion mean more than liberty and life.

There is a series of honor tragedies, *El médico de su honra*, *El pintor de su deshonra*, *A secreto agravio, secreta venganza*, etc., which would rank among the world's great tragedies if they did not offend the modern sense of pity by the sacrifice of innocent female victims to the requirements of a barbarous honor code. It is too much to be expected to sympathize with the Iagos rather than with the Desdemonas. These plays strikingly illustrate Calderón's limitations. He cannot achieve universality because he writes so exclusively for his locality and epoch.

Another masterpiece, *El mágico prodigioso*, deals with the legend of St. Cyprian of Antioch and his compact with the devil. The theme is similar to Mira de Amescua's *Esclavo del demonio*. This is Calderón's best religious play.

Calderón is most famous for *La vida es sueño*, his one great philosophical drama. Based on an old oriental tale, the "awakened sleeper" story, used also by Shakespeare in the Prologue to the *Taming of the Shrew*, it dramatizes the conflict between predestination and free will. Segismundo, the hero, is symbolic of humanity. The play

teaches that it is possible for man to better his nature, to
prevail over fate by assertion of the will, that all this life
is fleeting as a dream, but that good deeds wrought during
the dream are counted in one's favor against the awakening into the next life. This noble conception is partially
spoiled by the subplot, a commonplace palace-play intrigue. There are passages, like Segismundo's second
soliloquy, where the poet attains supreme heights; there
are others in which he takes the short step which separates the sublime from the ridiculous.

The autos.—The dramatic form on which Calderón
staked his reputation was the *auto sacramental.* He is the
leading writer of *autos.* For over thirty years he supplied
two of them annually to the municipality of Madrid. His
total output was in excess of seventy. They are now little
read—a pity, for in them the poet gave free vent to what
Fitzmaurice-Kelly calls his "lyrical splendor." But the
modern reader is repelled by a form which he fails to
grasp, by naïvetés which passed unnoticed in an age of
simple faith but which now seem irreverent. Most popular is *La cena del rey Baltasar.* The octaves spoken by
Death in this play are worthy of Milton and are one of
Calderón's finest achievements. *A Dios por razón de estado* may be cited as typical of the metaphysical *auto.*

Calderón's vogue.—Calderón achieved success early,
and through a stage career of sixty years knew no serious
rival. With his death the Spanish drama passes into a
state of abeyance. Third-rate imitators, like Antonio
Zamora (1660?–1728) and José de Cañizares (1676–1750),
continued his tradition into the eighteenth century. His
plays were frequently acted even during the period of
French ascendancy. There were more editions of them

accessible than in the case of any of his predecessors. To this his vogue during the Romantic period is partly to be ascribed. He was "discovered" by August Wilhelm and Friedrich Schlegel, the great critics of German Romanticism. For a time he was ranked with Shakespeare and Sophocles; but saner counsels now prevail. The Schlegels lacked literary perspective. Ignorant of the achievements of others, they ascribed to Calderón merits in which the whole Spanish school shared. Schack, the historian of the Spanish drama, placed Calderón in his proper setting. Grillparzer in Austria, Chorley in England, and Menéndez y Pelayo in Spain headed a reaction in favor of Lope de Vega. We now credit Lope with greater fertility of plot-invention, a fresher simplicity of diction, a wider human interest; Calderón, with a more exact knowledge of stage technique, less improvisation, greater lyric power, marred by more frequent sinning against the rules of good taste. Both are inferior to Ruiz de Alarcón in the comedy of character.

BIBLIOGRAPHY

CARRILLO, LUIS DE. "Obras," *BAE*, Vol. XLII.

GÓNGORA, LUIS DE ARGOTE Y. "Obras poéticas," ed. R. FOULCHÉ-DELBOSC, *Bibliotheca hispanica*, Vols. XVI, XVII. Also *BAE*, Vols. X, XXXII.

———. *Soledades*, transcribed into modern Spanish by DÁMASO ALONSO. Madrid, 1927.

———. *The Solitudes*, trans. E. M. WILSON. Cambridge, 1931.

THOMAS, L. P. *Don Luis de Góngora y Argote*. Paris, 1932.

———. *Le Lyrisme et la préciosité cultistes en Espagne. (Beihefte 18 sur Zeitschrift für romanische Philologie.)* Halle, 1909.

———. *Gongora et le gongorisme considérés dans leurs rapports avec le marinisme*. Paris, 1911.

KANE, ELISHA K. *Gongorism and the Golden Age*. Chapel Hill, 1928.

ALONSO, D. (ed.). *Las soledades*. Madrid, 1927. Study and version in contemporary Spanish.

———. *La lengua poética de Góngora*. Madrid, 1935.

PENNEY, CLARA L. *Luis de Góngora*. New York, 1926.

ARTIGAS, M. *Biografía y estudio crítico de don Luis de Góngora*. Madrid, 1925.

REYES, A. *Cuestiones gongorinas*. Madrid, 1927.

CHURTON, E. *Gongora*. 2 vols. London, 1862.

GRACIÁN, B. *El héroe*, ed. A. COSTER. Chartres, 1911.

———. *El héroe y El discreto*, ed. A. FARINELLI. Madrid, 1900.

———. *El criticón*, ed. J. CEJADOR Y FRAUCA. 2 vols. Madrid, n.d. Also *BAE*, Vol. LXV.

———. *El Criticón*, ed. M. ROMERA-NAVARRO. 3 vols. Philadelphia, 1938–40.

———. *Agudeza y arte de ingenio*, ed. E. OVEJERO. Madrid, 1929.

BELL, A. F. G. *Baltasar Garzián*. Oxford, 1921.

QUEVEDO, FR. DE. *Obras completas*, ed. L. ASTRANA MARÍN. 2 vols. Madrid, 1932.

———. "Obras completas," ed. M. MENÉNDEZ Y PELAYO. 3 vols. Sevilla: Sociedad de bibliófilos andaluces, 1897–1907. Also *BAE*, Vols. XXIII, XLVIII, LXIX.

MÉRIMÉE, E. *Essai sur la vie et les oeuvres de Francisco de Quevedo*. Paris, 1886.

CALDERÓN DE LA BARCA, PEDRO. "Comedias," ed. J. E. HARTZENBUSCH, *BAE*, Vols. VII, IX, XII, XIV.

———. *Comedias*, ed. KEIL. 4 vols. Leipzig, 1827–30. Both these editions are unsatisfactory, but there is nothing better except in the case of individual plays.

———. *Autos sacramentales*, ed. PANDO Y MIER. 6 vols. Madrid, 1717. Also *BAE*, Vol. LVIII.

———. *El mágico prodigioso*, ed. A. MOREL-FATIO. Heilbronn, 1877. The first critical text of a Spanish play.

———. *La vida es sueño*, ed. M. A. Buchanan. Toronto, 1909. The best edition.

MENÉNDEZ Y PELAYO, M. *Calderón y su teatro*. Madrid, 1881. The most important criticism.

VALBUENA PRAT, A. "Los autos sacramentales de Calderón," *Revue hispanique*, LXI, 1–302.

————. *Calderón: Su personalidad, su arte dramático, su estilo, y sus obras.* Madrid, 1941.

RUBIÓ Y LLUCH, A. J. *El sentimiento del honor en el teatro de Calderón.* Barcelona, 1882.

PARKER, A. A. *The Allegorical Dramas of Calderón.* Oxford, 1943.

COTARELO, E. *Ensayo sobre la vida y obras de don Pedro Calderón de la Barca.* Madrid, 1924.

FRUTOS CORTÉS, E. *Calderón de la Barca.* Barcelona, 1949.

CHAPTER XVIII

The
Eighteenth
Century

Tendencies, political and literary—The situation in Spain—
Feijóo—Luzán—His theories—Tadeo González—Nicolás Fernán-
dez de Moratín—Cadalso—Iglesias de la Casa—Samaniego—
Iriarte—Jovellanos—Meléndez Valdés—Cienfuegos—Quintana—
Gallego Blanco White—Lista—The neo-Classic drama—Other
neo-Classic dramas—Ramón de la Cruz—His critical self-justifica-
tion—The sainetes—Leandro Fernández de Moratín—His works—
El sí de las niñas—El Padre Isla—Torres Villarroel.

Tendencies, political and literary.—The beginning of
the eighteenth century found absolutism firmly entrenched
in most European countries. As the century advanced,
thought became liberalized. Rationalism was the prevailing philosophy. The questioning of old accepted
beliefs was not without its reaction on politics. The
century ends with the revolt of the American colonies
and the French Revolution. In literature, French standards of taste were everywhere accepted. French neo-
Classicism conquered the world.

The situation in Spain.—Charles II, the last degenerate ruler of the House of Austria, died in 1700. In this
same year the throne was filled by Philip V, of the French
Bourbon dynasty, who was able to maintain his position
only after a hard-fought war with his Austrian rival,
which further added to the miseries of the nation. The
following are the Bourbon kings who ruled during the

century: Philip V (1700–1746), Louis I (a brief period in 1724), Fernando VI (1746–59), Charles III (1759–88), Charles IV (1788–1808). During all this time Spain was economically prostrate and politically impotent. The close and cordial relationship between the rulers of France and Spain, sealed by a family compact, tended to make Spain a mere appanage of France. All these rulers were despots, Charles III the most enlightened of them. The age under discussion terminates with the Napoleonic invasion of 1808. Unlike other European nations of this period, there was little intellectual ferment in Spain. A few of the nobles, like the great minister Aranda, became rationalistic philosophers. The leading literary protesters against obscurantism were, however, not deists but priests, several of them Jesuits, and the Jesuit order was expelled from Spain in 1767. In literature, the beginning of the century offers the dregs of seventeenth-century ideas—uninspired imitations of Calderón and Góngora. Next comes the aping of the great Classic writers of France. The governmental endeavor to gallicize Spain was marked by such official acts as the founding of the National Library in 1712, that of the Royal Spanish Academy in 1714, and that of the Academy of History in 1735. But once again it was shown that Spanish individualism was to rebel against any attempt at standardization. Several writers reverted to the national tradition, and these are among the most interesting of a barren period. One may also note, as in other eighteenth-century literatures, anticipations of Romanticism. The beginnings of journalism also fall within this period—a development which was to affect literature profoundly in the years to come.

PHILOSOPHY AND CRITICISM

As the eighteenth century is a period of increasing enlightenment, even in Spain, it is well to consider first Spain's somewhat meager contributions to the ideas of the age.

Benito Jerónimo Feijóo y Montenegro (1676–1764) was a Galician who early joined the learned Benedictine order, and who for some forty years taught philosophy and theology in the University of Oviedo. His was an inquiring mind, scientific, critical, and, to a certain degree, skeptical. He considered it his life-mission to attack superstition and error. His chief work is the *Teatro crítico universal* (1726–39), eight volumes of miscellaneous content, containing essays on the natural sciences, mathematics, medicine, philosophy, law, economics, literature, philology, and popular superstitions. Feijóo is an encyclopedist who anticipated by many years the *Encyclopédie* of France. He was abreast with the thought of other countries. His style is trenchant, his ideas sane. He attacks with mordant wit national obscurantism, and that *españolismo* which made the infiltration of foreign ideas so difficult; but he is no less severe with those gallomaniacs who could see no good in their own country. As a literary critic, he believed in formal rules as a corrective of the then-existing anarchy; but he insisted that there is a *"no sé qué"* in literature which renders charming many a work which violates the formal Aristotelian rules. This indicated to him that the rules were too narrow and had not yet been correctly formulated.

Ignacio Luzán Claramunt de Suelves y Gurrea (1702–54) is the great exponent in Spain of the neo-Classic movement. A hard-headed Aragonese, educated in Italy and

with French contacts, he made it the task of his life to
discipline Spanish poetry. He saw that his countrymen
possessed talent, but too often lacked clarity, sense, and
taste. French neo-Classicism had supplied the needed
corrective to the unbridled exuberance of the French
Renaissance. In Spain that reaction had taken the form
of *culteranismo* which had struck deeper roots than the
similar movement of *préciosité* had done in France. It
was now high time to initiate a crusade in behalf of common sense. Mr. R. E. Pellissier has shown that this
veering toward French standards was not chiefly due to
the presence in Spain of a Bourbon dynasty. Spain was
merely going the way of all Europe.

His theories.—Luzán's famous *ars poetica* is entitled
*Poética, o reglas de la poesa en general y de sus principales
especies*, Saragossa, 1737. He makes no claim to originality of ideas, merely that he is preaching old doctrine
much needed in Spain. The work leans heavily upon
Italian interpreters of Aristotle and Horace. Boileau is
followed to a certain extent, but frequently disagreed
with. Luzán expounds the familiar doctrines of imitation,
verisimilitude, and the Horatian mingling of the useful
with the sweet. Unbridled imagination, he holds, belongs
solely to dreamers, fever patients, and madmen. The
drama should observe the three unities; the number of
characters should be limited, decorum observed. The
stereotyped characters of the old *comedia* should be
varied. Humor should not be the exclusive possession of
the clown. Attention should be given to costume, but
peasants should always wear gala garb. The *auto sacramental* is condemned as indecorous and irreverent. Blank
verse should replace rhyme, though the national ballad

meter is sanctioned as a close approach to prose. In discussing the epic, Luzán follows Tasso in substituting the "Christian marvelous" for the gods and goddesses of antiquity. A Romantic tenet has therefore slipped into the precepts of a Classic critic.

There is destructive criticism of Spanish authors. Góngora and Gracián are called the chief perverters of good taste. Luzán makes merry over the former's lines:

> . . . . memoria
> que sombras sella en túmulos de espuma,

in which the "shadows" signify printed letters and the "heaps of foam," white paper ready for the press. He rightly demands humor and common sense as a corrective for such extravagance. But he is fair minded enough to point out the good in Lope de Vega and Calderón. The latter is not considered obscure, and his careful workmanship is admired. His lukewarm attitude toward national idols caused Luzán to be regarded as unpatriotic in certain quarters; but he is essentially patriotic. He was the physician prescribing for an aggravated disease, the guide whom most writers of the century followed with more or less success. Few attained the crystal-clear simplicity which Luzán advocated. Neither did they refrain from copious allusions to Classic mythology. The national tendency toward inflated style and an occasional lapse into realism still persisted. But *culteranismo* was dead. In so far as this was accomplished Luzán's reform was a success. It failed to produce many masterpieces of literature, because neo-Classicism was a mold unsuited to the genius of the race.

Other philosophers and critics are best treated under different heads.

POETRY

Fray Diego Tadeo González (1733–94) formed one of a
group of poets called the Salamanca school, the leading
member of which was Meléndez Valdés. Tadeo González
successfully imitated the form of Luis de León, but was
unable to follow his master's lofty thought. His was a
gentle, effeminate nature. He was one of those worldly
abates of the century. His work suggests the harpsichord,
the bewigged gallants, and patched-and-powdered beauties of the circles he frequented. It is drawing-room
poetry. The love lyrics, addressed to various Melisas and
Mirtas, are achievements of formal frigidity. His best-
known poem, *El murciélago alevoso*, is unsurpassed for
deftness and lightness of touch, but humane readers
question whether the sufferings of a persecuted bat form
a proper subject for humor. No work better illustrates
the insensibility of certain Spaniards to animal suffering.
The marvelous description of the angry cat shows how
difficult it was for even the most Classic of Spaniards to
refrain from realistic touches.

Nicolás Fernández de Moratín (1737–80) was a premature romanticist. He attempted the Classic forms; he
even wrote a long didactic poem, *La caza*. But just as the
head of King Charles crept into the writings of Mr. Dick,
so Moratin was unable to escape the lure of chivalry, the
Middle Ages, the national past. His masterpiece, *Fiesta
de toros en Madrid*, illustrates this. So do various ballads
on national subjects. Moratín has been called a forerunner of the Duque de Rivas. His genius would have
thrived better after 1835.

José Cadalso (1741–82) was, according to Cejador, a
man who wrote Classicism and lived Romanticism. If

it is true that he bribed the guards of a cemetery to exhume the body of the lady of his love, Byron would have
envied him the exploit. Cadalso revived the anacreontic,
wrote a notable prose satire, *Eruditos a la violeta*, and,
in his *Noches lúgubres*, imitated from Young's *Night
Thoughts*, inaugurated in Spain that tendency toward
the mournful later so common with the Romantic poets.
His *Cartas marruecas*, 1789, is a successful imitation
of Montesquieu's *Lettres persanes*. Cadalso's fictitious
Moor finds much to criticize in the government of Spain,
the backwardness of education, and national manners
generally. Cadalso proved himself always an enlightened
thinker and a true patriot. He is a forerunner of Larra.

The mischievous genius of *José Iglesias de la Casa*
(*1748–91*) has caused him to be remembered as a worthy
disciple of Quevedo and the Góngora of the first manner.
He excels as satirist, parodist, and writer of epigram.
His serious verse, written after ordination to the priesthood, is now forgotten.

Félix María Samaniego (*1745–1801*) was a country
gentleman who resided in France long enough to become
a skeptic and a cynic. He introduced the versified fable
into Spain, a new literary form for his country. His
Fábulas morales, the printing of which began in 1781, is
a successful imitation of La Fontaine. Samaniego has
much of the Frenchman's *malice*, to which he adds a little
genuine Spanish *sal*.

Tomás de Iriarte (*1750–91*) was a stormy figure, embittered by his lack of popularity as a dramatist, and
wasting his talents in literary polemics. One cannot
understand why he was such a favorite with the gentle
Longfellow. Iriarte is now remembered chiefly for his

Fábulas literarias. He is probably the most successful imitator of La Fontaine outside of France. Unlike La Fontaine, Iriarte invents his own fables. Many contain covert attacks upon prominent men of letters. The versification shows the flexibility of the French model. The tone is brilliantly cynical; the morals are epigrammatic, like the following:

> Guarde para su regalo
> esta sentencia un autor:
> Si el sabio no aprueba, ¡malo!
> si el necio aplaude, ¡peor!

These fables are a mine of frequently quoted maxims.

Gaspar Melchor de Jovellanos (1744–1811), economist, sociologist, reformer, statesman, poet, was the greatest figure which the movement for national enlightenment produced during the eighteenth century. His *Informe sobre la ley agraria* marks him as a far-seeing patriot. His noble nature is shaken out of its serenity only when rendered indignant by a strong sense of justice. Intellectually an *afrancesado,* he died a martyr to the cause of Spanish nationalism, when the nation he loved was at war with the nation he admired. Though his literary activity was considerable, it was always an incidental employment. Jovellanos is a reflective poet, a typical Classicist in the supremacy of reason over emotion. He excelled in the Classic forms of didactic poetry, satire, and the epistle. His masterpiece is the epistle *Fabio a Anfriso,* written from the monastery of El Paular.

Juan Meléndez Valdés (1754–1817) stands for fluidity and sweetness. His artistic conscience, which led him to polish and repolish, makes him, perhaps, the most formally perfect of the neo-Classic poets. In his early manner he cultivated the anacreontic and the eclogue, not disdaining the national *romance*. Such charming trifles as *La flor del Zurguén* and *Rosana en los fuegos* will never drop out of the anthologies. Later, under the influence of Jovellanos, he became more philosophic, attempting ambitious didactic works like *La gloria de las artes*. Meléndez was strongly influenced by Young, Thomson, and Rousseau. With him the sentimental becomes naturalized in Spain. This is significant for the development of Romanticism.

Nicasio Álvarez de Cienfuegos y Acero (1764–1809) followed Meléndez in the direction of *sensibilité*, and may also be viewed as a precursor of Romanticism.

Manuel José Quintana (1772–1857) lived mostly in the nineteenth century; spiritually he belonged to the eighteenth. He witnessed the rise and fall of Romanticism, unaffected by that movement. A man of unblemished character, he knew but two passions: love of country and humanitarianism. His devotion to the cause of liberalism was not merely literary in its expression. Under Ferdinand VII he suffered persecution for his activity in behalf of a liberal constitution. Nature, love, and religion find slight expression in his poetry; he is primarily a poet of patriotism and liberalism. The Classic ode is his favorite form. His best-known odes are those entitled *A España después de la revolución de marzo* and *Al armamento de las provincias españolas contra los franceses*, both written in 1808. In these he clings to the externals of Classicism, while bidding adieu to Classic serenity. Reason is replaced by emotionalism. Written in a moment of intense excitement, these odes glow with a patriotism kindled to a white-hot heat. Love of Spain, hatred of France, fear for the future, mingled with a not-misplaced confidence in the race, make them something wholly different from most of the poetic productions of the neo-Classic school, in general so insipid. One regrets only an exaggeration of emphasis, reminiscent of Herrera. The rest of Quintana's poetry is wholly in the eighteenth-century tradition. As a critic he is a follower of Boileau. Mention should be made of his readable prose work, *Vidas de españoles célebres*, biographies of Spain's ancient worthies, the Cid, Guzmán el Bueno, El Gran Capitán, Roger de Lauria, Cortés, Pizarro, Balboa, etc. The author hoped that admiration for the deeds of the ancestors might bring into existence a new race of giants.

Almost the same criticism may be passed on the work of *Juan Nicasio Gallego (1777–1853)*, except that his verse is considered more correct and elegant. *El dos de mayo*, 1808, is the supreme expression of outraged Spain's indignation at the Napoleonic invasion. As in Quintana's patriotic odes, feeling shakes the poet's poise. Gallego wrote little, and well. He, too, imitates Herrera. As a priest, he was less influenced by French rationalistic thought. Late in life we find him flirting with Romanticism, translating Ossian and Manzoni, joining in the movement to write ballads on heroes of the past; but, with these few exceptions, his verse follows the Classic tradition.

José María Blanco y Crespo (1775–1841) was a poet of transition. His soul, according to Gladstone, was a battlefield where combats were waged between faith and skepticism. Leaving a comfortable benefice in Seville, where he was canon in the cathedral, he migrated to England, first turning Anglican, later Unitarian. Cardinal

Newman, whose conscience turned him to the opposite course, sympathized with this troubled doubter. In England, Blanco assumed the name of Blanco White. He there acted as editor, free-lance author, and Unitarian pastor. As a poet, he begins in the Classic style; but such poems as *Una tormenta nocturna en alta mar* evince a Romantic interest in nature's less peaceful aspects. Curiously enough, Blanco White's chief claim to fame rests upon an English sonnet, *Mysterious Night*, which may well compete with the best of Milton and Wordsworth:

> Mysterious Night! When our first parent knew
> Thee from report divine, and heard thy name,
> Did he not tremble for this lovely frame,
> This glorious canopy of light and blue?
> Yet 'neath a curtain of translucent dew
> Bathed in the rays of the great setting flame,
> Hesperus with the host of heaven came,
> And lo! creation widened in man's view.
> Who could have thought such darkness lay concealed
> Within thy beams, O Sun? or who could find,
> Whilst fly, and leaf, and insect stood revealed,
> That to such countless orbs thou mad'st us blind?
> Why do we then shun death with anxious strife?
> If light can thus deceive, wherefore not life?

Alberto Lista y Aragón (*1775–1848*) is the last important Classic poet and critic. With Blanco White and a few lesser lights he formed a group called the Sevillan school. Living in the last days of neo-Classicism, he waged a losing fight. He won a name for himself as the best schoolmaster of his time, and was the influence which turned Espronceda and Ventura de la Vega toward a life of letters. These brilliant pupils departed from the precepts of their teacher, who nevertheless continued to counsel them with kindly tolerance.

THE DRAMA

The neo-Classic drama.—The effort to write Spanish plays in the French manner dates from the middle of the century. The critical reform initiated by Luzán in 1737 was taken up by a journal, *Diario de los literatos*, and an organized group of cultured gentlemen, the Academia del buen gusto. The leading member of this academy, Agustín Montiano (1699–1764), besides writing two treatises on the drama, was the first to produce plays in accordance with the new theories. These were *Virginia* (printed in 1751) and *Ataulfo*. They were divided into five acts, written in blank verse, and decorously frigid. Not only are the three unities observed, but Montiano prided himself on the invention of a fourth, that of character. One character must always embody some one conspicuous trait, heroism, stoicism, piety, virtue, patriotism, etc. Thus all psychological subtlety is avoided and the dramatic personages become the veriest wooden puppets. It is noteworthy that from the first there was in Spain no attempt to avoid national or medieval subjects, as had been done in France. These plays were not acted in public theaters.

Other neo-Classic dramas.—Aranda, minister of Charles III, made various paternal efforts to reform the stage. For some years nothing better than translations from the French was to be had, until a group of litterati, the "tertulia de la Fonda de San Sebastián," resolved to supply the lack. Nicolás Fernández de Moratín was first in the field with *Hormesinda*, a tiresome piece, publicly performed in 1770, and withdrawn after six representations. The utmost that Aranda was able to effect could not keep it alive. The following year Cadalso's *Sancho*

García scored an even greater failure. The public could not endure the imitation of the French Alexandrine, and the "unity of character" was all too successfully observed. Greater success attended Vicente García de la Huerta's *Raquel*, 1778. The theme was that treated by Lope de Vega in his *Judía de Toledo*, and the romantic gallantry of the lines was a language intelligible to a Spanish audience. Jovellanos regarded the drama of his time as a "public pest." He would have liked to see the price of admission raised high enough to debar the common herd with their corrupting influence; but, as an exemplifier of what the drama should be, he is disappointing. *El delincuente honrado*, 1774, is a *comédie larmoyante* in the manner of Diderot. His *Pelayo*, written in 1769 and reworked and given to the public in 1792 under the title *Munuza*, is more Classic but of less merit. Iriarte deserves credit for producing the first successful Classic comedy, *El señorito mimado*, 1788. A later comedy, *La señorita mal criada*, was less favorably received, though of almost equal merit. These two sparkling plays are equipped with Molièresque theses. In them Iriarte pointed the way to a greater than himself, the younger Moratín. There is no need to swell the list of similar dramatic productions. Spain produced not a single noteworthy writer of tragedies in the French manner, no dramatist comparable to Alfieri in Italy. All the tragedies mentioned above suffer from the same faults; they are artificial and insipid, lacking French grace, clarity, precision, and psychological subtlety. There are occasional foreshadowings of Romanticism. The national subject is favored. In comedy at least one brilliant success was scored.

Ramón de la Cruz y Cano (1731–94).—If Spain failed
to produce an Alfieri, she did offer a rival to Goldoni.
Ramón de la Cruz represents a reaction against neo-
Classicism and a return to realism and the native dramatic tradition. He started as a writer of tragedies and
an adapter of foreign plays. He translated works by
Metastasio, Racine's *Bajazet*, and, through the French,
Shakespeare's *Hamlet*. Like the other cultivators of the
genre ennuyeux, he achieved nothing better than an occasional *succès d'estime*. Then he found his fitting means of
expression in the *sainete*. This was an amplification of the
old *entremés*, with more characters, more plot, written in
ballad meter, and depicting humorously realistic types.
He retained only this much of Classic doctrine, that a play
should instruct as well as please. Instruction took the
form of playful satire of existing foibles and abuses. In-
stantly Ramón de la Cruz attracted packed houses, and
became the object of bitter attack on the part of the "up-
lifters" of the drama, who were shocked at his catering to
the mob and envied his success.

His critical self-justification.—Jovellanos had stated
that modern writers were inferior to the ancient, because
the latter imitated nature, while the former imitated the
imitators. Ramón de la Cruz claimed the same right to
paint existing types that Plautus and Terence had had.
He might have added Molière. Frankly a realist, he proclaimed: "*Yo escribo, y la verdad me dicta.*" Decorum
might be sacrificed to realism. He defended his use of
coarse and ungrammatical expressions in the mouths of
his personages: "To copy vulgar actions and turn them
into ridicule, the poet must think like the sages and talk
like the common people." After a long interval democ-

racy was coming to the front again in Spanish literature.
He claims for himself historic accuracy: "In a word, all
those of you who have seen my *sainetes* . . . . say
whether or no they are copies of what your eyes see and
your ears hear . . . . and whether my pictures do not
represent the history of our century." All critics now
agree as to the fidelity of Ramón de la Cruz's three
hundred *sainetes*, and all compare him to the painter,
Goya. These two, each in his own way, depict an epoch.

The sainetes.—Every aspect of Spanish life in the
closing years of the eighteenth century is represented.
Some *sainetes* portray the hollowness of fashionable life,
that of a futile aristocracy, ignorant despite its veneer
of French polish. The ever present *abates* and *cortejos*,
those plagues of the epoch, are rendered odious. But
more interesting are those describing the life of the people.
The scene is the *patio* of a swarming tenement, a *plaza*
in the Avapiés district, or the banks of the Manzanares,
where *majos* and *majas* are assembled for merry-making.
The low-life characters talk dialect, exchange jests, wran-
gle, and fight realistically. They are not caricatures. Typical pieces are: *Las tertulias de Madrid, La maja majada,
Las castañeras picadas, El cortejo fastidioso, La casa de
Tócame-Roque, El fandango de candil, El Rastro por la
mañana, El Prado por la noche, La Pradera de San Isidro,
Los bandos del Avapiés, La Plaza Mayor por Navidad.*
Ramón de la Cruz's fame is confined to this minor genre
which he made his own. He never wrote a successful
comedy, still less a tragedy. But it is no slight achievement to have initiated a return to naturalness and to have
given permanent record to a form of life both picturesque
and fleeting.

Leandro Fernández de Moratín (1760–1828) represents
the culmination of the dramatic endeavor of the eighteenth century, though his masterpiece, *El sí de las niñas*,
was not produced until 1806. Moratín alone achieved
the perfect synthesis of the Gallic and the Hispanic
traditions. He was the only undoubted genius among
those writing plays in the French manner. He imitated
Molière without ceasing to be Spanish. The son of
Nicolás de Moratín, he early gave evidence of artistic
talent and was apprenticed to a jeweler; but literary inclinations led him to forsake this trade. He obtained various diplomatic appointments which supplied the necessary means and leisure for a life of letters. He learned
several languages and traveled extensively. Political
events wrecked a promising career. Previous to the
French invasion, a literary cabal had denounced Moratín's work to the Inquisition. It is small wonder that
he sided with the "Intruder King," Joseph Bonaparte,
who suppressed the Inquisition and gave Spain so many
other needed reforms. But with the fall of Bonaparte,
Moratín was forced to flee with the other *afrancesados*.
He had played into his enemies' hands. Henceforth he
lived a life of exile in France, absurdly overestimating his
unpopularity and living in dread of assassination. He
ceased writing for the stage at the moment when he
had found himself and had scored an artistic triumph.
His cowardly nature rendered him incapable of con-
tending against difficult situations. If his bulk of production had been greater, he would rank as one of
Spain's foremost dramatists. As it is, he enjoys a large
measure of fame as the result of a single masterpiece.

His works.—His lyric poetry is negligible. The prose

satire, *La derrota de los pedantes*, 1789, has some merit. It is an attack upon the belated *cultistas* and other corrupters of good taste. His *Orígenes del teatro español*, published posthumously, is the first attempt to write the history of the early Spanish drama. A wretched translation of *Hamlet*, 1795, is a literary curiosity. Moratín viewed Shakespeare as a barbarian, who, in spite of lack of art, occasionally achieved happy effects. More successful are his adaptations of Molière's *École des maris* and *Le médecin malgré lui*. Of Moratín's five original plays, *El viejo y la niña* and *El barón* rank as *juvenilia*. *La mojigata*, a hypocrite play reminiscent of *Tartuffe* and *Marta la piadosa*, evinces increasing powers. His second best play, *La comedia nueva, o el café*, is satire transferred to the stage. It is an attack upon Comella and his school of coarse, sensational writers, and from it grew enmities which occasioned most of Moratín's later troubles. One character, Don Hermógenes, the pedant, has become proverbial, like Dr. Pangloss.

El sí de las niñas stands in a class apart. It is written in prose for greater naturalness, and the three unities are rigorously observed without straining. The *utile dulci* principle is observed with the avoidance of prosy preaching. This is one of the first of modern thesis plays. The lesson taught is that parents and guardians should not arrange marriages without the young people's consent. Cervantes had insisted on this idea several times in his writings. The Classic division into five acts is abandoned for the traditional Spanish three. The characters number only seven, and each is carefully executed. They are convincing native types. The servants, Calamocha, Simón, and Rita, suggest the earlier *graciosos* and *gracio-*

sas. But humor is not confined to the clowns in the old way. Doña Irene, a variation of the old *beata* type, amuses with her pride of ancestry and silly garrulity. Both Don Diego, the elderly uncle, and Don Carlos, the young lover, are generous and chivalrous in the true tradition of Spain. Through it all runs a tender sentimentality, not found in Molière, which may be due to Rousseau, but just as probably may hark back to Cervantes. The language is simple and always in good taste. The low-life characters speak naturally, but without coarseness. Moratín alone showed how it was possible to retain the best to be found in the old drama and re-work it according to the rules of art. Romanticism was soon to place a premium on lawlessness again.

THE NOVEL

José Francisco de Isla y Rojo (1703–81), a Jesuit, is the one important novelist of the century. His *Historia del famoso predicador Fray Gerundio de Campazas, alias Zotes*, 1758, aimed to reform the pulpit oratory of Spain and did much to accomplish the result intended. The pulpit was the last refuge of *culteranismo*. Sacred oratory was as rococo as the eighteenth-century churches in which many of these preachers held forth. Obscurity, subtlety, sensationalism, and ingenious display of every sort had brought pulpit oratory into disrepute. In *Fray Gerundio*, Padre Isla laughs this kind of preaching out of existence, as Cervantes had done with the romances of chivalry. Fray Gerundio is a *pícaro*, but a *pícaro* in orders. There is little action and much whimsical philosophizing. The work is amusing in spots, but prosy as a whole. Isla's translation of Lesage's *Gil Blas* is better known and far more readable. The French novel is so thoroughly hispanicized that a former generation of scholars were convinced that Lesage, on his part, had merely translated into French a work originally Spanish. Besides these novels Isla wrote several satires. His *Cartas familiares*, directed to a sister, are a model of epistolary style. Isla's *Cartas* are the most important since those of Santa Teresa.

MEMOIRS

Diego de Torres Villarroel (1693?–1770).—Nobody knows the eighteenth century in Spain who has not read the picaresque memoirs of the charlatan, Torres Villarroel, as set forth in his *Vida*, 1743. The son of a Salamancan bookseller who desired to give his son an education, Diego refused to study, but learned to dance, play the guitar, fight bulls, write poetry, and pick locks. At twenty he ran away from home and led a life of ease as a false hermit. In Coimbra he turned dancing-master and practiced medicine without knowing the first word of the science. Next he enlisted, deserted, and toured Spain as a professional bull-fighter. At length the prodigal returned home. One day, finding in his father's shop a treatise on higher mathematics, he read it with passionate interest. Conic sections had for Diego all the charm of forbidden fruit, for mathematics were supposed to be related to magic, and the subject had remained untaught in Salamanca for one hundred and fifty years. In 1721 he wrote the first almanac ever known in Spain, and continued to write them the rest of his life. They were full of humbuggeries of all sorts, but, as a few of his random prophecies happened to come true, Torres achieved a

national reputation as a soothsayer. (In 1756 he predicted the French Revolution with the death of king and
dauphin set for the year 1790.) He applied for and obtained the position of substitute professor of mathematics at Salamanca, though as an undergraduate he had
never been able to take a degree. After hurling a quad-
rant at the head of an unruly student, he had no disci-
plinary difficulties. He was as popular with his students
as he was unpopular with his staid colleagues. Ousted
as a result of university politics, Torres set out in 1723
for Madrid. There he nearly starved, until, by exor-
cising a goblin which was disturbing the household of
the Condesa de Arcos, he won the patronage of that
noble family. In 1726 he was elected full professor of
mathematics at Salamanca. After five years of teaching,
he became involved in some obscure crime and passed
three years of beggary in France and Portugal, until a
royal pardon permitted him to resume his professorial
labors. Late in life he took orders and turned philan-
thropist. His ideas concerning hospitals and a national
academy of mathematics were excellent.

Thus Torres Villarroel depicts himself a second Guzmán de Alfarache. He is not above a lie, but in the
main the picture of himself and the society in which he
moved is truthful. In character he was vain, boastful,
quarrelsome, but marvelously frank. He had no illusions
respecting himself or others. He exploited without a
scruple the prevailing stupidity, but in the end tried to
ameliorate conditions. He is one of the few incredu-
lous characters that eighteenth-century Spain produced,
and so contributed his mite toward national enlightenment.

I well knew my ignorance and blindness; but I knew, too, that I was in the land of the blind; because Spain then suffered an obscurantism so disgraceful, that in no school, college, or university of its cities was there a man who could light a lamp to seek the elements of the sciences.

Conditions must, indeed, have been bad when a charlatan was one of the few who saw the need of culture and science. Only a handful of philosophers and artists strove to maintain standards. Neo-Classicism was bound to fail where education was so backward; and the general anemia of the nation was unfavorable for a strong manifestation of popular art. An epoch ended with the Napoleonic invasion of 1808; but the downfall of Spain's "old régime" could be nothing but a benefit.

BIBLIOGRAPHY

FEIJÓO Y MONTENEGRO, BENITO JERÓNIMO. *BAE*, Vol. LVI.

————. "Teatro crítico universal," ed. A. MILLARES CARLO, *Clásicos castellanos*. Madrid, 1923. Selections.

PARDO BAZÁN, E. *Examen crítico de las obras del P. Maestro Feijóo*. Madrid, 1877. Also M. MENÉNDEZ Y PELAYO, *Heterodoxos*, Vol. III.

PELLISSIER, R. E. *The Neo-Classic Movement in Spain during the XVIII Century*. Palo Alto, Calif.: Stanford University, 1918.

LUZÁN CLARAMUNT DE SUELVES Y GURREA, IGNACIO. *Poética*. 2 vols. Madrid, 1789. See M. MENÉNDEZ Y PELAYO, *Ideas estéticas*, Vol. III.

Parnaso español de los siglos XVIII y XIX, ed. A. BONILLA Y SAN MARTÍN. Madrid, 1917.

GONZÁLEZ, DIEGO TADEO. *Obras*, *BAE*, Vol. LXI.

FERNÁNDEZ DE MORATÍN, NICOLÁS. *Obras*, *BAE*, Vol. II.

CADALSO, JOSÉ. *Obras*. 3 vols. Madrid, 1821. Also *BAE*, Vol. LXI.

————. *Cartas marruecas*, ed. TAMAYO. Madrid, 1935.

CADALSO, JOSÉ. *Noches lúgubres*, ed. EDITH HELLMAN. Santander, 1951.

SAMANIEGO, F. M. *Obras*, *BAE*, Vol. LXI.

IRIARTE, TOMÁS DE. *Obras en verso y prosa*. 8 vols. Madrid, 1805. Also *BAE*, Vol. LXIII.

COTARELO Y MORI, E. *Iriarte y su época*. Madrid, 1897.

JOVELLANOS, G. M. DE. *Obras*, *BAE*, Vols. XLVI, L.

La Satire de Jovellanos contre la mauvaise éducation de la noblesse (*1787*), ed. A. MOREL-FATIO. Bordeaux and Paris, 1899.

SOMOZA GARCÍA-SALA, G. *Documentos para escribir la biografía de Jovellanos*. 2 vols. Madrid, 1911.

GONZÁLEZ BLANCO, A. *Jovellanos: Su vida y obra*. Madrid, 1911.

MELÉNDEZ VALDÉS, J. *BAE*, Vol. LXIII.

MÉRIMÉE, E. "Meléndez Valdés," *Revue hispanique*, I, 34–68, 217–35.

CIENFUEGOS Y ACERO, NICASIO ÁLVAREZ DE. *Obras*, *BAE*, Vol. LXII.

PIÑEYRO, E. "Cienfuegos," *Bulletin hispanique*, XI, 31–54.

QUINTANA, M. J. *Obras completas*. 3 vols. Madrid, 1897–98. Also *BAE*, Vols. VII, XIX, LXI, LXIII, LXVII.

PIÑEYRO, E. *Manuel José Quintana: Ensayo crítico y biográfico*. Paris and Madrid, 1892.

MENÉNDEZ Y PELAYO, M. "Manuel José Quintana, considerado como poeta lírico," *Estudios de crítica literaria* (5th series). Madrid, 1908.

GALLEGO, J. N. *Obras poéticas*. Madrid, 1854. Also *BAE*, Vol. LXVII.

BLANCO WHITE. *Obras*, *BAE*, Vol. LXVII.

PIÑEYRO, E. "Blanco White," *Bulletin hispanique*, XII, 71–100, 163–200.

LISTA, A. *Obras*, *BAE*, Vol. LXVII.

CRUZ Y CANO, RAMÓN DE LA. *Teatro*. 10 vols. Madrid, 1786–91.

———. *Teatro*, ed. A. DURÁN. 2 vols. Madrid, 1843.

———. *Sainetes inéditos en la Biblioteca Municipal de Madrid*, ed. C. CAMBRONERO. Madrid, 1900.

———. *Sainetes de Don Ramón de la Cruz*, ed. E. COTARELO Y MORI. Madrid, 1915.

COTARELO Y MORI, E. *Don Ramón de la Cruz y sus obras*. Madrid, 1899. The best biography and critical study of this author.

Pérez Galdós, B. "Don Ramón de la Cruz y su época," *Revista de España*, XVII, 200–227.

Fernández de Moratín, Leandro. *Obras, BAE*, Vol. II.

Isla y Rojo, J. F. de. *Fray Gerundio*, ed. V. Lidforss. 2 vols. Leipzig, 1885.

———. "Obras escogidas," ed. P. F. Monlau, *BAE*, Vol. XV.

Gaudeau, B. *Les Prêcheurs burlesques en Espagne au xviii⁰ siècle.* Paris, 1891.

Torres Villarroel, Diego de. *Obras.* 15 vols. Madrid, 1794–99.

———. "Vida," ed. F. de Onís, *Clásicos castellanos.* Madrid, 1912.

CHAPTER XIX

*The
Costumbrista
Movement*

History of the nineteenth and twentieth centuries—The costumbrista movement—Mesonero Romanos—Estébanez Calderón
—Larra—Lesser costumbristas.

History of the nineteenth and twentieth centuries.—The
War of Liberation against Napoleon (or, as the English
call it, the Peninsular War), lasted from 1809 to 1814.
During the greater portion of this time the tyrant's
brother, Joseph Bonaparte, occupied the throne. The
rey intruso initiated many needed reforms which the
majority of Spaniards received with ill grace from a
hated foreigner. In 1814 Fernando VII, one of the worst
kings Spain ever had, was restored to his throne.
The constitution was abrogated and the Inquisition
restored. A revolution headed by Riego succeeded in
restoring the constitution in 1820, which was again over-
thrown three years later, when the French Bourbons
sent an army into Spain to aid the hard-pressed Fernando.
There followed ten years of absolutism, during which
Spain's best thinkers and writers led lives of exile in
foreign countries. These returned in 1833, when Fernando died and was succeeded by his daughter, Isabel II.
Spanish Romanticism begins this same year as a full-
fledged movement. During Fernando's reign, most of the
Spanish-American colonies secured independence. The
first Carlist War, occasioned by the disputed succession
to the throne, occupied the years 1834–39. As the Carl-

ists were reactionaries, Isabel was forced to seek Liberal
support, but granted concessions grudgingly. She was
deposed in 1868, chiefly on account of personal unpopularity gained by a scandalous private life. There followed
six unsettled years of provisional government, the reign
of Amadeo de Saboya (1871–73), and the short-lived
republic of Castelar. The second Carlist War lasted from
1872 to 1876. During all this period there were numerous
minor military revolutions, *pronunciamientos*. There
was comparative peace after the Bourbon restoration of
1874. Alfonso XII reigned from 1874 to 1885. His post-
humous son Alfonso XIII was declared of age in 1902. In
1898 the war with the United States deprived Spain of
her last American and Philippine possessions. The heart-
searchings which followed that catastrophe gave rise,
with the Generation of 1898, to a vigorous literary movement. Spain's many political problems were by no means
solved during the reign of Alfonso XIII. Gen. Miguel
Primo de Rivera, in 1923, capitalizing on the discontent
of both army and nation with the muddling politicians
who had contributed to the disaster in Morocco, declared
himself dictator, and dissolved the Cortes. Growing dissatisfaction with the dictatorship resulted in a revolution,
and the king abdicated and hurriedly left Spain—never
to return—in 1931. The establishment of the Second
Republic, under the leadership of Niceto Alcalá Zamora,
was hailed with high hopes by liberals in Spain and
abroad. The painful history of the political ineptitude
of the well-meaning leaders, who proved unable to put
their ideals into practice, still lingers in many memories.
Throughout her history, Spain has leaned toward conservatism in Church and State. The rebellion of Gen.
Francisco Franco put an end to the Republic in 1936.

In literature the Generation of 1898 lingered on, but new tendencies began to manifest themselves.

The costumbrista movement.—The "sketch" as a literary form developed in England with the appearance of the newspaper. The *Spectator Papers* of Addison and Steele created a new genre. Often the sketch was a light, philosophical disquisition, often a little essay, sometimes the study of a familiar character or type, sometimes a short story. A series of them, like the *Sir Roger de Coverley Papers*, almost amounted to a novel. Washington Irving, in his *Sketch Book* and elsewhere, made the form famous in American literature. In France, Jouy, writing under the pseudonym of "L'ermite de la Chaussée-d'Antin," depicted Parisian life under the first empire. Mercier, in his *Tableau de Paris*, did the same. These last, now forgotten, were in their day widely popular, and Jouy exerted great influence in Spain. The sketch was a safe form under a rigid censorship. Ideas were considered dangerous and politics were taboo, but the *artículo de costumbres* was thought innocuous. The real initiator of the genre in Spain was Sebastián Miñano (1799-1845), who published his *Cartas del pobrecito holgazán* in 1820.

Ramón de Mesonero Romanos (1803–82) was a comfortably circumstanced man of affairs with a taste for antiquarian scholarship. He is the incarnation of the bourgeois spirit, shrewdly shunning politics, but public spirited and full of philanthropic ardor. A jovial disposition made him everybody's friend. Tact joined to common sense enabled him to effect many reforms. His style lacks brilliance, but charms by its good nature. At the age of nineteen, Mesonero published *Mis ratos perdidos*, 1822, sketches which he re-worked in a series of articles written for a literary journal called *Cartas*

españolas, published in the early thirties. These and
similar writings were later collected in three volumes,
Panorama matritense, Escenas matritenses, and *Tipos y
caracteres.* Mesonero thus became the chronicler of the
types and manners of the Madrid of his day. He may
have been influenced by Zabaleta. He certainly owed
something to Ramón de la Cruz and Jouy. Sometimes
he attempts the short story. He never tried his hand at a
novel. His archaeological interests found expression in *El
antiguo Madrid,* which still remains our best authority on
the history of the capital, its streets and plazas, churches,
and other architectural monuments. Mesonero was not a
romanticist. *El romanticismo y los románticos* was one
of the most amusing satires on Romantic extravagance
ever written. Mesonero's common sense kept him within
bounds, but he was sympathetic to the romanticists'
devotion to the past, and, as editor, republished many
masterpieces of the old literature. He did much to re-
create an interest in the drama of the Golden Age. His
Memorias de un setentón is a vivid picture of Madrid life
in the stirring times of the early nineteenth century. All
in all, *"El Curioso Parlante,"* as he called himself, is an
author whom one both respects and loves.

    *Serafín Estébanez Calderón (1799–1867), "El Soli-
tario,"* was one of the most active collaborators on the
staff of *Cartas españolas.* As a *costumbrista,* he does for the
life of his province what Mesonero had done for that of
the capital. His *Escenas andaluzas,* published in book
form in 1847, disappoints through its obscurity and affectation. It pleases by its abundant color. Estébanez was
first of the moderns to stake out a claim in Andalusia and
to exploit the picturesque life of that province for literary
purposes. To point the way to Fernán Caballero and

Juan Valera was no slight merit. Statesman and dilet-
tante scholar, Estébanez early abandoned literature. His
other writings are unimportant.

Mariano José de Larra (1809-37), "Fígaro," was the
greatest of the *costumbristas.* Educated partly in France
and partly in Spain, he was able to emancipate himself
from a narrow, nationalistic point of view without therefore ceasing to be genuinely Spanish. He alone of the
costumbristas saw beneath the surface and gave other
than shallow criticism of life. Intellectually Larra had a
mind at once penetrating and judicious. He was so far in
advance of his time that he seems to belong to the present.
He is the greatest critic of the Romantic period, fair in his
judgments, able to distinguish the good from the silly
in Romanticism and the liberal movement in politics.
Intellectually, he possessed poise; emotionally, he was
unstable. His private life was a series of violent passions
terminating with suicide at the age of twenty-eight. His
career was a war between a fine intelligence and an unrestrained temperament. He was one of the many Werth-
ers of the age.

Larra as a costumbrista.—Larra began to write early.
His first success was the publication of a little periodical,
a mere leaflet, *El pobrecito hablador* (August, 1832–
March, 1833). Fourteen numbers appeared, written entirely by the editor, when the publication expired. Nevertheless, its literary success had been phenomenal. Larra's
reputation was made. He later commanded salaries greater than those accorded other writers of the time. *El pobrecito hablador* contains several of Larra's most famous
articles: *El casarse pronto y mal, El castellano viejo,
Vuelva usted mañana,* and brilliant bits of dramatic
criticism. Here, too, are in evidence those qualities which

made Larra the best *prosista* of the early nineteenth century. He shuns the rotundity and amplitude dear to his countrymen, the so-called *"estilo académico."* The modern generation accepts him as a model. His sentences are short, pointed, and often barbed; for Larra is a satirist. He is so frequently caustic and bitter that the effect is not always pleasant. But he invariably interests, both for his thought and its manner of expression. Witty incisiveness is his chief trait. As a reformer, he fought without gloves and often drew blood. The jovial Mesonero, with his gentle ridicule and conciliatory spirit, doubtless accomplished more tangible results in bettering the life of Madrid; but as writer, Larra is incomparably the greater. His contributions as dramatist and novelist will be treated later.

Lesser costumbristas.—There was a host of lesser *costumbristas*. Scarcely a writer of the time failed to contribute to the genre. Mention should be made of a collective enterprise, *Los españoles pintados por sí mismos*, 1843, to which the Duque de Rivas, Bretón de los Herreros, Zorrilla and other notable authors contributed. Most of the work of this sort still lies buried in the files of old periodicals. The history of the movement is still to be written. The *artículos de costumbres* contain much of interest, but in the history of literature they are important chiefly as forerunners of the regional novel of manners.

BIBLIOGRAPHY

IMPORTANT NOTE.—For the nineteenth and twentieth centuries, and often for earlier periods, editions of authors are entirely current and available. In addition to good series of texts such as *Clásicos castellanos* (around 150 vols. to date), the *Colección Austral*, and others, several Spanish publishers, notably Aguilar, have published complete or selected works of all important authors. They can be bought, or found in the larger libraries.

ALTAMIRA, R. *A History of Spain*. Toronto, New York, and London, 1949. Good brief survey of the recent period.

CORREA CALDERÓN, E. *Costumbristas españoles*. 2 vols. Madrid, 1950–51. Good anthology and study.

LOMBA Y PEDRAJA, J. R. *Costumbristas españoles de la primera mitad del siglo XIX*. Santander, 1932.

MESONERO ROMANOS, R. *Obras*. 8 vols. Madrid, 1925–26.

PITOLLET, C. "Mesonero Romanos," *La España moderna* (October, 1903), pp. 38 ff.

ESTÉBANEZ CALDERÓN, S. *Escenas andaluzas*. Madrid, 1883.

CÁNOVAS DEL CASTILLO, A. *"El Solitario" y su tiempo*. 2 vols. Madrid, 1883.

LARRA, M. J. DE. *Obras completas*. Barcelona, 1886. They are not complete.

———. *Artículos . . .* , ed. J. R. LOMBA. 3 vols. Madrid, 1923–27.

———. *Postfígaro, artículos no coleccionados*, ed. E. COTARELO. 2 vols. Madrid, 1918–19.

BURGOS, CARMEN DE. *"Fígaro."* Madrid, 1919.

CHAVES, M. *Don Mariano José de Larra (Fígaro): Su tiempo, su vida, sus obras*. Seville, 1898.

CHAPTER XX

Romanticism

Romanticism as an international movement—Spanish Romanticism—The historical course of Romanticism in Spain—The emigrados—Martínez de la Rosa—*La conjuración de Venecia*—His other plays—Larra—El Duque de Rivas—*El moro expósito*—*Los romances históricos*—Don Álvaro, o la fuerza del sino—Espronceda —His Romantic Philosophy—*El estudiante de Salamanca*—*El diablo mundo*—His shorter poems—García Gutiérrez—Hartzenbusch—Gil y Zárate—Zorrilla—His lyrics—His drama—Gertrudis Gómez de Avellaneda—Juan Arolas—Enrique Gil—The historical novel—Bécquer—*Desde mi celda*—*Rimas.*

Romanticism as an international movement.—In the late eighteenth and early nineteenth centuries, all the literatures of Europe underwent a revolution. Under the term Romanticism numerous tendencies, some of them contradictory, are included. Classicism had generalized and was objective; Romanticism was subjective and stressed the ego. Poets became interested in themselves and expected their readers to share that interest. Unrestrained emotionalism replaced Classic reason and moderation. In politics most romanticists were Liberals and possessed of reformatory zeal, as, to be sure, had been the case with many classicists. But the strong impetus given to pity and sentimentality by Rousseau encouraged humanitarianism, and the new Romantic verse-forms were better fitted for impassioned utterance. In religion there were two opposing tendencies. Many romanticists, like Chateaubriand, contributed to a reaction in favor of Catholicism against the rationalism of the eighteenth century. Many men of letters were converted to Catholicism, particularly in Germany, and the most extreme of these, like Novalis, developed mystic tendencies. Christian allusions quite generally replace the outworn Classic mythology. Other writers, like Shelley, made a parade of irreligion and even atheism. As regards nature, the classicists had admired the peaceful, the well-ordered, the artificial. Formal gardens, like those of Versailles and La Granja, express the taste of the time. After Rousseau, the natural was admired, and beauty was seen in nature's more boisterous aspects. Wild mountain scenery, tempests, and nocturnal landscapes were favorite subjects of description. Romanticism was therefore a return to nature. It was also a return to the Middle Ages. Each nation displayed a keen interest in its national past. In Germany, Romanticism found important expression in scholarship. Comparative philology, Romance philology, and Germanic philology were born as scientific subjects. Each individual language and literature was studied with a method hitherto employed solely for the elucidation of the languages and literatures of Greece and Rome. Criticism was revolutionized. Bishop Percy in England found beauty in the despised popular ballad. Shakespeare gained at the expense of Addison and Pope. Lessing, Herder, the Schlegel brothers, the Grimms, and many another worked along the same lines in Germany. Goethe and Hugo found art in the Gothic cathedrals, previously considered barbaric. Everywhere horizons were widened. Interest was not confined to one's own literature, for it was held that each literature had its individuality and its own message to convey. Hence a growing interest in the exotic and local color. The colorful literature of Spain attracted much attention, especially after the Peninsular War had brought England and France into close contact with that nation. Southey, Lockhart, Bowring, Herder, Depping, the Grimms, Tieck, Abel Hugo, and others did much to popularize Spain's old romances, balladry, and drama. Calderón became a Romantic idol. With the return to the Middle Ages came an interest in chivalry. Sir Walter Scott is the best representative of this tendency. A less happy trend was the interest manifested in witchcraft, magic, the marvelous, and the morbid. Hoffmann's fantastic tales are a typical example. The age was not yet scientific. Many romanticists developed a pessimism (*mal du siècle*, *Weltschmerz*) which invested their writings with gloom. They looked upon themselves as misunderstood supermen at odds with society. Byron is the most famous exponent of this tendency. This unhappy frame of mind was genuine with some, with others it was a pose. Under the influence of Goethe's *Werther*, many committed suicide. The Romantic drama abandoned the three Classic unities. It was emotional, sensational, and melodramatic. French romanticists, more than those of other countries, were fighting for a less restricted metrical system.

Spanish Romanticism partook of most of the characteristics of European Romanticism, but had its points of difference. Neo-Classicism had never taken firm root in Spanish soil, had produced few masterpieces. The dramatists of the *siglo de oro* had never ceased to be represented on the Spanish stage, though frowned upon by a restricted group of intellectuals. Whereas in France the detractors of Corneille and Racine were regarded as antipatriotic iconoclasts, in Spain the Romantic critics were engaged in the pleasant task of rehabilitating glorious authors of the past. Only a handful of critics needed to be convinced; the bulk of the nation was predisposed to Romanticism already, and the hatreds aroused by the Napoleonic wars made the position of the *afrancesados* untenable. More of the Middle Ages had descended into modern life there than elsewhere; interest in the Spanish past had never died out. Rationalism had never been a widely spread philosophy south of the Pyrenees. There was no question of a return to Catholicism on the part of this Catholic nation. Neither could there be many writers to adopt the scoffing, irreligious pose. The quality of Spanish scenery, too, made it easy to treat nature in her grandiose aspects. The simplicity of Spanish character was against the development of the world-weary type. Only a few, like Espronceda, assumed the Byronic pose, or, like Larra, committed suicide. The marvelous and the fantastic were less cultivated in Spain than in the northern countries. It cost Spaniards little effort to throw overboard the three unities and other hampering rules. The poets avoided those verse-forms closely identified with Classicism, such as the ode and the epistle, developed a new genre, *la leyenda*, and invented many metrical innovations, but were already more metrically free than the French poets of their day. All conspired to give Romanticism an easy victory in Spain. For this very reason the movement is less significant there than elsewhere.

The historical course of Spanish Romanticism.—We have seen that many neo-Classic poets were addicted to sentimentality and melancholy, and that others gave way to emotionalism under stress of patriotic excitement. Many displayed an interest in the national past. Tomás Antonio Sánchez published *El poema del Cid* in 1779, and most of the other poetic monuments of Old Spanish literature a few years later. Thus Spain published her national epic years before France printed the *Chanson de Roland*, or Germany the *Nibelungenlied*. Bartolomé José Gallardo (1776–1852), the greatest of Spanish bibliographers, began early in life his scientific researches in the field of the older literature, resulting in the post-humous publication of his *Ensayo*. Johan Nikolas Böhl von Faber (1770–1836), German born, but long resident in Cádiz, served as the connecting link between Germany and Spain. He translated those portions of the writings of the Schlegel brothers treating of the Spanish drama, and, during the years 1814–19, maintained a heated controversy in behalf of Calderón with the neo-Classic critics José Joaquín de Mora and Alcalá Galiano. Faber was victorious in this quarrel and paved the way for the triumph of Romanticism in Spain. His *Floresta de rimas antiguas castellanas*, 1821–25, was the first modern anthology of Old Spanish poetry. His *Teatro español anterior a Lope de Vega* threw light upon the early drama. Agustín Durán (1793–1862) wrote, in 1828, a memorable defense of the native drama. He began publishing his famous *Romancero general*, still the most comprehensive ballad collection in existence, in 1828. The Preface is an intelligent revindication of the ballad as an artistic genre. This zeal for republication of the older literature culminated in the vast *Biblioteca de autores españoles*, the first volume of which was printed in 1846. The most significant manifesto of Spanish Romanticism was the Prologue to the Duque de Rivas' *El moro expósito*, written by Faber's old adversary, Alcalá Galiano, long since converted.

The emigrados.—Under Fernando VII, nearly all the leading men of letters were liberally inclined and forced to live in exile. Most of them flocked to London and Paris, where their political Liberalism was confirmed and their Classicism changed to Romanticism. The London group wrote extensively and published several excellent reviews. When, in 1833, Fernando VII died, the throne descended to his infant daughter, Isabel II. Isabel's claim was disputed by her uncle, Don Carlos, who rallied to his support the most reactionary elements of the nation. The queen regent, María Cristina, forced to seek Liberal support, relaxed the censorship and made it possible for the political exiles to return. The *emigrados* did return, in 1833, bringing with them much literary baggage and many novel ideas. Spanish Romanticism as a full-fledged, self-conscious movement dates from this year; but 1833 represents the flowering of Romanticism, not its beginning, for which no date may be assigned. The movement was at its height throughout this decade, but it was not long before other tendencies began to assert themselves.

Francisco Martínez de la Rosa (1787–1862), a statesman twice exiled for his Liberal views, later in life a cabinet minister and diplomat, was always an active man of letters. He was an eclectic rather than a Romanticist, an experimenter in various fields; yet he has to his credit the first important Romantic triumph on the stage. His early Classic lyrics show him a follower of Luzán. He even wrote his own *ars poetica* along similar lines. Most of his lyric verse, his political and biographical writings, his one historical novel, are now forgotten; but he will always remain a distinguished figure in the history of the Spanish drama.

"*La conjuración de Venecia*" was written in 1830, while Martínez was an exile in Paris. Its production with noisy acclaim, April 23, 1834, marked an epoch. Here was a drama, written in prose, with studied disregard for the unities, melodramatic and colorful. Its hero was a mysterious personage of unknown origin, a victim of fate; its heroine, a beauty in distress. Masked conspirators abounded. There was a love-making scene in a burial crypt in which the lovers were parted by hooded figures. The scene representing the carnival of Venice in the Piazza di San Marco required elaborate scenery and costuming. It is obvious that many of Martínez' innovations were puerile and in bad taste; but he set a fashion for the exotic and colorful. For some time after, the ladies of Madrid arranged their hair and dress according to the Venetian style.

His other plays.—Previously Martínez had written in French a play called *La révolte des Maures sous Philippe II*, which was produced with indifferent success at the Théâtre Porte Saint-Martin in 1830. This was turned into Castilian and produced in 1836 with the title *Aben Humeya*. This dramatic representation of the Morisco revolt gave no less opportunity for local color, but the play was a comparative failure. These are Martínez de la Rosa's two Romantic plays. His early plays imitated

Moratín and Alfieri. Even as late as 1832 he had returned to the Classic manner and produced his *Edipo*, which many consider the best neo-Classic tragedy produced by a Spaniard. Manifestly he had been a half-hearted convert to Romanticism; but he pointed out the path which others were to follow.

Larra wrote some ten plays, of no great significance as compared with his critical and satiric writings. Some of these were comedies in the manner of Scribe, others show the influence of the elder Dumas. His outstanding play is *Macías*, a four-act historical drama in verse, produced in 1834, shortly after *La conjuración de Venecia*. It deals with the tragic fate of that model for all unhappy lovers in Spain, Macías, the Galician troubadour. This play was more restrained than most of the sort, for Larra avoided the extremes of Romanticism.

Ángel de Saavedra (El Duque de Rivas, 1791–1865) was the writer who confirmed the triumph of Romanticism in Spain. Born in Cordova, the second son of an opulent and noble family, he early began to write Classic verse and to paint pictures. While a mere boy he shed his blood fighting against Napoleon. Later his active participation in favor of a Liberal constitution caused him to pass ten years of exile. Five of these years he lived on the isle of Malta, where he made the acquaintance of John Hookham Frere, sometime British ambassador at Madrid and an amateur of Spanish literature. This companionship was of capital importance in Saavedra's career. Frere introduced him to the works of Byron, Scott, and other contemporary poets, gave him the run of a well-stocked library, and finally suggested that he write a Romantic epic after the fashion of Scott's *Marmion* and *The Lady of the Lake*. The old legend of *los siete infantes de Lara* was proposed, and the youth acted upon the suggestion. Saavedra's shift over to Romanticism is evident in *El faro de Malta*, one of his best lyrics, written in 1828. A few profitable years were spent in Paris, painting pictures and writing verse. When free to return home in 1834, he brought with him several completed works. The death of his older brother this same year gave him a ducal title. He plunged actively into the Romantic struggle for the next few years. This was the period of his greatest productivity. Though occasionally dabbling in letters, his latter years were devoted to politics, government, diplomacy, and the management of his estates. With years he grew conservative. The Duque de Rivas was the best poised of any of the Spanish romanticists, and this despite the fact that he wrote the wildest of Romantic plays. He was always sane and wholesome in his private life. His elevated social position placed him above the ranks of Bohemia, but his lack of snobbery and native kindliness made him everybody's friend. His friendship with such a vagabond as Zorrilla was marked by no trace of condescension.

"*El moro expósito*" was published in Paris in 1834. The most distinctively new genre introduced by Romanticism was the *leyenda*, "legend." Poets of all lands began to ransack history and tradition for picturesque legends to be retold in prose and verse. The tendency continued many years. The Duque de Rivas was the first to attain conspicuous success in Spain by the cultivation of this genre. *El moro expósito* is generally referred to as a *leyenda*, but in view of its length may better be termed a Romantic epic. It retells the treacherous murder of the seven brothers with the vengeance wreaked upon the perpetrators by Mudarra, "the foundling Moor." The old ballads are followed, though with variations. Abundant use is made of the hendecasyllabic, a Classic meter, but the theme and treatment are wholly Romantic. The interest is well sustained, even though the work is too long for modern impatience. No other Spanish poet finished an epic legend of equal length, so that *El moro expósito* remains a work apart. Zorrilla's *Granada* is long, but lacks unity, being rather a collection of legends.

"*Los romances históricos.*"—If *El moro expósito* appeals to but few readers, Rivas' shorter *leyendas* have lost nothing of their interest, and will always be considered his masterpiece. *Los romances históricos* were not printed as a collection until 1841, though most had been written during the Paris period, and many had been published in periodicals. Rivas' intent was to revive Spain's past greatness in a series of ballads, each one of which was to represent some picturesque, great, or culminating moment of Spanish history. He treats such themes as the fall and execution of the favorite, Álvaro de Luna, the murder of Villamediana, the victory of Pavía, the tribulations of Columbus, the youth of Pizarro, the horrors of the reign of Peter the Cruel, and ends with the defeat of Napoleon's troups at Bailén. His training as a painter gave Rivas an unusually developed visual imagination. Before describing his scene he posed his models, carefully grouped, like a painter. He described in detail their costumes, weapons, and accouterments. Azorín and Mr. Allison Peers have commented on his strong sense of color. What he lacks is dynamic force. He fails to give us moving pictures; we have instead a series of striking tableaux. Where a change of scene or action is necessary, a new subdivision of the poem begins, still in ballad form but with change of assonance. Of all the writers of *le-yendas*, Rivas is the most historic and the least fantastic. He had considerable archaeological sense. Later, under the influence of Zorrilla, he wrote a few legends in which the supernatural figures, but these are not characteristic of his best manner. His most popular ballad is *Un castellano leal*, which tells how the punctilious Conde de Benavente burned his residence after it had been occupied, at the emperor's request, by the traitorous Constable Bourbon.

"*Don Álvaro, o la fuerza del sino*," though of less intrinsic merit, is Rivas' most important production from the viewpoint of literary influence. This play, written in prose in 1831, was re-written in mingled prose and verse and staged in 1835. It is the most typical of all Spanish Romantic plays. The sensation it created confirmed the success of Romanticism in Spain. Far more daring than *La conjuración de Venecia*, it had nine successive performances, not bad for the period. Don Álvaro is one of Romanticism's great characters, comparable to René, Werther, Manfred, Don Juan. He is a mysterious personage, a superman, a man of destiny pursued by a hostile fate. (For his use of fate Rivas is probably indebted to Hugo's *Notre Dame de Paris*.) There is a mingling of the comic and the tragic, commonplace realism with the sublime. The number of characters is large, many of them splendidly drawn Spanish types. The action is dislocated; sensationalism appears everywhere, reason nowhere. The hero's suicide is the final solution. Verdi made this play the libretto of *La forza del destino*, and in its operatic form *Don Álvaro* still holds the stage. A work of supreme importance in the history of Romanticism, *Don Álvaro* is too extreme and absurd to please the discerning. In spite of Menéndez y Pelayo's extravagant praise, *Don Álvaro* makes slight appeal to readers of mature intelligence. Rivas' success with this play was too great to be repeated. His other dramas are unimportant. One need mention only the Calderonian piece, *El desengaño en un sueño*, 1842.

José de Espronceda y Delgado (1808–42).—Romantic drama has not endured the test of time. The opposite is true of the lyric, that form in which unrestrained emotionalism may be indulged with least artistic loss. Espronceda is the greatest Spanish Romantic poet, and probably the greatest poet of his nation throughout the entire nineteenth century. He is also the most typical exponent of Romanticism in Spain. He lived Romanticism. The son of a general whose financial circumstances were comfortable, Espronceda enjoyed the least bad education which the times afforded, attending Lista's Colegio de San Mateo. Lista undoubtedly inspired his gifted pupil to write verse. Like all the Romantic poets, Espronceda's first attempts were in the neo-Classic manner. He early became a Liberal, and, when still a boy we find him playing the game of political conspiracy. Later he conspired in earnest and was forced to join the group of exiles, first in Lisbon, next in London, then in Paris. While abroad, he engaged in various filibustering expeditions, fought at the barricades of Paris, in 1830, had his sordid love intrigue with Teresa Mancha, read the English and French poets, and became a convert to Romanticism. Returning home in 1833, he proved himself too radical for the newly established Liberalism. He became a rabid journalist, and was several times jailed and banished from the capital for indiscreet writings. His literary work consisted mainly of scattered contributions to the newspapers. He became relatively famous in 1840 with the publication of his *Poesías*. He died two years later, a member of the Chamber of Deputies, on the point of contracting a prudent marriage, and giving indication that his storm-and-stress period was passing.

His Romantic philosophy and sources.—Espronceda was never a Bohemian; on the contrary, he was a dandy, like his hero Byron. His philosophy, as Bonilla has well pointed out, was the typical philosophy of Romanticism: doubt, the first principle of thought; sorrow, the positive reality of life; pleasure, the world's illusion; death, the solution of every problem. Byron was the source of most of his pessimism and Romantic irony. Throughout his verse there is evidence of pessimism and disillusion. More than any other Spaniard he suffered from the *mal du siècle*. How much of this was real, how much mere pose, is difficult to determine. Mr. Churchman has indicated how extensively he was indebted to Byron. M. Brereton has pointed out how much he owed to Béranger. From the latter he took the artistic use of the refrain, his admiration of the proletariat extending to the idealization of anti-social types, the idea of the political *chanson*. It is unfair to dub Espronceda "the Spanish Byron." In literature, as in love, there is safety in numbers; and he was also influenced by Tasso, Calderón, Tirso, Scott, Macpherson, and many others. He was clearly dominated by no one author.

"*El estudiante de Salamanca*" is Espronceda's one attempt at the *leyenda*, and the supreme expression of this genre. It is his most objective work. The legend recounted is that of Don Miguel Mañara, the man who witnessed his own funeral. Don Félix de Montemar, as the protagonist is styled, is a typical Romantic hero of the family of Don Juan Tenorio, irreverent, dissipated, cynical, superhumanly brave. He joins in the dance of death and weds his skeleton-bride with mockery on his lips and intrepidity in his heart. Metrically the poem is a *tour de force*. The poet essays nearly every possible meter and displays astonishing virtuosity. He is especially skilled at making music and rhythm fit the matter of his verse.

"*El diablo mundo*" is an unfinished masterpiece. The hero, Adam, is an old man miraculously rejuvenated, but with the mind of a child. Naturally good, he is thrown into a heartless world, where he undergoes a variety of experiences, always resulting in disillusion. There is much diversity of subject matter and meter. Caustic humor and Romantic irony abound. The influence of Byron's *Don Juan* is evident. The total effect is one of confusion, numerous magnificent passages thrown together pell-mell with little arrangement. Even if he had lived, an impetuous nature like Espronceda's could scarcely have carried so grand a scheme to a triumphant conclusion. As it is, the work remains a torso. The second of the six cantos, entitled *A Teresa*, written on the occasion of Teresa Mancha's death, is a bitter outpouring of the poet's disillusion with regard to love and women.

His shorter poems.—Equally typical of his subjective manner is *A Jarifa en una orgía. A la patria* and *Dos de mayo* are magnificent patriotic poems. The famous *Himno al sol* is typical of his early Classic manner. *Oscar y Malvina* betrays the influence of Ossian. His most famous short poems are the *canciones: Canción del pirata, El canto del Cosaco, El mendigo, El reo de muerte, El verdugo.* These alone would suffice to make Espronceda a great poet. In them he appears as a youthful revolutionary, exalting the social outcast, and preaching the nihilistic doctrine that wholesale destruction must precede the task of reconstruction. In this sort of verse he surpasses Béranger, his model. One may smile at the juvenile folly of his misdirected ardor, but there is no denying the vigorous grace of his art.

Espronceda's total output is small. He essayed other forms, a novel, and a few plays; but he is negligible outside the field of lyric poetry. His message is not so much personal as that of Romanticism in general. He interests through his reforming zeal, the intensity of his emotionalism, and his deftness as a craftsman. He will remain forever the outstanding representative of Romantic lyricism in Spain.

Antonio García Gutiérrez (1813–84) was a humble private in the army, when, in a borrowed coat, he appeared on the stage to acknowledge the applause accorded his play, *El trovador,* on its first representation in 1836. *El trovador* is one of the most important in the sequence of Romantic plays. In the form of Verdi's opera, *Il trovatore,* it is a hardy perennial, which though hackneyed, continues to please. García Gutiérrez was a fluent and correct versifier, less extravagant in his plots than many of his school. He lacked most of all the art of skilfully ordering his intrigues. He wrote voluminously for the stage, and several of his later plays are better than *El trovador*, but he never so satisfied the public as with this first success. He continued the Romantic historical play for decades after the vogue for it had passed.

Juan Eugenio Hartzenbusch (1806–80) was the son of a German cabinet-maker and a Spanish mother. He early evidenced scholarly tastes, and later contributed to the rehabilitation in popular esteem of the *siglo de oro* drama, both as editor and critic. He wrote much mediocre verse and certain fantastic tales, but shone principally as a dramatist. *Los amantes de Teruel*, 1837, was the definitive Romantic version of this famous legend. In other plays, like *La coja y el encogido*, Hartzenbusch followed the manner of Moratín. He excelled in dramatic construction, but was weak as a poet and in the creation of character.

Antonio Gil y Zárate (1796–1861) was an industrious playwright, who, beginning as a neo-Classicist, turned mildly Romantic. He sought his themes in Spanish medieval history. His masterpiece is *Guzmán el Bueno*, 1842.

José Zorrilla (1817–93), the spoiled child of Romanticism, was the troubadour who best catered to the taste of the masses. He recounts his bohemian career in *Cuentos de un loco* and the interesting but splendidly mendacious memoirs, *Recuerdos del tiempo viejo*, 1880. He achieved fame at the age of twenty, when, an unknown, ragged boy, he thrust himself forward at Larra's funeral to read his poetic tribute to that great writer. From that moment he was the idol of the Spanish-speaking world. He passed through life with singular lack of judgment, always making the wrong decision. His career was a long struggle with poverty, though if he had retained a royalty interest in his *Don Juan*, he would have been rich. But he never lacked friends upon whom to sponge. His life contained two tragedies: his relations with his father and an unhappy marriage. The faults of the son were all too evident to a hard-headed parent blind to his offspring's genius. Zorrilla adored his father and constantly strove to earn his good opinion. As the latter was a pronounced reactionary, the poet kept politics out of his writings. His marriage to the mother of one of his friends, a ridiculous and jealous person old enough to be his own mother, was a fatal step. In the end he deserted her to pass long years in Paris and Mexico, where he became a sort of poet laureate at the court of Maximilian. After the death of his wife in 1866, he returned to Spain to find that Romanticism was dead and new poets and literary tendencies in fashion. But as author of *Don Juan*, he retained a certain celebrity to the last.

His lyrics.—Zorrilla is pre-eminently the writer of *leyendas*. He lacks altogether Rivas' historic sense and power of visualization, is more inclined to the supernatural, and better skilled at creating atmosphere and mood. Two of his famous legends, *A buen juez mejor testigo*, and *Para verdades, el tiempo, y para justicia, Dios*, are already contained in his *Poesías*, 1837. With his *Cantos del trovador*, 1841, their number was considerably increased. His masterpiece in this genre is *Margarita la Tornera*. The medieval legend of how the Virgin replaces in her convent duties an erring nun has been treated by many poets from Gautier de Coincy down to Maeterlinck, but nobody has surpassed Zorrilla in tenderness of narration. *Granada*, 1852, tells the story of the conquest of that city by the Catholic monarchs, weaving into the substance of the narrative the numerous legends which cluster about the Alhambra. Pérez de Hita and Washington Irving are drawn from. Zorrilla is singularly barren of ideas. His merit is descriptive charm. Therefore he is best when he clothes in beauty some twice-told tale. As a craftsman he lacked painstaking effort. He is the modern representative of Lope de Vega's improvising method, facile, fluent, copious. His peculiarly Spanish qualities make him dearer to his race than he ever can hope to be with foreigners.

His drama.—His most successful plays are also based upon legends. Noteworthy is *El zapatero y el rey*, in two parts, 1840 and 1841, based upon a well-known legend about Peter the Cruel. The playlet called *El puñal del godo*, concerning Roderick the Goth, is equally famous. But *Don Juan Tenorio*, 1844, has had by far the most continuous success of any Romantic play. Throughout the whole Spanish-speaking world this play is acted in every important center during the first week of November. It never fails to please; it is at once a tradition and an institution. Zorrilla has given Don Juan his most successful modern reincarnation. This play, like his others, is full of inconsistencies and errors, constantly betraying the careless workman. It excels in color, emotion, mood, vigor, melodiousness of versification. Zorrilla died condemning this piece and wishing that he could blot out nine-tenths of what he had written. He will never fare well at the hands of critics; but, if he failed to gain the admiration of the élite, he won the love of a people. He was the last of the troubadours.

Gertrudis Gómez de Avellaneda (1814–73), a Cuban poetess whose career is chiefly identified with Spain.

combined an energy truly virile with the sense of pity to be expected of her sex. Thwarted in her one great passion, and later twice widowed, she pours her sorrows into her verse with a genuineness of emotion not to be questioned even in an age when so much Romantic melancholy was sheer pose. Religion is the other theme of her verse. She was influenced by Hugo and Lamartine. She enriched Spanish prosody by the introduction of long meters, successfully handled. Though negligible as a novelist, it is interesting to note that in *Sab* she anticipated Mrs. Stowe, though timidly, in writing an antislavery novel. As a dramatist she combines Classic pomp with Romantic vigor and formlessness. Her masterpiece is *Baltasar*, 1858.

Juan Arolas (1805–49) was Spanish Romanticism's most pathetic figure. A monk without vocation, in a Valencian monastery, he sought escape from his monastery cell by leading a life of fantasy. He conjured up in imagination ideal beauties to whom he wrote erotic verse. He fancied himself a traveler in India and China, surrounded by scenes of oriental richness. The end was madness. Arolas possesses a sensuous luxury of imagination suggestive of Keats. His masterpiece is the poem, *A una bella*. Along with the narcotic lusciousness of the description goes the refrain, "Sé más feliz que yo." The condensed pathos and Christian resignation of this prove that Arolas retained in him something of the priest after all.

TO A BEAUTY

Above thy azure pupil, drooping low,
Thy languid eyelid, falling drowsily,
Is like the pure and candid, driven snow

Upon the violets heaped high.
I ne'er have slept a sleep from sorrow free:
> Be happier than I.
  Thy voice, when lifted up in maiden prayer,
Is like the black-bird's song on India's shore,
Which, perched on some pagoda fair,
Sings vesper carols, soft as any sigh.
This prayer I send to heaven—nothing more:
> Be happier than I.
  Thy breath is like the lily's fragrant scent
Upon the banks of Arno's storied flood,
Such flowers as bloom among the rushes, bent
Low by the gentle zephyr wafting by.
I sense it not—nor any earthly good:
> Be happier than I.
  Love is a spirit formed of fiery air,
Who takes his guidance from the silent night,
And feeds alike on mortals' tears and prayer.
Hidden, thy crimson lips he hovers nigh.
Let him grant thee the bliss and me the blight:
> Be happier than I.
  Fair are thy lovely, youthful, dawning hours
As field of roses in the Orient.
I begged an angel for a gift of flowers;
He gave them me thy brow to beautify.
I said the while the wreathèd crown I bent:
> Be happier than I.
  Thy tender gaze suggests the turtledove.
Like poppy of the desert wilderness,
Thou causest ecstasy of frantic love,
Sweet houri fallen from a topaz sky.
My fate is hard, and bitter my distress:
> Be happier than I.

Enrique Gil y Carrasco (1815–46), whose untimely
death while minister to Berlin was a loss to letters, will live
as the author of one famous poem, *La violeta*. Dreamy

melancholy, sentimentality, and a touch of mysticism are Enrique Gil's characteristics as a poet.

The historical novel.—Just as Byron reigned supreme over the poets of the Romantic period, Scott ruled over the novelists. Translations of the Waverley novels, mostly through the French, were circulated in great abundance after 1831. Spanish versions of Chateaubriand, Cooper, and Manzoni were numerous. The historical novel became the fixed form for the Romantic novel. The first of Sir Walter's imitators was Ramón López Soler with *Los bandos de Castilla, o el Caballero del Cisne,* 1830. Nearly every writer of the time followed suit. Larra's *Doncel de Don Enrique el Doliente,* 1834, tells once again the story of Macías, a personage with whom the great satirist seems to have identified himself. Espronceda's *Sancho Saldaña,* 1834, is in many ways an imitation of *Ivanhoe,* although the style and spirit are quite different. Escosura's *Ni rey ni roque,* 1835, was one of the best. However, critics consider Enrique Gil's *El señor de Bembibre,* 1844, the very best of its sort. Most writers were content with one or two such ventures, but Manuel Fernández y González (1821–88) devoted his life to writing them. All told, he wrote about three hundred novels, making over five hundred volumes. The large number of historical novels written during the four decades following 1830 indicates a considerable market for such wares. No one of them is a work of permanent value. The historical novel was an unhappy interruption in the development of the realistic novel of manners inaugurated by the *costumbristas.* But, according to Azorín, it has made one lasting contribution. The imitators of Scott copied his landscape descriptions. Today the *paisaje,* developed with far greater art, is an important part of the novel. Such gifted painters of landscape as Azorín and Pío Baroja are heirs of Sir Walter Scott and the Romantic novel.

Gustavo Adolfo Bécquer (1836–70), a belated romanticist.—After Romanticism had died as a vital force, there appeared a gifted writer who embodied its spirit. Bécquer, a sensitive artist-soul, went to Madrid at the age of eighteen to follow the career of letters. For sixteen years he led a bohemian existence, constantly struggling with poverty and disease, unhappy in his marriage. He knew how to reconcile the insistent demands of journalism with the most careful craftsmanship. Bécquer's prose is perhaps the most artistic of any written during the century, down to the advent of the great contemporary stylists. The German poet Heine inspired much of his verse.

"*Desde mi celda,*" written from an old monastery, is a series of nine literary letters. Better known are Bécquer's prose *Leyendas.* Though eerie and mysterious, they are less fantastic than the tales of Hoffmann, but the atmosphere is that of fairyland. The supernatural abounds. The mood is that of dreamy melancholy. Bécquer possessed to the full that *Stimmung* so characteristic of German Romanticism. The world of fancy was to him a grateful refuge from an intolerable reality.

But his *Rimas,* published posthumously in 1871, constitute Bécquer's chief title to fame. There is the same dreamy melancholy here that one notes in his prose, but his verse is simpler and more subjective. Some of the *Rimas* are close adaptations of Heine, others are original. However, the cynicism is much milder than is the case with the German author. Mrs. W. S. Hendrix has caught Bécquer's simple charm in her admirable rendering of *Rima LIII:*

> The dusky swallows will hang their nests
> In your balcony once again,
> And with their wings they will lightly tap,
> As they flit past your window-pane;
> But those who paused in their eager flight
> And lingered our names to learn,
> That viewed your beauty and my delight . . . .
> Ah! these will not return!
>
> Dense honeysuckle will scale the walls
> Of your garden, and there once more
> Will show its blossoms when evening comes,
> Even lovelier than before;
> But those, dew-laden, whose drops we watched
> Now tremble and fall, alack!
> That we saw fall like the tears of day . . . .
> Ah! these will not come back!
>
> The burning, passionate words of love
> Once again in your ears will sound;
> And then your heart will perhaps awake,
> Will be roused from its sleep profound;
> But as one kneels at His altar, mute,
> Adoring, with head bent low,
> As I have loved you . . . . be undeceived,
> Ah! they'll not love you so![1]

BIBLIOGRAPHY

PEERS, E. A. *A History of the Romantic Movement in Spain.* 2 vols. Cambridge, 1940. A fundamental study. Indispensable.
———. *A Short History of the Romantic Movement in Spain.* Liverpool, 1949. One-vol. abridgment of above.
MARTINENCHE, E. *L'Espagne et le romantisme français.* Paris, 1922.

[1] First published in *Hispania*, October, 1922.

PEERS, E. A. "Some Spanish Conceptions of Romanticism," *Modern Language Review*, XVI, 281–96; XVIII, 37–50.

PITOLLET, C. *La Querelle caldéronienne de Bohl de Faber et J. J. de Mora.* Paris, 1909.

MARTÍNEZ DE LA ROSA, F. "Obras completas," *Colección de los mejores autores españoles*, Vols. XXVIII, XXXII.

MENÉNDEZ Y PELAYO, M. *Estudios de crítica literaria* (1st series), *Obras completas.* Santander, 1940–50.

RIVAS, DUQUE DE. *Obras.* 7 vols. Madrid, 1894–1904.

AZORÍN. *Rivas y Larra, razón social del romanticismo en España.* Madrid, 1916.

PEERS, E. A. *Rivas and Romanticism in Spain.* Liverpool, 1923.

———. "Angel de Saavedra, Duque de Rivas: A Critical Study," *Revue hispanique*, LVIII, 1–600.

ESPRONCEDA Y DELGADO, JOSÉ DE. *Obras poéticas.* Valladolid, 1900.

———. "Poesías y el estudiante de Salamanca," ed. G. MORENO VILLA. 2 vols., *Clásicos castellanos.* Madrid, 1923.

CASCALES MUÑOZ, G. *Don José de Espronceda: Su época, su vida, y sus obras.* Madrid, 1914.

CHURCHMAN, P. H. "An Espronceda Bibliography," *Revue hispanique*, XVII, 741–77.

———. "Byron and Espronceda," *Revue hispanique*, XX, 5–210.

BONILLA Y SAN MARTÍN, A. "El pensamiento de Espronceda," *España moderna*, CCXXXIV, 69.

FITZMAURICE-KELLY, J. "Espronceda," *Modern Language Review*, IV, 20–39.

GARCÍA GUTIÉRREZ, A. *Obras escogidas.* Madrid, 1866.

ADAMS, N. B. *The Romantic Dramas of García Gutiérrez.* New York, 1922.

HARTZENBUSCH, J. E. *Obras.* 3 vols. Madrid, 1888–92.

CORBIÈRE, A. S. *Juan Eugenio Hartzenbusch and the French Theatre.* Philadelphia, 1927.

ZORRILLA, J. *Obras completas.* 4 vols. Madrid, 1905.

ALONSO CORTÉS, N. *Zorrilla: Su vida y sus obras.* 3 vols. Valladolid, 1916–20.

GÓMEZ DE AVELLANEDA, G. *Obras literarias.* 4 vols. Havana, 1914–18.

——. *Autobiografía y cartas de la ilustre poetisa, hasta ahora inéditas,* ed. L. CRUZ DE FUENTES. Huelva, 1907.

WILLIAMS, E. B. *The Life and Dramatic Works of Gertrudis Gómez de Avellaneda.* Philadelphia, 1924.

COTARELO, E. *La Avellaneda y sus obras.* Madrid, 1930.

AROLAS, JUAN. *Poesías religiosas, orientales, caballerecas y amatorias.* Valencia, 1883.

LOMBA Y PEDRAJA. *El Padre Arolas: Su vida y sus versos.* Madrid, 1898.

GIL Y CARRASCO, E. *Obras ahora por primera vez reunidas en colección,* ed. G. LAVERDE. Madrid, n.d.

SAMUELS, D. J. *Enrique Gil y Carrasco.* New York, 1939.

ZELLERS, G. *La novela histórica en España,* 1828–1850. New York, 1938.

BÉCQUER, G. A. *Obras completas.* Madrid, 1942.

SCHNEIDER, F. *Gustavo Adolfo Bécquer: Leben und Schaffen.* Leipzig, 1914.

GUILLÉN, J. "La poética de Bécquer," *Revista hispánica moderna,* VIII (1942), 1–42.

CHAPTER XXI

The
Nineteenth-Century
Regional Novel

The regional novel—Fernán Caballero—Antonio de Trueba—
Juan Valera—Pedro de Alarcón—José María de Pereda—Benito
Pérez Galdós—Emilia Pardo Bazán—Leopoldo Alas (Clarín)—Armando Palacio Valdés—Luis Coloma—Jacinto Octavio Picón—Vicente Blasco Ibáñez.

The regional novel.—After the first fervor of Romanticism had spent itself, Spaniards were not slow to return
to Realism, that natural bent of the race. The *costumbristas* had shown the way. It remained merely to expand
the sketch into a longer work of fiction. Spanish Realism
is the expression of a sane and simple race. It is rarely
pessimistic like that of France and Russia. Humor almost
invariably enters in to provide an atmosphere of optimism. Foreign influence counted for little in the early
novels of this sort. Late in the century several novelists,
under the influence of Zola, drifted into Naturalism with
its emphasis of the repulsive; but such experiments have
been less objectionable than has been the case in France
and Italy. It was inevitable that the modern novel of
manners in Spain should be regional. Life is not uniform
in Spain. The country is still a grouping of the old
reinos, each with its traditional customs and manners. A
given novelist therefore describes the life of his *patria
chica*. Many have attempted literary pilgrimages outside
the bounds of the native province, but almost invariably

with loss of power. Galdós remains the one great novelist who is Spanish rather than regional; and even he is at his best in depicting the life of the capital.

Cecilia Böhl von Faber (Fernán Caballero, 1796–1877) initiates the regional novel. She was the daughter, by a Spanish mother, of the distinguished scholar and critic, Johan Nikolas Böhl von Faber. Her interest in folklore was doubtless inspired by her German father, who in his native land had seen a new lyric spring from the *Volkslied*. Andalusia was an unworked mine of such material. Fernán Caballero (it is convenient to use the pseudonym in the case of a lady of such frequent change of name) early became interested in peasant lore—the proverbs, the stories, the songs and ballads, the superstitions, and the simple piety of the people. Some of these she incorporated in her first stories, written in bad German and French, without thought of publication. *La Gaviota* was translated from its original French and published in 1849. This, the first of the regional novels, had the charm of novelty to a generation wearied of the historical novel. Estébanez Calderón with his *Escenas andaluzas* had pointed the way, but here was a sustained novel, racy of the soil of Andalusia with recognizable types and customs. It tells the unhappy story of a German surgeon who marries a peasant songstress. She becomes a famous opera singer, falls in love with a bull-fighter, and ends by marrying the village barber, when the surgeon dies of a broken heart and the *torero* perishes in the arena. The plot is romantic and silly; the interest lies in the realistic descriptions of peasant life. *La familia de Alvareda* is more popular. *Clemencia, Lágrimas, Un servilón y un liberalito*, and a long series of similar works followed.

Her ideas and style.—Fernán Caballero's ideas are so old fashioned and reactionary as to be silly. She hates republics, liberal monarchies, Americans, and heretics. She scolds these institutions and individuals most vehemently; but, after all, she is democratic in her sympathy for the people, and wholesome in her advocacy of simple things. As a writer she possessed color, but lacked clarity. At times she is so ungrammatical as to suggest illiteracy. Today she appeals almost exclusively to the folklorist. But hers is the glory of redirecting the modern Spanish novel into its proper channel. Gertrudis de Avellaneda, as novelist, imitated George Sand unsuccessfully. Fernán Caballero, imitating nobody, is the George Sand of Spain.

Antonio de Trueba (1819?–89) did for the Basque provinces, on a lesser scale, what Fernán Caballero did for Andalusia. Most of his *cuentos* are based upon folklore, and reflect the naïveté of peasant character.

Juan Valera (1827–1905) was an aristocrat from the south whose career was diplomacy, whose avocation was literature. He traveled much and gained a tincture of cosmopolitanism without on that account losing his national flavor. He served as minister at Lisbon, Brussels, and Washington. There is an air of urbanity in all his writings. A cheerful contentment renders him one of the most agreeable of authors. His style has the salt and sunshine of his native Andalusia.

His works.—His first novel, *Pepita Jiménez*, 1874, is also his most famous. It was the fruit of the author's readings in the field of mysticism. The hero, Luis de Vargas, studying for the priesthood, falls in love with the charming widow Pepita, not realizing what is happening to him. His emotions and scruples are conveyed to a clerical uncle in the form of letters. He finally gives up his contemplated career, marries Pepita, and settles down to the life of a landed proprietor. Characters and descriptions are excellent. *Doña Luz* treats of the platonic love of an elderly priest for the heroine. *El comendador Mendoza* and *Juanita la larga* are also pictures of Andalusian life. *Las ilusiones del doctor Faustino* and *Morsamor* are next in importance. The latter is a fantastic narrative set in the era of navigation and discovery. Valera's plots are simple, his characters well drawn, his style pleasing, his pictures of manners convincing. He exerted considerable influence as a critic, though too kindly by far to mediocre writers, and sometimes glaringly at fault in his judgments. In reading Valera one gets no impression of greatness, but rather that feeling of satisfaction which comes from meeting a well-bred intelligent man of the world.

Pedro Antonio de Alarcón y Ariza (1833–91).—With Alarcón, Andalusia comes to the fore again. This the most colorful of provinces was earlier exploited by writers than other regions. Alarcón's literary career opened with *El final de Norma*, written at the age of eighteen—fantastic trash but still enjoyed by the very young. He first won fame with narratives of travel: *Diario de un testigo de la guerra de África*, 1860, and *De Madrid a Nápoles*, 1861. The novelist came fully into his own with the publication of *El sombrero de tres picos*, 1874. The source was a popular ballad, *El molinero de Arcos*, which Alarcón retold with the utmost originality. *El sombrero de tres picos* will always rank as one of the world's greatest masterpieces of humor. In every other respect Alarcón is deficient as a novelist, but in humor he stands supreme among modern Spanish writers of fiction, nearly every one of whom is richly endowed with that quality. This work, like the almost equally popular *El capitán Veneno*, is a novelette. Alarcón also excelled in the short story, a genre in which modern Spain has been surprisingly weak. Many of his *Novelas cortas* are excellent. *El libro talonario*, for example, is inimitable. In the novel proper he was less successful. *El escándalo*, 1875, is the best of these. *El niño de la bola* followed in 1880, and *La pródiga* in 1882. All of these offer agreeable reading, but lack composition and sustained interest. Alarcón continues to be one of Spain's most widely read novelists, but his merit is due almost exclusively to his humor, and he is at his best in the short story and novelette.

José María de Pereda (1833–1905), the chronicler of the Montaña district, is in many respects the greatest of the modern Spanish realists. Born of a noble and well-to-do family, he inherited the conservative ideas of his caste. Intending first to follow a military career, he abandoned this plan, doubtless because his Carlist sympathies made it impossible for him to serve except against the existing government. He next tried politics and served a term as deputy, but was too squeamish to endure rough contacts with corrupt politicians. He therefore returned to his loved Santander and founded a journal, *La abeja montañesa*, in which he published his first fiction, a series of *cuadros de costumbres*. These were republished in 1864 with the title, *Escenas montañesas*. Pereda is the writer who best illustrates in his work the evolution of the *artículo de costumbres* into a novel.

His works.—Even in these early efforts Pereda's

characteristic manner is in evidence. He is the sympathetic historian of the Santander fisher-folk and the primitive farmers of the hilly hinterland. "La leva," one of the stories in *Escenas montañesas,* was considered by Menéndez y Pelayo the best Spanish short story since Cervantes. It is a little preachment against conscription, and the idea that fortune lies afar. One should be content with one's lot and one's surroundings. This was one of Pereda's pet ideas. After several essays in the drama, all unsuccessful, Pereda wrote his first long novel, *El buey suelto,* 1878. This attacks the selfishness of celibacy and inculcates the duty of marriage. *Pedro Sánchez,* 1883, forsakes the mountain region to describe the life in Madrid of an unscrupulous journalist and politician. It is the greatest of modern picaresque novels. As one novel followed another, Pereda gave evidence of growing power. *Sotileza,* 1885, his most popular work, is the finest novel of the sea written by a Spaniard. *La puchera,* 1889, brings in both the water and the land. *Peñas arriba,* 1895, describes the farmer's life among the hills. Though less popular than *Sotileza,* it is regarded by critics as Pereda's masterpiece. Its plot is simple. The interest lies in its descriptions and the charmingly developed philosophy of the simple life.

Pereda's ideas.—Pereda had aristocratic prejudices, but also the virtues of his caste. As a youth the corruption of politics had disgusted him with democratic institutions. His solution was a feudal regimentation of society, with a contented peasantry living under paternally benevolent landlords. He hated cities and their demoralizing ways. The hero of *Peñas arriba,* a blasé young city aristocrat, finds happiness only by casting in his lot with his tenants and sharing their simple joys. Away from the city and back to the farm is one of Pereda's reiterated themes. In general, Pereda hated the middle class. In *Sotileza*, the fish-girl heroine has all the fine feelings of a lady, while Luisa, the daughter of the bourgeoisie, is a vulgar little snob. He was not interested in what the world calls progress. His admiration was for the virtuous poor and those few nobles with a sense of *noblesse oblige*. He had a fine scorn for everything mean. He saw no surer way to attain happiness than by following the teachings of the church. This conservatism has caused Pereda to lose caste with the younger generation of critics who do not always distinguish carefully between an author's ideas and an author's art. Admitting that many of Pereda's views are old fashioned and ill advised, they are for the most part wholesome. There is a restfulness in his writings which is refreshing after the feverishness of the young radicals of the present.

His style.—Pereda is gifted as a creator of living types. His characters are never caricatures. Many of them are, however, slightly idealized. He is a realist and never a naturalist. Peasant characters speak and act in natural fashion, but the principle of artistic choice is always observed. Pereda will not descend to coarseness. The richness of vocabulary and the frequent use of dialect make him a difficult author for foreigners, and even for Spaniards. That is because he is so wholly of his province that he has lost a certain degree of universality. There is no affectation to mar his style; all is simplicity and naturalness. Valle-Inclán and Azorín are now accounted greater stylists; but there is often a straining for effect in their best prose. Pereda has greater ease, is simpler and less mannered. He is king of the regional novelists, classic in his poise. His Realism is humorous and optimistic. He loved the region and the types described. *Realidad idealizada* is the phrase employed by Menéndez y Pelayo to sum up Pereda's manner.

Benito Pérez Galdós (1843–1920) is the apostle of progress among the nineteenth-century novelists. He interests by his sane Liberalism, his crusading spirit, his ability to depict Spanish life. He is not a regional novelist, rather the novelist of all Spain. He has described the life of every province with one exception—that of the Canary Isles, his birthplace. He left Las Palmas at fifteen, and henceforth lived in Madrid. Frequent journeys gave him a cosmopolitan outlook. He knew the life of each of the great European capitals, and toured every region of Spain in third-class carriages so as to establish close contacts with the people. He had an inquiring mind, was gifted as interviewer and reporter, and came to know his country and countrymen as few have known them.

"Episodios nacionales."—Galdós' first work, *La fontana de oro*, 1870, was a historical novel describing life in the early nineteenth century. He conceived the idea of writing a series of historical romances dealing with the troubled history of the nineteenth century. The first of these, *Trafalgar*, appeared in 1873. Sequels followed almost down to the author's last year, continuing the story to the time of Cánovas del Castillo. These novels, arranged in five series, number forty-six. Galdós had marvelous historic imagination and power to evoke the spirit of an age gone by. The popular tumults, revolutions, and battles of the past are made as vivid as if they were affairs of today. Through it all runs the lesson that

mere revolution without education of the masses affords no relief. The democracy only shifts the burden from one shoulder to another. Every student of Spanish literature should read the graphic description of the *première* of *El sí de las niñas* in *La corte de Carlos IV*, the account of the patriotic revolt against the French and of the most famous of modern sieges, told, respectively, in *El 19 de marzo y el 2 de mayo* and *Zaragoza*. The Carlist wars are narrated no less graphically. All these novels supply an excellent background for the understanding of contemporary Spain. Yet in spite of their obvious merits, it is hard to comprehend the enthusiasm of Spanish critics for the *National Episodes*. The boy-hero of the first series is a preposterous prodigy, always prominently to the fore wherever great events are stirring. Most of the fictitious personages are caricatures. One may even find absurdities, and there are many signs of excessive haste in the writing. There are flashes of brilliance, but there are glaring faults in the *Episodios*.

Novels of social reform.—*Doña Perfecta*, 1876, broaches the religious question. It is a dramatization of the spirit of progress at grips with tradition. The characters are symbolic: Pepe Rey, of progress; Doña Perfecta, of bigotry leading to crime; the Penitenciario, of obscurantism; Rosario, who loses her reason as a result of the differences of the rest, stands, perhaps, for the afflicted Spanish nation. The novel contains excellent types, but the total effect is false. The characters have been too carefully chosen in support of a thesis. *Gloria*, 1877, propounds the question of race. A bigoted Catholic is unable to marry a cultured Jew whom she loves, on account of difference of creed. *La familia de León Roch*, 1879, describes the wrecking of a marriage through the religious differences of husband and wife. These novels created a stir at the time of their appearance, but Galdós is moderate in his attitude. He is not attacking religion, not even Roman Catholicism, merely clericalism and bigotry. A crucifix always hung on the wall of the novelist's bedchamber. In politics, he was not a Socialist. What he pleaded for was education, enlightenment, honesty, practical improvements. All these things could not be attained over night, and he was content with slow results. He lacked the bitterness and revolutionary spirit of certain contemporary reformers.

His later works.—Artistically these works are marred by the intrusion of theses. Galdós is best when he describes life without *arrière-pensée.* And the life he knew best was that of the capital, especially that of the middle and lower classes. His masterpiece is the four-volume novel, *Fortunata y Jacinta,* the story of two unhappily married women, one of the bourgeoisie, the other of the proletariat, whose lives are fatally intertwined. At times Galdós becomes mildly naturalistic, as in *Tormento, Lo prohibido,* and *La desheredada.* Again he betrays, as in *Nazarín,* the influence of Tolstoy. Among his best productions are *Ángel Guerra* and the four books of the "Torquemada" series, the latter a psychological study of the effects of usury upon character.

Galdós' merits and defects.—Just as Pereda's conservatism has caused him to be undervalued by the Generation of 1898, so Galdós' enlightened progressivism has caused him to be overestimated by the same critics. Both men should be valued according to their art, rather than according to their ideas. Of the two, Galdós is certainly the more enlightened patriot; Pereda is beyond comparison the greater writer. Galdós prepared for his novels carefully and wrote them carelessly. He seldom produced less than four a year. This is perhaps excusable in the case of one who lived by his pen in a country where a restricted reading public rendered incessant productivity a necessity; but the fact remains that Galdós wrote hastily and often incorrectly. His ideas are good, his style mediocre. His propensity for caricature may be due to the influence of Dickens. This is less in evidence in his riper work. So, too, are the melodrama, the emphasis, the forcing of the note which mar so many of his works. But in spite of his faults, Galdós is a forceful and admirable character for whom the reader forms an affection. The intimate friendship which united two such opposites as Galdós and Pereda was honorable to both.

La Condesa Emilia Pardo Bazán (1852–1921), the regional novelist of Galicia and introducer of Naturalism into Spain, was the most distinguished female novelist of her country. Her career as a writer begins with the publication of *Pascual López,* 1879, naïve in plot, but already giving evidence of that vigor and color which were to distinguish her later writings. A woman possessed of considerable culture in contemporary European literature and art, she knew little of the older Spanish literature. This became apparent with the publication of *La cuestión palpitante,* 1883, a critical volume in which she sought to introduce the Naturalism of Zola into Spain. This, like her other critical productions, is superficial and of little permanent value.

Naturalistic novels.—Pardo Bazán's two strongest works, those in which she attempts to put Naturalism

into practice, are *Los pazos de Ulloa*, 1886, and *La madre
naturaleza*, its sequel, 1887. Doña Emilia, though daring
at times, avoids the extremes of Zolaesque pornography.
Hers is a poetized Naturalism. In *Madre naturaleza* there
is a pantheistic conception of nature carried to the point
of justifying incest. Such sentimentalizing over the un-
clean disgusts in its way as much as Zola's balder crudi-
ties. One wishes that Pardo Bazán had had the good
sense to remain feminine; but, as with many other female
novelists, it was a matter of coquetry with her to appear
more virile than the males. In spite of all, the two works
mentioned are great novels. They study the progressive
degeneracy of a noble family, gradually descending to
the level of their peasant tenants, while the estate goes
to rack and ruin. The peasant types are convincing, the
nature-setting attractive, the plots interesting.

Other works.—Other regional works are *La tribuna,
El cisne de Vilamorta, Insolación, La piedra angular,
Morriña*, and many short stories. *La quimera*, 1905, one
of her most ambitious novels, is interesting for its autobiographic reminiscences. It contains an element of
symbolism and is more cosmopolitan in tone and setting
than most of her other works. Her last novel was *Dulce
dueño*, 1911. Her criticism and narratives of travel were
of ephemeral interest. Pardo Bazán is relatively weak in
humor, but far less pessimistic than her chosen models,
Zola and Tolstoy. Her vocabulary is rich, her style
colorful and energetic, if a bit too diffuse. Spanish critics
make a good point when they scold her for her mistaken
belief that Spain needed foreign models for Realism. She
never went the full length of Naturalism, but her fame
would have been greater if she had been content to apply

the realistic method of the other regional novelists to
the unworked field of her native province.

Leopoldo Alas (Clarín, 1852–1901) was a regional
novelist of Asturias. Like Pardo Bazán, he was an enthusiastic advocate of Naturalism, though in his later
work he became an idealist. His long novel, and most
considerable work, *La Regenta*, 1884–85, is a mixture of
the naturalistic and the psychological novel. It is a
picture of life in Oviedo, documented and carefully
studied down to the last detail. Nearly every phase of
the city's life is represented by some character. The
clerics attached to the cathedral and the idle frequenters of
the Casino are admirably drawn. The principal interest
consists in the pitiless analysis of the heroine's false
mysticism. Alas also wrote many short stories, often fantastic, but always inculcating some moral or philosophic
lesson. He was primarily a thinker. For many years
he served in the University of Oviedo as professor of
political economy. Under the pseudonym of Clarín he
wrote criticism of contemporary literature. Often called
"a second Larra," he outrivaled his predecessor in trench-
ancy and abusiveness of style, if not in brilliance. Alas
was liberal, anticlerical, progressive. He was too prone to
engage in polemics, but his destructive criticism counter-
acted beneficially the urbane flatteries of Juan Valera
and the like. The younger generation has profited by
Clarín's fight in behalf of standards.

Armando Palacio Valdés (1853–1938) is also a regional
novelist of Asturias. He is even more popular abroad
than at home. William Dean Howells recognized in him a
kindred spirit, and did much to make his writings known
in this country. In fact, Palacio Valdés' best manner is

very like that of Howells—a realism rich in humor and avoiding the sensational. He began his career as a novelist in 1881 with *El señorito Octavio*. This as well as *Riverita* and *Maximina* are interesting for their autobiographic details. His masterpiece is *Marta y María*, 1883, in which the mystic and domestic virtues as exemplified by the two heroines are delightfully contrasted. The writer's preference, and inevitably the reader's, is for the less saintly and more normal of the two. Almost equally popular is *José*, like *Sotileza*, an idyl of the life of fisherfolk. *El cuarto poder* deals with provincial newspaper life. The scene is localized in Oviedo. In *La hermana San Sulpicio*, Palacio Valdés leaves his *patria chica* to describe life in Seville. No one of the Andalusian writers has better caught the atmosphere of that delightful province. In *La alegría del capitán Ribot*, Valencia is portrayed with equal success. In a few novels, Palacio Valdés made an unhappy experiment with Naturalism. *La espuma* is a bold exposé of the immoralities and futilities of Madrid's smart set. *El maestrante* and *La fe*, though less objectionable, contain naturalistic elements. The true Palacio Valdés is to be sought elsewhere. Optimism, not pessimism, is his forte. Though Spain has produced greater novelists, she has given the world few more delightful.

Luis Coloma (1851–1914), Jesuit *padre*, need be mentioned for only one work, his mildly naturalistic novel, *Pequeñeces*, 1891. Like *La espuma*, this is a satire on the aristocracy. It achieved "a success of scandal," for its characters were readily identified with real personages. Its style is undistinguished, but the book has permanent value as a witty comment on the life of the times.

Jacinto Octavio Picón (1853–1924) wrote anticlerical

novels, showing more acrimony than Galdós had done, and initiates the *novela erótica*. Though less popular than most of his contemporary novelists, his works created a stir and possess permanent value for their artistic form and polished style.

Vicente Blasco Ibáñez (1867–1928) is the novelist of Valencia. Starting life as a Republican and Socialist politician, he participated in revolutionary conspiracies and suffered exile and imprisonment. Later he served in the Cortes as a Republican deputy and founded in Valencia a radical journal, *El pueblo*. His first literary efforts were serials written in that newspaper. The storm-and-stress period soon passed, and increasing years, fame, and wealth so tempered his views that so good a Socialist as John Dos Passos once called him "an inverted Midas." Nevertheless, he spent his last years actively propagandizing against the military dictatorship. Though somewhat less radical, he remained to the end a sincere liberal.

The Valencian novels.—*Arroz y tartana*, 1894, was Blasco Ibáñez' first important novel. It centers around the market-place of Valencia, and was evidently suggested by Zola's *Ventre de Paris*. The influence of Zola is marked in his early works. From Zola he got his Naturalism, his technique of handling plot (monotonously the same always), and his ability for describing crowds. *Flor de mayo* is another novel of the life of fishermen, inferior to *Sotileza* and *José*. *Cuentos valencianos* and *Entre naranjos* also center about Valencia. *La barraca*, 1898, is undoubtedly Blasco Ibáñez's masterpiece. The theme is that of Sudermann's *Der Katzensteg* —a virile personage at odds with an entire countryside.

The setting is the beautiful *huerta* of Valencia. The characters are the half-Moorish peasants of the region, vindictive in their animosity toward the stranger. *Sonnica la cortesana*, 1901, is a historical novel dealing with the siege of ancient Saguntum. The civilizations of Greece, Rome, and Carthage, converging upon the ancient Levantine city, are vigorously portrayed. Spain has produced no better historical novel. *Cañas y barro*, 1902, ranks as his second-best work of fiction.

The sociological novels.—The next series consists of sociological and socialistic preachments in which art is sacrificed to propaganda. The author now leaves his native province and seeks to be the novelist of all Spain, losing much power when he describes backgrounds less familiar. *La catedral* is localized in Toledo and centers around the cathedral life of the primate church of Spain. The church, the army, and the monarchy are savagely attacked. *El intruso* is a study of trade-unionism in Bilbao. *La bodega* describes the hardships of the Andalusian peasant. *La horda* pictures the proletariat of Madrid. *Sangre y arena*, 1906, is the completest account of the bull-fight which has appeared in fiction. Bull-fighting is displayed objectively with all its horrors, but not attacked until the final sentence, where the crowd of spectators is likened to a monster. *Los muertos mandan*, 1909, contains charming descriptions of the Balearic Isles.

Novels of South America and the war.—Having devoted a novel to almost every important Spanish center, Blasco Ibáñez set out for South America, like an Alexander bent on conquering new worlds. He intended to devote a novel to each of the South American nations. *Los Argonautas*, 1914, dealing with Argentina, had just appeared when the outbreak of the Great War interrupted this scheme. Returning to Europe, Blasco Ibáñez wrote his war novel, *Los cuatro jinetes del Apocalipsis*, 1916, which was a fabulous success on account of its timely interest and its enthusiastic advocacy of the cause of the Allies. As literature it is mediocre. There followed *Mare nostrum*, 1918, a prose poem on the Mediterranean. It describes the history of the inland sea, ancient and modern, its flora and fauna, and everything that has to do with the cities on its shores. The whole is an indigested mass of encyclopedic information, enlivened by a few thrills supplied by the activities of German spies and submarines. Blasco Ibáñez' most recent production has been hackwork. *La reina Calafia* gives some of the author's impressions of California.

His style.—Many complained because Blasco Ibáñez was so well known in English-speaking countries to the exclusion of so many other Spanish novelists better deserving of recognition. His merit is vigorous forcefulness, but he is crude, ungrammatical at times, and always without polish. He is commercial and too prolific. Delicacy and finesse are not to be found in his writings. He interests chiefly by the attractive descriptions of Valencian life in his early novels.

BIBLIOGRAPHY

GONZÁLEZ BLANCO, A. *Historia de la novela en España desde el Romanticismo a nuestros días.* Madrid, 1909.

GÓMEZ DE BAQUERO (ANDRENIO). *El renacimiento de la novela en el siglo XIX.* Madrid, 1924.

BLANCO GARCÍA, F. *La literatura española en el siglo XIX.* 3 vols. Madrid, 1891–94; 2d ed. Madrid, 1899.

VÉZINET, F. *Les Maîtres du roman espagnol contemporain.* Paris, 1907.

FERNÁN CABALLERO. *Obras completas.* 17 vols. Madrid, 1893–1914.

GONZÁLEZ BLANCO, A. *Antonio de Trueba: Su vida y sus obras.* Bilbao, 1914.

VALERA, JUAN. *Obras completas.* 57 vols. Madrid, 1905–35.

AZAÑA, M. *La novela de Pepita Jiménez.* Madrid, 1927.

BALSEIRO, J. A. *Novelistas españoles modernos.* New York, 1933.

ROMANO, P. *Antonio de Alarcón el novelista romántico.* Madrid, 1933.

BELL, A. F. G. *Contemporary Spanish Literature.* Rev. ed. New York, 1933.

MADARIAGA, S. DE. *Semblanzas literarias contemporáneas.* Barcelona, 1924.

CAMP, JEAN. *José María de Pereda: Sa vie, son oeuvre et son temps.* Paris, 1937.

COSSÍO, J. M. DE. *La obra literaria de Pereda.* Santander, 1934.

GULLÓN, R. *Vida de Pereda.* Madrid, 1944.

ALAS, L. *Páginas escogidas de Clarín,* with Prologue by AZORÍN. Madrid, n.d.

WALTON, L. B. *Pérez Galdós and the Novel of the Nineteenth Century.* London, 1928.

BERKOWITZ, H. C. *Benito Pérez Galdós: Spanish Liberal Crusader.* Madison, 1948.

CASALDUERO, J. *Vida y obras de Galdós.* 2d ed. Madrid, 1951.

PATTISON, WALTER J. *Benito Pérez Galdós and the Creative Process.* Minneapolis, 1954.

EOFF, SHERMAN H. *The Novels of Pérez Galdós.* St. Louis, 1954.

MENÉNDEZ Y PELAYO, M. *D. Benito Pérez Galdós considerado como novelista, Estudios de crítica literaria* (5th series), *Obras completas.*

SÁINZ RODRÍGUEZ, P. " 'Clarín' y su obra," *Revista de las Españas,* Vol. II (1927).

GONZÁLEZ LÓPEZ, E. *Emilia Pardo Bazán: Novelista de Galicia.* New York, 1944.

BALSEIRO, J. A. *Vicente Blasco Ibáñez: Hombre de acción y de letras.* San Juan, 1935.

CRUZ RUEDA, A. *Armando Palacio Valdés: Estudio biográfico.* Jaén, 1924.

CHAPTER XXII

The Post-Romantic
Drama of the
Nineteenth Century

The various currents—Bretón de los Herreros—Gorostiza—
Ventura de la Vega—Florentino Sanz—Tamayo y Baus—López de
Ayala—Núñez de Arce—Echegaray—El género chico—Enrique
Gaspar—Pérez Galdós—Dicenta.

The various currents.—Simultaneously with the Romantic drama certain writers carried on the tradition o
the younger Moratín. Bretón de los Herreros devised a
drama of social satire which is reminiscent in many of its
characteristics of *siglo de oro* drama. The thesis play
develops with Tamayo y Baus and López de Ayala. The
Romantic historical play continues to be cultivated,
though the excesses of Romanticism are avoided. Foreign
masters, like Scribe, Dumas fils, Augier, and Ibsen exert
a slight influence. Echegaray develops a new form of Romantic drama. Toward the end of the century Dicenta
introduces Naturalism to the stage.

Manuel Bretón de los Herreros (1796–1873) represents
a return to old traditions. He is a nineteenth-century
Lope in his fecundity, versatility, and facility as a versifier; but, like Ramón de la Cruz, he sought to adapt
the old formulas to modern conditions. His 175 plays
are of every sort. He translated Racine and Voltaire; he
readapted Lope, Tirso, and Calderón; he wrote a Romantic drama. But he soon perceived that Romanticism
did not fit his peculiar genius and became one of the most

brilliant satirists of that school. The younger Moratín
was his chief source of inspiration. His earliest play,
A la vejez, viruelas, 1824, satirizes the elderly lover. *Marcela, o ¿cuál de los tres?* 1831, is a sprightly play which will
always remain a classic. Marcela is forced to choose
between three suitors, a talkative busybody, a glutton,
and *un melancólico.* She sensibly gives them all the
mitten. As time progressed, Bretón developed a more
individual manner. Among his numerous plays the following deserve mention: *Muérete y verás, ¿Quién es ella?
La escuela del matrimonio,* and *A Madrid me vuelvo.*
Bretón at his best and most characteristic is a clever
satirist of middle-class society. He has wit, lightness of
touch, and charm.

Manuel Eduardo de Gorostiza (1789–1851), a Mexican
domiciled in Spain, continued the tradition of Moratín.
His best play is *Indulgencia para todos,* 1818. His most
popular one, *Contigo pan y cebolla,* 1833, with its caricature of Romanticism, still continues to please.

Ventura de la Vega (1807–65) was a native of Argentina and fellow-student with Espronceda under Lista.
Unlike Espronceda, he was not a convert to Romanticism, but belonged to the school of Moratín. His dramatic masterpiece is *El hombre de mundo,* 1845, in which a
rake, after marriage, is made to feel the pangs of jealousy.

Eulogio Florentino Sanz (1825–81) is remembered for
one admirable historical play, *Don Francisco de Quevedo,*
1848. This is interesting for its philosophic treatment of
the great satirist's romantic career.

Manuel Tamayo y Baus (1825–81), after writing sentimental Romantic plays, historical dramas, and what is
called the last of the Classic tragedies, *Virginia,* 1853,

found his true bent in the comedy of manners. He is said to have inaugurated the thesis-play in Spain under the influence of Dumas fils and Augier; but the debt to these writers was slight, and Moratín's example was no less significant. Only a few of his plays may be said to contain theses, and the lesson he would teach is always some sound precept of morality. *La bola de nieve*, 1856, makes jealousy odious; *Lo positivo*, 1862, is an attack upon materialism; *Lances de honor* condemns the duel. *Un drama nuevo*, 1867, is one of the greatest of Spanish tragedies. The characters are Shakespeare, Yorick, his clown, and other members of Shakespeare's troupe. It is an extraordinary piece with its play within a play, and simulated jealousy and murder becoming real. The rôle of Yorick has made many an actor's reputation. A professional player in his early years, Tamayo possessed a practical knowledge of technique.

Adelardo López de Ayala (1829–79) insists more than Tamayo on the moral thesis. His *El tanto por ciento*, 1861, anticipates the latter's *Lo positivo* by a year. The theme is the same—love versus money. López de Ayala was influenced by Ruiz de Alarcón, and, like that master, attempts character types of a general nature. He is less successful in depicting sharply individualized personages. Though a prolific writer, he was careful in his workmanship and versification. He loomed large in a period of mediocrity. His first play, *Un hombre de estado*, 1851, is possibly his best.

Gaspar Núñez de Arce (1834–1903), more famous as a lyric poet, produced one of the best of Spanish historical plays, *El haz de leña*, 1872. The theme is the tragic death of the Infante Don Carlos, son of Philip II. The author, in attempting a subject already treated by Enciso, Quintana, Schiller, and Alfieri, produced a work fit to stand comparison with those of his predecessors. While he does not adhere to history so closely as to destroy all romance, and adds fictional elements of his own, Núñez de Arce has violated history less than the other dramatists named. The play contains striking situations, and drives home the lesson of religious tolerance. The title is suggested by an alleged utterance of Philip II, to the effect that if his own son were guilty of heresy, he, the father, would provide the first faggot for his burning.

José Echegaray (1832–1916), professor of mathematics, engineer, and statesman, was king of the stage from 1873 down to the advent of Dicenta and Benavente in the nineties. In the main he represents a return to Romanticism. He did not turn toward the Middle Ages or the fantastic, but gave expression to melodramatic passion. Modern criticism reacts strongly against him. Much of his work is sheer fustian; his dramatic situations are forced and sensational. He must be allowed skill as a technician—that is his chief merit. He attempted the problem play, but in most instances the problems propounded are unlikely to arise in real life. Of his scores of plays most are now dead. *El hijo de Don Juan* is one of the few Spanish plays inspired by Ibsen. It is a study of the effects of inherited disease. *O locura o santidad*, one of Echegaray's masterpieces, has for its hero a quixotically honorable gentleman, who is considered crazy by family and friends when he attempts to make over his fortune to its rightful owners. The cynical thesis that the world considers honorable conduct insanity is strange doctrine for a Spaniard to preach. *El gran Galeoto*, 1881, has been acted in America and every European country with conspicuous success. It is a "triangle" play, but unlike most of the sort, all three persons concerned are actuated, at the start at least, by honorable motives. The world with its heartless calumny drives even the virtuous to sin. The idea is ingenious and cleverly developed. Doubtless it was the fame of this play which gained Echegaray the Nobel prize—the first won by any Spanish writer.

El género chico.—No account of the drama during the nineteenth century would be complete without mention of the *zarzuela*, a form of operetta which has continued to be the most widely popular form of dramatic entertainment in Spain. Most *zarzuelas* are clever, but only occasionally does one of them attain to the dignity of literature. Important writers in this genre are Ricardo de la Vega, Javier de Burgos, and, more recently, Miguel Ramos Carrión, Pina y Lumbreras, and Camprodón.

Enrique Gaspar (1842–1902) paved the way for the modern realistic drama. He abandoned verse and rhetoric and cultivated pure realism. *La levita* shows how stylish attire may hide a multitude of faults. *Las circunstancias* shows how environment determines conduct for good or evil.

Benito Pérez Galdós (1843–1920) did not equal, on the stage, his fame as a novelist. Some of his novels are said to be too dramatic. On the other hand, his plays are alleged to be too novelistic. *Doña Perfecta* reads as if it were written with a view to staging, and indeed whole passages were transferred to the like-named play with little change. Pérez Galdós' first play was *Realidad*, 1892, followed by *La loca de la casa*, 1893. This last is a drama-

tization of part of the plot of *Ángel Guerra.* Most of
Galdós' plays are stagings of his novels, and contain the
same social theses. His best play is *El abuelo,* 1904, derived from the like-named novel. In this an elderly
aristocrat, puffed up with the pride of family, is human-
ized by his affection for an illegitimate granddaughter.
La de San Quintín is another noteworthy play. Two
ruined aristocrats find their salvation when won to the
idea of useful employment. *Electra,* 1901, while not
Galdós' best play, was the most sensationally successful
of all both at home and abroad. It dramatizes once
again the conflict between obscurantism and progress.

Joaquín Dicenta (1863–1917) is the Blasco Ibáñez of
the stage. He is the creator of the proletarian drama in
Spain. His most significant works attack social injustice
from the socialistic viewpoint. *Juan José,* 1895, depicts
the evolution of an honest workingman into a murderer
by reason of the persecutions of a hardhearted employer.
This was the greatest success of the late nineteenth century from the point of view of gate receipts. As a work
of art, it is distinguished by excellent handling of plot,
good characterization, and strong dramatic situations.
It produces an impression of crude strength. The people
speak their natural dialect; there is, of course, no attempt
at elegance. *El lobo,* 1913, shows a callous convict redeemed and turned into a hero by love. Evidently,
Dicenta, in spite of his realism, could not entirely shake
free of Romanticism. He followed the tradition of Echegaray, adding more realism, and finding his heroes in the
populace.

Other nineteenth-century dramatists may best be
treated in another chapter.

The Post-
Romantic
Drama

BIBLIOGRAPHY

Bretón de los Herreros, M. *Obras.* 5 vols. Madrid, 1883–84.

Le Gentil, G. *Le poète Manuel Bretón de los Herreros et la société espagnole de 1830 à 1860.* Paris, 1909.

Gorostiza, M. E. de. *Obras.* 4 vols. Mexico, 1899–1902.

Roa Bárcena. "Datos y apuntamientos para la biografía de Don Manuel Edurado de Gorostiza," *Memorias de la Academia Mexicana,* I, 89–204.

Vega, Ventura de la. *Obras poéticas.* Paris, 1866.

Leslie, J. K. *Ventura de la Vega and the Spanish Theatre, 1820–1865.* Princeton, 1940.

Tamayo y Baus, Manuel. *Obras.* 4 vols. Madrid, 1898–1900.

Cotarelo y Mori, Emilio. *Estudios de historia literaria de España,* pp. 363–403. Madrid, 1901.

López de Ayala, A. *Obras,* ed. M. Tamayo y Baus. 7 vols. Madrid, 1881–85.

Goldberg, I. "Benito Pérez Galdós," *The Drama of Transition.* Cincinnati, 1922.

CHAPTER XXIII

Criticism, Erudition, Philosophy, History, and Oratory during the Nineteenth Century

Spanish intellectual life during the nineteenth century—Ceán Bermúdez—Navarrete—Clemencín—Gallardo—Durán—Salvá—Balmes—Donoso Cortés—Bello—Ferrer del Río—Gayangos—Milá y Fontanals—Lafuente—Amador de los Ríos—La Barrera—Castelar—Menéndez y Pelayo—Cuervo—Rodríguez Marín—E. Cotarelo y Mori—Pérez Pastor—Bonilla y San Martín—Cejador y Frauca.

Spanish intellectual life during the nineteenth century.— During the early nineteenth century intellectual life in Spain was at a low ebb. Ticknor, in his Preface to the *History of Spanish Literature,* describes graphically conditions of that time, when those few intellectuals who were the nation's pride were victims of persecution or exile. From this inauspicious beginning the recovery has been slow but sure. The century produced no outstanding philosopher, and, toward the close, only one great critic, and a single historian of importance. Little original work was done in the natural sciences; little in the study of foreign languages and literatures. But much was accomplished by Spaniards in the study of their own literature. Scholarship often took the form of that archaeological research so unjustly satirized by Galdós (*Doña Perfecta*) in the character of Don Cayetano. Great bibliographers, philologers, and literary researchers are fairly numerous. It would be ungrateful not to mention the names and works of a few of these men so helpful in our field.

Ceán Bermúdez' (*1749–1829*) *Diccionario histórico de los más ilustres profesores de las bellas artes en España*, 1800, is still the best guide to the fine arts in Spain.

Martín Fernández de Navarrete (*1765–1844*), in his *Vida de Miguel de Cervantes Saavedra*, 1819, wrote the first scientific biography of Spain's greatest writer, making available many new documents bearing on Cervantes. His *Colección de los viajes y descubrimientos, que hicieron por mar los españoles desde fines del siglo xv, etc.*, Madrid, 1825–37, was the pioneer history of American exploration.

Diego Clemencín (*1765–1834*) was the first great Spanish commentator on *Don Quijote*. His famous edition appeared in 1833. It leans heavily upon the first exhaustive commentary, that of the Englishman, Bowle, but contains much that is original. Clemencín's shortcomings as an annotator are due to the fact that he lacks scientific knowledge of the older Spanish language, finding fault with Cervantes because he did not write in nineteenth-century style. Clemencín essayed the rôle of a Malherbe, using his commentary as a means of standardizing Spanish grammar.

Bartolomé José Gallardo (*1776–1852*) was the greatest of Spanish bibliographers. He spent a lifetime viewing rare old books, and, after the irreparable loss of his first set of *papeletas*, began the task anew. The result was one of the most indispensable of reference books, the *Ensayo de una biblioteca española de libros raros y curiosos* (4 vols.), published posthumously in 1863–69. The still inedited portion should be printed by a grateful nation. Galdós,

for once, was singularly obtuse when he stated, in *Cádiz*,
that this diligent worker *"no hizo nada de provecho."* He
was merely another Don Cayetano. Gallardo's literary
journal, *El criticón*, which, starting in 1835, perished
after eight numbers, contained valuable literary studies.

Agustín Durán's (1793–1862) importance as a Romantic critic and as an aid in the revival of interest in the
older literature has already been mentioned. His fame
rests chiefly on his monumental *Romancero general*, the
printing of which began in 1829.

Vicente Salvá (1786–1849) was a collector and vender
of rare books, long established in London. The *Catálogo de
la biblioteca de Salvá* (2 vols.), 1872, brought to completion
by the author's sons, is an important bibliographical
guide.

Jaime Balmes (1810–48) revived philosophical studies
in Spain. His system is based upon that of Thomas
Aquinas, and he is naturally an ardent defender of Catholicism. His chief work is *El protestantismo comparado con
el catolicismo en sus relaciones con la civilización europea*,
1844.

Juan Donoso Cortés (1809–53), famous as an orator,
was a leader of conservative thought. He played the
same rôle in Spain as did De Maître and Chateaubriand
in France, that of champion of the nineteenth-century
Catholic reaction.

Antonio Ferrer del Río (d. 1872), in his *Galería de la
literatura española*, 1846, published the biographies of the
leading writers of the first half of the century. This remains a source book from which we derive much of our
knowledge of the authors in question.

Andrés Bello (1781–1865), a Venezuelan and a gifted

poet, published the first edition of his *Gramática castellana* in 1847. This was superior to any other Spanish grammar ever written, and, as revised and augmented by the great Cuervo, remains today our best Spanish grammar.

Pascual de Gayangos (*1809–97*) was an active but ill-trained scholar. He specialized in Arabic. He is especially noted for the publication of various works of Old Spanish literature then inaccessible, and as the translator into Spanish of Ticknor's *History of Spanish Literature.*

Manuel Milá y Fontanals (*1818–84*) was a scholar of far greater caliber. He is especially noted for his researches into the origins of the Spanish and Catalan epic and ballad. Some of his discoveries were epoch making. His two most important books are *De los trovadores en España*, 1861, and *De la poesía heroico-popular castellana*, 1874. It was not the least of Milá's achievements to have been the teacher of Menéndez y Pelayo.

Modesto Lafuente (*1806–66*), in the thirty volumes of his *Historia de España*, 1850–57, has written the most comprehensive history of his country ever undertaken by a Spaniard. However, the work is superficial, uncritical, and seldom based upon primary sources.

José Amador de los Ríos (*1818–78*) was a distinguished medievalist. He edited the works of the Marqués de Santillana, wrote *Estudios históricos, políticos y literarios sobre los judíos de España*, 1848, and then embarked upon his *Historia crítica de la literatura española* (7 vols.), 1861–65. The scheme was vast, comprising Latin authors born in Spain, as well as Mohammedan and Jewish writers there resident. The history is carried through the reign of the Catholic monarchs. The portion devoted to the Middle Ages is based upon first-hand investigation. Much in the work of Amador de los Ríos has since been superseded, but such a monument of literary pioneering will always have its lasting value.

Cayetano Alberto de la Barrera (1831–72) was a student and bibliographer of the drama. His *Catálogo bibliográfico y biográfico del teatro antiguo español*, 1860, is the *vade mecum* of every student of the Spanish drama. It is more than a list of plays, containing, as it does, the best biographies to be found anywhere of many of the writers of the *siglo de oro*. His biography of Lope de Vega, constituting the first volume of the Academy edition of Lope's dramatic works, was the first exhaustive account of that author's life.

Emilio Castelar (1832–99), statesman and, in 1873, president of the short-lived Spanish republic, is inaccurate as a historian and of slight consequence as a writer of historical novels. He was the most famous orator of his age. John Hay, in *Castilian Days*, describes the effect produced upon him by Castelar's stupendous talent as a public speaker. His was the old-fashioned, orotund, flowery style, and he wrote as he spoke. According to Azorín, the effect of Castelar's style upon other writers of the epoch was mischievous.

Marcelino Menéndez y Pelayo (1856–1912) was the greatest Spanish critic of the century, a modern humanist and polygraph. Possessed of far more erudition than his critical rivals, Valera, Alas, and Pardo Bazán, he also had a saner outlook and a surer taste. His method is partly historical, partly aesthetic. His erudition will not bear the test of minute inspection, but correctness in every detail is not to be expected of a man whose enterprises were so vast. His chief defect as a critic is his *españolismo*, characterized by a strong national and religious bias which in his earliest work approaches fanaticism. He lacked the cosmopolitan outlook. But one respects him for a devotion to country and church which resulted in so many labors of love. Menéndez' collected works are a storehouse wherein are gathered innumerable newly acquired facts about a host of authors, as well as critical valuations of those authors which are all but definitive. The style is lucid, simple, always interesting, though a bit rhetorical.

Menéndez' achievement.—Early in life Menéndez determined to write a history of Spanish literature. Nobody was better fitted for the task; but, lacking a body of scholarly monographs on which to base the work, he decided that the task must be undertaken *a pedazos*. He achieved a history of Spanish criticism, the epic and ballad, early lyric poetry, the early novel, covered much of the history of the drama, and filled gaps with many a detailed study. Publishing incessantly from the age of twenty, he dispersed his energies in many vast undertakings some of which were left incomplete. The first important work was *La ciencia española*, 1876, since expanded, in which Menéndez answers the century-old question: What has Spain contributed to civilization in philosophy, science, and invention? It must be admitted that a strong case for Spain has not been established; but a host of forgotten names are rescued from oblivion and credit restored where due for their many contributions to civilization. *Horacio en España*, 1877, is a study on the influence of the Latin poet upon the Spanish lyric. A work of wider scope was *Historia de los heterodoxos españoles*, 1880–82, in which Menéndez enters the field of philosophy and theology. *Calderón y su teatro,* 1881, begins a critical campaign to deflate Calderón's exaggerated reputation and to award first place of honor to Lope de Vega. His *magnum opus* is the *Historia de las ideas estéticas en España* (9 vols.), 1883–89. This is a complete history of Spanish criticism to the date of writing. In 1884 he began his *Estudios de crítica literaria,* a collection of scattered monographs of the utmost value. Between 1890 and 1902 appeared the thirteen volumes of the *Obras dramáticas de Lope de Vega,* published by the Academy under Menéndez' editorship, and containing instructive studies of the individual plays printed. The merit of these studies outweighs the very deficient textual criticism which characterizes these volumes. No less important is the *Antología de poetas líricos castellanos* (13 vols.), 1890–1908, which offers a history of Spanish poetry, lyric and epic, down to and including Boscán and Garcilaso. (The volume on Garcilaso was written by another.) The *Orígenes de la novela,* 1905–10, carries the history of the novel genre down to the picaresque novel. It is ever to be regretted that death prevented Menéndez from writing on this last-mentioned form. In addition to these huge works, many too vast in scope for one man to complete, Menéndez published short studies touching almost every phase of Spanish literature. He was keenly interested in contemporary literature and the poetic production of Spanish-American writers. It was said that he did not administer the National Library of which he was director, but that he read it. He had indeed read almost everything touching his wide interests, and his marvelous memory retained most of what he read. The sum total of his achievement is prodigious. Don Marcelino was a Lope de Vega turned scholar, a Spanish Sainte-Beuve.

Rufino José Cuervo (1834–1910), a Columbian, was the most distinguished philologer of his time. His three great works are *Apuntaciones críticas sobre el lenguaje bogotano*, 1867, and frequently reprinted (the scope is far wider than the title suggests), the "Notas" written to Bello's *Grámatica*, and the *Diccionario de construcción y régimen de la lengua castellana* (2 vols), 1886–93. This dictionary of syntax extends only through the letter *d*. The remaining portion is preserved in manuscript at Bogotá. It should be published as a monument to South America's greatest scholar. Cuervo, though mostly self-taught, is noted for his rigid scientific method.

Francisco Rodríguez Marín (1855–1943) is noted as folklorist, editor of texts, and for important researches concerning Espinosa, Mateo Alemán, Cervantes, and others. His editions of *Rinconete y Cortadillo* and *El celoso extremeño* are noteworthy. His large edition of *Don Quijote* is the best of modern editions, though imperfect in its philological commentary. Rodríguez Marín is an authority on all that concerns his home city, Seville. He is typically Andalusian in his wit.

Emilio Cotarelo y Mori (1868–1936) was a prolific researcher in the field of literature, particularly that of the drama. His biography of Tirso, his edition of the inedited plays of that author, and his studies on Iriarte and Ramón de la Cruz are his most important efforts. His two volumes of the *entremés* added much to our knowledge of that interesting genre. Cotarelo had industry, enthusiasm, and much native talent.

Cristóbal Pérez Pastor (1843–1908) had a passion for

bibliography and delving in ancient archives. The amount of new data by him brought to light concerning Cervantes, Lope de Vega, Calderón, many minor authors, and the actors of the Golden Age is astounding. To few other scholars of his time are Spanish letters more beholden than to this diligent worker.

Adolfo Bonilla y San Martín (1875–1926) was equally at home in law, philosophy, and literature. On him fell to a considerable extent the mantle of Menéndez y Pelayo, for Bonilla stood for an all-embracing humanism rather than for the modern ideal of specialization. Among numerous valuable contributions, one may instance *Luis Vives y la filosofía del renacimiento,* 1903, as his best. With Puyol y Alonso he wrote one of the best of historical novels, *La hostería de Cantillana,* 1902.

Julio Cejador y Frauca (1864–1926) was amazingly industrious. His exhaustive philological works are unsound and of slight value. The *Historia de la lengua y literatura castellana* (14 vols.) is the most extensive history of Spanish literature ever written, and is as exasperating as it is useful. Ill-arranged, indigested, hastily compiled with the aid of scissors and paste, it nevertheless has its merits. It is especially useful for information concerning lesser authors, neglected in works of restricted scope, for its information regarding South American writers and the contemporary schools. Much can here be found elsewhere difficult of access. As a critic of literature Padre Cejador is reactionary. He delights in everything popular and *castizo.* His religious bias is less objectionable than his chauvinism, for he decries everything foreign and progressive. The impression made is one of vigorous narrow-mindedness.

404

BIBLIOGRAPHY

MENÉNDEZ Y PELAYO, M. *Obras completas.* 18 vols. Madrid,
1911–30; New ed. Santander, 1940–50.

BONILLA Y SAN MARTÍN, A. *Marcelino Menéndez y Pelayo (1856–
1912).* Madrid, 1914.

ARTIGAS, M. *La vida y la obra de Menéndez y Pelayo.* Zaragoza,
1939.

TORRE, G. DE. *Menéndez Pelayo y las dos Españas.* Buenos Aires,
1943.

LAÍN ENTRALGO, P. *Menéndez Pelayo: Historia de sus problemas
intelectuales.* Madrid, 1944.

SÁINZ RODRÍGUEZ, P. "Don Bartolomé José Gallardo y la crítica
de su tiempo," *Revue hispanique,* LI, 211–595.

BUCHANAN, M. A. "Notes on the Life and Works of Bartolomé
José Gallardo," *Revue hispanique,* LVII, 5–46.

MILÁ Y FONTANALS, M. *Obras completas.* 8 vols. Barcelona,
1888–96.

CHAPTER XXIV

Post-Romantic
Poets of the
Nineteenth Century

A period of transition—Campoamor—Núñez de Arce—Bartrina—Rosalía de Castro—Gabriel y Galán—Vicente Medina—
The Modernist movement—Rubén Darío—His works and influence upon Spain.

A period of transition.—Between the two movements
of Romanticism and Modernism lies a period of transition. An age of fancy was giving way to an age of
science. Poetry tended to become more philosophical.
A new form of pessimism appeared, that arising from
loss of faith. A few regional poets appear. But there was
no clearly defined school of poetry. Each poet was feeling
his way. At the end of the century comes the Modernist
revolution.

Ramón de Campoamor (1817–1901), physician, politician, philosopher, and poet, was the first distinguished
poet of the century to break with Romanticism. Caring
little for form, he attached supreme importance to the
thought embodied in his verse. "*El arte por la idea*" was
his motto. Campoamor prided himself on being the
inventor of several new poetic forms. The *dolora*, the most
important of these, is a poetic composition combining
sentiment with lightness, concision with philosophic importance; or, as he otherwise defined it: a transcenden-
tal fable in which eternal verities are symbolized, char-

acterized by brevity, delicacy, pathos, and philosophic teaching hidden beneath irony. The *pequeño poema* is an amplification of the *dolora*. The *humorada*, of two, three, or four lines, is not to be distinguished from the epigram. In fact, Campoamor's originality consists chiefly in finding new names for old things. Two examples will illustrate the *dolora* and Campoamor's manner:

TWO MIRRORS

Into my mirror's glass I gaze
  At forty years of age,
And find myself so worn with days
  I break the glass in rage.

And then I turn my gaze and peer
  Across my mirrored soul;
And see within my conscience clear
  My woes beyond control.

The loss of faith, of love, of youth —
  I see my mortal curse!—
Within my mirror—evil truth;
  And in my conscience—worse!

—Thomas Walsh

TRADITIONS

I marked a cross upon a lonely spot
  One day when in the country I took air;
A passer told me—"A base robber shot
  And killed a soldier there."

O false tradition—once again I passed
  The site upon that lonely plain;
Another stranger told me, as the last—
  "A robber herē was by a soldier slain."

—Thomas Walsh

Campoamor's most famous *dolora* is *¡Quién supiera
escribir!* the story of an illiterate and lovelorn peasant
girl dictating a love-letter with the aid of a worldly wise
but uncomprehending priest. This and many others of
his poems were committed to memory by cultured Spaniards of Campoamor's generation. A poet who is sentimental and tells a story has many admirers. The modern
generation of critics, with the exception of González
Blanco, has reacted sharply against him. Campoamor
fails to satisfy their higher standards of art, and his old-
fashioned morality excites their scorn.

Gaspar Núñez de Arce (1832–1903) is the other outstanding poet of the transition period. He, too, did not
disdain to tell a story in verse. *La pesca*, a love-story of
fisher-folk, suggests *José*, except for its tragic ending.
Maruja, in which an aristocratic couple find contentment
by adopting a beggar waif, is similar in theme to Galdós'
El abuelo. But the most charming of this poet's works
is *Un idilio*, a tale of love thwarted by death. Into
none of his poems has the poet put more of himself.
The theme is Romantic, the treatment Classic. The
plains of Castile have seldom been better described than
in these polished stanzas. Núñez de Arce's most important collection of lyrics is *Gritos del combate*, 1873. In
these he reveals himself a poet of disillusion. His pessimism differs from the *mal du siècle* of the romanticists. It
is a product of the new trend of thought brought about
by the Darwinian theory of the mid-nineteenth century.
Núñez de Arce was a man who longed to possess religious
faith, but was unable to find intellectual justification
for it. Hence his despair. *La última lamentación de lord
Byron* shows him in sympathy with certain phases of

Byron's thought. In *La visión de fray Martín*, he praises
Luther as an apostle of doubt. The poet's despair in-
cludes politics as well as religion. He participated in
politics and served as deputy and minister. Association
with dishonest self-seekers caused him to doubt the possibility of effective reform. Núñez de Arce, better than
any other Spanish poet, voices the disintegrating effect
of scientific discovery upon the old theologies.

Joaquín María Bartrina (1850–80) is also a poet of
materialistic pessimism. His chief collection of lyrics,
Algo, 1876, is noteworthy for epigrammatic acuteness.
The following *quintilla* is often quoted:

ARABESCO

Oyendo hablar a un hombre, fácil es
acertar donde vió la luz del sol;
si os alaba a Inglaterra, será inglés,
si os habla mal de Prusia, es un francés,
y si habla mal de España, es español.

Rosalía de Castro (1837–85), unlike Campoamor and
Núñez de Arce, enjoyed little fame during her lifetime;
but criticism now proclaims her the greatest Spanish
poet of her generation. She is the tragic soul of Galicia.
Descendant of an illustrious family, the irregularity of
her birth (she was a priest's daughter) and an unhappy
marriage imparted a note of gloom to her writings. These
were the vent for an intensely emotional nature. She
wrote in both Galician and Castilian. Her early works
are rare. Her dying injunction upon a sister was to destroy all unpublished manuscripts. This was done, and
the family has even opposed the reprinting of existing
editions. Her two most important works are *Cantares
gallegos,* 1863, and *En las orillas del Sar.* 1884. She also

wrote stories and regional novels of Galician life. There
is nothing artificial in Rosalía de Castro's verse. This
simplicity is what causes her to be esteemed by the
modern school, whom she anticipates in many ways. She
possessed the sentimentality of the Galician race, but an
unforced sentimentality, the reflex of a suffering soul.
The genuineness of her poetry will ensure its endurance.

José María Gabriel y Galán (1870–1905), though his
poems were printed in the twentieth century, really
belongs to the nineteenth. He has nothing in common
with the Generation of 1898, unless it be a passion for
simplicity. He was born into a family of comfortably
circumstanced peasant-farmers, received a good education, taught in country schools, contracted a happy
marriage, and took up farming. If it is true that he is a
disciple of Luis de León, it is still truer that his chief
source of inspiration came from the peasants whom he
loved and of whom he felt himself one. His first important work, *El ama*, 1901, inspired by the death of his
mother, won the prize at the *juegos florales* of Saragossa,
and established his reputation as a poet. The last few
years of his life were active. He published several beautiful collections of verse, *Castellanas, Nuevas castellanas,
Extremeñas, El Cristu bendito*, etc. *Religiosas* was issued
posthumously in 1906. Some of his work is in Extrem-
aduran dialect. His principal themes are family affection,
love of nature and the common people, and religion.
His style is serene and tender. He is an apostle of *con-
formidad* rather than of revolt. Discontent may be
"divine" for some, but not for Gabriel y Galán. For him
religion is the sovereign remedy. This poet is therefore a
traditionalist. Few have entered into the peasant mind

so well as this regional poet of Central Spain. He is a
Spanish Robert Burns. And the proof of this is that
scores of his poems are committed to memory and recited
by the peasants of his region, and, with the alterations
due to oral transmission, have passed into folklore. No
greater compliment than this can be paid a poet. That
one of his poems to which the anthologies have given
widest circulation is *Los pastores de mi abuelo*, very
characteristic of his best manner.

Vicente Medina (*b. 1866*), a poet all too little known,
is, like Gabriel y Galán, a regional poet and a laureate of
the lowly. He writes in the dialect of the Murcian *huerta*,
a speech easy for even the foreigner to comprehend. He is
like Gabriel y Galán in his sympathy for the poor, but
his inferior in serenity and poise. Socialism, rather than
religion, is his remedy. Yet he does not parade his social
outcasts defiantly before the reader after the fashion of an
Espronceda. He sympathizes with them and makes the
reader share his sympathy. His two most important
collections are *Aires murcianos*, 1898, and *La canción de
la huerta*, 1901. In these he sings of the struggles of the
poor with poverty and disease and the loves of youthful
peasants. Medina has a vast fund of human sympathy,
and relies for his effects upon the simplest means. He is a
genuine poet of democracy, not only the friend of the
friendless, but, as he shows in his free-verse poem *Naide*,
he is also the lover of the loveless:

NOBODY

I know she does not love me; that is not my trouble.
If it were that alone, I almost could rejoice.
My trouble is not one of those which rend the heart.
And yet at times are cured.

Mine is no swift delivered wound,
Which trickles blood.
My trouble is not deep;
My trouble is not great;
But it is a trouble,
Which, with its sadness, will not let me rest.
It is a gnawing bitterness,
Which I carry in the shadow, which I carry in the air!
I know she does not love me; that is not my trouble.
My trouble is of such a sort there's no appeasing it.
I've set my eyes on all the girls, on all of them!
And no one of them all will look at me!
She is not the only one who does not love me.
Neither she, nor any one of them! Nobody loves me!

The eternal triangle of mother, sweetheart, and the man has never been described with more condensation than in the following quatrain:

No he tenido carta tuya;
pero de mi madre sí. . . .
¡y aún no he escrito a mi madre
y otra vez te escribo a ti!

Such poetry, with its purely human appeal, stands in striking contrast to the more sophisticated forms of art soon to appear.

The Modernist movement in poetry comes into Spanish literature at the close of the nineteenth century, specifically in the year 1898. The intellectual Renaissance led by the so-called Generation of 1898 is almost coincident with Modernism. Most of the writers of the group have been influenced by it, and it should be studied apart before taking up the larger movement which was soon to revolutionize Spanish literature. Modernism, as a tendency in Spanish and Spanish-American literatures, derives from the French Parnassians and the poets of the decadent-symbolist group. Poe, Whitman, and a few English and German writers also served as models. The Parnassians, headed by Leconte de Lisle, revolted against the subjectivity of Romanticism. They retained that school's color, but cultivated Classic detachment. Above all they sought marmoreal perfection of form. They appealed to a visual rather than to an aural imagination. Against them the decadents and symbolists (two names applied to different wings of what is essentially the same group) reacted in turn. They reasserted the claims of the individual. Their appeal was chiefly to the ear—"Music above everything else" was Verlaine's demand. Metrical innovations of all sorts were introduced. They took far greater liberties with meter than any romanticists had ever dared to do. Suggestion was preferred to clear statement. *Nuances* were preferred to color. Their work was shadowy and vague, rather than clear. Many symbolists resorted to ridiculous extremes, but the total effect of their effort was to enrich and free French poetry. The influence of Leconte de Lisle, Baudelaire, Verlaine, Rimbaud, Jammes, Kahn, and others was manifest in South America long before it was in Spain. The South American nations have always been more under the intellectual dominance of Paris than has been the case with Spain. Remote though they are, for that very reason they lack the prejudice of a next-door neighbor. Modernism is the name given to a recent form of poetry and poetic prose deriving from both the Parnassian and the Symbolistic schools. It is the synthesis of the two, aiming to achieve form, color, and music, and appealing both to the eye and the ear. It is like Romanticism in its demand for individual freedom; like Classicism in its culti-

vation of form; like *culteranismo* in its effort to enrich a
poetic vocabulary worn threadbare, by the introduction
of colorful and expressive words. First of the *modernistas*
were the Mexican, Manuel Gutiérrez Nájera; the Cubans,
José Martí and Julián del Casal; and the Colombian,
José Asunción Silva. But Nicaragua produced a poet
transcending all these, Rubén Darío, and he it was who
brought Modernism to Spain.

Rubén Darío (1867–1916), in his interesting autobiography, describes a troubled existence which leaves
the impression of one long series of political revolutions,
earthquakes, and love affairs no less volcanic. Even as a
boy he achieved a reputation as a poet. Zorrilla was his
first model. Study and imitation of the old masters of
Spanish poetry preceded his familiarity with French
models. These opened new worlds to him, as was evident
with the publication of his first great work, *Azul*, 1888.
This, written while in Chile, gained him instant fame.
Henceforth this poet was an object of adoration. Like
Zorrilla he traveled extensively in the New World and the
Old, always sponging upon some admirer, or filling a
consular sinecure especially created that he might live
in Paris or Madrid. A voluptuary and an inebriate, he
led a bohemian existence. But he was not a slovenly
Bohemian. The poet must be an aristocrat, he thought.
Patent-leather shoes were as essential a matter as the
proper scansion of a verse. Rubén Darío is not the poet
of Nicaragua, nor even of South America. "I am a
Spaniard of South America and a South American of
Spain," he proclaimed. He was more than that—a cosmopolitan at home in every capital, but especially in his
element in Paris.

414

A poet of color and of sound.—On the formal side
Rubén Darío is the greatest recent poet employing the
Spanish tongue. Never before had there been such
witchery and magic of versification. He is polychrome and
symphonic. Each word is carefully chosen for harmonious
effect. The *mot recherché* was painstakingly pursued.
Words like *libélula, nelumbo, hipsipila,* and *nefelibata*
abound; but they are introduced with discretion. The
poetic vocabulary is renovated without producing an impression of pedantry or obscurity. Darío displays an
aristocratic preference for elegant things. There is constant reference to gold, ivory, marble, silk, lace, roses, and
swans. The period of history he most admires is the seventeenth and eighteenth centuries of France. But it is the
France of Watteau and Fragonard rather than that of Corneille and Racine. An aesthete, he wrote only for the fas-
tidious. Darío's metrical innovations and renovations are
of vital importance in the history of modern Spanish
poetry. These are listed by Cejador.[1] Darío's philosophy
is frankly epicurean and hedonistic. He sings of sensual
love. He loves life and fears death. He possesses every
beauty except the highest of all—moral beauty. Cejador
puts it happily when he says that this poet built an Alhambra, not a cathedral.

His works and influence upon Spain.—*Azul,* 1888,
was Darío's first revolutionary performance. Blue was
to him the color of art and dreams. The selections in this
short volume are partly in prose, partly in verse. All
are poems. Of the prose pieces, *El velo de la reina Mab*
is most famous. The poetic section, entitled *Lyric Year,*
describes love in the four seasons of human life. It may

[1] *Historia,* X, 113–14.

have suggested to Valle-Inclán his famous *Sonatas. Azul*
gave fullest evidence of the poet's exquisite sensitive-
ness, his marvelous assimilative faculties, and what has
been called his "verbal aristocracy." It was admirably
reviewed by Juan Valera. The next important collection
of verse is *Prosas profanas*, 1896. *Prosa* is here used in
the medieval sense of "poem in the vernacular," according
to Goldberg. It means rather a religious poem, so that
the word "*profanas*" joined to it has the force of paradox.
This collection evidenced a growing power, which reached
its height with *Cantos de vida y esperanza*, 1905. Most of
Darío's best work is included in these last two collections.
Special mention may be made of only two poems: the
famous *Sonatina*, the most musical poem in Spanish,
and his greatest piece, *Canción de otoño en primavera*.
In the latter he voices the sensualist's lament over departing youth. Darío wrote much prose, an autobiography,
an autobiographical novel, *El oro de Mallorca*, and many
articles of criticism and travel. His prose is always as
exquisite as his verse. Darío's influence upon Spain becomes important after the publication of *Prosas profanas*
and his residence in that country in 1898. How great
that influence was will become apparent in the next
chapter.

BIBLIOGRAPHY

CAMPOAMOR, R. DE. *Obras poéticas completas.* Madrid, 1942.
HILTON, R. *Campoamor, Spain and the World.* Toronto, 1940.
GONZÁLEZ BLANCO, A. *Campoamor: Biografía y estudio crítico.*
    Madrid, 1912.
NÚÑEZ DE ARCE, G. *Obras escogidas.* Barcelona, 1911.
ROMO ARREGUI, J. *Vida, poesía y estilo de don Gaspar Núñez de
    Arce.* Madrid, 1946.

Post-Romantic Poets

BARTRINA, J. M. *Obras en prosa y verso escogidas y coleccionadas* . . . , ed. J. SARDÁ. Madrid and Barcelona, 1881.

CASTRO, ROSALÍA DE. *Obras completas*. 4 vols. Madrid, 1909–11, 1944.

PROL BLAS, J. S. *Estudio bio-bibliográfico-crítico de las obras de Rosalía de Castro*. Madrid, 1917.

SANTAELLA MURIAS, E. *Rosalía de Castro, vida, poética y ambiente*. Buenos Aires, 1942.

GABRIEL Y GALÁN, J. M. *Obras completas*. Madrid, 1941.

REVILLA MARCOS, A. *José María Gabriel y Galán: Su vida y sus obras*. Madrid, 1921.

GONZÁLEZ BLANCO, A. "Vicente Medina," *Los contemporáneos*, Primera serie, pp. 240–75. Paris, n.d.

DARÍO, RUBÉN. *Obras poéticas completas*, ed. A. MÉNDEZ PLANCARTE. Madrid, 1952.

CONTRERAS, F. *Rubén Darío: Su vida y su obra*. Barcelona, 1930.

TORRES-RÍOSECO, A. *Rubén Darío, casticismo y americanismo*. Cambridge, Mass., 1931.

MAPES, E. K. *L'Influence française dans l'œuvre de Rubén Darío*. Paris, 1925.

SALINAS, PEDRO. *La poesía de Rubén Darío*. Madrid, 1948.

DÍAZ PLAJA, G. *Rubén Darío*. Barcelona, 1930.

ONÍS, F. DE. *Antología de la poesía española e hispanoamericana (1882–1932)*. Madrid, 1934.

VALBUENA PRAT, A. *La poesía española contemporánea*. Madrid, 1930.

CHAPTER XXV

The
Generation
of 1898

The war of 1898 and its consequences—Ángel Ganivet—Joaquín Costa—Giner de los Ríos—The Generation of 1898—Their social program—Their artistic program—Lyric poetry—Marquina —Manuel Machado—Antonio Machado—Ramón Jiménez— Villaespesa—The drama—Benavente—The Brothers Álvarez Quintero—Linares Rivas—Marquina—Villaespesa—Martínez Sierra—Grau—The novel—Pío Baroja—Valle-Inclán—Ricardo León—Concha Espina—Felipe Trigo—Criticism, philosophy, history, and erudition—Martínez Ruiz (Azorín)—Unamuno— Altamira—Menéndez Pidal.

The war of 1898 and its consequences.—The war between Spain and the United States was remarkable in that it ended leaving both participants better friends than before. Spaniards displayed not the slightest trace of animosity toward their late antagonists. In the United States an increased interest in "the things of Spain" dates from that year, in striking contrast to the attitude of Americans after World War I, who then manifested a foolish prejudice toward the language and literature of Germany. But in Spain the disasters of Cavite and Santiago de Cuba were bitter. It was a time of heart-searching. Something must be wrong with Spain, and something must be done about it. Out of the travail of souls grew a patriotic, intellectual, and artistic Renaissance. The leaders in this movement of many phases call themselves the "Generation of 1898." Before stating their doctrines, it is well to consider a few of their predecessors; for the year 1898 merely crystallized tendencies which had been long forming.

Ángel Ganivet (1865-98) as a consular agent in northern lands gained a detached and cosmopolitan point of view. His two political-philosophical novels are entitled *La conquista del reino de Maya,* 1897, and *Los trabajos del infatigable creador Pío Cid,* 1898—whimsical books rich in ideas. More important is his *Idearium español,* 1896, so frequently quoted in the first chapter. This is a searching analysis of the national character. Like a skilful surgeon, Ganivet does not hesitate to cut deep and inflict pain when necessary. The chief fault of Spain, according to him, is a weakening of the national will. Spaniards, individually and collectively, must cultivate will-power or the nation is lost. From Ganivet derives the doctrine of *la voluntad,* so insisted upon by Azorín, Pío Baroja, and other writers of the new school. The heroes of most contemporary novels are either exponents of will or horrible examples of its lack. Ganivet died in the fulness of his powers, just as his teachings were about to bear fruit.

Joaquín Costa (1846-1911) was a specialist in the philosophy and history of the law. His writings are mostly on legal, political, and economic topics. Descended of sturdy, Aragonese, peasant stock, he was an educated man of the people, the uncompromising foe of administrative inefficiency and political jobbery. Powerful as was the influence of his writings upon the rising generation, his virile personality on the lecture platform produced an even greater effect. His message to the nation was an appeal for Europeanization, or the "deafricazation of Spain," as he so frequently expressed it. Spain must assimilate from other nations those ideas and methods which had made them successful. To accomplish this she must break with her past and abandon quixotic adventure. New times demanded new ideas. *Españolismo* was an obstacle. His frequently iterated war-cry was: "A double turn of the key to the Cid's tomb" (*"Doble llave al sepulcro del Cid"*). Break with the past. This became the slogan of the new school. But breaking with the past meant to them only the abandonment of certain evil tendencies. They retained from the past whatever appealed to them as good.

Francisco Giner de los Ríos (1840–1915), at one time professor of the philosophy of law in the Universidad Central, was irked by official restrictions, and driven from his chair by hostile politicians. The great idea of his life was the reform of Spanish education. Not content with propaganda, he put his ideas into practice by founding as early as 1870 the Institución libre de enseñanza. Giner de los Ríos was an unselfish altruist who devoted his life to philanthropy. His disciples liked to call Don Francisco a modern St. Francis, and he did resemble the saint of Assisi in his love for nature and humanity. He liked English ways, believed in fresh air, soap and water, and sports as a means of forming character; but his practical side was balanced by his appreciation of the beautiful. Everything fine appealed to him. His model school became a focus of the new thought. Azorín writes:

"What do we owe to the Free Institute of Teaching?" we are wont to inquire; and the usual answer is: "Little." . . . . Little! when all the literature, all the art, much of politics, a large part of our pedagogy have been renovated by the spirit emanating from that Institute? Slowly in the course of forty or fifty years, the radiation from that select nucleus of thinkers and school-teachers has extended through all Spain. The work continues its progressive march. The spirit of the Free Institution—that is to say, the spirit of Giner—has determined the group of writers of 1898; that spirit has aroused the love of nature, and consequently for the landscape and for things Spanish, Castilian—a love which has renewed our painting (Beruete, Sorolla, Zuloaga, etc.); that spirit has caused our gaze to revert to the traditional, literary values, and our poets to be restored to life, editions of the classics to be reprinted, as formerly was not the case, a new school of philologers and criticism to arise, informed with a spirit which formerly did not exist. From neatness in attire and cultivation of good manners to the love for an old city or a primitive poet, what a fertile and human gamut of *nuances* and aspects Spanish culture owes to that little old man!

Another altruist who influenced the youth of his time was the Catalan, Pi y Margall; and the Liberalism of Pérez Galdós was constantly bearing fruit.

The *Generation of 1898* initiated a national Renaissance. The movement was as conspicuous a flowering of genius as the recent literature of any nation could boast. The group included at least five distinguished lyric poets: Marquina, the Machado brothers, Pérez de Ayala, and Juan Ramón Jiménez; dramatists like the world-famous Jacinto Benavente, the Álvarez Quintero brothers, Linares Rivas, Marquina, and Villaespesa; novelists like Valle-Inclán and Pío Baroja. Unamuno was their philosopher and essayist; Martínez Ruiz, their critic. The brilliant journalist Ramiro de Maeztu fought for their ideas. Rafael Altamira was a distinguished historian and publicist. Ramón Menéndez Pidal and his school represented them on the side of erudition. Many other worthy names might be added. Other brilliant writers were de-

tached from the group or hostile to it; because a break
with tradition cannot be accomplished without offense to
many.

Their social program.—The program of the Generation of 1898 was multiform. Each individual represented
a different phase of the movement. Some were concerned
with practical reforms; others, solely with art (and every
artist sees art in his own way). Nevertheless, there was
a community of purpose in a desire to better the national
life, though the means to that end were various.

In politics, for example, some were conservative,
others, socialistic; but all were united in a fine scorn for
the boss system (*caciquismo*) and the political jobbery
which had so afflicted the nation. Some of them continued Galdós' fight against clericalism, and many
stood for tolerance in religious matters. Owing to his
outspoken opposition to the tyranny of the dictatorship,
Unamuno suffered the martyrdom of exile. Many of the
group were courageous fomenters of the revolution,
which, when established, honored them with office. Unhappily, the second Spanish Republic proved unable to
put its series of highly commendable ideals into practice.

Since a general opinion prevailed among the men of
1898 that most of the evils of Spain were due to the sheer
ignorance of the masses of the people, it was natural that
great attention should be paid to education. It seemed
evident that the Cortes would not and really could not
provide the enormous sums necessary to overhaul
primary and secondary education. Therefore, they
tried to start at the top, furthering the plan of
Giner de los Ríos on a larger scale. An effort was made
to train numbers of devoted, intellectual leaders whose
influence would penetrate to the masses. The bureau-

cratic, official university system was suffering from dry rot. To attain results an extramural university was held necessary. One would like to tell in detail the story of the founding of the Centro de estudios, that worthy successor to the Institución libre de ensañanza, through the efforts of that practical idealist, José Castillejo. This institution was subsidized by the government, but enjoyed an atmosphere of freedom not to be found in the old universities. There was no religious test; no discrimination as to sex. It was a place where the most enlightened youth of Spain came into contact with the nation's best scholars. Many of these, like Menéndez Pidal, also held university chairs. The Centro was concerned with the training of teachers according to the most advanced principles of pedagogy, with the scientific study of agriculture, technical training in all branches, and the most unutilitarian forms of research. Its list of scholarly publications was distinguished. It yearly sent forth a group of able students to study in the universities of Germany, France, England, and the United States. This was a practical way to counteract *españolismo* and to train a corps of scientific workers. All this occasioned bitter opposition from reactionaries. Naturally the Franco régime changed the system entirely, substituting its own form of organization, which has numerous achievements to its credit.

Their artistic program.—The literary endeavor of the Generation of 1898 has been termed *"el movimiento de bien escribir."* Naturally each author had his own idea about what constituted good writing; but all were united in the belief that the worst vices of Spanish writing, careless improvisation and pompous inflation, should be avoided. In this respect there was a very sharp break with the past. They also avoided literary *españolismo*.

Spanish writers, they felt, should be free to seek inspiration abroad. Many of the group became modernists.
Two main trends should be noted. First, the tendency
toward *preciosité* in the poets following the lead of Rubén
Darío, and in prose-writers like Valle-Inclán. Second, the
reaction toward simplicity, of which the poetry of Juan
Ramón Jiménez affords the most striking example.
Benavente, Azorín, and Baroja showed a modern contempt for patterns. In general, they believed that a play
or novel should take the haphazard course of the average
human life. It was an article in the creed of most of these
writers to avoid rhetorical figures as much as possible, to
rely for effect upon the evocative power of simple description. Great importance was attached to the *paisaje*,
"landscape." These ardent young moderns took the
keenest aesthetic delight in viewing and painting the
tawny, arid plains of Central Spain, and its picturesquely
dilapidated, stagnant old cities. Never before had the
physical and spiritual values of the nation been so admirably portrayed. Literary radicals in other countries
are too prone to despise all but the "last cry" in literature. Such was not the attitude of the Generation of
1898. They loved their old authors, except those characterized by the faults above mentioned, just as they
adored their ruined cities. They read them eagerly for the
messages they contained for the present. They strove to
be modern while retaining the aesthetic values of the
past.

LYRIC POETRY

Eduardo Marquina (1879–1946), a Catalan who preferred to write in Castilian, was the first conspicuous poet
of the Modernist school in Spain. Beginning with *Odas*,

1900, he afterward produced *Églogas, Las vendimias, Vendimión,* etc. Marquina is an aristocratic poet, sane and optimistic, distinguished for his perfect mastery of form. The principal theme of his early verse is love, a passion which, as Marquina conceives it, transforms the lover of woman into a lover of all created things—a sort of neo-Platonism. In his later volumes, *Canciones del momento,* 1910, and *Tierras de España,* 1914, he gives expression to social and political problems. He accepts Spanish degeneracy as a fact and seeks to find the remedy. In this line of activity he is in a sense a follower of Núñez de Arce, though with very different technique and greater artistry. His achievements as dramatist will be considered later.

Manuel Machado (1874–1947) was fully identified with the Modernist movement. From the French he learned the use of the *trait juste* and the *mot propre.* He is technically dexterous, light, and at times frivolous. His best work is his first, *Alma,* 1902. *Apolo* is an attempt to describe the masterpieces of the Prado Museum. Photographic reproductions of the paintings appear on one page, the poetic description opposite. His *Felipe IV* is so successful a performance, that, if Velázquez's painting were destroyed, the pen portrait would almost suffice to restore it. Other important collections of verse are *Caprichos, El mal poema, Mueso, Trofeo,* etc. In *Castilla* he poaches on the preserves of his more famous brother Antonio, with greater success than might have been anticipated. Manuel Machado is one of the most successful followers of Rubén Darío. He initiated a tendency, strong among the Generation of 1898, of portraying the great characters of the sixteenth and seventeenth cen-

turies. His power of historic evocation is unsurpassed.
He excels in the descriptive sonnet, as the following will
show:

THE HIDALGO

In Flanders, Italy and Franche-Compté
And Portugal he made his twelve campaigns;
Now he is forty, and in all the Spains
He is the oldest soldier, so they say.

Retired with honors, now he passes through
The arches of the plaza, solemnly,
The sunlight shedding native glory due
Unto his medals—stately champion he.

Claiming the battlefield of Nancy still
As lost but at the Duke of Alba's will,—
His daughter's hand refusing haughtily

To rich Don Bela's scant nobility;—
Telling his deeds of prowess on a scroll
To Olivares for the pension roll.

—Thomas Walsh

Antonio Machado (*1875–1939*) had only slight contacts with the modernists. He has been called a symbolistic poet possessed of Parnassian perfection; but what
he owes to France is slight:

Adoro la hermosura, y en la moderna estética
corté las viejas rosas del huerto de Ronsard;
mas no amo los afeites de la actual cosmética,
ni soy un ave de esas del nuevo gay trinar.

And as between content and form he values the former:

Dejar quisiera
mi verso, como deja el capitán su espada,
famosa por la mano viril que la blandiera,
no por el docto oficio del forjador preciada.

The fact that he uses form to clothe a serious message is
what has given Antonio Machado his reputation as a
truly great poet of the twentieth century.

Born in Seville, the vicissitudes of his profession, that of a teacher of French, established him in the heart of Castile. There he found a landscape more in harmony with his serious, pensive nature than the joyous province of his birth could afford. This Andalusian is the poet of Castile. *Soledades*, his first work, dates from 1903. His second, and most characteristic, is *Campos de Castilla*, 1912. He renders admirably the spirit of that austere landscape. He views it admiringly as the theater of epic exploit, sadly as the abode of present desolation in contrast with past grandeur. He sees its wastes peopled with a race of semibarbarous peasants, with limitless possibilities for good or evil. Into this landscape he projects his mood; but his moods and thoughts are not so much stated as hinted. Landscape and mood being in harmony, Antonio Machado arrives at mood through nature.

Antonio Machado belongs to the Generation of 1898 through his fondness for landscape, simplicity, and sincerity. His artistic conscience was well developed, and he wrote little. Mr. Thomas Walsh has happily rendered one of the shorter poems:

COUNSELS

Learn how to hope, to wait the proper tide—
    As on the coast a bark—then part without a care;
He who knows how to wait wins victory for his bride;
    For life is long and art a plaything there.
But should your life prove short
    And never come a tide,
Wait still, unsailing, hope is on your side.
    Art may be long or, else, of no import.

Juan Ramón Jiménez (1881–1958) was a native of the far south of Spain, but there is little discernible Andalusianism in the poetry which he steadily produced through his long and inspired career. He began as a Modernist, and it was Darío who suggested the title of the volume published before the young poet was twenty years old: *Almas de violeta. Ninfeas* (*Waterlilies;* the title was suggested by Villaespesa) was published in the same year, 1900. Before long Juan Ramón—as he came to be almost universally called—reacted against prettiness and marmoreal perfection of form in the direction of simplicity, even though he forever retained the quality of elegance. Sainte-Beuve once said (*Causeries du lundi,* Vol. III): "I detest that self-styled beautiful poetry which has only form and sound, for fear that it may be mistaken for true poetry and usurp its place." Some such thought must have come to the Spanish poet. In speaking of his Muse, he says:

> She came to me first pure, clad in innocence, and as a boy I loved her. Then she kept putting on I know not what garments; and I began to hate her without knowing it. She came to be a queen, pompous in her wealth. What bitter and senseless anger! But she began to strip, and I smiled upon her. She was left with the tunic of her former innocence. I believed in her anew. She removed the tunic and appeared all naked. Oh, passion of my life, naked poetry, mine forever!—Trans. from a poem in *Eternidades,* 1918.

It is indeed true that Juan Ramón Jiménez devoted his life with singular devotion to poetry, seeking, in his frequently quoted phrase, *"la depuración de lo mismo."* He eschewed rhetorical figures almost entirely, and abandoned "proud words" with no intrinsic content. He was perfectly capable of writing in conventional poetic forms (*Sonetos espirituales,* 1917), but ordinarily he forsook rhyme and even assonance for his own rhythmic forms and cadences. It was the essence which he was constantly seeking, not pomp and external beauty; simplicity rather than ornateness. The poet has himself explained that by simple he means that which is achieved with the fewest separate elements, that spontaneity must come from long discipline and experience if it is to be artistically valid. Juan Ramón Jiménez wrote voluminously, but he did not gush effervescently like a Zorrilla. He constantly polished and burnished.

His tone is generally sad, though without Romantic self-pity. One has only to read the titles of some of his volumes of verse: *Arias tristes, Elejías, Poemas májicos y dolientes, Melancolía.* He is characterized by delicacy rather than by sturdiness, but his melancholy is a product of his nature and not trumped up.

Juan Ramón Jiménez could also write most delicate prose. The account of his alleged wanderings in Andalusia with his highly poetized little donkey was published first in 1917, and is called *Platero y yo.* It was twice capably translated into English in the late 1950's, one of the most delicate European items to reach these shores.

Since the production of this poet was voluminous, it may be best to read him in anthology. He himself selected a *Tercera antología poética*, which contains selections from thirty-nine volumes of verse and itself contains 1,115 small pages.

It is not beside the point to note that the beautiful volume just mentioned is dedicated "*A Zenobia de mi alma.*" The reference is to the poet's talented wife, translator of Rabindranath Tagore, Zenobia Camprubí Aymar. She was Juan Ramón's constant inspiration and support, without whom his accomplishment would surely have been limited or impossible. Unhappily, in their exile in Puerto Rico from Franco Spain, she did not live to share in the poet's final official triumph.

Juan Ramón Jiménez was awarded the Nobel Prize for literature for 1956.

NOCTURNE: FROM PIEDRA Y CIELO

My weeping and the starlight
Together met, and joining swift,
Became as though one tear,
Became as though one star.

And I grew blind—and heaven
Grew blind of love—And all the world
Was nothing more than sorrow
Of a star, and glitter of a tear.

—THOMAS WALSH

Francisco Villaespesa (1877–1936) was a poet of the second rank, who sought to portray the joyful life of Moorish Spain. In this he follows in Zorrilla's footsteps, adding realism, and taking a few, but only a few, hints from the Modernists. He began with *Intimidades* and *Flores de almendro*, in 1898, and afterward wrote voluminous lyric poetry, novels, and poetic dramas. He is most distinguished in the latter field, and his plays will be treated elsewhere. He excels in the descriptive sonnet:

AFTER LAS ANIMAS

The aged castellan beside the fire
Bends o'er his parchment leaves, in his desire
To learn the wise old proverbs of the past

That speak of gerfalcon's and hawks' wild cast;
  The chatelaine her rosary unwinds
In sleepy fingers; and the buffoon binds
His bells in imitation, for a laugh,
Shaking his ruddy hood and tinkling staff.
  In silence the fair damsel draws the threads
Of silk and gold; beneath her lashes sheds
Her glances on the ruddy page who stands
  Below her dais smiling half in glee,
The while he plucks the hound's ear aimlessly,
Until a hollow growl sounds 'neath his hands.

—Thomas Walsh

THE DRAMA

Jacinto Benavente (1866–1954) was king of the drama
during this period—the one outstanding figure. He was a
native of Madrid, the son of a successful physician. Comfortable family circumstances permitted him to devote
his life to letters. He enjoyed a good education and the
benefits of travel. His knowledge of both the older and
newer dramas of Europe is profound. Benavente owes
nothing to the *siglo de oro* drama, and his break with the
school of Echegaray was sharp. His methods are modern.
From Lavedan, Donnay, Curel, and other contemporary
French dramatists he learned the art of social satire; but
he is far from imitating the typical "well-made" play of
France. He studiously avoids threadbare theatrical con-
ventionalities. The strong situation is rare in his plays.
Action is slighted. Interest depends upon character and
dialogue. He is not without technique, but it is a new
technique, in some respects analogous to Shaw's. Yet
one may agree with Federico de Onís that Benavente is
less an idealogue and far more of an artist than Shaw.
He is less interested in theses. His attitude toward med-

dlesome, pharisaical reformers is hostile, as a reading of
Los malhechores del bien will show. Temperamentally and
politically he is a conservative. But he sees much that is
rotten in state and society and applies his analytic scalpel
to all sorts of abuses, including the abuse of misdirected
reform. Innate skepticism prevents Benavente from
seeking solace in any radical fools' paradise. Hence his
criticism is destructive rather than constructive. His
plays are always thought provoking; but the solution is
usually left to audience and readers.

Plays of social satire.—Only a few of Benavente's
plays—they exceed eighty in number—can here be mentioned. His career began in 1894 with an insignificant
production, *El nido ajeno.* His second piece, *Gente conocida*, 1896, proclaimed the advent of a new genius. This
is the first of a long series of plays satirizing the aristocracy and rich bourgeoisie of Madrid. In these Benavente
does very much what Padre Coloma had done in *Pequeñeces*, but with infinitely more finesse. Realism is most
evident in this series, because the author is dealing with a
social group to which he belongs and which he knows
through and through. When the scene changes to the
provinces, Benavente lets his fancy play, and his method
is often more symbolic. He does not understand the
small-townsman or the peasant as he does the Madrileño.
High society always enjoys the spectacle of its foibles
transferred to the stage, and the lower orders are nothing
loath to see their masters pilloried. The success of *Gente
conocida* was instantaneous. The author repeated with a
long series of similar plays. *Por las nubes* discusses the
high cost of living. *Lo cursi*, 1901, one of the best of the
sort, satirizes the false standards of the rich arising from

the fear of being held "second-rate." *La gobernadora* unmasks social hypocrisies.

Children's plays.—Benavente's father was a specialist in children's diseases. His bust has been placed in that portion of the public park where the children of Madrid play. From his father the dramatist inherited a fondness for children, which found expression in a form of play called *el teatro para los niños*. A series of dramatized fairy tales display a charming side of Benavente's genius. Like the best of juvenile fiction they make appeal also to the elders. *El príncipe que todo lo aprendió en los libros* depicts a prince who believes his fairy stories, journeys out into the world, and finds the personages of the tales existing in real life. The ogre, for example, is the social oppressor. Other charming little pieces of this sort are *Ganarse la vida* and *El nietecito*.

Los intereses creados, 1909, is commonly accepted as Benavente's masterpiece. It is a return to the Italian masqued comedy. The characters are Polichinelle, Harlequin, Pantaloon, Columbine, etc., each symbolic of a human type. The two chief personages are Leander and Crispin, who typify, respectively, the good and evil elements of the human soul. The servant controls his master like another Mephistopheles. The title is explained by these words of the author: *"Para crear afectos en la vida lo mejor es empezar por crear intereses."* Mr. de Onís states the thesis as follows:

> We have to do with a pessimistic work in which the power and necessity of evil are recognized and affirmed. Although love, purity, and generosity are not denied, and even end triumphant, they do not triumph through any virtue of their own, but thanks to the machinations of all-powerful evil.

"*La Malquerida,*" *1913.*—The *Bonds of Interest,* when acted by the Washington Square players, gained only an artistic success. The thought was too subtle to be readily apprehended; the technique was something new to American audiences. But *The Passion Flower* (a poetic but inaccurate rendering), graced with the acting of Miss Nance O'Neill, took America by storm. That is because this play, though not among his best, is the one most nearly approaching conventionality of form which Benavente has written. It is a tragedy of peasant life, after the manner of the Catalan, Guimerá. The theme is a stepfather's guilty love for his stepdaughter. This play proves that Benavente can handle plot and strong situations when he cares to.

Señora ama, 1908, is the play which Benavente himself considered his masterpiece. There are many who agree with him. The interest is psychological. The heroine is a saintly character, who shows generosity to her erring husband's mistresses and illegitimate children, so long as she herself is childless. On becoming a mother, she turns egotistic.

When Echegaray was awarded the Nobel prize, certain young intellectuals made demonstrations of disapproval. When the same honor fell to Benavente in 1922, it was felt to be a national triumph. He is the most versatile and supple dramatist that Spain has produced in modern times. His range is wide; his manner original. He has many of the marks of universality.

The Brothers Serafín (1871–1938) and Joaquín (1873–1944) Álvarez Quintero were not great, but very pleasing. These gifted collaborators bring to the stage the sunshine, flowers, and laughter of their native Seville. Sometimes

they wander away from Andalusia in the choice of a subject, but the spirit is always the same. Tragedy and social thesis are banished from their writings. They aim
to amuse, not to instruct. With true Spanish fecundity
the brothers produced over one hundred plays and
zarzuelas; significant are *Los galeotes*, 1900; *El patio*,
1900; *El amor que pasa*, 1904; and *Doña Clarines*, 1909.

Manuel Linares Rivas (1867–1938) imitated Benavente in the comedy of social satire. He is more super-
ficially clever than his model, with more froth and less
substance. His is Gallic wit rather than Spanish humor.
An air of sophistication characterizes all his work. His
best pieces are *El abolengo*, 1904; *La garra*, 1914; *El
caballero lobo*, 1919; and *La casa de la Troya*, 1919. Sometimes, as in *Lady Godiva*, he attempts fantastic flights.

Eduardo Marquina (1879–1946), already treated as a
lyric poet, successfully revived the *teatro poético*. Many
of his subjects are epic, like *Las hijas del Cid*, 1908; *Doña
María la Brava*, 1909. His masterpiece, *En Flandes se
ha puesto el sol*, 1910, deals with the wars in Flanders
under Philip II. The diametrically opposite national
ideals of Dutch and Spaniards are weighed in the balance
with perfect fairness. Marquina has equal respect for the
thrifty industry of the Lowlanders and the noble, if
quixotic, crusading spirit of his own race. He has a sense
of dramatic situation, and invests an epic subject with a
lyric charm.

The poet *Francisco Villaespesa* also cultivated the
poetic drama. As in his shorter poems, he turns by preference to Moorish Granada. *El alcázar de las perlas*, 1911,
pleased by its romantic colorfulness. Later attempts,
Doña María de Padilla, La leona de Castilla, Abenhumeya,

El rey Galaor, etc., were less successful. Villaespesa has
less dramatic effectiveness than Marquina. His plays
delight the reader, but often lack power on the stage.

Gregorio Martínez Sierra (*1881–1948*) and his de-
cidedly gifted wife, *María de la O Lejárraga* often collaborated in the works which bear the signature of Martínez
Sierra. Doña María, a lady as modest as she was talented,
refused to share in her husband's glory, but it is thought
that her contribution to the firm's success was large. To
her may be due the note of feminity characteristic of all
of Martínez' work. *Flores de escarcha*, 1900, is a noteworthy collection of verse. There followed a series of
novels, no less poetic and distinguished by a fine feeling
for nature, a few of which are *Almas ausentes*, 1900;
Pascua florida, 1901; *Sol de la tarde*, 1904; *Tú eres la paz*,
1907; *El amor catedrático*, 1910; etc. However, Martínez
Sierra was most successful as a dramatist. *Canción de
cuna*, 1910, is a delicate depiction of convent life. In this
two-act drama in prose, realism is tempered by sympa-
pathetic imagination. There is next to no action; the author merely desired to transfer a picture to the stage.
Here, as elsewhere, one notes Benavente's influence. The
first act represents the nuns all in a flutter over the ac-
quisition of a foundling infant left at their doorstep.
They accept the charge, and the second act, eighteen
years later, represents the baby, grown to womanhood,
on the eve of her wedding, about to forsake the convent
for the world. The way in which the thwarted maternal
instinct of the nuns is made to find expression is as delightful as it is human. Like Benavente, Martínez Sierra
cultivates the dramatized fairy tale. *El palacio triste* is a
charming plea for nature as against artificiality. Mar-

tínez Sierra was one of Spain's most distinguished stylists.
He was full of color, exquisite in form and thought, and
possessed a delicate sense of the *nuance*. He shared with
his contemporaries their fondness for landscape. The
influence of Maeterlinck has been denied, but there is an
undoubted resemblance.

Jacinto Grau (1877–1959), a Catalan, won great critical respect though not popular acclaim as a dramatist.
El conde Alarcos, 1917, is evidence that the old ballads
still serve as a source of inspiration to the Spanish playwright.

THE NOVEL

Pío Baroja (1872–1956), a Basque, who drifted from
medicine to the proprietorship of a bakery in Madrid,
and then to literature, began as a regional novelist of the
Basque provinces. *Vidas sombrías*, 1900, later revised
with the title *Idilios vascos*, gave evidence of talent. *La
casa de Aizgorri*, 1900, is a dialogued novel of Basque
industrial life, and *El mayorazgo de Labraz*, 1903, describes a dead city of the north. *Zalacaín el aventurero*,
1909, betrays that interest in the Carlist wars so keen in
every Basque. These are among the novelist's best works;
but, like Blasco Ibáñez, Baroja scorned to remain a
regional novelist. The "Paradox" series is a fantastic
critique of existing notions of government and social
organization. *Camino de perfección*, 1902, is Baroja's best
novel. He takes his neurasthenic hero on a pilgrimage
through the old cities of Central Spain, and nowhere have
the plains and towns of that region been better described.
Baroja is supreme in his *paisajes*. Next came the trilogy,
La Busca, *Mala hierba*, and *Aurora roja*, novels of the

Madrid proletariat, as forceful as they are disagreeable, and in which the author makes parade of anarchistic leanings. The sincerity of Baroja's radicalism is often open to question. He has a childish desire to shock his readers. *La feria de los discretos* depicts Andalusian life with slight success. Baroja is temperamentally unfitted to enter into the spirit of that province. Most of his stories are novels of the road, and there are few corners of Spain which he leaves unexplored. He even sought to rival the *Episodios nacionales* of Galdós with a series of historical novels on the first Carlist War bearing the collective title, *Memorias de un hombre de acción.*

Baroja's literary method.—Baroja was influenced by Zola, Balzac, and the Russians, but his style is individual. There is no artificially arranged plot. Things happen to the characters, haphazard, as they do in real life. In Baroja's opinion, the novelist must not usurp the rôle of destiny. In form, or rather lack of form, his novels resemble the *novela picaresca.* The story moves rapidly, abruptly. Transitions are avoided. The style is jerky, hurried. Baroja writes for the impatient reader of a restless age. It is a style which should have been invented by an American rather than a Spaniard. The tone is pessimistic without attaining to the gloom of the Russian masters. Baroja's humor is grim and satiric. He charms by his magnificent descriptive power. As a stylist he obtains effects of forceful directness, never of elegance. He interests by his endeavor to give the novel a new form suited to modern life.

Ramón María del Valle-Inclán (1869-1936), above all a stylist, did for modern Spanish prose what Rubén Darío did for verse. This Galician surrounded his

early years with so much mystery that one suspects that
they were commonplace. He would have us believe that
he passed some years in a monastery, served as a soldier
of fortune in South America, when, "on board *La Dalila*,
I recall it with pride, I assassinated Sir Robert Yones.
It was a vengeance worthy of Benvenuto Cellini. I will
tell you how it was, even if you are incapable of comprehending its beauty; but it will be better not to tell you;
you might be shocked." Valle-Inclán is a neo-romantic
in his fondness for pose and his delight in "startling the
bourgeois." In latter years, a longhaired, bespectacled,
one-armed bit of picturesqueness, he browbeat and insulted admiring café coteries after the fashion of a Dr.
Johnson. His arm was lost in an encounter with an an-
tagonist far more formidable than the mythical Sir Robert Yones. He liked to be thought a modern Casanova.
His literary forebears, besides Rubén Darío, were Barbey
d'Aurevilly, D'Annunzio, and Eça de Queiroz; but from
these he merely derived hints for the enrichment of a
highly original literary personality.

A stylist of sensationalism.—Valle-Inclán began with
Femeninas, seis historias amorosas, 1894, distinguished for
nothing but eroticism. With the famous four *Sonatas*,
1902–5, his characteristic style is formed. These novels,
named after the four seasons, correspond to four periods
in man's amatory experience. The hero is the Marqués
de Bradomín, the complete realization of the author's
suppressed desires. *Sonata de primavera*, the most charming of the four, describes the dawn of love in the spring-
time of life, with the setting of an Italian château. Love
is luridly satisfied in Mexico in the *Sonata de estéo*.
The scene changes to Spain in the last two of the series,

those devoted to middle-aged and senile love. *Sonata de
otoño* is the greatest of the four, and, with the possible
exception of *Romance de lobos*, is his masterpiece. Valle-
Inclán is a degenerate in his eroticism and Sadic cruelty
It is a commonplace of criticism that degenerate art
makes an end of the means. Style is no longer the handmaid of thought, but rules over it as queen. Ideas interest
Valle-Inclán little. He is primarily a sensationalist, and a
past master in arousing moods and emotions, pleasant
and unpleasant. "The characteristic condition of all
modern art," he writes, "and very especially of literature,
is a tendency to refine sensations and increase them in
number and intensity." His vocabulary is choice, every
sentence clear and rhythmic. He avoids the hackneyed.
It is his constant endeavor to *"ayuntar dos palabras por
primera vez."* Music and color concern him as much as
meaning. "Some words are like diamonds, others emit
phosphoric glow, others float like a mist." Valle-Inclán's
undoubted virility, however, saves him from becoming a
mere exquisite. Style serves as an embroidery for the tra·
ditional Spanish realism, and this realism gives body to
much which might otherwise pass for aesthetic trifling.
The *Sonatas* were followed by the *La guerra carlista* trilogy,
1909–10, in which the aesthete delights in painting scenes
of barbaric cruelty. Other important works are *Flor de
santidad*, *Cofre de sándalo*, and *La lámpara maravillosa*, in
which a tendency toward occultism is manifest. Valle-
Inclán has also written excellent verse and several plays
which have won slight favor, because they lack dramatic
force, and their supersubtle refinements are lost upon the
audience, though they may please the reader. Valle-
Inclán has achieved effects wholly new. He will be re-

membered in future ages as the leading prose stylist of the early twentieth century. Henceforth a higher standard of art will be demanded of every prose-writer who hopes to gain attention.

Ricardo León (1877–1943) was not highly regarded by the Generation of 1898, because his manner was traditional and he pinned his faith to mysticism rather than to practical reform; but many readers liked his rhetoric and his plots. He was widely known abroad. *Casta de hidalgos*, 1908, with its poetic descriptions of the town of Santillana, is one of the best of modern novels. In *Alcalá de los Zegries*, 1909, the novelist turns to the south, localizing the action in Ronda. *El amor de los amores*, a study in mysticism, recounts the career of an imaginary St. Francis of modern times.

Concha Espina de la Serna (1877–1955), in *La esfinge maragata*, 1913, staked out a new claim for herself, becoming the regional novelist of the mysterious race of Maragatos, who inhabit the region around Astorga. In *El metal de los muertos*, she laments the misfortunes of the mine-workers of the south. A novelist of no great power or significance, Concha Espina pleases by her feminine sense of pity.

Felipe Trigo (1865–1915) was the leading exponent in Spain of *la novela erótica*. His spicy novels were the "best sellers" of their day. Trigo's work, though frequently pornographic, is not to be dismissed as mere trash. He was an artist. Nevertheless, his work is unpleasant and not in the best Spanish tradition. He had been preceded in this sort of novel by Eduardo Zamacois (b. 1873).

Gabriel Miró (b. 1879) is a symbolistic and impressionistic novelist. He will be discussed later.

CRITICISM, PHILOSOPHY, HISTORY,
AND ERUDITION

José Martínez Ruiz (Azorín, b. 1874) is the leading
critic, and, next to Valle-Inclán, the chief prose stylist
of the Generation of 1898. First acquaintance with one of
Azorín's books is an event in any reader's life. It is like
one's first introduction to Anatole France. One admires
his sanely progressive ideas, his patriotism, the wistful,
yearning melancholy of his style. This last is highly
personal. He reacts against the too easy fluency of the
past. His sentences are short. He eliminates the over-
worked particle *que*, and is the sworn enemy of similes,
metaphors, and other tropes. But he abuses the rhetorical
question, has a mania for repetition, and has other peculiarities which degenerate into mannerisms. This becomes evident on reading widely in his works, for
Azorín lacks versatility and range. Mood and manner
never vary. In the end, his style cloys, like any other
sweet thing.

Novels and stories.—La voluntad, 1902, and *Antonio
Azorín,* 1903, may be considered novels, with some lati-
tude of definition. Plot, there is none; characterization
is slight. The chief personage is Azorín himself, uttering
his own thoughts and experiencing his own delicate impressions. The whole charm lies in the descriptions of
somnolent cities lost in their memories, rural exteriors and
interiors, and native human types. Azorín, with the
possible exception of Baroja, is first of modern Spanish
painters of landscape. Nobody better evokes the past
and interprets it to the present. He has evolved a new,
delightful form of short story. He lets his imagination
play around some character in the old classics and carries

on the story. Thus, he has written a charming sequel to *El licenciado Vidriera*, and has happily resurrected the cap-manufacturers of Toledo—those kindly girls, barely mentioned in *Lazarillo de Tormes*, who shared their luncheons with the starving *pícaro*. Best of all is *Las nubes*, in which those famous lovers, Calisto and Melibea, reappear. Through it runs the thought that love, like the clouds, manifests itself throughout the ages in ever changing form, but always essentially the same.

Descriptive pieces.—The novel has always appeared too artificial a form to Azorín. "It should have no plot," he says. "Life has no plot; it is multiform, undulant, contradictory . . . . everything except symmetrical, geometric, rigid as it appears in novels." This too, we have seen is Baroja's view. Azorín speedily abandoned a form for which he had little talent to gratify his readers with his wonderful descriptive power. In works like *Los hidalgos, El alma castellana, Los pueblos, La ruta de Don Quijote, España,* and *Castilla* he is at his happiest. Levantine Spaniard though he is, Castile interests him more than other provinces, as the one most typical and where more than elsewhere the national type has been evolved. No Spaniard has ever loved Spain and the Spaniards better, or better interpreted their soul. Cejador's denunciation of Azorín for alleged Gallomania is as silly as it is shallow. Merely because an enlightened thinker holds that a few lessons may be learned from foreign lands. If Azorín takes aesthetic delight in Spain's noble past and picturesque present, he never loses sight of the possibility of a better future. This vision saves him from being an aesthetic decadent. It is no slight feat to enthral a reader by works purely descriptive. This Azorín has done.

Azorín as critic.—Azorín is as fond of old books as he is of old cities. He has written several distinguished works of criticism, *Los valores literarios, Al margen de los clásicos,* and others. His method is largely impressionistic, and has the inconsistencies and vagaries of all subjective criticism. The tenets of the Generation of 1898 are his only external criteria. The aesthete and the reformer are at odds. Literature to Azorín has value only if it conveys a message to the present generation. This somewhat utilitarian standard minimizes the importance of works which are merely beautiful without practical meaning. Azorín is also narrow in his judgments of certain genres which he detests, notably the drama, and toward the previous generation of writers and those opposed to his school. When he attacks Menéndez y Pelayo, he is assailing a critic vastly greater than himself. The most scholarly and cultured of Spanish-American critics, Pedro Henríquez Ureña, has applied the needed corrective. On the other hand, Azorín delights in lifting out of obscurity inconspicuous mediocrities and assigning to them undue importance. But, aside from these faults, Azorín is the most ingratiating of critics. He knows how to impart to others the fascination of his favorite authors. He has made many sound revaluations. And here, as in all his other writings, he invests everything with that indefinable charm characteristic of his genius.

Miguel de Unamuno (1864–1936) might have been a great philosopher, a great poet, or a great novelist; but he so dispersed his energies that he never attained the highest rank in any field. Yet this sturdy Basque, who filled the chair of Greek at Salamanca, was once the most potent intellectual force of Spain. His novels, *Paz en la guerra,* 1897; *Niebla,* 1914, etc., contain vigorous strokes of realism, sparkling wit, and original ideas. Unamuno called them *"nivolas,"* a term he coined for a novel in which each character voices the author's views. Obviously, such works are little more than popularized philosophical tracts. He wrote some excellent verse, but his proper form of expression was the essay. The *Ensayos* (6 vols.), 1916–18, are very stimulating criticisms of education, religion, literature, politics, and similar subjects. Many are paradoxical, for Unamuno has a tendency to fly in the face of accepted beliefs. But socialism has no charms for him. Unamuno is a typical Spaniard in his individualism. He has an abiding faith in humanity and confidence in the ability of the individual to lead the masses onward and upward. He has a cosmopolitan culture, intellectual curiosity, independence of judgment, and expresses his thoughts with trenchant vigor. Above all, he loves Spain, believes in her capabilities for good, and fights for her advancement. His idealism comes to the fore in *Vida de don Quijote y Sancho,* 1905, a spiritual commentary on Cervantes' great novel. No recent writer has influenced more profoundly the youth of his nation.

Unamuno's philosophy.—Unamuno never crystallized his thought in any hard-and-fast philosophic system. One must seek it in his greatest work, *Del sentimiento trágico de la vida en los hombres y en los pueblos,* 1913, in his *Ensayos,* and here, there, and everywhere throughout his scattered writings. Often his views change, for Unamuno reserves the right to alter his opinions. He is a voluntarist, and on occasion shows pragmatic leanings. He is consistent only in his opposition to everything that fetters, and attacks dogma and governmental tyranny fearlessly. Race and nation are to him, as to the socialists, hampering concepts of the human mind. Humanity is his race, the universe his country. But he does not attack the concepts of race and nation because they stand in the way of collective action, but because they hamper the individual. This does not mean that he holds aloof from that fraction of humanity known as Spaniards; but he feels that their interests will be best served by abandoning their *casticismo* and *españolismo*. He anticipated Ganivet in diagnosing the national disease, and even in the use of the term *abulia*.[1] His remedy is less aloofness and more democracy: *"Tenemos que europeizarnos y chapuzarnos en pueblo."* Being such a pronounced individualist, Unamuno cannot brook the thought of the annihilation of the ego. He believes in a future life, and is a Christian, but a most undogmatic one. Always liberal and ever courageous, many regarded him as Spain's grand old man. He has his detractors, but was undeniably important.

Rafael Altamira (1866–1951) was the greatest Spanish historian of his generation. His *Historia de España y de la civilización española* (4 vols.), Barcelona, 1900–1913, is not so much a political and military history as a history of Spanish culture—architecture, sculpture, painting, literature, etc., though the story of the nation is briefly sketched. It contains the best working bibliography of Spanish history that we have. Altamira gained wide influence in Spain and America as publicist and lecturer. He was an energetic Liberal, always fighting in the van of progress. He was first attached to the University of Oviedo, going later to Madrid. He won international positions and was held in world-wide esteem, as a philosopher of law and as a historian.

[1] *Ensayos*, I, 207.

Ramón Menéndez Pidal (b. 1869), with his publication
of *La leyenda de los infantes de Lara*, 1896, appeared before the world as a scholar of the first rank. Today he is
recognized as not only the leading Spanish authority on
letters and linguistics, but the world's greatest romance
philologist. Later appeared his wonderful edition of *La
primera crónica general;* the *Cantar de Mio Cid* (3 vols.),
containing texts, grammar, and vocabulary; the *Manual
de gramática histórica española: L'Epopée castillane*, in
French; *El romancero español; Documentos lingüísticos;
La España del Cid;* and numerous monographs of all
sorts. He has served as director and general editor of the
monumental *Historia de España*, which marks one of
Spain's most serious efforts in historiography. The mere
listing of the titles of the great scholar's publications
would fill a great many large pages. One observes that
in this vast accomplishment, there has been no slighting
of detail, Menéndez Pidal founded in 1914 the fundamental journal devoted solely to Hispanic studies, the
Revista de filología española. He imparted his modern
philological method to a galaxy of brilliant disciples—
Américo Castro, Antonio G. Solalinde, Navarro Tomás,
Alfonso Reyes, Homero Serís, Gómez Ocerín, Federico de
Onís, and many others almost, if not as fully, as distinguished. Amid the stormy waves breaking on Spain and
the world, Don Ramón Menéndez Pidal has ever stood
like a rock of scholarly stability.

BIBLIOGRAPHY

Torrente Ballester, G. *Panorama de la literatura española con-
    temporánea.* Madrid, 1956. Studies and selections.
Laín Entralgo, P. *La generación del noventa y ocho.* Madrid,
    1945.

JESCHKE, H. *Die Generation von 1898 in Spanien.* Halle, 1934.

LEVI, E. *Figure della letteratura spagnuola contemporanea.* Florence, 1922.

VALBUENA PRAT, A. *La poesía española contemporánea.* Madrid, 1930.

BARJA, CÉSAR. *Libros y autores contemporáneos.* Madrid, 1935.

CANSINOS-ASSENS, R. *Poetas y prosistas del novecientos.* Madrid, 1919.

——. *La nueva literatura.* 4 vols. Madrid, 1917–27.

BALSEIRO, JOSÉ A. *Nueve escritores españoles contemporáneos juzgados por un crítico angloamericano.* Havana, 1926.

FERNÁNDEZ ALMAGRO, M. *Vida y obra de Angel Ganivet.* Valencia, 1925.

ESPINA, A. *Ganivet: El hombre y la obra.* Buenos Aires, 1942.

CIGES APARICIO, M. *Costa, el gran fracasado.* Madrid, 1930.

MONSERRAT, S. *Antonio Machado: Poeta y filósofo.* Buenos Aires, 1940.

PEERS, E. A. *Antonio Machado.* Oxford, 1940.

PÉREZ FERRERO, M. *Vida de Antonio Machado y Manuel* Madrid, 1947.

MULLERT, W. *Azorín.* Halle, 1926. Spanish trans. Madrid, 1930.

GÓMEZ DE LA SERNA, R. *Azorín.* Madrid, 1930.

ONÍS, F. DE. *Jacinto Benavente.* New York, 1923.

STARKIE, WALTER. *Jacinto Benavente.* Oxford, 1924.

AZORÍN. *Los Quinteros y otras páginas.* Madrid, 1925.

FERNÁNDEZ ALMAGRO, M. *Vida y literatura de Valle-Inclán.* Madrid, 1943.

GÓMEZ DE LA SERNA, R. *Don Ramón María del Valle-Inclán* Buenos Aires, 1944.

SALINAS, P. *Significación del esperpento o Valle-Inclán, hijo pródigo. del 98.* Mexico, 1947. Taken from *Cuadernos americanos.*

AGUSTÍN, FR. *Ramón Pérez de Ayala, su vida y obras.* Madrid, 1927.

BALSEIRO, J. *Cuatro individualistas de España.* Chapel Hill, 1949. Blasco Ibáñez, Unamuno, Valle-Inclán, Baroja.

ORTEGA Y GASSET, J. "Ideas sobre Pío Baroja," *El espectador,* Vol. I (1916).

TREND, J. B. *Pío Baroja and His Novels.* London, 1920.

HELMUT, D. *Pío Baroja: Das Weltbild in seinen Werken.* Hagen, 1937.

ROMERA-NAVARRO, M. *Miguel de Unamuno: Novelista, poeta, ensayista.* Madrid, 1928.

MARÍAS, J. *Miguel de Unamuno.* Madrid, 1943.

FERRATER MORA, J. *Miguel de Unamuno: Bosquejo de una filosofía.* Buenos Aires, 1944.

PALAU DE NEMES, GRACIELA. *Vida y obras de Juan Ramón Jiménez.* Madrid, 1957.

GICOVATE, B. *La poesía de Juan Ramón Jiménez.* San Juan, 1959.

CHAPTER XXVI

The Twentieth Century. The Civil War to the Present

General—Thinkers and essayists—Scholars—Later essayists and critics—The drama after Benavente—The novel after 1898—The later twentieth-century novel—The short story—Lyric poetry—Poetry after World War I—Poets of the thirties and later.

GENERAL

The division of literature into neat periods by years may be useful, but it is inaccurate. The Renaissance did not suddenly burst into blossom with the fall of Constantinople in 1453. Sainte-Beuve pronounced Romanticism dead in 1850, but many Romantics thought they were still alive. The Generation of 1898 did not utter a convenient death rattle with the firing of the first gun in the Spanish Civil War. Lyric poetry did not suddenly expire with the foul murder of García Lorca in July, 1936.

It may be safely said, however, that the members of the so-called Generation of 1898 had nothing really new to offer after the late 1920's. They continued to produce into the late 1950's, and one or two, very old, are still happily alive as this is written. Three or four generations, representing different general tendencies, can and do coexist, as in Spain. And no very satisfactory names have yet been found to designate them. The confusions, the centripetal tendencies, of the contemporary world make classification all the more difficult.

Somewhere after the first decade of this century or around the time of the First World War one can observe some change in spirit, even some protest against those who began writing around 1898, although these younger men were chronologically younger by only a few years, and a substantial number of literary historians prefer to attach them to the Generation of 1898. It is fair to say that they were in general men of greater academic culture, more intellectualized, more Europeanized, less subjective, more inclined to accept facts, and less likely to utter anguished cries of protest than their predecessors. Their medium of expression was characteristically the prose essay rather than verse or drama. The dominant spirit of the time was Ortega y Gasset, whose influence came to be considerably greater than that of Unamuno.

THINKERS AND ESSAYISTS

José Ortega y Gasset (1883-1955) came from a family distinguished on both sides in literature and politics. He did not have to struggle to get an education, and he got an excellent one. Like the sons of many liberal and intellectual families—Pérez de Ayala for example—he received his early training from the Jesuits. After earning his doctorate in philosophy from the University of Madrid in 1904, he studied for a few years in Germany. At Marburg he was initiated into neo-Kantianism by Hermann Cohen, and the influence of his German teachers remained strong in his thinking. In 1910 he assumed the chair of metaphysics in the University of Madrid, and proceeded, with much success, to create in Spain an atmosphere in which philosophical studies could flourish. He applied his keen intelligence to all aspects of life and art, with a broad criterion and enormous suggestiveness. Fundamental in his philosophy is his definition of the individual: "Yo soy yo y mi circumstancia." That is, we act as the result of the interplay between subjective and objective reality. The "radical reality" which Ortega emphasizes defines life as the reaction of the whole being, not just the pure rational faculty, to external things. Ortega's own style, always zestful and often filled with metaphors, is the natural expression of his own attitudes. He himself has said that he constantly sought to bring all aspects of life and art "along the shortest road to the plenitude of their meanings," to approach all problems with "intellectual love."

Many disagreed with Ortega's expressed opinions, some of which were surely fallible, such as his statement that the modern novel is doomed to disappear, for lack of subjects. Pío Baroja, who differed with Ortega (and with practically everyone else) on many matters, nevertheless viewed him as "the only possibility that we have of philosophy in Spain." Admiration for Ortega was not confined to his own country, but became fully international.

After numerous contributions to highly respectable dailies and magazines, Ortega's first book was his very suggestive *Meditaciones del Quijote*, 1914. From 1916 to 1934 he published eight volumes of essays in a collection which he called *El Espectador*. One observes the significance of the attitude implied in the title. In 1923 Ortega founded the most important review of modern Spain: the *Revista de Occidente*, which unhappily had to be suspended in 1936. *España invertebrada*, 1921, had raised something of a furor in Spain, because in it Ortega tried to explain Spain's decadence. One idea displeased many: that Spain, like other nations, languished for lack of directing "select minorities," which have been evident, he said, in all nations in their plenitude.

The two books by Ortega which have probably had the greatest resonance abroad are *La deshumanización del arte*, 1925, and *La rebelión de las masas*, 1930. The first is a lucid analysis and by implication a defense of anti-realism in modern art, of the tendency to depersonalize what is expressed in painting, sculpture, music, or literature. In the second, called in English *The Revolt of the Masses*, the author pitilessly analyzes the debasing influences of mob dictatorship upon government, art, and literature. Though he often disagrees with Spengler, he is at one with the gloomy German in predicting degeneracy and ruin for civilization. Ortega holds, first, that humanity has devised no better form of government than liberal democracy; second, that this is not the best conceivable form of government; third, that to revert deliberately to a worse form, such as communism or fascism, means racial suicide.

Most of the numerous works of Ortega can be found in the six volumes of his so-called *Obras completas*, 1946–47, but publication still goes on of many manuscripts which he left upon his death in 1955.

Many Spaniards disagreed with Ortega's ideas, often on political or religious grounds. None, however, could fail to admire his supple, rich, elegant, and suggestive style.

The acute German critic E. R. Curtius spoke advisedly in calling Ortega y Gasset, "one of the Twelve Peers of the European spirit."

Eugenio d'Ors (*1883–1954*), who used the pen-name
"Xenius," should not be neglected because of the Fran-
coist-Fascist ideology which he displayed in his later
years. Born in Barcelona, he wrote his first works (*Glosa-
ri*) in Catalan. His later works, *Glosarios*, even a *Novísi-
mo glosario*, were written in extremely expressive Castilian. He also wrote in French. Even though he was
deservedly overshadowed by his towering contemporary
Ortega y Gasset, Ors merits serious attention for his
stimulating writings on politics, science, philosophy, literature, and especially on art. Many consider his art
criticism the best part of his work. He was the most
noted advocate of *Novecentismo*, a variously defined and
mainly conservative movement which championed order
and renewal within the classical canons of art. The delicately chiseled prose of his "classical" period and the
deliberate artifice of his "baroque" phase are of interest
to the student of style. Critical opinions concerning Ors
have varied. Angel Valbuena Prat finds considerable
depth under the surface of the Catalan's "sencillo juego
de ideas." To Ángel del Río, Ors's work gives an impression of dilettantism and his style the feeling of affected
preciosity. It is permissible to wonder how high he will
be ranked by critics in the future.

Salvador de Madariaga (*b. 1886*), a true cosmopolite
who happened to be born in Spain, has been primarily
interested in spreading a knowledge of his native country
to the rest of the world. He writes with idiomatic facility
in Spanish, English, and French and has published in all
three languages. He has written very informative biographies of Hernán Cortés, Columbus, and Bolívar, and the
title *Shelley, and Calderón and Other Essays on English*

and Spanish Poetry, 1920, shows a little of the breadth
of his interests. His *Guía del lector del Quijote*, 1926, is
keenly written and has probably improved the lectures
of many a professor of Spanish literature. It was supplemented by his *Don Quixote: An Introductory Essay in
Psychology* in 1934. His *Englishmen, Frenchmen, Spaniards* is an interesting commentary on national characteristics. It is possible that his most important book has
been the historical interpretation *España*, published in
various editions in different languages. He has been professor at Oxford and has lectured widely throughout the
world. Since his ideas are, in general, democratic and
liberal, he never returned to his native country after the
advent of Generalissimo Francisco Franco.

Manuel Azaña (1880–1940) is thought of chiefly as
the prime minister and later president of the unhappy
Second Spanish Republic, but he was also an intellectual
figure of real stature and a novelist (*El jardín de los frailes*,
1927), essayist, dramatist, and literary historian. He is
particularly known for his illuminating studies of Juan
Valera.

Gregorio Marañón (b. 1886) helps to prove the statement that Spanish doctors are far more likely than their
American, or, for that matter, their British, French, or
German counterparts, to be interested specifically in literary and general cultural problems. Dr. Marañón published highly respectable studies connected with his pro-
fessorship of endocrinology at the University of Madrid,
but he has also enriched literary scholarship and criticism. Many of his numerous books supplement biography
and history with medical knowledge. He has written on
Amiel, Henry IV of Castile, Tiberius, the myth of Don

Juan, the Count-Duke of Olivares, Antonio Pérez, and
El Greco. His prose is smooth and readily comprehensi-
ble. A man of liberal ideas, he has undoubtedly been for
long years one of Spain's most considerable intellectual
figures.

Manuel García Morente (1886–1942) was from 1912
to 1936 an esteemed professor of philosophy in the University of Madrid, and dean from 1931 until he was dismissed at the beginning of the Spanish Civil War. He
spent his exile in Paris and in Argentina. After a spiritual
crisis, he returned to Catholicism and was ordained priest
in 1940. In addition to many essays, he published studies
of Kant and Bergson. His most important work was
published after his death as *Fundamentos de filosofía.*

SCHOLARS

Among the older scholars inspired by Menéndez Pidal, some have already been mentioned, such as *Américo
Castro (b. 1885).* Long a professor at the University of
Madrid, Castro transferred his rich scholarly activities
to America and taught there, mainly at Princeton, later
at Houston. He steadily published an extremely large
number of learned and critical articles and books on many
phases of Spanish literature and culture. If one had to
pick just two books to remember him by, they might be
his fundamental study, *El pensamiento de Cervantes,* 1925;
and his historical interpretation of Spain first published
in Spanish in 1948, then in English in 1954, finally again
in Spanish in 1957 under the title *La realidad histórica de
España.*

Frederico de Onís (b. 1885) was professor at Oviedo
and Salamanca and in 1916 became professor of Spanish

at Columbia University. After his retirement there, he went to the University of Puerto Rico. He published numerous studies, essays, editions, and independent books. Particularly useful is his *Antología de la poesía española e hispanoaméricana (1882–1932)*, Madrid, 1934. Another pupil of Menéndez Pidal is *Tomás Navarro Tomás (b. 1884)*. He produced extremely important works on Spanish phonetics, dialectology, and metrics. *Homero Serís (b. 1879)* made great contributions to Spanish bibliography. *Antonio G. Solalinde (1892–1937)* did admirable work on medieval literature, especially on Alfonso el Sabio, at the University of Wisconsin until his untimely death. His work is being continued by a most capable group of American scholars there.

Dámaso Alonso (b. 1898) is not only an admirable poet, but is also one of the scholars and critics who do most honor to their master, Menéndez Pidal, and whose scholarly achievements have been most honored in Spain and abroad. He has particularly enriched the study and appreciation of Spanish poetry, from the *kharjas* onward to the modern epoch. His studies of Góngora (a prose version of the *Soledades* in 1927, *La lengua poética de Góngora* in 1935) are particularly noteworthy, and attitudes toward the great baroque poet have been better informed and more comprehending ever since the publication of those works. His anthologies, going from *Poesía de la Edad Media y poesía de tipo tradicional* (1935) to *Poetas españoles contemporáneos* (1952), are most discriminating. His studies on San Juan de la Cruz, Francisco de Medrano, his commentaries on the works of Erasmus, of Gil Vicente, and on many other important

figures have been wide'ly influential. Julián Marías has
termed Alonso's *Ensayos sobre poesía española* (1944),
supplemented by *Poesía española* (1950), *"una espléndida
colección de estudios concisos y perspicaces."* Dámaso
Alonso generously guided and aided younger scholars,
both native and foreign.

Samuel Gili Gaya (b. 1892) has made valuable contributions to linguistic and philological studies, as did
Amado Alonso (1896–1952) in Spain, Buenos Aires, and
at Harvard University. *Joaquín de Entrambasaguas (b.
1904)* has covered a wide field of scholarly endeavor and
is particularly known for his studies of Lope de Vega.
Rafael Lapesa (b. 1908) has devoted himself mainly to linguistic studies but has also produced a valuable study of
Garcilaso and others. *Antonio Rodríguez-Moñino (b. 1910)*
has not confined himself solely to studies of literary figures of his *patria chica*, Estremadura. He too is noted for
encouraging younger aspirants to scholarship and letters.
He founded a good review, the *Revista española*, in 1953.
José Manuel Blecua (b. 1913) has studied Spanish poetry
from Juan de Mena through Jorge Guillén, in addition to
producing other studies.

Ángel Valbuena Prat (b. 1900) is particularly known
for Calderonian studies, but he has also published many
other works and is well known for his *Historia de la literatura española*. His son Ángel Valbuena Briones is following in the paternal footsteps. *Guillermo Díaz-Plaja (b.
1909)* and *Fernando Díaz-Plaja* have enriched literary
and historical studies. *Martín de Riquer (b. 1914)* has
published prestigious studies of many aspects of Spanish

literature. His work on the epic is highly respected
throughout the world.

One of the most noted lexicographers and philologists
of the century is *Joan Corominas (b. 1905)*. He has
taught at the University of Barcelona, at the Universidad
Nacional de Cuyo, Argentina, and has since 1946 been
Professor of Romance Philology at the University of Chicago. He published various works on Romance dialectology and linguistics, but his great achievement is to be
found in his remarkable *Diccionario crítico-etimológico de
la lengua castellana*, 1954, a true monument of modern
scholarship. It is amazing to reflect on the broad knowledge and zealous industry which enabled Sr. Corominas,
almost single-handed, to produce a work running to four
large volumes and about 4,000 pages. It is an indispensable standard etymological dictionary of Spanish, and
will undoubtedly remain so for decades, perhaps for generations.

No doubt the names of many other worthy scholars
are ungraciously omitted. It is ungracious, too, not to
mention the names of foreign Hispanists who have made,
and are making, noteworthy contributions to Spanish
linguistic and literary scholarship. They may exist in
greater numbers in the United States and in Latin America, but one should not forget the large number also in
Canada, Great Britain, France, Germany, Holland, and
elsewhere.

LATER ESSAYISTS AND CRITICS

Censorship cannot block thought, though it may be
rough on the thinker. Not everything published during
the Franco regime has been officially approved propa-

ganda. It is true that certain men have been punished
for expressing themselves; and some remain in exile.

Pedro Laín Entralgo (*b. 1908*) is another doctor who
is vastly interested in general cultural problems. He had
excellent training in medicine and psychiatry, in Spain
and in Vienna. As professor in the University of Madrid,
he published numerous medical works and directed a
series called *"Clásicos de la Medicina."* He was rector of
the university until he was relieved of his position for opposing official government attitudes. The titles of a few
works show his broad interests and help to explain why
he has had considerable influence on younger men: *Sobre
la cultura española; Menéndez Pelayo*, 1944; *Las generaciones en la historia*, 1945; *La generación del noventa y
ocho*, 1945; *España como problema*, 1949.

Xavier Zubiri (*b. 1898*), Doctor of Philosophy and
Theology, studied in Madrid, Louvain, and Freiburg. He
acknowledges Ortega and Heidegger as his masters. He
has written widely on philosophical subjects, and some of
his best work will be found in the collection *Naturaleza,
historia, Dios*, 1944.

Guillermo de Torre (*b. 1900*), able critic, essayist, and
journalist, has always been in the forefront of advanced
literary and artistic movements, which he has interpreted
and furthered. He translated Max Jacob, Verlaine, Stra-
vinsky, and others and published studies of Apollinaire
and Picasso. In 1920 he wrote the *Manifiesto vertical ul-
traísta*, and *Literaturas europeas de vanguardia* in 1925.
From his residence in Buenos Aires he edited the complete works of his friend García Lorca. Though some
might regard him as a wild man of art, his contributions

have been highly useful for gaining an understanding of newer artistic aspirations.

José Luis Aranguren (*b. 1909*) has been professor of ethics in the University of Madrid. He is regarded as one of the better interpreters of modern Catholic thought in Europe. Many of his attitudes will be found in his *Catolicismo y protestantismo como formas de existencia*, 1952.

José Ferrater Mora (*b. 1909*) has lived in exile since 1939. Quite outside the bounds of Catholic orthodoxy, he has produced several philosophical works, such as his useful *Diccionario de la filosofía*, 1941; *Unamuno*, 1944; *Cuestiones españolas*, 1946; and *Ortega y Gasset*, 1957.

Julián Marías (*b. 1914*), pupil and interpreter of Ortega y Gasset, has done useful and diligent work in philosophy and literary criticism, much of which has appeared regularly in the valuable publication *Ínsula* and in other journals. He has taught and lectured widely in various foreign countries. Among his numerous publications are: *Historia de la filosofía*, 1941; *Miguel de Unamuno*, 1943; *Introducción a la filosofía*, 1947; *Filosofía española actual*, 1949; *Aquí y ahora*, 1952; plus studies of Ortega and numerous translations, anthologies, and editions of philosophers from Plato through Dilthey.

THE DRAMA AFTER BENAVENTE

Most critics described Spanish drama of the thirties and forties as being in a state of acknowledged decay. It is customary to quote the statement of Benavente, who lived and wrote plays until 1954, to the effect that he had buried four generations of critics who opposed his theater. There have been at least a few playwrights of talent in the 1930's or later.

Alejandro Casona (*b. 1903*), the pen name of Alejandro Rodríguez Álvarez, made a hit in Republican Spain with *La sirena varada*, published in 1934. *Nuestra Natacha* was a great hit in 1936. Casona went into exile in 1937 (Mexico, Havana) and has lived in Buenos Aires since 1939. He has there had several successes: *La dama del alba*, 1944; *La barca sin pescador*, 1945; *Los árboles mueren de pie*, 1949; *Siete gritos en el mar*, 1951. Casona has an excellent knowledge of theatrical technique and shows a pleasant mingling of realism and fancy.

Enrique Jardiel Poncela (*1901–52*) had a good sense of humor even if his plays were not fully effective on the stage, and he died saddened because the theatergoing public apparently had grown tired of him. He also wrote novels. It has been suggested that his best play is *Angelina, o El honor de un brigadier*, a satire on late nineteenth-century manners. Other plays are *Eloisa está debajo de un almendro* and *Los ladrones somos gente honrada*.

Joaquín Calvo Sotelo (*b. 1905*) is a lawyer turned dramatist, as was Linares Rivas. His first success on the stage came with *El rebelde*, 1934. *Plaza de Oriente* has by some been considered his best. *Criminal de guerra* came in 1951, *María Antonieta*, in 1952. *La muralla*, 1954, was also successful.

José López Rubio (*b. 1903*), in collaboration with Eduardo Ugarte, won success in 1928 with a pleasant fancy called *De la noche a la mañana*. *La casa de naipes* came in 1930. After a period of work in motion pictures, the dramatist returned to the legitimate stage with *Alberto*, in 1949. Some judge *Celos del aire*, 1950, to be his most finished play. *La otra orilla*, like Ferenc Molnar's *Liliom*, brings dead characters back on the stage to con-

front the living. In 1954 López Rubio won the Premio
Nacional de Teatro with his *La venda en los ojos*.

No matter whether dramatic fare in Spain is very
tasty or not, there is no dearth of aspiring playwrights.
In 1954, for example, 254 plays were submitted in com-
petition for the Premio Lope de Vega. Choice among numerous names may be arbitrary, but one may mention
the polygraphic champion of conservatism in Church and
State, *José María Pemán (b. 1898)*. He has written
voluminously in every field of literature, including drama.
Perhaps *Édipo*, 1954, is his best play. Among others,
there is Miguel Mihura, who has a gay and very un-
subtle sense of humor. Antonio Paso has written and
collaborated extensively for the stage. Carlos Llopis is
thought of as one of the foremost comic dramatists. Vicente Soriano de Andía, J. A. Giménez Arnau, Felipe
Sassone, J. I. Luca de Tena, V. Ruiz de Iriarte, C. de la
Torre, and Antonio de Lara have been successful in various plays. These pages could be considerably extended
with a mere list of prize winners for drama in Madrid
and Barcelona alone.

Perhaps more solid values are offered in the seriously
wrought plays of *Antonio Buero Vallejo (b. 1916)*. Rising
superior to unhappy personal vicissitudes, he won the
Premio Lope de Vega in 1949 with his *Historia de una
escalera*. It skilfully presents the problems of various
groups of people who pass down the stair of the same
apartment (tenement) house at various periods in their
lives. *En la ardiente oscuridad*, 1950, enjoyed less popularity. *La tejedora de sueños* is based on the *Odyssey*. *La
madrugada*, 1953, helped to consolidate the author's

reputation. *Hoy es fiesta,* 1956, is a combination of symbolism and realism.

Les cartas boca abajo, 1957, is a psychological drama. Here is one estimate by the Spanish critic José María Castellet, as of 1955: *"En realidad, en esos diez y seis años, creemos que sólo dos obras literarias colman los requisitos de* revelación y propuesta: 'La colmena, *novela de Camilo José Cela, e* Historia de una escalera, *drama de Antonio Buero Vallejo.'"* Quite possibly.

Among dramatists still relatively young, the name of *Alfonso Sastre (b. 1926)* has been suggested as the most promising. Time will tell. Perhaps he has the not un-unusual *afán de singularizarse,* since he is reported to use only red and green ink for his manuscripts. Not mauve at any rate. He has been praised especially for *Escuadra hacia la muerte.* Other plays of his have been *La mordaza, La sangre de Dios, Muerte en el barrio.* Even if there have been no modern Lopes and Calderóns in Spain, we may reflect that the rest of the world has not recently produced any rivals to Shakespeare either. Spanish drama may yet be revitalized.

THE NOVEL AFTER 1898

To Spanish literature produced just after the Generation of 1898 began to be consolidated the term *Novecentismo* has been applied, as we have seen, by Ortega and others. It has no great significance as a term but may be convenient, like the preceding *Modernismo.* There was, as has been suggested, a somewhat subtle but recognizable change in authors' ideals and methods. In the essay, it would be represented by Eugenio d'Ors, not to mention Ortega himself.

Ramón Pérez de Ayala (*b. 1880*) is often thought of
as a slightly younger member of the Generation of 1898.
He is much more intellectual than his immediate predecessors, and his poems, articles, and novels all present his
critical, often ironic but comprehending, view of persons
and institutions. Despite his intellectualism, he is capable of deep feeling. If he seems to be the most realistic
of the realists, he nonetheless possesses warm human sympathy for the sufferings of bumbling human beings who
inhabit or clutter the globe.

Ayala received an excellent education in Jesuit board-
ing schools and at the University of Oviedo, and he traveled extensively and read widely. Madariaga has pointed
out that Ayala's native Asturias looks outward upon the
sea, and inward toward the heart of Spain, and that its
inhabitants are especially likely to combine cosmopolitan
and traditional Spanish points of view.

Pérez de Ayala published his first volume of poems,
La paz del sendero in 1903; his second, *El sendero innumerable*, in 1916; and a third, *El sendero andante*, in 1924.
They are mature, thoughtful, and display true poetic
sensitivity, but the author is not seeking mere effects of
musicality and sensual suggestiveness as did the Modernists who immediately preceded him. He can be happily
evocative, but he can also be ironical. His style is individual, and he ranks high among contemporary poets.

Ayala was also an excellent critic. *Política y toros*,
1918, offers criticism, often severe, of two national pre-
occupations. The two volumes of *Las máscaras*, 1917,
1919, contain keen criticisms of contemporary drama and
are by no means favorable to Benavente.

Pérez de Ayala never abandoned his poetic, speculative, and critical tendencies, but it is as a novelist that he won his greatest fame. *Tinieblas en las cumbres*, 1907, is a delightful combination of poetic feeling, intellectual meditation, and bawdy episode. *A.M.D.G.*, 1910, is based on the author's own school experiences and constitutes a violent attack on the Jesuits and their system of education in Spain. The book is written with too much passion to achieve successful artistic effect, though it contains admirable passages and sharp characterizations. *La pata de la raposa*, 1912, and *Troteras y danzaderas*, 1913, follow the subsequent career of Alberto Díaz de Guzmán, the Bertuco of *A.M.D.G.*, a young man who suffers from lack of will and from aimlessness in life. Various other characters are skilfully presented, and the arrangement in the novels seems pleasantly helter-skelter. The scene is mainly in the literary backwashes of Madrid, and the conversations as well as the activities of the characters cover a wide range. *Luna de hiel, luna de hiel* and its second part, *Los trabajos de Urbano y Simona*, 1913, are what one might call therapeutic novels concerning marriage.

Earlier short stories of Ayala were gathered and published under the titles *Bajo el signo de Artemisa* and *El ombligo del mundo*. A few are obviously juvenilia, but some are fully realized episodes and character sketches.

In 1916 Ayala entered a period of true maturity as a novelist with his *Tres novelas poemáticas* (*Prometeo, Luz de domingo, La caída de los Limones*). Each one is a short novel or novella rather than a mere short story, and each is related with somber intensity. Each one offers an example of tragedy stalking unfortunate individuals, through no particular fault of their own. The characters stand sharply outlined against the dark background, and the style is admirably adapted to the material. These are definitely three of the best stories in modern Spanish literature. Each section in the stories is prologued by a poem deftly and impressively giving a foretaste and generalized summary of the events which are to follow. The verses which appear in *La caída de los Limones* are the most impressive and summarize the picture which Ayala paints in Ribera-like colors of a Spain fallen from her high estate, of characters who retain from traditional glories only the aristocratic bearing and gesture. A picture of depressing degeneration, though beautifully executed.

Belarmino y Apolonio, 1921, is the intricately contrived story of two cobblers, the first an introverted philosopher-dreamer, and the second an extrovert with a high sense of the dramatic. In the novel, which some have considered Ayala's best, the author's extraordinary abilities in characterization, narration, dialogue, humor, caricature, and philosophical reflection appear at their finest. The same literary gifts are perceived in Ayala's *Tigre Juan* and its sequel, *El curandero de su honra*, both 1926. The scene is the imaginary city of Pilares, which suggests the author's native Oviedo in many respects and which appears as the background of other stories. The characters live before us with singular intensity, especially the protagonist, whose conflicting qualities are partly summarized in his very name: Juan Guerra Madrigal. The novel presents him as really more than life-size, but he and the other inhabitants of Pilares, including the visiting Don Juan of the piece, are truly human and are characterized with bold and sure strokes of the literary brush.

The literal and spiritual geography of the novel is specifically Spanish, but the implications are universal. Tigre
Juan lived to middle age possessed of terrible Calderonian
ideas about honor; life, his own experience, reflection, and
conversation with his earthly and sensible friend the
mountaineer Nachín de Nacha converted him to reasonable attitudes. In this novel Ayala's great ability in description, humorous expression, and characterization and
and his deft and vigorous style show at their best. The
amazing richness of his vocabulary was long ago praised
by Ayala's friend, the aged Galdós. There is little doubt
that Pérez de Ayala possessed more native and acquired
gifts as a novelist than anyone else of his time. It has
seemed tragic to his great number of admirers that he
wrote no more novels after 1926.

Gabriel Miró (1879–1930) has been said to represent
the symbolistic novel, displaying lyric pessimism along
with the bejeweled prose of a Valle-Inclán. He was always the uncompromisingly conscientious artist, writing
with apparent simplicity and unremitting elegance. His
impressionism is stylized, connected with his immediate
predecessors; some of his ideals are like those of the later
devotees of *poésie pure*. He was born in Alicante, but his
style and manner are at the farthest possible remove
from those of his fellow Levantine a little to the north,
the indelicate Blasco Ibáñez. Gabriel Miró's was a delicate art, hardly appealing to the great public. Some
novels—or perhaps we should call them *estampas*, "en-
gravings," as he often did—are *La novela de mi amigo*,
1908; *Las cerezas del cementerio*, 1910; *Figuras de la pasión
del Señor*, 1916 (translated into English); *El libro de Si-
güenza*, 1917; *El humo dormido*, 1919; *Nuestro Padre San*

Daniel, 1921; *El obispo leproso*, 1925; and *Años y leguas*, 1928.

Ramón Gómez de la Serna (b. 1888), despite his cultivated eccentricities, has always been, in the vulgar phrase, "crazy like a fox." What if he did once lecture in a circus in blackface, from a trapeze? Suppose he did keep in his apartment a highly verisimilitudinous wax female nude to greet unsuspecting visitors? He has always known what he was trying to do, and he possesses very great talent. One might say that his positively Lopean long list of works is one vast series of metaphors. To find a startling, new metaphor for each sentence, RAMÓN, as he apparently preferred for his friends and admirers to call him, needed no gift of serendipity. The gods had already given it to him at his birth.

Gómez de la Serna's typical form is the *greguería*, which he himself has defined as "humorismo + metáfora." Many of them are startlingly original and vivid. "The cricket measures the pulsations of the night." "The garden puts fallen leaves into its pipe and smokes them." "After every discharge, the cannon recoils as though startled by what it has just done." "Violets are the dark circles under the garden's eyes." "Lightning is a kind of angry corkscrew." "Bottle, wine's coffin." "Grapes are the nipples of the earth, virginal and small nipples." Many *greguerías* are longer and more elaborate.

The influence of Gómez de la Serna has been more widespread than one would suspect from the apparent insouciance of his works. He entitled his autobiography *Automoribundia*. The title suggests the gladiators' *Morituri te salutamos* and the attitudes of the Spanish-born Stoic, Seneca.

Those who have any real interest in Gómez de la
Serna will do well to thumb through some of his numerous volumes. At the worst, one will encounter highly man-
neristic quirkishness, at the best, a new attitude toward
reality, toward life with all its absurdities and grotes-
queries. In one way Gómez de la Serna stems from and
follows the Generation of 1898, in another he marks the
dissolution of the novel. One of his books bears the attractive title, *Seis falsas novelas*, 1926. They are: Occasionally he almost achieves continuity of plot, as in
El torero Caracho, 1926, but generally there is none. One
would hardly expect plot in a whole book devoted to
Senos, 1923, which is somewhat overblown. Gómez de la
Serna also wrote several biographies of writers and other
artists: Oscar Wilde, Azorín, Carolina Coronado, Valle-
Inclán, Lope de Vega, El Greco, Valázquez, Goya. They
are all unconventional.

THE LATER TWENTIETH-CENTURY NOVEL

The most respected novelist of the twentieth century
in Spain was unquestionably Pío Baroja, who did not die
until 1956, at the age of eighty-four. He had survived
four serious wars in his lifetime without changing his
manner. He was too sturdy a Basque to be blown about
by new winds. There were hardly any aesthetic winds of
gale force anyway. For a long time, even after the Spanish Civil War, one does not observe any transformation
of novelistic techniques. As far as influence was concerned, the highly artistic prose of a Valle-Inclán or a
Miró was dead. Broadly speaking, the novel was and
still continues to be realistic in one form or another.

The statement is true, for example, of *Arturo Barea*

(*1897–1957*). His origins were of the humblest, but he was gifted. He vigorously served the Republic until he went into exile in England. His chief work was published there, first in three separate parts, then together, in 1951, as *The Forging of a Rebel*. Mainly autobiographical and forcefully written, it is an admirable presentation of conditions in Spain in the earlier part of the century and should be required reading for anyone who wishes to know how life was then and there by one who lived through it. Barea was also a good critic. He greatly helped foreigners to understand the essentially Spanish character of a great poet in his *Lorca: The Poet and His People*.

Ramón Sender (*b. 1902*) is another ardent liberal, who now has the honor of being equally vituperated by Francoists and Communists. Despite his undeniable merits and his importance, he is seldom mentioned in his native country. The large and useful Bleiberg-Marías *Diccionario de literatura española* does not even list his name, though it treats hundreds of lesser authors, past and present.

Yet Sender is quintessentially Spanish and remains so in his exile on the hot (or quite cold) steppes of New Mexico, like the true hardheaded Aragonese that he is. His production is large and he has had the honor of translation into several languages, an honor not shared by many of his contemporaries in Spain or in exile. His first great success came with *Imán*, 1929, a vivid and unsparing account of his experiences during military service in Morocco. He had joined the staff of the great liberal Madrid newspaper *El Sol* in 1924. He was imprisoned by Primo de Rivera, but naturally came into great favor with the establishment of the Republic in 1931. In 1935 he received the Premio Nacional de Literatura. He served as a soldier—as a Loyalist, of course—in the Civil War, and his *Contraataque*, 1937, translated as *Counterattack in Spain*, was one of the most impressive books to come out of that conflict. His extensive works include books of travel, a life of St. Teresa, short stories, a work on Hernán Cortés, and novels with Spanish or Mexican settings. One of the better constructed is *El lugar del hombre*, 1939. It is a good study in human relationships, concerning the stir created in a village when a man supposedly murdered suddenly emulates Enoch Arden and reappears. In 1942 Sender published *Epitalamio del Prieto Trinidad*, translated as *Dark Wedding*, which is thought by perhaps more than one critic to be worth a dozen or so contemporary novels rolled together. *La esfera*, 1947, has a "spherical technique" which caused comment.

Some of Sender's works are actually stylized autobiography. Among these is one of his most delicate and sympathetic works, the *Crónica del alba*, 1942. It is an extraordinarily sensitive account of the actions and feelings of an eleven-year-old boy in Spain and paints a quite unforgettable portrait. Other later autobiographical material is utilized in *Los cinco libros de Ariadna*—published in Spanish in New York in 1957 under the aegis of *Ibérica*, to which Sender frequently contributes—and in the work in English, *Before Noon*, of the same year. The last contains translations of *Crónica del alba*, *Hipogrifo violento*, and *La quinta Julieta*.

Sender's style is not invariably a model of care. The author has not given new directions to the course of the Spanish novel, but he possesses great vigor and evoca-

tive power, vividness, sincerity, a fine eye for detail. It
is not without significance that he is a gifted and imaginative amateur painter. So far he has kept his poems unpublished.

The question "Who is the greatest novelist living in
Spain today?" would probably be answered: *Camilo José
Cela (b. 1916)*. He never received the Premio Eugenio
Nadal for the novel, which has been awarded to many
lesser novelists, male and female. Great celebrity came
to Cela on the publication of *La familia de Pascual Du-
arte*, 1942. It is the grim, imaginary autobiography of a
criminal awaiting execution, filled with deeds of senseless
violence—super-realistic, stark, vigorous. The novel is
a good example of what is called *tremendismo*, in vogue
also with other authors. Equally grim reading will be
enjoyed also in *La colmena (The Hive*, 1951). The human beings who people the hive of modern Spanish society have more cruel instincts and undergo with more
resigned or vigorous desperation the sufferings of which
they are victims than do real bees. The queen is the terrible Doña Rosa, who owns and runs the cheap café
into which the poor and extraordinarily numerous characters (has someone counted 164 of them?) come and
go seeking surcease from their ills. Many suffer from
sheer hunger, like little Lazarillo de Tormes. Incidentally, Cela wrote his own modern continuation of
Lazarillo, in which he satirizes many classes of contemporaries, except men of religion, who seem to enjoy
literary sacrosanctness in present-day censored Spain.
The title of the work is *Nuevas andanzas y desventuras
de Lazarillo de Tormes*, 1946. Other works are *Pabellón
de reposo*, 1944 (life in a sanatorium for tuberculous pa-

tients); *Viaje a la Alcarria*, 1948; *Del Miño al Bidasoa*. 1952; *Mrs. Caldwell habla con su hijo*, 1953.

Cela's style, often rough on purpose, is vigorous and vivid. Julián Marías, after commenting on Cela's virtues, has expressed the hope that his future books will be *"más complejos e íntimos, menos arbitrarios, con menos caprichosa condescendencia con el humor de lo truculento y repelente. ..."* Future readers will see whether Cela has taken his critic's admonitions to heart.

Juan Antonio de Zunzunegui (b. 1902) usually describes in his novels the comfortable upper-middle-class life to which he was born in Bilbao. Zunzunegui was educated partly in England, France, and Italy, but he shows little cosmopolitanism in his works, in which he mainly follows the tradition of nineteenth-century realism. His admitted master is Galdós. He has been accused of portraying life too much from the outside, too photographically. He began in 1926 by publishing regional sketches, and his first novel, *Chiripi*, appeared in 1931. *El chiplichandle*, 1939, is concerned with types in Bilbao. *La quiebra*, 1947, describes tricky procedures in the world of business. *El supremo bien*, 1950, presents more idealistic characters. Other titles are *Esa oscura desbandada*, 1951; *La vida como es*, 1954; *El hijo hecho a contrata*, 1956. Zunzunegui, popular at home, seems to have attracted little attention abroad.

Such is not true of *José María Gironella (b. 1917)*. He attended a theological seminary in his native Gerona, left to work in a distillery, a grocery store, a clothing store, and a secondhand bookstore. In his "teens" he became a soldier for Franco in the Civil War. With his novel *Un hombre*, translated into English as *The Soil Was*

Shallow, he won the Nadal Prize in 1946. *La marea* came in 1948. To date his most important novel has been *Los cipreses creen en Dios*, 1951. The scene is really Gerona, and it is a detailed account of conditions in Spain just before the Civil War. The narration of events tends to diminish interest in the characters, and it may be hard to tell where history leaves off and art begins. The novel has run through many editions in Spain, and *The Cypresses Believe in God* was successful in English. Perhaps the author may publish from abroad sequels which go through the Civil War and after. He has talent, and one awaits his future work with interest.

Juan Goytisolo (*b. 1931*) is by some regarded as the major novelist of contemporary Spain after Cela. It is to be observed that he was too young to participate in the Civil War, and his impressions may have been not unlike those of our Civil War felt by Americans born around 1860. His *Duelo en el Paraíso*, 1955, is a good account of the life and activities of a group of refugee children in a small Spanish village during the Civil War and must have been based on experience. *La resaca*, the last novel by Goytisolo to come to attention to the date of this writing, was published in Paris and banned by the busy censors in Spain. In English, *The Young Assassins*, 1959, was well received. It is a translation of *Juegos de manos*, 1954. The work confirms Cela's picture of rather desperate conditions in the Spain of recent years. It is evident that Goytisolo is a novelist of real promise.

Luis Romero (*b. 1916*) received the Premio Nadal in 1951 for *La noria*. The technique is not unlike that of Cela's *La colmena*, and so many characters appear that

it is hard to know them, despite the general interest of
the material.

Enrique Azcoaga (b. 1912) is an art critic and poet,
but he has published a highly praised novel, *El empleado*,
1949. It is a portrayal not just of an individual but of a
whole type, the average employee, without much ambi-
tion or much hope or much joy. Azcoaga has been resid-
ing in that largest Spanish-speaking city in the world,
Buenos Aires.

Tomás Salvador (b. 1921) has utilized his experiences
as a member of a sort of Spanish FBI as the basis for
most of his novels which draw on direct observation.
The best of his dozen or so works so far is, in his own opinion, *Cuerda de presos*, 1953. Cervantes dealt with a more
picturesque *cuerda* of the sort. *Cabo de vara*, 1958, seems
of importance.

Carmen Laforet (b. 1921) won the first Nadal Prize
with *Nada*, 1944. The simple story of the experiences of
a young girl who comes to live in Barcelona, the work
enjoyed considerable popularity. *La isla y los demonios*,
1952, is more smoothly written. The scene is the Canary
Islands. *La mujer nueva*, 1955, is divided into two parts:
I, the adulterous woman; II, her regeneration through
religion. The first part is more interesting than the second. Carmen Laforet is definitely on the side of virtue.

Among the fairly numerous women novelists in Spain,
some prefer *Elena Quiroga (b. 1921)*. Her *Viento del norte*
won the Premio Nadal in 1950. It has the Galician background of Pardo Bazán's *Los Pazos de Ulloa* and a kinship in method to Buero Vallejo's *Historia de una escalera*.
Algo pasa en la calle, favored by other readers, shows an
interesting technique: the revelation of the character of

a deceased personage through the thoughts of those who view his corpse. *La enferma* and *La careta* came in 1955. Elena Quiroga's principal concern is with love as the prime motive for human actions.

Miguel Delibes won the Premio Nadal in 1947 with a book bearing the attractive title *La sombra del ciprés es alargada.* (The American swamp cypress is not nearly so alluring as the standard European variety.) He won the Premio Nacional de Literatura in 1956 with *Diario de un cazador.* His importance as a novelist has been debated, but he is worth watching.

José Suárez Carreño (*b. 1915*) won the Lope de Vega drama prize (*Condenados,* 1952) and the Nadal novel prize in 1949 with *Las últimas horas,* translated into English as *The Final Hours. Ignacio Agustí* is a journalist who first wrote verses in Catalan and won fame with his novel *Mariona Rebull,* 1943. It was the first of a series planned to portray the Catalan capitalistic class. *Ignacio Aldecoa* shows an admirable knowledge of the Spanish countryside. Rafael Sánchez Ferlosio won the Nadal Prize in 1955 with *El Jarama.* The well-observed action is supposed to take place in a single Sunday afternoon. The prize was won in 1956 by *J. L. Martín Descalzo,* with *La frontera de Dios.* Its blurb says it "*posee la fuerza y audacia de la moderna novela católica extranjera y encierra al mismo tiempo una visión serena y trágica de la vida española.*" In 1957 the prize was won by *Carmen Martín Gaite*—already known for three or four novels— with *Entre visillos;* in 1958 by *José Vidal Cadellans,* with *No era de los nuestros.* These novels seem a bit effortful, *efectista. El Jarama* offers most interest.

It would be very easy to list the names of at least

six dozen novelists now practicing their art in Spain. A consensus of opinion would be that good novels are now being produced, but not great ones. Unrecognized geniuses may be appearing. Did many Spaniards in 1584 recognize great promise in the author of *La primera parte de la Galatea?* And as late as 1604 Lope de Vega spoke scathingly of *Don Quijote* and its author. It is hoped that the lines above are written with the modesty which is obligatory for any critic of contemporary literature in any language.

THE SHORT STORY

Since the publication in 1613 of the *Novelas ejemplares* Spain has not been without cultivators of the genre, but it is well to note that in recent years the short story has grown in popularity and numerous highly gifted *cuentistas* have published their brief narrations in various media. Many of the novelists previously mentioned have published short stories as well as novels, and so have some dramatists and poets. The total list of those who have published admirable brief fiction in recent years would be long indeed. Their pardon is asked for not giving them the attention which they deserve. Professor William H. Shoemaker has performed an excellent service in presenting to American students a volume entitled *Cuentos de la joven generación*, New York, 1959, with good introductions to the sixteen *cuentistas* represented. The average quality of the stories, all published since 1950, is high. Mr. Shoemaker adds the names of nine other authors worthy of representation. He finds that, in the stories which he has considered, the authors have regularly avoided humor, that they reflect the grim times after the Spanish Civil War. Many of the stories illustrate the cult of cruelty and violence, of frustration and hopelessness, which characterizes the movement known as *tremendismo*. Further, the authors in general do not seek regional picturesqueness or the expression of subjective emotion as did their nineteenth-century forebears. They try to convey, often in extremely brief form, some aspect of universal experience. Good samples can be found in *Los mejores cuentistas españoles*, edited by Pedro Bohigas, Madrid, 1946, and *Antología de cuentistas españoles contemporáneos*, edited by F. García Pavón, Madrid, 1959. Short story writers themselves, the editors supply valuable introductions to their anthologies.

LYRIC POETRY

When Spanish literature of the first half of the twentieth century is evaluated more accurately, say, in the year 2000, it is most likely that Spain's greatest contribution to the world's literary art will be thought to have been in lyric poetry, which even now constitutes a real glory. The remark is not made merely because Juan Ramón Jiménez was deemed worthy of the Nobel Prize for 1956.

The poetry of the Generation of 1898, through Darío the Machados, and Jiménez himself, was impressive enough, but they were to have most excellent successors, and the proportion of poets born every year bulks unusually large in the total fairly high birth rate of Spain.

Certain aspects of the transition from Modernism are well represented by *Enrique Díez-Canedo (1879–1944)*, who, reacting against the excesses of Rubén Darío's inferior imitators, strives successfully for a lyrically restrained poetic expression of intellectualized emotion. Díez-Canedo's own poems may appear minor, though he published several volumes, beginning in 1906 with *Versos de las horas*. Other volumes of verse were *La visita del sol*, 1927; *La sombra del ensueño*, 1910; *Imágenes*, 1910; *Algunos versos*, 1924; and *Epigramas americanos*, 1928. He translated various modern French and English poets, plus works of Montaigne, John Webster, and H. G. Wells. He was no doubt even more important as a critic, because he was in charge of literary and theatrical criticism on *El Sol*. Those who eagerly clipped that lamented newspaper in happier days have large files. Díez-Canedo knew Europe and he knew Latin America, for he filled various diplomatic posts. Some of his prose articles were published in collections. In 1935 he was justifiably elected *Académico de Número de la Academia Española*.

A good account of post-Modernist poetry in Spain has been given by Federico de Onís, already mentioned, and by *Ángel del Río* (*b. Soria, 1900*), both of Columbia University, a vantage point from which they have been able to interpret Spanish literary art far and wide. The latter is also widely known for his interpretations of modern Spanish literature or, more generally, for his admirable *Historia de la literatura española* (2 vols.), New York, 1948. The careful reader will see that a number of Del Río's excellent suggestions have contributed to this present chapter.

We remember that Rubén Darío published his splendid *Cantos de vida y esperanza* in 1905. In less than a decade afterward, we observe the rise of younger poets who mark a transition between Modernism and post–World War I poetic movements. It is not to be forgotten that Juan Ramón Jiménez, the Machados, and others were reaching their plenitude during the same time and that they continued their rich production for a long time. As transitional poets we may mention particularly *José Moreno Villa (1887–1955), Juan José Domenchina (b. 1898),* and *León Felipe (b. 1884).* Though different from each other, they all show the influence of Jiménez, Antonio Machado, and perhaps Unamuno, and they all tend to Hispanize Darío's French accent, also to give their poems more content, with less attention to sheer formal beauty. Moreno Villa began with *Garba* in 1913 and in succeeding volumes of verse displayed various tendencies, even surrealism, though always with his own personal stamp. He was also a literary and art critic (he translated Wölfflin), editor (Lope de Rueda, Espronceda), and painter.

Juan José Domenchina began publishing verse while still in his "teens"; *Del poema eterno* appeared in 1917. He has been called baroque in form and cerebral in content, as one might divine from the title of one of his volumes of verse, *La corporeidad de lo abstracto.* He is certainly far from Darío. His volume *Exul Umbra* was published in Mexico. León Felipe, three years older, began writing poems later; *Versos y oraciones del camino* won fame in Spain in 1920. His expression has constantly been relatively simple, direct, highly personal. Influences on him extend from the Bible through Walt Whitman, whom he translated. His restless activity has made him an actor in Spain, a druggist in Africa, a professor in America, a political agitator during the Republic, a vigorous singer of Spain's tragedy in his exile in South America (*El español del éxodo y del llanto*). His verse may be

sampled in his *Antología rota, 1920–1947,* published in
Buenos Aires. There were many other poets whom one
might classify in the group. Among them perhaps the
best known were Mauricio Bacarisse, Antonio Espina,
and Ramón de Basterra.

POETRY AFTER WORLD WAR I

Spanish poets were constantly seeking a renovation,
and after World War I we observe various tendencies.
First, they were influenced by new movements and artistic aspirations in evidence all over Europe—some of them
definitely exaggerated, even wild—applied to all the arts.
Spanish poets were also subject to the influence of the
masters of the preceding generation. The influence of
Juan Ramón Jiménez has ever been of great importance;
and, in the realm of general ideas, that of Ortega y Gasset
has been significant. Yet those who began by rebelling
against traditional Spanish values finally came to accept
them, to seek guidance from poets of the Renaissance and
Golden Age such as Garcilaso and Góngora, and from the
romancero.

The years immediately after World War I have been
frequently called "The Epoch of the Isms." There were
indeed plenteous isms, and Spaniards fleetingly and
briefly adopted them all and added some of their own.
To list a few (not to exaggerate them, we put them in low-
er-case letters): futurism, dadaism, surrealism, vanguardism, expressionism, imagism, freudianism, joyceanism,
cubism, creationism, neogongorism, ultraism—not to
mention fascism and communism as underlying inspira-
tions for some. The list could be extended. Some poets
flitted from one ism to another, and domination by any

ism over any poet was likely to be of brief duration. Poetic life gradually settled down. We shall here briefly discuss only some of the admittedly greater poets. The reader who wishes to know more poets and to read samples of their work is strongly advised to consult a book such as F. C. Sáinz de Robles, *Historia y antología de la poesía española* (2d ed.), Madrid, 1950. It contains no less than 2,268 pages, and is a rich treasury indeed, with good critical introductions.

The manifesto of ultraism, a definitely vanguardist movement, was signed early in 1919 by a group of young writers including the nineteen-year-old Guillermo de Torre, who is reputed to have coined the word by which the movement is designated and who has been previously mentioned in these pages for his subsequent achievements. An older member of the group was the novelist and critic Rafael Cansinos Assens. The manifesto called for a complete break with the past, for the creation of the "pure" poem shorn even of logic and of emotion, and was definitely influenced by the dadaists (Tristan Tzara and André Breton, who were later to found surrealism). The movement and the numerous little magazines to which it gave rise were of short duration. Of the poets involved, only Gerardo Diego, Juan Larrea, and José Luis Borges (Argentine) afterward produced noteworthy verse.

It should be observed that, somewhat before, a vigorous protest against the elegant school of Darío had already been uttered. It was the famous sonnet of the Mexican doctor and poet Enrique González Martínez, *Tuércele el cuello al cisne*, published in 1911. The recommendation proclaimed was that more attention be paid to the owl of knowledge and wisdom.

Perhaps creationism, though less noisy, was more important. It stemmed in 1916 from the poetic doctrines of the Chilean poet Vicente Huidobro, in collaboration with the Frenchman Pierre Reverdy. The book *Manifestes* was published in 1925. The ideal was "to create a poem as nature creates a tree"—that poetry should exist in and for itself, independent of externalities. Gerardo Diego and Juan Larrea were proponents of the movement. Ortega y Gasset clarified their artistic aspirations and those of other innovators in his *La deshumanización del arte*.

One might pick the year 1927 as marking the incorporation of this *"literatura joven," "de vanguardia"* into the more general body of literature. That year witnessed the foundation of the *Gaceta Literaria*, which, be it said aside, made rather strange reading for some American professors of Spanish, perhaps nurtured on Campoamor and Núñez de Arce. The files now smell rather musty.

It is time to speak of important poets: two from academic circles, Salinas and Guillén, and two products of more popular inspiration, Alberti and Lorca.

Pedro Salinas (1892–1951) had a rich career as professor, scholar, critic, and poet. He taught at Seville, Murcia, the Sorbonne, Cambridge, Madrid, Puerto Rico, Johns Hopkins, and elsewhere. He wrote books of scholarly criticism (on Jorge Manrique, Rubén Darío; *Reality and the Poet in Spanish Poetry, Literatura española, siglo XX*) and translated the *Cid* into modern Spanish verse. Yet it is his own poetry by which he will be best remembered. Some poetic volumes: *Presagios*, 1923; *Seguro azar*, 1929; *Fábula y signo*, 1931; *La voz a ti debida*, 1934; *Razón de amor*, 1936; *El contemplado mar*, 1946; *Todo más claro y otros poemas*, 1949; *Poemas escogidos*,

1953 (*prólogo* by J. Guillén). A collection called *Poesía
junta* was published in Buenos Aires in 1942.

The fundamental theme which unifies all Salinas'
verse is love, but very differently conceived from, say,
Garcilaso or Bécquer, or the sensual Darío. To Salinas
the external world seems chaotic as well as transitory, and
he seeks to transform reality, everyday objects, familiar
scenes, into something permanent because they are shared
with the beloved. The poet speaks to her, with her, and
not about her, like a Zorrilla. He does not dress her up in
verbal finery but seeks experiences shared with her.
There is deep emotion, but it is not worn on the sleeve.
His love seeks not so much fruition as shared happiness.
The expression is vastly different from Elizabeth Barrett
Browning's lush "How do I love thee? Let me count the
ways." Salinas might seem at first glance to be prosaic,
but far from it. There is a poetic transformation of reality, feeling, complicated thought, which Leo Spitzer
once referred to as *"conceptismo interior."* The poetry of
Salinas requires perceptiveness on the reader's part.
The effort is worthwhile.

Jorge Guillén (b. 1893), who was born in Valladolid,
shows, at least apparently, something of the austerity
(but also of the "diaphanous air," as Del Río says) of
his native Castile. His professional career has been
teaching: the Sorbonne, Murcia, Seville, Oxford, and,
for many years, Wellesley College, until his retirement,
after which he occupied the Charles Eliot Norton chair
at Harvard. For a long time his poetic work was confined to one volume called *Cántico*, first published in 1928,
but it was considerably enlarged in successive editions,
until the fourth (Buenos Aires, 1950), containing 334

poems. In 1957 he published *Maremágnum (Clamor)*, in
1958 *Viviendo y otros poemas*. Some of the poems in the
latter had appeared in the former.

Guillén is usually mentioned as the most "Classic"
modern Spanish poet. In form and sobriety of expression, yes. His work is not quite as varied as that of his
friend Salinas. In a way, it displays greater optimism,
greater satisfaction with all creation as reflecting some
sort of higher order dominating the world and the individual. He himself has said that he seeks *"una poesía pura,
ma non troppo."* He stoutly avoids ornamentation, and
one is positively startled to see the large predominance of
nouns over adjectives, even over verbs, in his lines.
Critics have connected him with Paul Valéry and have
suggested similarities to the simpler Góngora, and to
Luis de León in less Horatian moods. Instead of seeking
the interpretation of an object through metaphor, Guillén
tries to establish its "poetic presence." The process may
not be readily apprehensible to the man in the street, and
Guillén is undoubtedly a poet *"de minorías."* Many find
his poetry difficult, even though the words seem plain.
The poetry is there.

Rafael Alberti (b. 1902) came from the Province of
Cadiz, a region which had already known civilization for
some three thousand years (as contrasted with Virginia's
or New England's three hundred). Truly gifted, well-
educated and well-read, he absorbed and often combined
the popular lore of Lower Andalusia with inspiration from
the most advanced modern European movements. He
can versify, and has, like a simple poet of the old *roman-
ceros* or the most exaggerated surrealist; he even became
a super-protelarian propagandist, only to return nostalgi-

cally in his later years to the poetic themes and manner
of his youth. Like some others, he took up communism
and later rebelled and was expelled from the party. As
one of thousands and thousands of refugees from Franco
Spain, he went to France and finally settled in Argentina.

Some critics consider his early volumes his best:
Marinero en tierra, 1925; *La amante,* 1926; *Cal y canto,*
1927; *Sobre los ángeles,* 1928. Often quoted are little
songs of popular savor from the first:

> ¡Quién cabalgara el caballo
> de espuma azul de la mar!

> Si mi voz muriera en tierra,
> llevadla al nivel del mar
> y dejadla en la ribera.

Sobre los ángeles is surrealistic, with perhaps a bow to
Jean Cocteau and Rainer Maria Rilke. The volumes of
his middle period are less impressive. Among later publications in exile, may be mentioned: *Retornos de lo vivo
lejano,* 1945; *A la pintura,* 1948 (Alberti is also a painter);
Ora marítima, 1954.

Alberti's poetic talent was great, popular, and highly
sophisticated. He is certainly one of the foremost of his
generation.

Federico García Lorca (1898–1936) lived and wrote
richly and died tragically. He was one of the great gifts
that the gods gave to Andalusia, Spain, and the world
which his genius conquered. He came from a rather well-
off farming family near Granada, the traditional city
where he spent much of his youth and where he met his
death. Death hovered over much of his verse—blood,
and death, which he viewed with so much poetic dread.

His love of the dramatic showed early. In his very
tender years, he staged puppet shows in his own house,
where he was fortunate to have an old servant who would
weep at all the proper moments. He was educated mainly
in Granada. His conversational and musical talents there
made him most welcome at *tertulias* of his elders. The
remarkable professor of law Fernando de los Ríos,
learned, sympathetic, and one of the best Spanish orators
of all times, encouraged and aided him. Lorca actually
took his degree in law in 1923. From 1919 onward he was
mainly in Madrid, living at the liberal *Residencia de Estu-
diantes*. In 1930 he came to New York, a city which in
many ways horrified him, but gave him new poetic motifs,
as well as new friends and admirers. In 1931, in co-opera-
tion with Eduardo Ugarte, he founded a barnstorming
group of players in Spain who went about putting on
Golden Age plays and who were called *La Barraca*. In
1933–34 he was in Argentina. In the early days of Franco's rebellion, having no political affiliations, he went to
Granada for safety. In early July, 1936, he was taken
from his home by Rebel sympathizers, dragged near a
cemetery, and basely assassinated. There were five shots.
The tragedy was not merely for the poet and his family
and friends; it caused a grievous loss to Spanish poetry
and to all of the relatively young poet's passionate admirers throughout the world.

Because Lorca's poetry is so appealing, one may find
it difficult to make dispassionate evaluations of his productions. His first book was a prose account of a student trip through Castile, published in 1918 as *Impre-
siones y paisajes*. It was forgotten. In 1920 Lorca put
on his first play, *El maleficio de la mariposa*, which failed

and was not even printed. In 1921 came his first and still immature verse, *Libro de poemas*, which, however, suggested his personal poetic slants. *Canciones* came in 1927. The extremely important *Romancero gitano*, containing some of the most popular Spanish poems of all times, was published in 1928. It is a date to remember. *Poema del cante jondo*, 1931; *Llanto por Ignacio Sánchez Mejías*, 1935; *Seis poemas gallegos*, 1935; *El diván de Tamarit*, 1936. Other titles will be found in his *Obras completas*. We shall speak of the plays, too, but not list them bibliographically. They are easily accessible, in Spanish or English, or in other languages.

Whatever a very sober critical estimate of Lorca may be, it is a fact that he has had more appeal abroad than any other Spanish poet of his day, possibly of any day. Far more, for example, than the Nobel Prize–winning Juan Ramón Jiménez, whose influence on younger Spanish poets was unquestionably greater than Lorca's. Let us leave a precise estimate to the future. It is the belief of this critic that Federico García Lorca will be considered one of the best Spanish poets of all time.

Lorca had great appeal to the illiterate (the fact is attested) and to the highly educated. So did Lope de Vega, even Góngora, in their heyday. Did Lorca seek cheap approbation? Never. One never senses any grasping for effect. Julián Marías has suggested three qualities possessed by Lorca: a great sense of popular rhythms; a talent for rich and unexpected metaphors; the suggestion of vague and mysterious emotions which may obsess human beings in the dark of the night, or even in daylight. The combination of qualities is unusual in poets of any language. The word "haunting" has been badly overused in criticism, but it is not misapplied to many of Lorca's poems.

As one properly says to the interested in so many cases: read and see for yourself. It is worth learning Spanish just to read Lorca, and the experience to those with any sensitivity at all will be most rewarding. Oh, yes, he has been translated, but not always with the best success. To gain the joy of knowing him, it is desirable to have some background in Spanish language and culture.

It is unfortunate that Lorca has not had more successful followers in his conscious or unconscious efforts to bring about a much-needed renovation of the Spanish theater. His plays share the qualities of his poems and have been much admired abroad. They have, frankly, not lured the *"gran público,"* but they have undeniable merit. Did Lorca, for all his knowledge of the soul of the Spanish people, for all his poetic resources, for all his intensity of emotion, just miss the touch of a Lope de Vega? Most probably. And Lope de Vega was willing to make great concessions to lower popular tastes, and his plots were in general more lightly, more deftly, constructed.

Lorca shows a delightful fancy in the prettily stylized *La zapatera prodigiosa*, 1930, and what some consider his most characteristic play, *El amor de don Perlimplín con Belisa en su jardín*, 1931, the same year as the *Retablillo de don Cristóbal* and *Así que pasen cinco años*. *Mariana Pineda*, skilfully portraying the fate of that actual personage, had come in 1925. *Bodas de sangre*, 1933—somber, intense, tragic—dramatizes the simple episode of a bride who flees with her former lover Leonardo instead of marrying her fiancé. The moon stops its rising when Leonardo is murdered by the irate groom. Symbolic woodcutters and a beggar are figures from some mysterious nowhere. This brooding play has been frequently put on abroad. *Yerma*, 1935; *Doña Rosita la soltera*, 1935; and the posthumous *La casa de Bernarda Alba*, 1936, deserve better analysis than we can here give them. It is too bad that no dramatist has arisen since Lorca to follow and perfect the directions which he suggested.

Moreover, other poets about contemporary with García Lorca, or younger, have made much less impression on the world and must be mentioned with a brevity which is no doubt unfair to many of them. We shall not bother to classify them according to particular schools or groups or the special poetry magazines to which they were attached.

Vicente Aleixandre (*b. 1900*) has led a rather retired life devoted to poetry. His first volume was *Ambito*, 1928. He has said that his verse *"se dirige a lo permanente en el hombre."* His *Historia del corazón*, 1954, is a characteristic volume. His *La destrucción o el amor*, 1935, was a significant title, very different from the amorous moonlight poems of the Romantics of the 1830's. Aleixandre was affected by modern tendencies such as surrealism, but they were not intrinsic in his work. In general he prefers long, free lines in his verse, rather than formal stanzas.

Luis Cernuda (*b. 1904*) published his first volume of verse, *Perfil del aire*, in 1927. *Donde habita el olvido* came in 1935, *La realidad y el deseo*, in 1936. Cernuda was forced into exile after the Civil War and taught at Glasgow. In 1943 he published one of his best works, in lyric prose, *Oknos, el alfarero*. Also in prose is his *Variaciones sobre un tema mexicano*, 1952. Cernuda was early influenced by Jorge Guillén. He has been touched by surrealism. Perhaps in his vigorous expression he displays intellectualism complicated by Romanticism. His talent is undeniable, his feeling intense. Torrente Ballester says of him: *"No participamos en esa poesía, no nos importa."* Extraordinarily strange criticism, to which many will offer vigorous dissent. Cernuda is in many ways a most admirable poet.

Aleixandre and Cernuda were born in Seville. Also Andalusian are *Emilio Prados (b. 1899)* and *Manuel Altolaguirre (1904–59)*. They early came under the influence of Juan Ramón Jiménez, and both were connected with the important Malagan poetic journal called *Litoral*. Since 1939 they have lived in exile in Mexico. Both have the ability to utilize popular and sophisticated elements in happy fusion in their verse. The emotions of exile have perhaps increased their depth. A few volumes, Prados: *Tiempo*, 1925; *Vuelta*, 1927; *Llanto subterráneo*, 1936; *Mínima muerte*, 1939; *Jardín cerrado*, 1946. Altolaguirre: *Las islas invitadas*, 1926; *Vida poética*, 1930; *La lenta libertad*, 1936; *Nube temporal* and *Fin de un amor*, 1949.

Adriano del Valle (b. 1895) is another native of Seville. Though contemporary with vanguardism, he followed more traditional routes in his facile and rather joyous verse, less subjective than that of many contemporaries. Attractive titles of his volumes are: *Primavera portátil*, 1934; *Los gozos del río*, 1940; *Arpa fiel*, 1942.

Dámaso Alonso (b. 1898) has already been mentioned as a noteworthy scholar and critic. He is also a poet of note, original, intense, finished in expression. His first volume of verse was *Poemas puros; Poemillas de la ciudad,*

1921. *Oscura noticia* came in 1944. Most important is *Hijos de la ira*, 1944. The serious manner has religious overtones, expressed in a modern manner.

POETS OF THE THIRTIES AND LATER

Most of the poets mentioned in this chapter continued their production through the thirties, forties, and even the fifties. It is hard to generalize about modern trends, but there seemed to be in post–Civil War poetry a tendency to return to simpler and more Classic forms of expression, to compose less dehumanized verse, even to pay more attention to love as a theme. The foundation of the journal called *Garcilaso* shows at least one aspiration.

The names might first be mentioned. *Luis Rosales* (*b. 1910*), in his volume *Abril*, 1935, showed Classic influences, including that of Garcilaso. His poems, as in his *Rimas*, 1951, are generally personal, often religious. *Leopoldo Panero* (*b. 1909*) wrote his *Canto personal*, 1953, all in tercets. They mark a simple and direct expression of everyday experiences and feelings. His brother *Juan Panero* (*1908–37*) was noted for both depth and delicacy. He usually wrote in long meters. *Luis Felipe Vivanco* (*b. 1907*) is an architect turned poet, surely an unusual combination. He translated Paul Claudel and Rilke. His *Continuación de la vida*, 1948, is the clear and simple expression of mainly religious feelings. He has happily been called a more melodious Unamuno.

The strange case of *Miguel Hernández* (*1910–42*) has interested many. He was a farm laborer and goatherd who familiarized himself with the poetry of Spain's Golden Age, and his own poems greatly attracted his contemporaries. His *Perito en lunas* was published in Murcia in

1933. The next year he went to Madrid and was received by older poets and critics with the enthusiasm which his genius deserved. His untimely death cut short a truly promising career.

Dionisio Ridruejo (*b. 1912*) has made solid contributions to Spanish culture, and Americans will not object to the attitudes and activities which have got him into hot water at home. As a poet he has approached almost all subjects. The expression is regularly simple. He received the Premio Nacional de Literature in 1950 for his poems collected under the title *En once años.*

It is manifestly impossible to consider the scores of Spanish poets who are now writing, often richly. A new Juan Ramón or another Lorca may spring forth at any minute. Here are a few names of poets who have already, some for several years, produced admirable verse, and all these and more have their admirers: Victoriano Crémer (b. 1910), Gabriel Celaya (b. 1911), José Luis Cano (b. 1912), Ernestina de Chapourcin (b. 1905), José García Nieto (b. 1914), Germán Bleiberg (b. 1915), Vicente Gaos (b. 1919), Rafael Morales (b. 1919), Carlos Bousoño (b. 1923; his reputation seems to grow steadily), Eugenio de Nora (b. 1923), José María Valverde (b. 1923), Concha Zardoya, José Hierro, Blas de Otero, Ángela Figueroa, Gloria Fuentes, Ramón de Garcisol, Carmen Conde. José Luis Hidalgo (1919–47) died very young. The names of others should be added. Apologies are offered to them for not expressing the esteem they deserve.

It cannot be predicted whether the poetic bird in future Spain will have the voice and the plumage of the nightingale, the thrush, the linnet, the swan, or even the raven. One remembers, however, the last words of Bécquer's familiar: *"No me digáis que agotado su tesoro. ..."* Still always, *"habrá poesía."*

BIBLIOGRAPHY

BLEIBERG, GERMÁN, and MARÍAS, JULIÁN. *Diccionario de literatura española*. 2d ed. Madrid, 1953. Extremely useful for information concerning contemporary as well as past authors.

TORRENTE BALLESTER, G. *Panorama de la literatura española contemporánea*. Madrid, 1956. Valuable.

CASTELLET, J. M. *Notas sobre literatura española contemporánea*. Barcelona, 1955.

VALBUENA PRAT, A. *Teatro moderno español*. Zaragoza, 1944.

TORRENTE BALLESTER, G. *Teatro español contemporáneo*. Madrid, 1957.

ALBORG, J. M. *Hora actual de la novela española*. Madrid, 1958.

SÁINZ DE ROBLES, F. C. *La novela española en el siglo XX*. Madrid, 1957.

NORA, E. DE. *La novela española contemporánea, 1898-1927*. Madrid, 1958.

ALEIXANDRE, V. *Algunos caracteres de la nueva poesía española*. Madrid, 1955.

ALONSO, DÁMASO. *Poetas españoles contemporáneos*. Madrid, 1952.

CERNUDA, L. *Estudios sobre poesía española contemporánea*. Madrid, 1957.

AUB, MAX. *La poesía española contemporánea*. Mexico, 1954.

VIVANCO, L. F. *Introducción a la poesía española contemporánea*. Madrid, 1957.

The number of full-length studies of particular authors is large and steadily increasing. Briefer but significant critical articles appear steadily in various periodical publications.

General
Bibliography

MOST ESSENTIAL BIBLIOGRAPHIES OF
SPANISH LITERATURE

SIMÓN DÍAZ, J. *Bibliografía de la literatura hispánica.* 4 vols. to date. Madrid, 1950——.

SERÍS, HOMERO. *Bibliografía de la literatura española.* 2 vols. to date. Syracuse, 1948——.

BLEIBERG, GERMÁN, and JULIÁN MARÍAS. *Diccionario de literatura española.* 2d ed., Madrid, 1953. Large, invaluable for ready reference.

NEWMARK, MAXIM. *Dictionary of Spanish Literature.* New York, 1956. Defective. May be useful for American students.

SÁINZ DE ROBLES, F. C. *Ensayo de un diccionario de la literatura,* II, *Escritores españoles e hispanoamericanos.* 2d ed. Madrid, 1953.

Working bibliographies will be found in many of the histories and journals mentioned below.

NICOLÁS ANTONIO. *Bibliotheca hispana vetus* and *Bibliotheca hispana nova.* 4 vols. Madrid, 1788. For old and rare books only.

GALLARDO, B. J. *Ensayo de una biblioteca española de libros raros y curiosos.* 4 vols. Madrid, 1863-89.

SALVÁ Y MALLEN, V. *Catálogo de la biblioteca de Salvá.* 2 vols. Valencia, 1872.

FOULCHÉ-DELBOSC and BARRAU-DIHIGO. *Manuel de l'hispanisant.* 2 vols. New York, 1920-25. Discontinued.

PALAU Y DULCET, A. *Manuel del librero hispano-americano.* 7 vols. Barcelona, 1923-27.

THOMAS, H. *Short-title Catalogue of Books Printed in Spain and of Spanish Books Printed Elsewhere in Europe before 1602.* London, 1921.

Bibliographie hispanique. 13 vols. New York, 1905-17. Discontinued. Good only for the years given.

FITZMAURICE-KELLY. *Spanish Bibliography.* Oxford, 1925. Fuller than in his history.

PENNEY, CLARA L. *List of Books Printed before 1601 in the Library of the Hispanic Society of America.* New York, 1929.

GRISMER, LEPINE, and OLMSTED. *A Bibliography of Articles on Spanish Literature.* Minneapolis, 1933.

FARINELLI, A. *Italia e Spagna.* Torino, 1929.

LA BARRERA Y LEIRADO, C. DE. *Catálogo bibliográfico y biográfico del teatro antiguo español, desde sus orígenes hasta mediados del siglo XVIII.* Madrid, 1860. Still the most serviceable bibliography on the drama.

LEADING HISPANIC JOURNALS

Revista de filología española. (Spanish.) Contains by far the best current bibliography.

Revista de archivos, biblioteca y museos. (Spanish.)

Boletín de la Real Academia Española. (Spanish.)

Revue hispanique, 1894–1929. (French.) Discontinued.

Bulletin hispanique. (French.)

Hispania. (French.)

Hispania. (American.)

Bulletin of Hispanic Studies. (British quarterly.)

Nueva revista de filología hispánia. (Argentina, Mexico.)

Boletín de la Biblioteca Menéndez y Pelayo. (Spanish.)

Nueva revista hispánica moderna. (Argentina, Mexico.)

Revista de Occidente. (Spanish.) Discontinued.

Indice. (Spanish.)

Insula. (Spanish.)

Revista de literatura. (Spanish.)

Hispanic American Reports. (American.)

Asomante. (Puerto Rican.)

Hispanic Review. (American.)

Iberica. (German.)

ROMANCE JOURNALS CONTAINING
SPANISH MATERIAL

Zeitschrift für romanische Philologie. (German.) Best annual Romance bibliography.

Romanische Studien. (German.)

Litteraturblatt. (German.) Good current bibliography.
Archiv für das Studium der neueren Sprachen und Literaturen. (German.)
Modern Language Review. (British.)
Modern Language Notes. (American.)
Modern Philology. (American.)
Romania. (French.)
Bulletin of Studies. (British.)
Romanic Review. (American.)
Publications of the Modern Language Association of America.
Philological Quarterly. (American.)
Revue de littérature comparée. (French.)
Comparative Literature. (American.)
Romance Notes. (American.)
Hispanic American Report. (American.)

MOST IMPORTANT HISTORIES OF SPANISH LITERATURE

TICKNOR, G. *History of Spanish Literature.* 6th ed.; 3 vols. Boston, 1891. A pioneer work but still valuable. The German trans. by Julius, Leipzig, 1852 and 1867; and the Spanish by Gayangos, Madrid, 1951–56, contain additional notes.

WOLF, F. *Studien zur Geschichte der spanischen und portugiesischen Nationalliteratur.* Berlin, 1859. Highly important, especially for the ballad and drama.

AMADOR DE LOS RÍOS, J. *Historia crítica de la literatura española.* 7 vols. Madrid, 1861–65. Covers medieval period only.

BAIST, G. "Die spanische Literatur," *Grundriss der romanischen Philologie.* Strassburg, 1897. Authoritative for the Middle Ages.

FITZMAURICE-KELLY, J. *A New History of Spanish Literature.* Oxford, 1926.

MÉRIMÉE, E. *Précis d'histoire de la littérature espagnole.* Paris, 1922. Now best to be consulted in Morley's English revision: Mérimée-Morley, *A History of Spanish Literature.* New York, 1930. The bibliographical footnotes indicating special studies on each author are valuable.

CEJADOR Y FRAUCA, J. *Historia de la lengua y literatura castellana.* 14 vols. Madrid, 1915–22. Vast in scope, but uncritical and to be used with caution. Useful for its extensive bibliography, and for its treatment of obscure authors omitted in smaller works, also for South American writers and those of the recent period.

BARJA, C. *Literatura española: Libros y autores clásicos.* Brattleboro, 1922; 3d ed. 1932.

———. *Libros y autores modernos.* New York, 1924.

———. *Libros y autores contemporáneos.* Madrid, 1935.

PFANDL, L. *Spanische Literaturgeschichte.* Leipzig and Berlin, 1923. A brief handbook for use in the German schools. Extends through the reign of Charles V. Accurate and scholarly.

FITZMAURICE-KELLY, J. *Chapters on Spanish Literature.* London, 1908. Brilliant studies on a few important genres and authors.

HURTADO, J., and GONZÁLEZ PALENCIA, A. *Historia de la literatura española.* 6th ed. Madrid, 1949. Pp. 1,102. Highly useful for information and bibliography. Apparently not proofread.

VALBUENA PRAT, A. *Historia de la literatura española.* 4th ed.; 3 vols. Barcelona, 1953. Somewhat uneven. Stimulating criticism.

BOGGS, R. *Outline History of Spanish Literature.* Boston and New York, 1937.

DÍAZ PLAJA, G., *et al. Historia general de las literaturas hispánicas.* 4 vols. in 6. Barcelona, 1949–57.

ROMERA NAVARRO, M. *Historia de la literatura española.* 2d ed. (little changed). Boston and New York, 1949.

DEL RÍO, A. *Historia de la literatura española.* 2 vols. New York, 1948. Stimulating. One of the best.

BRENAN, GERALD. *The Literature of the Spanish People.* Cambridge, 1951, 1953; Meridian Books, 1957. Personal opinions. Delightfully written. Highly recommended.

ADAMS, N. B., and KELLER, J. E. *Spanish Literature: A Brief Survey.* Paterson, N.J., 1960. A short guide for the uninitiated.

ADAMS, N. B. *The Heritage of Spain.* Rev. ed. New York, 1959. General background, mainly literature. Illustrated.

TEXT COLLECTIONS

Biblioteca de autores españoles (BAE). 71 vols. Madrid, 1846–80.
  Contains the greater part of Spanish literature. The most important collection, though badly edited, still being added to.

Nueva biblioteca de autores españoles (NBAE). 22 vols. Madrid,
  1905–28. Better edited.

Bibliotheca hispanica. 22 vols. Barcelona, Madrid, and New York,
  1900–1921. Well-edited reprints of early texts.

Bibliotheca romanica. A cheap, but well-printed and edited collection of the masterpieces of Romance literature, printed in Strassburg by the firm of Heitz and Mundel; contains many Spanish works.

Clásicos castellanos. A series begun in 1910, offers cheap, well-printed, and, on the whole, well-edited reprints of the Spanish classics. About 150 vols. to date.

Collección de libros raros o curiosos. 24 vols. Madrid, 1871–96.

Libros de antaño. 15 vols. Madrid, 1872–98.

Sociedad de bibliófilos andaluces. 44 vols. Seville, 1868–1907.

Sociedad de bibliófilos españoles. Madrid, 1866——. In course of
  publication.

Sociedad de bibliófilos madrileños. Madrid, 1909——. In course of
  publication.

Biblioteca universal. Numerous reprints, badly done, whose only merit is their cheapness.

Colección universal, Calpe.

Colección Austral. A great many texts in good paper-covered editions.

As noted, various Spanish and Spanish American publishers, notably Aguilar, have steadily issued good, well-printed and well-bound editions of older and modern Spanish authors. They should be found in all good libraries.

TRAVELS: SOME OLDER STAND-BYS

AMICIS, E. DE. *Spain and the Spaniards* (trans. from Italian).
  Philadelphia, 1895.

D'AULNOY, MME. *Relation du voyage d'Espagne.* Paris, 1691. Nu-

merous later reprintings. Valuable for the culture history of
the seventeenth century.

BORROW, GEO. *The Bible in Spain.* New York, 1908.

ELLIS, H. *The Soul of Spain.* London, 1908.

FORD, R. *Handbook for Travellers in Spain.* 2 vols. London, 1845,
1898.

GAUTIER, TH. *Voyage en Espagne.* Paris, 1845 and later. First
pub. as *Tra los montes.* Paris, 1845.

HAY, JOHN. *Castilian Days.* Cambridge, 1903.

HOWELLS, W. D. *Familiar Spanish Travels.* New York and London, 1913.

A FEW MORE RECENT TRAVEL BOOKS

MARTÍNEZ RUIZ, J. (AZORÍN). *El paisaje de España visto por los
Españoles.* Madrid, 1917.

UNAMUNO, M. DE. *Por tierras de Portugal y de España.* Madrid,
1911.

———. *Andanzas y visiones españolas.* Madrid, 1922.

TREND, J. B. *Spain from the South.* London, 1928.

MAUGHAM, W. S. *Andalusia.* New York, 1920.

MORTON, H. V. *A Stranger in Spain.* New York, 1954.

BRENAN, GERALD. *South from Granada.* New York, 1957.

———. *The Face of Spain.* New York, 1956.

STARKIE, WALTER. *The Road to Santiago.* New York, 1957.

CROCKETT, LUCY H. *Kings without Castles.* New York, 1957.
Excellent. Honest opinions.

TRACY, HONOR. *Silk Hats and No Breakfast.* New York, 1958.

PRITCHETT, V. S. *The Spanish Temper.* New York, 1954. Travel
and opinions.

Index of Proper
Names and Titles

[Where there are several references, the most important are indicated by italicized numerals. Cross-references are provided when necessary. In a few instances where variant titles are in use for the same work, both are given.]

508

Index

510

Index

512

Index

Index

Guía del lector del Quijote (Mada-
riaga), 454
Guía de pecadores (Luis de Grana-
da), 196
Guido delle Colonne, 62, 91
Guillén, Jorge, 457, *484–85*, 491
Guimerá, A., 433
Gutiérrez Nájera, Manuel, 413
Guzmán; *see* Pérez Guzmán
Guzmán de Alfarache (Alemán),
180–82
Guzmán el Bueno (Gil y Zárate),
360

Haedo, Diego de, 251
Hamlet (Shakespeare), 328, 331
(Las) Harpías en Madrid (Castillo
Solórzano), 188
Hartzenbusch, Juan Eugenio, *360*
Hay, John, 399
(Las) hazañas del Cid (Castro), 287
(El) haz de leña (Núñez de Arce),
390–91
*(Los) hechos de Garcilaso de la Vega
y moro Tarfe* (Lope de Vega),
256
Heidegger, 459
Heine, H., 256, 366
Helias, 92
Hemans, Felicia, 33
Hendrix, Mrs. W. S., 367
Henríquez Ureña, Pedro, 443
Herberay des Essarts, 147
Herder, J. G., 219, 346, 347
(La) hermana San Sulpicio (Pala-
cio Valdés), 383
(La) hermosa fea (Lope de Vega),
272
(La) hermosura de Angélica (Lope
de Vega), 230, 269
Hernández, Alonso, 236
Hernández, Miguel, *492*
Hernani (Hugo), 355
(El) héroe (Gracián), 304

Herrera, Fernando de, *142–44*, 209,
324
Herrera y Tordesillas, Antonio de,
208
Hidalgo, José Luis, 493
(El) hidalgo (M. Machado), 425
(Los) hidalgos (Azorín), 442
Hierro, José, 493
*(La) hija de Celestina, o la ingeniosa
Elena* (Salas Barbadillo), 172,
182
(El) hijo de Don Juan (Echega-
ray), 391
(El) hijo hecho a contrata (Zunzune-
gui), 473
Hijos de la ira (Alonso), 492
Hildebrandslied, 27
Himno al sol (Espronceda), 359
Hipogrifo violento (Sender), 471
Hispania victrix (López de Gó-
mara), 206
*Historia crítica de la literatura espa-
ñola* (Amador de los Ríos), 398
*Historia de Carlo Magno y de los
doce pares*, 91
Historia de España (Lafuente), 398
Historia de España (Mariana),
204–5
*Historia de España y de la civiliza-
ción española* (Altamira), 445
*Historia del Abencerraje y de la
hermosa Jarifa, 157–58*, 262, 263
Historia de la filosofía (Marías), 460
*Historia de la lengua y literatura
castellana* (Cejador), 403
Historia de la literatura española
(Del Río), 479
Historia de la literatura española
(Valbuena Prat), 457
*Historia de las ideas estéticas en
España* (Menéndez y Pelayo),
401
Historia de las Indias (Las Casas),
206–7

Index

Index

Index

Index

528

Index